IT'S ALL ABOUT JESUS!

IT'S ALL ABOUT

JESUS!

Faith as an Oppositional
Collegiate Subculture

*Peter Magolda and
Kelsey Ebben Gross*

STERLING, VIRGINIA

COPYRIGHT © 2009 BY
STYLUS PUBLISHING, LLC.

Published by Stylus Publishing, LLC
22883 Quicksilver Drive
Sterling, Virginia 20166-2102

Library of Congress Cataloging-in-Publication-Data
Magolda, Peter Mark.
   It's all about Jesus! : faith as an oppositional collegiate sub-
culture / Peter Magolda and Kelsey Ebben Gross.
      p. cm.
   Includes bibliographical references and index.
   ISBN 978-1-57922-354-0 (hardcover : alk. paper) —
ISBN 978-1-57922-355-7 (pbk. : alk. paper)
1.   Church and college—United States. 2.   College
students—Religious life—United States. 3.   Public
universities and colleges—United States—Religion.
4.   Evangelicalism—United States. 5.   Subculture—United
States.   I. Gross, Kelsey Ebben, 1982- II. Title.
   LC383.M324 2009
   248.8'34—dc21

                                    2008054643

13-digit ISBN: 978-1-57922-354-0 (cloth)
13-digit ISBN: 978-1-57922-355-7 (paper)

Printed in the United States of America

All first editions printed on acid-free paper
that meets the American National Standards Institute
Z39-48 Standard.

Bulk Purchases

Quantity discounts are available for use in workshops
and for staff development.
Call 1-800-232-0223

First Edition, 2009

10   9   8   7   6   5   4   3   2   1

For Marcia and Charlie
The two greatest influences on my life—PMM
For Peter and Andy
Your encouragement and faith in me are a true blessing—KEG

ACKNOWLEDGMENTS

While conducting and completing this research study, we received support from numerous individuals who educated us in dramatic and profound ways. Those to whom we owe the greatest debt of gratitude are members of the Students Serving Christ (SSC) organization. SSC students and staff allowed us unrestricted access to their lives. More important, they took risks and opened their hearts and minds to us as we regularly frequented their safe space to observe and record their private and vulnerable moments. Having the opportunity to interact with these students over a prolonged period was undoubtedly the highlight of this undertaking. We cannot mention these individuals by name, but we hope they recognize their unique and important contributions.

Numerous colleagues encouraged and assisted us as we conceptualized this study. First, we thank Carol Varano and Lora Warner, two research colleagues who collaborated with us on an earlier research project that spawned this undertaking. We recognize and appreciate their strong work ethic and dedication to inquiry. David Stanfield and Naomi Callahan encouraged us to explore the unfamiliar world of evangelical collegians despite our lack of expertise and initial uneasiness as strangers in a strange land. They also continued to provide critical feedback and enthusiasm for our work throughout the entire process. Thank you, David and Naomi—it was worth the risk.

Sarah Steward, Kari Taylor, Jenny Williams, and Celia Ellison carefully read numerous drafts of this manuscript. Their significant conceptual and cosmetic recommendations enhanced the book's key arguments and readability. These colleagues' theoretical questioning and attentiveness to details resulted in a clearer and more efficient presentation of our arguments. Larry Braskamp and Alyssa Bryant sent us interesting readings, including their own scholarship, that kept us up-to-date on contemporary faith issues in higher education and expanded our intellectual horizons. John von Knorring of Stylus offered creative and candid suggestions about the book's content and organization. We especially appreciate John's patience in waiting for us to decide when to publish this book.

Our families and friends provided ongoing support and keen sensitivity at critical times during this 4-year journey. For Peter, Marcia Baxter Magolda has and continues to be a supportive spouse and sage research counsel. Marcia offered both unvarnished praise and criticism, both her trademarks—and godsends. Cara Magolda Tucker, Peter's niece, frequently shared her first-hand experiences as a member of several collegiate evangelical subcultures. These insights gently guided our fieldwork observations and analysis. Kelsey is grateful for her spouse, Andrew Gross, who was a source of constant encouragement, patience, and inspiration while she was immersed in this project. She also thanks her parents, Tim and Vicki Ebben, for their support; they are two expert teachers who have always modeled a strong dedication to learning and educating others. That passion for education sustained Kelsey throughout the inquiry and writing process. All these individuals' labors have helped us immensely and have enhanced the quality both of this book and of our lives.

In *Jim and Casper Go to Church: Frank Conversation about Faith, Churches, and Well-meaning Christians* (Henderson & Casper, 2007), Jim, a seasoned minister, invites Casper, an atheist, to join him on a road-trip to visit 12 diverse Christian churches in the United States. In this faith travelogue, this odd couple visits institutions ranging from opulent megachurches with fog machines and state-of-the art light shows to down-and-out missions. They listen to, discuss, and critique worship services, ministers, and biblical messages, showcasing Casper's outsider critiques. For non-Christian readers, the book makes the strange familiar and provides both poignant and occasionally humorous vicarious experiences of a multitude of contemporary church experiences. For Christian readers, the story makes the familiar strange by offering disorienting interpretations that challenge "normal" church conventions, which evokes a wide range of reactions and emotions. Throughout the text Jim and Casper model ways for those with diametrically opposing views to reflect on, describe, and defend their beliefs, celebrate their biases, engage in meaningful and respectful dialogue, and learn from awkward and counter-intuitive situations.

Much like *Jim and Casper Go to Church*, *It's All about Jesus: Faith as an Oppositional Collegiate Subculture* makes the strange familiar for non-Christian readers and the familiar strange for Christian readers. We offer a contemporary view of collegiate evangelicals by interviewing members; experiencing, discussing, and critiquing organizational programs; and deconstructing intended issues that matter to the organization and its members. Throughout the endeavor, we acknowledged and monitored our outsider status and perspectives. For non-evangelical readers, *It's All about Jesus* makes the unfamiliar familiar by allowing readers to vicariously experience the organization's day-to-day workings by focusing on the leaders' agenda, curriculum and pedagogy, as well as members' reactions to the organizations' offerings. For evangelical readers, the story makes the familiar unfamiliar by offering outsiders' secular interpretations of these evangelical offerings.

This book, a 2-year ethnographic study of a collegiate evangelical student organization on a public university authored by two "non-evangelicals," fills a void in the higher education literature. As Lowery (2000) explains,

> Despite the size of the evangelical movement, little research has been conducted in an effort to understand the experiences of evangelical students in public higher education. Researchers have most commonly focused upon students attending evangelical colleges and seminaries (Cummings, 1997; Dobson, 1986; Hunter, 1987; Mayer, 1997; McGinn, 1995; Powell, 1994). Additional accounts of the experiences of evangelical students, including those in public higher education, exist, but are quite dated and were written for the evangelical community (Gilbert, 1933; Orr, 1971; Quebedeaux, 1974). (p. 9)

Following Jim and Casper's lead, we attempt to model ways for those with differing views to reflect, make public their beliefs, acknowledge their biases, evoke meaningful and respectful dialogue, and—most important—learn from "the other." As was the case with *Jim and Casper Go to Church,* we expect our book will evoke a wide range of reactions and emotions from its readers. Banks (cited in Nasir and al-Amin, 2006) argued that "[o]ne of the challenges to pluralistic societies is to provide opportunities for cultural and ethnic groups to maintain components of their community cultures while at the same time constructing a nation-state in which diverse groups are structurally included and to which they have an allegiance. A delicate balance of unity and diversity should be an essential goal of democratic nation-states" (p. 27). Accepting pluralism and forging unity between diverse groups necessitates public discourse, something rare in American higher education. It is our hope this scholarly work will extend existing public discourses centering on religion in public higher education.

JESUS AND HIGHER EDUCATION

Rituals of Faith

Let the Weekend Begin

The steady exodus of collegians on their Thursday-evening pilgrimage from their middle-size public university campus to downtown is unmistakable. Hundreds of students prematurely dressed in summer uniforms—shorts, T-shirts, and sandals—mill around on street corners and at the entrances to the many taverns that occupy the strip. The coffee shops are brimming with activity; copy shop and bookstore fronts are vacant. The windy and unseasonably cool evening does not appear to dampen students' spirits as they haphazardly cross the streets and avoid the steady stream of the busy two-way traffic.

On campus, the soaked streets—the result of an April storm—are mostly deserted. Many campus buildings appear temporarily abandoned, although street parking, even at night, remains at a premium. We approach Wister Auditorium and feel our anticipation rise as we prepare to attend FaithNite, a weekly 2-hour worship service that the largest Christian student organization at this 16,000-student public university sponsors. In order to enrich our understanding of collegiate Christians in general and the Students Serving Christ student organization (the focus of this book) in particular, we occasionally attended other organizations' public meetings, such as the FaithNite event.

Hundreds of students attend this weekly event, so the mini-traffic jam does not surprise us. Automobiles slow to scan the many nook-and-cranny–like parking enclaves, seeking coveted convenient parking spaces. We opt for the larger (and hopefully less crowded) parking lot a bit farther from the auditorium to ensure that we arrive a few minutes before the 9:00 p.m. weekly event.

Inside the lobby, two greeters smile as they distribute programs; we accept their goods and nod appreciatively as we pass. The organization boasts a membership exceeding 1,000 active members; it appears 600 members are present as the auditorium nears capacity. Students cram the center and two side aisles, making it nearly impossible to move about the auditorium. Judging by the spontaneous hug-fests near the stage, attendees do not appear inconvenienced by the crammed conditions. Like their downtown peers, attendees' attire for this event is casual, yet stylish. Men sport shirts, baggy cargo shorts, and flip-flops, and tops and floral print skirts are the preferred garb of women. Women outnumber the men by an approximate ratio of 2:1. An aura of camaraderie fills the air as the start of FaithNite approaches.

The scene resembles a rock concert more than a worship service. Band members situate guitars, a drum kit, keyboards, and percussion instruments on the stage. They wander around as sound technicians check the stage microphones. The lighting director tests the stage lights as two men in the back of the hall focus their PowerPoint slides, which they will project on the jumbo screen once the program commences. The high quality of the sound and audio-visual systems suggests that this organization spares no expense to produce this weekly event. The heavy, dusty, and dilapidated velvet curtains (which seem to serve as mildew magnets) contribute to the musty room odor. It is difficult to ascertain what is more annoying—the dank smell or the overcologned and overperfumed attendees sitting nearby.

We select two seats toward the back of the room to ensure an observational vantage point that will allow us to appreciate the activities taking place on stage as well as those taking place in the audience. Nearby, a student introduces her father to her friends. The older man appears out of place.

At 9:06, a technician turns off the lights as a familiar countdown film clip abruptly appears on the screen. "❹ . . . ③ . . . ❷ . . . ① . . . " Immediately, images of students walking across campus appear on the screen as Steppenwolf's 1970s song "Born to Be Wild" blares through the temporary sound system situated on stage. We—two researchers, both born and bred Catholics—confess that this faith-based gathering is a bit disorienting. The raucous studio audience crowd yells and cheers; it is clear to us that this is not "your father's weekly worship program."

Following the mini-movie showcasing collegians and campus landmarks, a primitive cartoon with an ant-like bug grasping a little cup and a huge spoon appears on the screen. The character says in a humorous, granny-like voice: "My spoon is too big." The ant repeats this phrase several times. Then a banana character appears on the screen and, in an equally bizarre dialect, declares, "I'm a banana," repeating the phrase three or four additional times. Immediately following, a subtitle flashes on the screen that reads, "The following video was never meant for public viewing." The collective roars of laughter from the audience suggest that the producers of this hip video understand their 20-something constituents.

As the cartoon concludes, two men appear on the screen to reenact the scene. They rehearse the scene at least a dozen times, each time getting a bit closer to accurately mimicking the cartoon characters. The audience's mounting applause and shouts of approval signal to the thespians they are approaching perfection. Suddenly a slide appears on the screen—"Welcome to FaithNite"—as *Born to Be Wild* resumes. It seems a bit odd that students selected *Born to Be Wild* as the theme song for the program's introduction. The song seems better suited for their classmates headed to the Thursday evening downtown party scene than for this evangelical gathering. Yet, the frenetic, partylike atmosphere of FaithNite grows as band members casually retrieve their instruments strewn across the stage and methodically tune their guitars.

As the band begins to play, accompanying lyrics appear on the screen, replete with Christian references. This would likely be outsiders' first clue about the primary focus of this event. The lyrics lag behind the tempo as the band performs a rendition of a 1980s song with contemporary Christian lyrics. Attendees appear to relish the experience, singing loudly and proudly praising the Lord. Immediately following the second song, an emcee appears on the stage and yells, "It's so exciting to see a full house here!" Sporting shorts and a polo shirt, his hands in his pockets, he reveals he has been the master of ceremonies for 3 months. The emcee extols the band, eliciting extreme applause from the audience. As he exits the stage, the emcee announces, "Chuck is going to talk next. I want to hear what he has to say." An older man in his late 30s appears. Nearby students retrieve their notebooks and Bibles. Chuck recounts a story about his daughter who recently participated in her second dance recital that her Christian elementary school sponsored; she assumed the role of a skunk. Chuck explains that a few weeks following the recital, he attended an open house at his daughter's school, where the teacher asked him to offer a prayer since he is "a professional Christian." Chuck continues:

> I was overwhelmed by the goodness of God. . . . I was crying because I realized my privilege. . . . I have a friend who is helping pay for my daughter to attend this special Christian school. . . . Too often I take a lot for granted. . . . You do this as well, like take for granted your college education. . . . Anyway, it's an honor to be at this worship service. . . . Too often, I take for granted that 600 people show up each week to praise the Lord. . . . Give thanks for what we have, and be reflective about our lives.

As we assimilate Chuck's content and study his presentation style, we conclude that he is the organization's director. His age, family size, job as a professional minister, and poised storytelling style all contributed to our drawing this tentative conclusion, which we confirmed during the next segment of the program.

Chuck awkwardly pauses for a moment before shifting gears to talk about ministry fund-raising:

> We need money to pay for this ministry. . . . We are fortunate to have many different people who give to this ministry, including business people, alumni, and parents. . . . We hope this summer you will consider giving a pledge to give back to the ministry. . . . This is the only time this year we talk about money. If you have been around and have been benefiting from this ministry to improve yourself spiritually, please consider pledging some of the money you earn.

Chuck instructs staff situated around the perimeter of the auditorium to distribute pledge cards. The staff complies as Chuck explains the donation process. He repeats the instructions four times for the unruly audience, which appears uninterested in the process, as evidenced by the 50 or so simultaneous side-conversations. Chuck has to keep saying, "Shhhhh, please listen!" The scene is reminiscent of an elementary school lesson gone amuck. He encourages attendees to take a card and ask the Lord for guidance. He continues,

> If you don't want to or cannot give anything, don't worry . . . If 100 of you give $100.00 each, we would raise $10,000. And this money would go back

to you. We need money to do creative things. If you need more time, turn in the pledge packet next week. Or, find me later tonight and I can work out a plan.

After a brief pause, Chuck introduces tonight's featured speaker, who immediately appears on stage and addresses the crowd. Cheers and clapping ensues as Jack reveals that he is a senior business major who intends to graduate, get married, and move to Chicago. Jack, dressed in a clean-cut shirt, khakis, and sandals, looks like the many upper/middle-class, White undergraduates who compose this university's dominant demographic. He continues,

> I am honored to be up here. I knew I wanted to talk about something that has impacted my life over the past 4 years. . . . Well, something I'm still learning about is the grace of God. If we want to know God deeply, we have to experience His grace in our lives. I am not a fountain of wisdom. I still don't know about everything but God has taught me what I know. Tonight I want to talk about the grace of God. We as Christians talk about grace a lot, and we don't know much about it.

Jack bows his head and prays aloud. "Lord, thank You for the opportunity to speak to all these people here. Thank You for Your word, which is *truth*. Thank You for Your grace. . . . In Your name, Amen. If you have your Bible, turn to Ephesians 2:1-10." A slide of Ephesians 2:1–10 appears on the screen with a popular quote from the Protestant tradition: "For it is by grace you have been saved, through faith—and this is not from yourselves, it is the gift of God— not by works, so that no one can boast." Jack continues,

> The definition—"It's kindness to someone who doesn't deserve it." It's a free gift. This describes four truths about God's grace. God's grace saves us from ourselves. We're all imperfect people. We let our culture and selfish desires dictate our life. There's war, poverty, crime, materialism, meaningless sex. . . . Some of us think we do okay. It's like God is completely perfect—our flawed selves keep us separated from Him. But because God loves us, [through] His grace, God made us alive. Our old selves are spiritually dead, separated from God. God's forgiveness through Christ makes us alive. His grace saves us from ourselves and we begin a relationship with Him. All it takes is prayer backed up with attitude from the heart. If you haven't made the decision yet, I encourage you [to]—it'll change your life.

We wonder how many attendees actually "have yet to make the deci-sion" to accept a relationship with Jesus and whether Jack's fast-paced ser-mon style is understandable to outsiders. We struggle to keep up with the enthusiastic, amateur preacher's wandering sermon. It appears that his sen-iority as a veteran organization member has earned him the respect of his peers. Jack pauses, then introduces his second major point: how God's grace gives flawed humans a new identity that does not fade or change over time. Jack quickly shifts to his third argument and explains that God's grace keeps us humble. He reads Ephesians 2:8–9 and then resumes his extemporaneous commentary:

> We are forgetful people. As Christians we accept God's grace, but we battle with temptation to make it all about us. We get rid of bad habits, go to church, and begin to think God's grace is "just for starters." So, we do good works—and then spiritual pride takes over. Spiritual pride is one of the greatest barriers to experiencing God's grace. . . . Well, what did I struggle with most when I accepted Christ? You got it, pride. God did some things in my life—I overcame some sin, met Christian friends—but God reminded me I couldn't brag about anything in my life. . . . God's grace will always be undeserved.

Jack continues his lengthier-than-expected remarks with his fourth and final point. He argues that God's grace produces a life of influence and that Christians show gratitude by the way they live. Jack reminds attendees that they are God's masterpiece, created to give glory to Him. Christians' good works show the world the love and grace of God. He asks, "Where is God calling you to lead a life of influence? I don't know where you are [on this journey]. Keep seeking Christ. . . . While we're here we can live every day and remember God created us to do great things." He concludes,

> If you're here seeking, if you find your identity in something other than Christ, or if you've known Christ for a long time but have pride. . . . I'm confident God has a message for *you* in grace. It's by His grace that I am a different person. Now, I'm thinking about how to serve God in the work-place, and I'll be married to a beautiful woman who loves God.

Loud cheers resound from the crowd as Jack exits the stage and the emcee reappears to introduce a student who will give her testimony. Wearing a skirt and blouse, Erin appears on stage; she has brunette curly hair and glasses.

> Hi. I am Erin. I am a junior science major. I am here to give my testimony—how I became Christian. . . . I only have 6 minutes, so here we go.

> I now view my life as a play in two parts. Pre-Christian life is Act 1 and Act 2 is once I became a Christian. Act 1—It might sound like bragging, but you will understand later that I am not. It makes me uncomfortable talking about my accomplishments, but it is important for the big picture. I was valedictorian in my high school. I received a scholarship to attend this college. I have a wonderful family. I also have a sister who is my best friend. My father is a doctor; so let's just say money was never an issue. Erin in Act 1 was agnostic. I did not believe we could know about God. I thought Christians had no idea what they are talking about. I thought they were hypocrites.

Erin confessed that as a first-year student she immersed herself in the party scene and "lived the college dream." She explained she partied 3 days a week and still managed to maintain a 4.0 grade point average in pre-med.

> I had everything going for me, but one thing was missing; I never had a boyfriend. I was deeply embarrassed that no one wanted to date me. I figured I was not cute, or I was bad at flirting. I am still bad at flirting; that is true. I learned that guys were attracted to me if I was drinking, so I drank. I felt ashamed of what I did when I was drunk.

Erin revealed that she worried all of the time about failing tests, making awkward statements, having body odor, trying to be funny around her friends. For a while, she struggled to get out of bed and she even entertained thoughts of suicide, but she kept these feelings to herself.

> I was miserable. I put on an act of being happy. My sister saw through my act, and she prayed for me. She also wept at my pain. I believe that because of prayers, God brought Kim into my life. Kim lived next to me last summer. . . . She was kind to me. I was comfortable talking to her. The topic of faith came up a lot. She was Christian, and I was agnostic. I asked many questions. She patiently listened and gave me answers that made sense.

Erin indicated that she lost her way and that Kim planted seeds that opened her mind. Erin began to pray for God to make her believe. When she returned home, she surprised her family by attending church services. Over time, Erin opened her heart to Jesus, and her faith strengthened.

> In Erin Act 2, I hardly ever worry. It is a miracle. I take Jesus at His word. Don't worry. I learned to love without anything in return. I now can feel love. God is the only person who can love me. I believe Him. I have nothing to lose. I would like to end with a quote from Mother Teresa. "We must be loved by God first and then we can give to others. His love has no boundaries." Thanks for listening. God bless.

Loud clapping and cheering follow. Erin breathes a sigh of relief and quickly vanishes from the stage. Her candor about normally taboo topics—insecurities, anxiety, and suicide—in front of 600 peers stuns us. Judging from the appreciative applause, it appears Erin's decision to fully disclose her story is a normal and accepted practice among group members.

The band runs on stage and spends a few minutes retuning their instruments. Attendees wait, though a bit restless. Multiple side-conversations arise throughout the auditorium. The band plays a four-song medley, and then the bandleader again offers a brief prayer. "Thank you God. . . . We don't have an identity we have to change. We're perfect in your eyes."

At the conclusion of the music and prayer, the emcee returns and makes a few final announcements: "Women Bible Study leaders—you must turn in your packets, don't forget! We still need 30 people to write devotionals for days of summer." As the nearly 2-hour program concludes, the emcee screams, "Thanks for coming!" Let the weekend begin!

About the Research Study

Religion, Faith, and Public Higher Education

Christian organizations are prevalent at public universities across the United States. More than a decade ago, Spaid (1996) noted that the number of religious organizations on college campuses had continually increased during the early 1990s; so, too, had student enrollment in religious studies seminars. Ten years later, collegians' interest in religion and spirituality continues to expand (Finder, 2007). Coomes (2004), summarizing survey results from the

Spiritual Life of College Students Preliminary Report (UCLA Higher Education Research Institute, 2003), found that "more than two thirds of third-year undergraduate students demonstrate a substantial level of religious engagement and commitment" (p. 22), evidenced by their interest in prayer, attendance at religious services, and discussions of religion or spirituality with peers. Further, a high percentage of collegians describe themselves as Christian. The *Spiritual Life of College Students Report* (UCLA Higher Education Research Institute, 2005) found that 41 percent of college students classify themselves as protestant Christians (i.e., 17% mainline Protestant, 13% Baptist, 11% other Christian), and of these students, the *evangelical* brand of Christianity continues to grow. For instance, *Newsweek* (Adler, 2005) found that 28% of Americans age 18–39 consider themselves to be *evangelical* Christians (p. 48); a Harvard Institute of Politics poll (Calhoun, 2007) indicated that 35% of college students call themselves "born again," and 22% identify, again, as *evangelical* Christians.

These religious students expect opportunities to explore and deepen their faith while in college. The *Spiritual Life of College Students* survey (UCLA Higher Education Research Institute, 2005) concluded, "As they begin their college experience, freshmen have high expectations for the role their institutions will play in their emotional and spiritual development. They place great value on their college enhancing their self-understanding, helping them develop personal values, and encouraging their expression of spirituality" (p. 3). Similarly, Dalton (2001) argued that "[f]or most students, the college years are a time of questioning and spiritual searching in which there is particular emphasis upon two dimensions of spirituality: making connection with ultimate life purpose and finding an inward home" (p. 17). These dimensions are obvious components of FaithNite and other evangelical gatherings we attended throughout our 2-year ethnographic study.

Although students' interest and involvement in religion in general and evangelism in particular continue to grow, public universities remain both tepid and uncomfortable with mixing public education with faith-based initiatives, both inside and outside the classroom. Although overt hostility toward faith-based student organizations is rare, a pervasive uneasiness persists, the roots of which are complex. Marsden (1997, cited in Lowery & Coomes, 2003) notes that although religious groups founded many American higher education institutions, during the first half of the 20th century, institutions began to shed their religious qualities, a trend fueled by the desire to fully separate church from all other aspects of American society.

An uneasy historical tension between religion and public institutions' academic mission persists today in higher education (Schwehn, 2005). Public education's core values, such as the open exchange and acceptance of diverse ideas, inclusion, and the creation of academic communities celebrating difference rather than homogeneity, are often at odds with the dogmatic ideologies of faith-based organizations. Within their academic curricula, public universities remain steadfast in separating the secular from the sacred. Although universities sanction religious studies majors and seminars, rarely do faculty in other disciplines broach the topic of faith. Discussing Christian students, Riley (2005) elaborates on the impact of these reserved public higher education institutional practices:

> Students who do arrive on campus their freshman year with some traditional religious identity quickly find themselves a beleaguered minority both in the classroom, where their beliefs are derided as contrary to the principles of tolerance and 'diversity' (since they are not accepting of every lifestyle and don't believe that every viewpoint deserves equal consideration), and in their extracurricular lives, where their sensibilities are consistently offended by what they regard as the amoral behavior of their peers and its tacit approval by college officials. (p. 1)

Typically, in the cocurriculum (i.e., life outside the classroom), institutions recognize the existence of faith-based student organizations and allow them to use campus facilities for meetings; seldom do they fund these organizations. According to Hunt (1993), university administrators' reluctance to support religious initiatives is not always born of hostility but rather of indifference. Jones (2005) notes that as a result of many colleges' uncertainty about how to support students' religious needs, national faith-based associations (with paid staff who are not affiliated with the university) establish and manage student organizations with highly sophisticated organizational infrastructures to fill this void.

This is especially true of evangelical Christians. Although evangelical organizations' missions, levels of influence, and effectiveness vary, collectively their ministries continue to expand as they maintain their high-profile presence on many public university campuses. National organizations that

sponsor these parachurches (i.e., interdenominational evangelical organizations) on college campuses (Butler, 1989) provide students a much-desired
"safe space" to explore their belief systems. "Some of these organizations are
intellectually vibrant and spiritually formative; others border on faddish fool-
ishness or frightening fundamentalism. All of them exist outside the intellectual debates and discussions that shape the curriculum as well as the research
and writing of scholars" (Jones, 2005, p. 35).

The academy remains largely ignorant about the intricacies of evangelical organizations and uncertain how to meet the unique needs of evangelical
students while remaining true to core, secular institutional values. Miller and
Ryan (2001) assert, "Despite statistics suggesting that the majority of students
themselves say that spirituality and religion are important to them, public
universities have chosen to leave religious and spiritual activities largely to
religious denominations and the students themselves with a minimum of collaboration" (p. 41). For example, on the campus of 16,000 students where we
conducted our fieldwork, the organizational sponsor of FaithNite has an
active membership of more than 1,000 students. Thirty-five full-time professionals manage the organization and regularly interact with students. The
intersection of the evangelical staff with the university administrators,
although cordial and professional, is infrequent.

Evangelical programs, such as FaithNite, are unusual and confusing.
They resemble neither a "normal" student organization program at a public
university, such as a concert or lecture, nor a "normal" or traditional religious
gathering, such as a Sunday worship service. Instead, evangelical organizers
blur the sacred and secular by purposely cooking up a recipe for both college
success and salvation that includes the ingredients of *faith, fellowship,* and
fun. FaithNite student speakers call for attendees to abandon their self-
centeredness and strengthen their relationship with and faith in Jesus. However, even though faith is a key ingredient, a puree of faith, fun (e.g., the
cartoon reenactments), and fellowship (e.g., socializing prior to FaithNite
programs) provide evangelical attendees the minimum daily allowance of
spiritual nourishment. Overwhelmingly, Christian students "try it and like
it," as evidenced by their organizations' burgeoning membership on
American college campuses.

A centerpiece of this faith, fellowship, and fun ideology is an evangelical
cocurriculum and pedagogy that: [1] values and advocates learning outside
of the classroom and [2] encourages students to act as both teachers and

learners as they collaboratively learn about Jesus. Evangelical-sponsored events such as FaithNite, replete with songs, sermons, and peer testimonies, demonstrate that these organizations are keenly aware of the power and importance of student learning and of peers teaching peers. Calhoun (2007) commented on the importance of faith-based organizations for student learning:

> "Parachurch" organizations . . . may or may not be formally recognized affiliates of specific campuses; they usually are not organized under chaplaincies. But they are centers of religious engagement—and importantly, this is often intellectual engagement. Students in these organizations discuss how to interpret the content of their courses—often without the knowledge of their instructors—as well as how to understand the big issues of the day. And—contrary to stereotypes—this is an active part of life at schools like Princeton, not just at less elite and more explicitly religious institutions. (para 3)

Because of their focus on student learning, evangelical organizations' cocurriculum affirms Miller, Bender, and Schuh's (2005) argument that "students need to embrace the ethos that a college education is more than just attending classes, and institutional practices need to stimulate that understanding" (2005, p. 91). Additionally, these organizations' pedagogy echoes Astin's (1993) conclusion that peer teaching contributes to learning, because, "First, students are held accountable by their peers for achieving certain learning outcomes. Second, students assume a certain degree of responsibility for assisting their peers in achieving the same learning goals. These two peer group phenomena may well serve to motivate students to invest additional time and energy in the learning process" (para 13).

Although seldom explicitly acknowledged as a *political agenda*, implicit in evangelical organizations' cocurriculum and pedagogy is a politically based mission to spread the Word of Jesus. A prerequisite for mobilizing students to enact this agenda is meaningful, in-depth, and sustained student involvement. As they blend faith, fellowship, and fun, evangelical organizational leaders encourage interested students to pray to Jesus and ultimately select an evangelical organization to place at the epicenter of their collegiate experience. The fact that more than 600 students continue to attend the FaithNite weekly event suggests that the program is meaningful, which ultimately aids the organization in its political quest. In addition to FaithNite, leaders sponsor programs such as Bible studies that allow students to deepen and prolong their involvement.

Christian organizations mobilize members by capitalizing on members' shared sense of marginalization. Beyond sponsoring creative and responsive programs that facilitate significant and sustained student involvement, evangelicals often position themselves as cultural *outsiders*—distinct from the dominant campus culture that does not share their religious and moral beliefs (Lowery & Coomes, 2003). As a result of this joint marginalized status, campus Christians draw upon their collective strength to resist challenges from the dominant culture. Parachurch organizations serve as "safe spaces" for students to express their faith within the larger secular university setting. This sense of safety is clear in the opening story; students shamelessly shared personal stories about their struggles and their love of Jesus, stories that would not be acceptable in other campus contexts.

Warren (2002), author of the popular Christian book *The Purpose Driven Life,* states, "You must make a counter-culture decision to focus on becoming more like Jesus. Otherwise, forces like peers, parents, coworkers, and culture will try to mold you into their image" (p 177). Accordingly, campus evangelical leaders eschew sinful collegiate activities such as excessive alcohol consumption. Organization leaders purposely schedule FaithNite on Thursday evenings, a night that college students typically designate as a time for socializing in bars. Therefore, the Thursday night gathering reinforces a perception that FaithNite attendees are not "normal." Campus Christian organizations simultaneously provide students a sense of solidarity and a structure for organized resistance to the dominant culture.

Ironically, Christian students represent the religious majority on this particular campus; according to the Cooperative Institutional Research Project results (UCLA Higher Education Research Institute, 2005), 41.5 percent of students on this campus listed "Christian" as their religious preference; this was the largest percentage reported. Of religious student organizations on campus, 77 percent profess a Christian tie. This particular demographic mirrors national trends among college students. Yet, as *outsiders,* evangelicals lead lives distinctively different from their mainstream peers while engaging in political behaviors that mirror that of other marginalized student subcultures. This sense of marginalization becomes even more puzzling when combined with Christian organizations' overwhelming racial and ethnic homogeneity on this campus. Although the Christian organizations we studied appeared to be inclusive and inviting, the ranks of participants remained largely White—which is yet another dominant demographic of this campus (multicultural students make up 8 percent of the student body). Evangelical students' political agenda, homogeneity, and somewhat ironic and self-proclaimed outsider status are three topics that we frequently revisit.

Purpose and Focus

Ethnographic examinations of evangelical students are rare (Bramadat, 2000; Bryant, 2005; Bryant, 2006; Bryant, 2007a; Bryant, 2007b; Cherry, DeBerg, & Porterfield, 2001; Ebben & Magolda, 2007; Kim, 2006; Magolda & Ebben, 2006; Magolda & Ebben, 2007; Moran, 2007). This book, which includes stories and analysis of evangelical events such as FaithNite, provides a glimpse into the lives of college students who join evangelical student organizations and who subscribe to an evangelical way of life during their college years. *It's All about Jesus* offers empirically derived insights about how students' participation in a homogeneous evangelical student organization enhances their satisfaction with their collegiate experience and helps them develop important life lessons and skills.

We intend the narratives and interpretations to not only enrich understanding of a particular student organization but also, which is more important, to spark intellectual discourse about the value of faith-based organizations within public higher education. The role of religion in public higher education, student involvement in the cocurriculum, and peer education are three examples of critical issues in higher education for which this idiosyncratic case study offers broad understanding.

The FaithNite introductory narrative generates an eclectic collection of questions that we both pose and answer throughout the text: What is it like to be a collegian involved in a Christian organization on a public college campus? What roles do Christian organizations play in the lives of college students enrolled in a public college? How do evangelical student organizations recruit members, welcome them into their community, sponsor educational programs, and facilitate leadership development? What are evangelical student organizations' political agendas, and how do they mobilize members to advance these agendas? How do leaders form and sustain these evangelical organizations? What counts as *normal* within these organizations? What is the optimal relationship between universities and evangelical student organizations? What is the optimal equilibrium between the secular and the sacred within public higher education? What constitutes *safe space* for evangelical students and who should provide this space? What role does *being on the margins* play for evangelical students? Is there a place for evangelizing within public higher education?

In light of the increased interest in religion in higher education—coupled with an increased presence of evangelical Christians on campus—answering these complex questions is timely and essential. We acknowledge that as Rorty (1999) comments, religion can be "a conversation-stopper" during discussions with "those outside the relevant religious community" (p. 171). Yet, despite the tension that accompanies a book like this one, religion in higher education must be addressed, as Rice (2006) notes:

> [discussions of religion] trigger deep-seated antagonisms, tensions, and intellectual rifts in what many of us call a community of scholars. Addressing religious issues in the contemporary context also has the potential to further fray the sometime fragile relationships that exist between the academy and the larger society. Despite these difficulties, however, these conversations can no longer be avoided. Silence is not an option. (para 2)

We hope the stories and analyses that follow, although difficult for some, will not be a conversation-stopper. We concur with Rice: silence is not an option. Although the proliferation of campus Christian organizations continues, published scholarly research about collegiate evangelicals lags behind (Lee, 2002), especially scholarship that embraces an ethnographic genre of writing. This text fills this void.

Research Setting

To answer the aforementioned questions, we embarked on a 2-year study of a medium-sized interdenominational Christian student organization, Students Serving Christ[1] (SSC), situated on a medium-sized public, 4-year residential college in the Midwest. As a medium-sized organization, it was not only easier to access for research purposes but also provided an interesting contrast to the larger organizations, which often have a stronger identity and presence on American public university campuses.

Students Serving Christ, which is affiliated with a national Christian organization, has a membership of approximately 80 students, two full-time staff coordinators, and one staff intern. Three values guide the organization's practice: [1] following Jesus with passion, truth, and sincerity by focusing on prayer, witnessing, fellowship, the Bible, and discipleship, [2] loving God and people, and [3] aligning one's values and priorities with the values and priorities the Bible espouses. SSC sponsors weekly worship meetings, Bible study groups, prayer sessions, and leadership training. The SSC also designs and implements ongoing evangelical training, coordinates one-on-one spiritual training and mentoring activities, and organizes regularly scheduled fellowship activities.

Theoretical Frameworks

To gain understanding of this faith-based organization and Christian students' everyday lives, we participated in many of the SSC sponsored events and programs and found that these social scenes seemed to possess ritual-like characteristics. Thus, we use *ritual* as our interpretive framework throughout the book to organize our discussion of the SSC values and behaviors. Through the careful presentation and analysis of the daily rituals of this unique SSC subculture, we reveal the core values of the organization and its members.

McLaren (1986) and Quantz (1999), positing that rituals play a crucial role in education, lament researchers' and practitioners' tendencies to ignore rituals. Rituals "[1] are seldom scrutinized, [2] are important sources for revealing social and cultural conditions, [3] reveal much about the ritual organizers and participants, and [4] are political acts that communicate expectations and norms for behavior and performance (that is, transmit culture)" (Magolda, 2000, pp. 32–33). By experiencing and analyzing these SSC social scenes, the organization's identity and distinctiveness, power structures, political priorities, norms, and mobilization strategies aimed at sustaining and growing the organization come into focus.

"The term *ritual* is a diffuse and often impalpable concept—one that has been beset with problems of definition that have haunted it for years" (McLaren, 1986, p. 44). Despite the challenges associated with defining ritual, we align our view of ritual with Quantz and Magolda (1997), who explain that ritual is a formalized, symbolic performance.

Ritual is a *performative* act. As such it is marked by physically acting out something for an audience; the action is intended for others to observe. For example, the student testimony is an act intended for others to view. In this drama, participants play distinct roles. Typically, the testifier's role is that of a once wayward Christian who has now found a new life with Jesus. Other attendees, too, are included in this ritual performance. Evangelical peers assume the role of encouragers and thus affirm the students' life-changing decision. This ritual's purpose is to create a "reality" that conveys to those inside and outside the organization the difference that Christ has made in one's life.

Ritual also involves transmitting information through *symbols*—mechanisms that convey meaning indirectly. The Christian organization's request for students to donate their earnings to their organization is symbolic of the organization's desire that students put *God's needs* and the development of their faith first before secular summer fun and entertainment. As organization leaders present this information, they convey organizational values centered on prayer as a means of discernment, sacrificing for God, and living a Christian lifestyle.

Finally, symbolic performances have a *recognizable* and *expected form*. Someone is likely to recognize whether a ritual is performed correctly. When someone attempts to perform a ritual act but violates some important aspect of the form, the violation is likely to call into question the legitimacy of the performance. For example, students giggling and engaging in side-conversations during a prayer beginning a Christian organization gathering, or the person leading the prayer joking and using profane language would violate important aspects of the form. Embedded in these symbolic performances are explicit and implicit "rules" that convey to participants whether the ritual was done correctly. Doing it correctly legitimizes the ritual. For people to embrace the ritual and its implicit meaning, the ritual must follow form and be convincing; if it does not, it loses its power. Over time, rituals acquire "a sense of rightness" (Young, 1999, p. 11).

The analyses in the chapters that follow—focusing on macro, grand, and more defined social scenes (e.g., a student sharing the Bible with a non-Christian), as well as the more amorphous, micro, and sometimes more "mundane" events (e.g., a greeting between the evangelist and the soon-to-be evangelized)—reveal much about the evangelical culture, including its knowledge, beliefs, morals, customs, and enculturation (i.e., the internalization of other normative habits that members acquire over time). Rituals also reveal the mutual influence of environment and participants on each other and the organization's power structure and political struggles to teach members (McLaren, 1985; McLaren, 1986). Through these performance analyses, the evangelical subculture's identity (i.e., the ways in which the organization positions and differentiates itself from both non-Christians and other Christian organizations) and ideology (i.e., political and moral view of the world) become apparent. Viewing a student evangelical subculture through a ritual lens is a unique contribution of this book.

Audiences

It's All about Jesus targets multiple audiences—both sacred and secular. For readers unfamiliar with evangelical collegiate organizations and the students they serve, we hope the narratives make the unfamiliar familiar and the dubious obvious. For evangelicals, we first hope that the thickly described narratives make the familiar more familiar and the obvious more obvious. Second, we intend our analyses and findings to make the familiar unfamiliar, the obvious dubious, and the hidden obvious by uncovering the tacit meaning embedded in these familiar but seldom examined subculture rituals.

For parachurches in particular, we hope this book spurs discussion on topics such as campus power and politics, how their organizations interact with the secular world around them, and how they can improve their organizations. Additionally, this text urges secular readers in higher education to consider the many benefits, as well as liabilities, of parachurches as cocurricular learning sites on campus. Both religious organizations and secular higher education can benefit from thinking more deeply about the position of religion on campus, for the continued growth of parachurches—illustrated in the opening story, featuring a group with 1,000 members—can no longer be ignored.

We acknowledge at the outset that writing this book is risky business in light of the polarizing discourses surrounding the topic of evangelicals in public higher education. Many evangelical readers, understandably, are likely to be suspicious of secular academicians studying, writing about, and evaluating their sacred collegiate initiatives. Likewise, some academicians are likely to dismiss a book about Christianity—in particular, about its expanding role in public higher education. Our goal is neither to offer romanticized portrayals of the SSC nor to offer a "slash and burn" critique of evangelicals such as the SSC. Instead, we hope our interpretations and analysis will raise a series of questions worth pondering and discussing. We lay bare our interpretations and evaluative commentary, and we invite readers to formulate their own interpretations of our narratives and interpretations, drawing their own evaluative conclusions and themes. We hope that readers will become more informed about their own beliefs and assumptions about religion, student organizations, Christianity, student learning, and "the other" (e.g., collegiate Christians)—information we argue will improve higher education.

Chapter Summaries

In each of the subsequent chapters, we adopt Eisner's (1998) four-part framework for educational criticism (i.e., description, interpretation, evaluation, and thematics) to present our findings. To begin each chapter, we first provide thickly described narratives about an SSC ritual that offers insights into the values of the subculture. Second, we use diverse theoretical concepts to introduce our interpretation of the narratives. Interspersed within each chapter are evaluative comments pertaining to the content. Finally, at the conclusion of each chapter and in the final chapters of the book, we introduce thematics (i.e., sensitizing concepts) for readers to consider as they apply these findings to their own contexts.

In Chapter 2, *Research Processes: Rituals of Inquiry,* we discuss the origins of the study, processes for gaining access, data collection and analysis procedures, quality assurance safeguards, and fieldworker dilemmas. In Chapter 3, *Researchers' Tales: Rituals of Disclosure,* we lay bare our subjectivities as researchers as we reveal aspects of our lives that influenced our observations and interpretations of the SSC.

In Chapter 4, *Evolving Christians: Precollege Evangelical Rituals,* we introduce students' narratives that provide a glimpse into precollege experiences that were instrumental in their desire to affiliate with a collegiate Christian organization. In Chapter 5, *God's Squad: Rituals of Recruitment,* we reveal the ways in which SSC recruits, socializes, and initiates members; we also discuss the characteristics SSC students prefer when selecting a Christian student organization. In Chapter 6, *Praise Jesus: Rituals of Difference,* we explore the ways in which SSC and its counterparts on campus create a distinctive organizational niche and situate themselves in opposition to other Christian and secular student organizations. In Chapter 7, *Getting to Really Know Jesus: Teaching and Learning Rituals,* we describe a higher level of commitment to which students can pledge their time beyond the weekly worship gatherings: namely, the Bible study. In Chapter 8, *Bridging the Gap Between Evangelicals and Nonbelievers: Outreach Rituals,* we explore SSC students' transition from inward Jesus scholars to outward evangelists via a month-long training program aimed at mobilizing students to implement SSC's agenda. In Chapter 9, *Leading by Following Jesus: Servant Leadership Rituals,* we showcase ways in which the SSC prepares students on the Servant Leadership Teams to reach out to peers via evangelism and discipleship. In Chapter 10, *From College Seniors to Real-world Evangelicals: Transition Rituals,* we describe a 5-week program aimed at helping SSC seniors transition from student Christians to "life Christians." In Chapter 11, *The Chosen: Rituals of Vocation,* we highlight the lives of six SSC members who chose to extend their SSC experience by devoting their professional lives to Jesus.

In Chapter 12, *SSC Revelations and Reconciliations: Rituals of Understanding,* we integrate and synthesize key themes and tensions we present in the book. In Chapter 13, *Capstone Principles: Exit Rituals,* we offer recommendations for higher education, evangelical organizations, and evangelical and secular collegians. In Chapter 14, *It's All about Jesus: The Last Word,* SSC members offer their interpretations of and reactions to our findings, as well as final thoughts about their experiences in SSC. In total, it's all about Jesus.

2

RESEARCH PROCESSES

Rituals of Inquiry

Resolutions[1]

"How's everyone doing? Glad to be back in classes? Did you make your New Year's resolutions?" Matthew, the 20-something spiritual leader and campus director for Students Serving Christ (SSC) commands the attention of attendees, who this week number around 50 students, mostly women. "Did you know over 60 percent of resolutions are broken within 7 days? If you made it through the first week without breaking them, congratulations." The congregation sits silently as Matthew paces in front of the altar. It is the first Friday of winter term, and it appears that the regulars continue to make their weekly pilgrimage to the chapel for the 90-minute service. "What changes is God calling us to make as a ministry?" Matthew pauses, not expecting a response to this rhetorical question, then continues,

> How can we improve as a ministry? I've lost sleep pondering this question. We should be seeing more fruitfulness in our ministry. Our ministry goal is to learn about Christ and spread his word. The first part we are doing okay; part two we are not holding up our own [end]. We cannot and must not neglect our mission. Let us pray.

Matthew bows his head and stares at his Bible, which fits into the palm of his hand like a glove, as he recites an extemporaneous prayer. Students, many casually dressed in jeans and sweatshirts, bow their heads until the prayer concludes. Warmth and a sense of solidarity fill this quiet sanctuary, more than compensating for this cold and dreary winter evening.

During his sermon, Matthew urges his congregation to take seriously their New Year's resolutions and enact them. He encourages attendees to reflect on their past, identify changes God is calling them to make, and change to improve both the ministry and themselves.

In this chapter, we heed Matthew's advice. We reflect on and describe the research processes and procedures we employed throughout the SSC study, identify processes and procedures we would sustain as well as alter, and offer resolutions for change as we contemplate future research initiatives. To accomplish these aims, we discuss the origins of the study; the philosophical foundations of the inquiry process; the research methods for collecting, analyzing, and representing the data; and the criteria for judging the quality of the findings and interpretations. We conclude with a discussion of the three fieldwork dilemmas that perplexed us most throughout the study.

Research Specifics

Research Origins

Originally, the SSC subculture was one of four collegiate student organizations we selected for a 3-year ethnographic study aimed at examining the roles of student governance in higher education. Of particular interest were the political actions of students participating in these organizations, such as the tactics and strategies members use to gain and sustain authority, influence, and power.

Upon approval of the University's Institutional Review Board, we contacted student organizational leaders and advisers to introduce them to the study and seek their permission to study their group. The SSC was one group we initially contacted, and they agreed to participate.

The decision to select the SSC for inclusion in this qualitative study was both ideological and pragmatic. On the ideological front, nontraditional governing organizations interested us. We intended to design and implement a research study about the political actions of college students that did not simply feature the "usual suspects"—for example, high-profile, conventional student governance organizations. The four organizations we initially approached about participating in the study, and which eventually accepted our invitation to participate, included three traditional-governance organizations (i.e., a campuswide student government association, a sorority, and residence hall governing board) and the SSC, the sole nontraditional organization. We classified the SSC as a nontraditional organization because SSC members did not readily describe their organization as a governing society or political entity.

Second, the issue of marginalization interested us. We knew from collegewide surveys that Christianity was by far the most popular religious affiliation among students on this campus. Yet, from the outset, SSC members described and positioned Christianity and their organization on the margins of campus life. The irony of a Christian organization describing itself as a fringe organization initially confused and intrigued us.

Third, ignorance and curiosity about this ever-growing and commanding force within American higher education influenced our decision to study this particular student subculture. Our lack of familiarity with a self-proclaimed conservative student organization piqued our intellectual curiosity, influencing our final decision to include the SSC in the study once members agreed to participate.

Jorgensen (1989) explains, "The decision to participate in a setting . . . sometimes is based on opportunity and convenience" (p. 41). Both opportunity and convenience, along with other practical considerations, guided our decision to include the SSC in the study. On a pragmatic level, the size of SSC was ideal. SSC was not overly small or overly large, allowing us to focus on depth rather than breadth. Second, Matthew, the SSC's director, allowed us access to all SSC programs and training. Third, the SSC was geographically proximate to our homes and places of work, giving us easy and frequent access to SSC events.

During the first year of the study, the research team attended one or two events per week that each of the four student organizations sponsored. Gradually, the research team realized that the SSC was not only an ideal context for the multisite student governance/politics study, but also a fascinating stand-alone study in its own right. As a result, we dramatically increased our fieldwork involvement with the SSC and extended our involvement with this group from 12 to 24 months, beginning in October 2004 and concluding in September 2006. This ethnographic text reflects the fruits of our expanded labors with the SSC student subculture.

Research Methodology

Schwandt (2001) defines ethnography as a

particular kind of qualitative inquiry distinguishable from case study research, descriptive studies, naturalistic inquiry, and so forth by the fact that it is the process and product of describing and interpreting cultural behavior . . . . [B]oth anthropological and sociological definitions of ethnography stress the centrality of culture as the analytic concept that informs the doing of ethnography.

Ethnography unites both process and product, fieldwork and written text. Fieldwork, undertaken as participant observation, is the process by which the ethnographer comes to know a culture; the ethnographic text is how culture is portrayed. There is general agreement that culture is not visible or tangible but is constructed by the act of ethnographic writing. Hence, understanding what it means to 'write' culture (i.e., literal representation, inscription, transcription, textualization, and cultural translation) is a critical concern in ethnography. (p. 80)

From the outset, we envisioned our SSC ethnographic study to be, as Schwandt describes, both a process and product involving the study of the SSC organization and the cultural behavior of its members. The fieldwork component of the study allowed us prolonged engagement with members of this student subculture, which resulted in numerous opportunities to come to know this organization.

This ethnography is also a product that integrates and synthesizes how we perceived and constructed the SSC student subculture. The text reflects the outcome of the ethnographic process and our social construction of this ideographic subculture. In order to create a useful ethnographic product, researchers must follow distinctive processes for data collection and analysis, processes based in a formalized research ideology. Schwandt (2001) delineates these components as research methods and research methodology. The former includes procedures, techniques, and tools used to gather and analyze data. We discuss our research methods later in this chapter. We begin with a discussion of methodology, which according to Schwandt (2001) is

a theory of how inquiry should proceed. It involves analysis of the assumptions, principles, and procedures in a particular approach to inquiry (that, in turn, governs the use of particular methods). Methodologies explicate and define the kinds of problems that are worth investigating; what comprises a researchable problem, testable hypothesis, and so on; how to frame a problem in such a way that it can be investigated using particular designs and procedures; how to understand what constitutes a legitimate and warranted explanation; how to judge matters of generalizability; how to select and develop appropriate means of generating data; and how to develop the logic linking problem-data generation-analysis-argument. (p. 161)

Methodologically speaking, we situate this research study within an interpretive worldview (Guba & Lincoln, 2005; Schwandt, 1990) with critical theory leanings (Quantz, 1992). Interpretive researchers solicit and document the multiple realities of the researcher and respondents; value and attend to the local context and its history; recognize that knowledge is partial, positioned, and incomplete; and value and celebrate subjective interpretation while recognizing that these interpretations are socially constructed and influenced by the researcher's position and perspective (Schwandt, 2001). In short, by adopting an interpretive lens, we sought to fully engage with participants in the SSC setting in order to capture various members' understanding of themselves, their organization, their values, and the world around them. We recognize as researchers that our own understandings of the SSC, the world, and ourselves influence our interpretations as well as our interactions with SSC participants. Because we created these interpretations, they are "partial and incomplete"; we claim no purchase on the "reality as is" in the SSC subculture.

In addition to interpretivism, we also acknowledge our critical social science (i.e., critical theory) leanings. The critical influence in this SSC study is evident in three distinct ways. First, we infused the issue of power into the interpretive tapestry; specifically, the book focuses on subculture power relations on campus and reveals how power operates within the SSC context. Second, we clearly acknowledge our own presence, position, politics, and subjectivity—acknowledging we are intimately involved with the research context and with SSC participants in the creation of knowledge. Third, we use difference and conflict, rather than similarities and consensus, as organizing concepts in our analysis. The book hopes to, as Foley (2002) recommends,

create a practical, value-laden science that generates the knowledge needed to foster a democratic society and a critical citizenry . . . such knowledge production is part of a long dialogic consciousness-raising process. Such knowledge production should have an "emancipatory intent" . . . that challenges the status quo in some way. (p. 472)

Every subculture holds an *ideology,* or a certain set of beliefs and values guiding social action. But until members understand the complexities and contradictions of their ideologies, Foley's (2002) emancipatory goals for social change remain elusive. Researchers' ability to convey a subculture's complexities to members is made difficult by the fact that often ideologies are implicit rather than explicit. For example, people are more likely to instinctively enact their ideologies than they are to be able to articulate them. A goal of this study is to help SSC members and readers understand what we think are the contradictions inherent in the SSC ideology; in essence, we share what we think is "really going on" and then work with individuals to act on these new realizations and improve the organization. Our obligation is to make the hidden obvious and serve as a resource for change; ultimately, though, change rests with participants and with readers.

Research Methods

We employed a variety of procedures, techniques, and tools to gather and analyze our fieldwork data. In addition, we adopted an emergent research design, in which we had no pre-determined set of research procedures; rather, the actions of SSC participants guided the trajectory of the study and influenced the tools we used to collect data. In this section, we introduce and retrospectively make sense of research procedures that ultimately emerged and the methods we ultimately employed.

Gaining Access

The chances of getting permission to undertake the research are increased when the researcher's interests appear to coincide with those of the subjects. . . . In the course of getting in, researchers must present not only themselves but also their proposed research. . . . Access will be shaped by the cultural and ascriptive differences between the field researcher and the researched. When these differences are minimal, access and even acceptance are likely to be enhanced. (Shaffir & Stebbins, 1991, p. 26)

During our initial meeting with the SSC director, differences in our faith-based beliefs were obvious and significant. There were few ideological similarities between the SSC director and us. Our greatest barrier to gaining access to the SSC was that we were nonbelievers[2] in the eyes of SSC evangelicals. As outsiders desiring to study a student subculture that has historically been maligned by educational researchers and journalists, we needed to take extra care to explain the goal of our study and possible consequences for the group. Evangelical insiders are understandably leery of outsiders writing about their culture, fearing the investigators will misinterpret the culture or offer analyses filled with not-so-flattering stereotypes. Our status as nonbelievers was an initial barrier that we predicted would result in the SSC, as well as other evangelical campus groups, declining our invitation to participate in the study. Fortunately, we were incorrect.

Ironically, it was the evangelical mission of the SSC—to spread the Word of God to nonbelievers—that influenced the director's decision to permit us to study the SSC. The director's willingness to practice what he preached regarding forging relationships with non-Christians eclipsed the fact we were nonbelieving researchers. Ultimately, we forged a respectful partnership with Matthew and his congregation that we sustained throughout the study.

Collecting Data   Throughout our fieldwork, we employed three qualitative data collection techniques: observation (Angrosino, 2005; Spradley, 1980), formal and informal interview (Fontana & Frey, 2005; Spradley, 1979), and document analysis (Hodder, 2000).

OBSERVATIONS   Our fieldwork observations included attending more than 50 events and programs, such as public and private ministry services, evangelical training sessions, Servant Leadership meetings, and Bible study gatherings. We began with generic and unfocused observations, which allowed us to gain preliminary impressions and the "lie of the land." Over time, we sharpened our observational focus by keying in on specific domains of interest (e.g., marginalization) and events (e.g., Bible study).

The moderate size of the organization and the length of the study increased the probability that most SSC members understood the purpose of our overt research study and the reasons for our attendance at their programs. SSC members' passion for and expertise in spreading the Word of God to nonbelievers accelerated the acquaintanceship and data collection processes. Both of these factors ultimately enhanced the quality of our observations.

Spradley (1980) identifies five degrees of participation for researchers: *complete, active, moderate, passive,* and *nonparticipation*. We began our fieldwork as *passive* participants. For example, during Bible studies we sat outside the circle of aspiring biblical scholars and took copious notes. Our initial role as spectator at private and public SSC events seldom appeared to disrupt these gatherings. Gradually, we assumed a *moderate* participatory role in the field. For example, we would join conversations prior to the start of meetings and hang out with members after their Friday worship service.

In Chapter 14, SSC members comment that we did not step outside of our observer roles and engage enough with them and therefore did not gain complex understanding of the organization. Perhaps we should have become "complete" or "active" participants in this organization. Yet accomplishing this outcome was difficult because of our lack of content expertise (e.g., familiarity with the Bible and SSC practices). We accept this explicit criticism. An implicit SSC criticism with which we take exception is that if researchers get closer to research participants and phenomena of study, the researchers' interpretations would more closely align with research participants' interpretations. We do not position our interpretations as "privileged" in relation to the participants; rather, we position them simply as different, the result of the influences of our life experiences.

Lincoln and Guba (1989) indicated that the nature of qualitative inquiry is such that the relationship between researcher and respondent is paramount, taking precedence over traditional goals such as the quest for truth. We keenly understood the importance of rapport and trust with respondents. With each observation opportunity, we gradually and diligently extended our relationships with respondents to create relationships built upon difference, dignity, and respect. As a result of our observations, we not only identified patterns of behaviors but also gradually established trust with respondents. Ultimately, we learned first-hand how well the SSC enacted its espoused values.

We documented our observations in a notebook or laptop computer and fleshed out these notes shortly after each event. We also kept individual personal field journals, in which we recorded our personal experiences, impressions, ideas, problems, questions, and preliminary interpretations and hypotheses. These journals augmented our more factual field notes.

INTERVIEWS We conducted more than 30 formal interviews/focus groups and countless informal interviews with SSC students and staff. Formal interviews began 6 months after our participant-observations began. This delay allowed us to gradually understand the organizational norms and establish trust and rapport with SSC members before we solicited their input.

We heeded the advice of Whyte (1997), who noted, "People need time to get used to having a participant-observer around and to feel that they can trust the researcher not to do anything to harm them" (p. 25).

The interview protocol remained relatively constant throughout the study. Patton (1990) identified several variations in ethnographic interviewing, ranging from informal conversational interviews, in which questions emerge from the context, to a standardized open-ended interview, in which wording and a sequence of questions are predetermined. SSC interviews were informal, open-ended, unstructured, and conversational (Lincoln & Guba, 1985). Although we did not pose predetermined questions, we acknowledged to interviewees our predetermined domains of interest (e.g., evangelical leadership training). This format provided interviewees maximal degrees of freedom to set the agenda and discuss what they deemed important.

During each interview, we explained the purpose of the study, informally introduced the notion of reciprocity, acknowledged risks, discussed confidentiality and its limits, and explained informed consent. We solicited the written consent of each interviewee to conduct the interview and audiotape it; all SSC interviewees signed the consent form and allowed us to audiotape the sessions.

Minimally, each interview consisted of three parts: [1] "Tell me a story that might sensitize me to what it is like to be part of the SSC organization"; [2] "If you were to embark on a study of the SSC how might you conceptualize it—what would you observe, with whom would you talk?"; [3] "Identify people who might share your conceptualization of the SSC and people who would have a different view than yours."

The intent of our initial "Tell me a story . . ." request was to solicit from interviewees seldom-told stories about their life experiences and their SSC-related experiences. Adults are natural storytellers, although they have often learned to suppress their urge to tell stories as a way of knowing (Witherell & Noddings, 1991). Through these solicited stream-of-consciousness stories, we eventually gained a focused and in-depth understanding of the SSC.

The second research question solicited input from respondents regarding ways to modify the study to improve the quality of data we might collect and to improve the quality of our interpretation. Interviewees offered numerous insightful recommendations, which sharpened the focus of the study. The aim of the final interview question was enlisting interviewees' assistance in identifying diverse and information-rich key informants. The aim of this snowball sampling technique (Patton, 2002) was gathering as many differing perspectives as possible. Predictably, SSC interviewees had an easier time identifying individuals who shared their views than those who held opposing views, because the group is relatively homogeneous. With that said, interviewees' sampling recommendations helped us identify a diverse array of SSC members holding various viewpoints.

PHYSICAL ARTIFACTS   "Records, documents, artifacts, and archives— what has traditionally been called 'material culture' in anthropology— constitute a particularly rich source of information about many organizations and programs" (Patton, 2002, p. 293). We collected and carefully studied numerous written materials, such as the SSC Web site, e-mail announcements to members, training manuals, and handouts. These documents helped us confirm and refine our blossoming interpretations and also introduced new areas for investigation.

Analyzing Data   After we expanded our field notes, transcribed interviews, and wrote summaries of physical artifacts we reviewed, we analyzed our data using a cultural analysis framework (Geertz 1973) that allowed us to systematically review data to optimally understand how SSC members make sense of their experiences. We acknowledge at the outset that there is no "getting to the bottom" of the SSC subculture, as Geertz (1973) notes:

> Cultural analysis is intrinsically incomplete. And, worse than that, the more deeply it goes the less complete it is. It is a strange science whose most telling assertions are its most tremulously based, in which to get somewhere with the matter at hand is to intensify the suspicion, both your own and that of others, that you are not quite getting it right. (p. 29)

Geertz aptly describes the "messy," dubious process researchers undertake in analyzing qualitative data. However, despite this "messiness," researchers follow a relatively structured system for sifting through data and forming temporary hypotheses, which they then reanalyze in light of additional data. Specifically, for this study, we began by extracting key units of meaningful information, such as phrases, sentences, and paragraphs, from our three types of data sources (Lincoln & Guba, 1985).

Then, we analyzed data using Glaser's (1965) constant comparative method, which intertwines coding and analysis to generate "a theory which is integrated, consistent, plausible, close to the data. . . . The constant comparative method is concerned with generating and plausibility, suggesting (not provisional-testing) many properties and hypotheses about a general phenomenon" (pp. 437–438). Glaser's method hinges on the process of categorizing data and then integrating categories to create a theory. LeCompte and Preissle (1993) further describe this categorization process as "perceiving, comparing, contrasting, aggregating and ordering, establishing linkages and relationships, and speculating" (p. 238).

Through this process of establishing relationships between data and "playing with ideas," theory inductively emerges from the field experience. For example, it was only after interviewing members about how they study the Bible, attending Servant Leader Team training sessions in which members worked collaboratively on a variety of initiatives, and reading e-mail messages to members encouraging them to attend summer workshops that we came to a fuller understanding of the value the SSC placed on peer teaching and learning. We hope that readers, too, can use LeCompte and Preissle's (1993) suggestions to form their own theories about the narratives and data we present.

Writing We used narrative or storytelling conventions to present our findings. Harrison (2002) describes the perils of embracing a narrative tradition in educational research:

> Most curriculum designers, researchers, and theorists are slow to embrace the use of storytelling because it tends to break the mold of traditional thinking. It is somewhat different—possibly even suspect. The subjectivity in narrative causes both a sense of freedom and uneasiness—freedom in that some of the rules are relaxed and the writer has some license but uneasiness because of believability (credibility of source, text, and events). (p. 73)

Despite the liabilities Harrison noted, we subscribed to a storytelling mode of re-presentation because it [1] challenged our ways of knowing, [2] connected the events, actors, storytellers, and readers to each other, [3] taught and fostered learning, and [4] acted as a springboard for action. Our narratives describe SSC students' experiences and include our own reflections and interpretations. We attempted to depict complex phenomena in an authentic way while remaining self-analytical, political, aware, and honest.

Richardson (2000) identified five criteria for a well-crafted ethnographic text: [1] *substantive contribution* (i.e., does the writing contribute to readers' understanding of the phenomena being investigated?); [2] *aesthetic merit* (i.e., does the use of creative analytic practices result in an interesting and moderately disorienting written document, causing readers to pause, reflect, and generate multiple interpretative responses?); [3] *reflexivity* (i.e., is the author's self-awareness and self-exposure evident, allowing the readers to judge the goodness of the author's perspective?); [4] *impact* (i.e., does the writing affect the reader emotionally and intellectually, and does it generate new questions for readers, moving them to action?); and [5] *expression of reality* (i.e., is the text a credible account of the culture, and does the text embody a sense of lived experiences?).

While writing, we purposely used these five criteria as guides. We sought to craft stories that were interesting, accessible, credible, provocative, moderately disorienting, and educational. We attempted to lay bare our political, ethical, pedagogical, and methodological subjectivities while inviting readers to do the same by reflecting, generating their own interpretative responses, and, most important, acting on these new insights.

One writing issue with which we grappled was protecting the anonymity of the SSC members and their organization. Protecting the anonymity of individual members was easier than protecting the anonymity of the organization. We changed the names of participants, and we asked them to notify us of any glaring personal descriptions that might compromise their identities. We then deleted or modified these references. Although members within the SSC might readily identify individual members, this identification task would be more difficult for outsiders.

Protecting the identity of the SSC was more challenging. Our aim of writing stories replete with thick and rich descriptions of the SSC increased the chance that we will inadvertently reveal and compromise the identity of the organization. We have acknowledged this possibility to SSC members and leaders throughout the study. Despite our valiant efforts, "We know that privacy, anonymity, and confidentiality are virtually impossible to guarantee in qualitative case studies that are of high fidelity" (Lincoln & Guba, 1989, p. 221). Thankfully, Matthew agreed that the benefits of this publication are numerous; thus, he trusted our honest efforts to protect the group while sharing our interpretations in the hopes that this book might benefit readers.

Sandra Harding (1991) wrote, "No one can tell the one, eternally true, perfect story about the way the world is; but we can tell some stories about ourselves, nature, and social life which can be shown with good evidence to be far less partial and distorted—less false—than the dominant ones." (p. 60). This quote demonstrates the power of qualitative inquiry and the way stories provide fresh insights into social life. The process of interpreting events and relationships is a natural activity for humans, which makes stories accessible for readers; stories also often tap into shared avenues of human understanding. Yet the way each storyteller's identity influences her or his story yields many possible interpretations. Again, although we do not believe our interpretations to be "true," we hope readers find them plausible and use them as a basis for further research, discussion, and storytelling.

Research Quality

Ensuring High-Quality Data   To address the issues of quality and subjectivity, we triangulated data, used peer debriefing, conducted member checks with respondents, and created an audit trail (Creswell & Miller, 2000). In the following sections we briefly discuss each of these components.

TRIANGULATION   To establish credibility of the data, we used the process of triangulation. Denzin (1989) identified four kinds of triangulation, all of which we employed in this study. *Data triangulation* refers to the purposeful and systematic use of different data sources involving different individuals at different times and at different places. We regularly solicited the perspectives of the SSC's past and present members, including both those in leadership positions and lower-profile members, many of whom were consumers of SSC programs. We also interacted with former members who strayed from the SSC flock, as well as members of other Christian organizations who explored SSC offerings but ultimately joined different Christian organizations. We interacted with individuals—some numerous times—in a variety of contexts.

Investigator triangulation involves the use of multiple researchers to minimize subjectivities of a single researcher. In the SSC study, although we shared similar faith upbringings rooted in Catholicism, Kelsey began the study as a practicing Catholic, whereas Peter no longer claims an affiliation with the Catholic faith. Differences in gender, age, and accumulated years of research experience between us were obvious, and in the SSC context, they served as assets. Kelsey's closeness in age to many SSC members allowed her to more quickly establish rapport with students than Peter. Kelsey was particularly effective in establishing relationships with many women who were "regulars" at the Bible study sessions she attended. In turn, Peter's familiarity with higher education acted as a gateway to several first-generation college students who joined the SSC. These differences did not simply result in a convenient division of labor based on areas of expertise, but also allowed systematic comparisons of differing and sometimes competing interpretations of issues, rooted in our different life histories.

Theory triangulation is the third kind of triangulation in Denzin's schema. Throughout the study, we viewed the data through interdisciplinary theoretical lenses (e.g., subculture theory, generational theory) to extend the possibilities for generating and disseminating knowledge. We acted as *bricoleurs* (Hebdige, 1979), for we assembled interpretations rooted in these various discourses into an interrelated, coherent system of rich meaning. In essence, the tapestry of data collected from multiple theoretical lenses helped us present previously accepted ideas in a new way—a goal of the study.

Methodological triangulation involves both within-method and between-method forms of triangulation; we included both forms of triangulation in our study. For example, when interviewing the same respondent multiple times, we initially employed an open-ended interview protocol, which provided interviewees maximal degrees of freedom to focus the conversation. In some subsequent interviews, we were more direct in our attempts to collect data about a topic of which we had less understanding. These differing interview protocols, exemplifying method triangulation, yielded important differences. Previously, we discussed between-method triangulation, which involved regularly combining observations with interviews and document analysis. Denzin (1989) argues that the "triangulation of method, investigator, theory, and data remains the soundest strategy of theory construction" (p. 236); we concur.

PEER DEBRIEFING   We regularly debriefed what we were learning about the SSC immediately following observations, which allowed us to continually fine-tune the observation and interview schedules. This emergent design permitted us to connect what we were learning from one fieldwork setting to subsequent contexts (Lincoln & Guba, 1985) and to improve the quality of data we gathered.

MEMBER CHECKS   Periodically, we solicited feedback from SSC participants about our findings and interpretations; this practice is respondent validation, also known as member checking (Schwandt, 2001). This process was particularly important to the outcome of the study, because, "[t]he success or failure of either report or full-blown ethnography depends on the degree to which it rings true to natives and colleagues in the field" (Fetterman, 1998, p. 11). We used these member checks to help correct errors of fact, but, more important, to allow respondents to critique our tentative conclusions. Through this hermeneutic and dialectic process (Guba & Lincoln, 1989) we shared, understood, considered, critiqued, and acted upon these different interpretations, claims, concerns, and issues. Still, researcher–respondent differences persist, showcased in Chapter 14 (when we showcase SSC members' reactions to our published interpretations of their organization).

Member checking did not help us get it "right" or get closer to truth, but it allowed us to monitor and lessen the power gap between respondents and ourselves. Although we desired an egalitarian relationship with respondents, we could not avoid unequal power dynamics privileging us as the researchers. Member checking was one technique we used to minimize the power differential between researchers and respondents. By allowing (for example) SSC participants to critique our interpretations and provide feedback on our manuscripts, we were able to establish a more equal, mutually beneficial exchange of information. As a result of these member checks, we made numerous changes to our manuscript before submitting it for publication.

AUDIT TRAILS   To provide evidence that our inquiry decisions were logical and defensible and that our data could confirm our results and conclusions, we established an audit trail (Lincoln & Guba, 1985) including raw data such as tapes, interview notes, documents, debriefing summaries, and correspondence.

VALIDITY   To address issues of goodness criteria and subjectivity concerns, we sought *face validity* (Lather 1986a; Lather 1986b) by inviting select research participants to review and react to the research findings. To address *content validity,* which focuses on theory construction (Lather 1986a; Lather 1986b), we constantly compared our preconceived theoretical perspectives with the data to ensure that the data has influenced our original theories. To address *catalytic validity* (Lather 1986a; Lather 1986b), which focuses on how well the research undertaking contributes to social change (not simply to abstract knowledge), we shared findings with the

SSC in the hope that dialogues (and social change) based on the interpretation of this subculture will result.

Navigating Fieldwork Dilemmas   Inevitably accompanying each fieldwork experience are dilemmas with which the fieldworker must grapple. This was true in our case. Throughout this chapter, we have acknowledged several of these quandaries (e.g., gaining access, being outsiders) and have briefly revealed how we resolved them. In this section, we introduce and discuss one challenge with which we struggled throughout the study. This issue regularly appeared in our personal journals and was a frequent topic of conversations during our debriefing meetings. We acknowledge at the outset that we do a better job of sensitizing readers to this complex challenge than of offering a tidy solution.

MAJOR DIFFERENCES IN RESEARCHERS' AND PARTICIPANTS' ONTOLOGIES AND EPISTEMOLOGIES   A major methodological issue we encountered was navigating the tensions between our own and SSC members' ontological and epistemological beliefs. Guba and Lincoln (1989) define ontology as an individual's fundamental view of the nature of reality. As interpretivists (with critical theory leanings), we subscribe to a *relativist ontology*, which means that we believe there are multiple, socially constructed realities.

Most members of the SSC, however, subscribe to a *realist ontology*, which holds there is a single reality that "operates according to immutable natural laws" (Guba & Lincoln, 1989, p. 84). In essence, many SSC members believe in the indelible Word of God as Truth, whereas we believe truth is something that is socially constructed, or created by humans to make sense of their world. Because humans do not have license on any certain "reality," multiple explanations for phenomena exist. Often when these ontologies clashed, they proved very disorienting to both SSC members and us.

We also struggled with conflicting epistemologies, which Guba and Lincoln (1989) define as "the relationship of the knower to the known" (p. 83). As interpretivists, we assert a *subjectivist epistemology* in which the researcher and participants jointly participate in the creation of knowledge. For example, we spent time participating in SSC meetings and speaking directly with SSC students in order to collectively create knowledge. This knowledge-construction process is sometimes complex because it allows for the competing subjectivities of both researcher and participants to enter into conversation. On the other hand, many SSC members hold a *dualist objectivist epistemology* in which there is a distinct way to understand God's Truth (i.e., through the Bible). From this perspective, individuals shun personal and societal values as ways of creating knowledge. Instead, SSC students turn to the Bible for answers about how to conduct every aspect of their daily lives.

Daily quandaries arose from these differences. Often, we wondered whether it was futile to study the SSC group, given that our constructed reality (i.e., our interpretations) of the group may not be valid in the eyes of SSC members, for whom God's Word was the only authentic source of wisdom. We worried that we might not be able to fulfill a major goal of the study, which was to share our interpretations with the SSC in the hopes that social change might occur.

Occasionally, we became frustrated when participating in SSC activities. For example, SSC Bible study participants spent a significant amount of time interpreting and debating the meaning of the Bible. These robust meaning-making activities appeared to be aligned with our subjectivist epistemological belief system. However, these meetings frequently ended with Bible study leaders sharing the "definitive interpretation" of God's Word—a dualist, objectivist process for studying the Bible. We gently broached this topic with participants (usually during formal interviews) and asked, "How can you find value in spending hours debating Bible verses, when in the end you learn the one 'True' answer?" Diplomatically posing these important questions was no easy task since we did not want to convey that we thought their trust in God's word was *wrong*.

We recognize and appreciate the value of differing ontologies and epistemologies; yet, as interpretivists, we found coming to understand and accept SSC members' views to be, at times, ironic and challenging. Peshkin (2000) asserts: "I judge what I have managed to learn to be useful or not, I judge where it can fit in my line of reasoning, and I judge what extent of qualification I must attach to what I believe I can conclude" (p. 9). Toward these ends, we have purposely made an effort in this book to acknowledge the limitations and strengths of both the SSC's and our own ontological and epistemological belief systems. We leave it to individual readers to evaluate the merits of each. We also sought to provide substantial evidence for our interpretations and to qualify our ontologically based and epistemologically based opinions.

3

RESEARCHERS' TALES

Rituals of Disclosure

Strangers in a Strange Land[1]

As the Friday evening worship service reaches a mid-point, Christa returns to the altar and instructs the congregation to form prayer circles. As students comply, Christa distributes handouts about Vanuatu, an island in the South Pacific. She announces that attendees are going to pray for the people of Vanuatu in honor of the Students Serving Christ's (SSC's) weekly fellowship activity of watching the reality TV show *Survivor: Vanuatu*. Two women invite me (Kelsey) to join their circle, and I accept their offer. I study the handout, which includes vital statistics about the country and the number of missionaries of various religious denominations working there. I learn that Christians comprise only a small percentage of natives. I am simultaneously uncomfortable and fascinated. As a consumer of anthropology texts, I resist and dislike the idea of proselytizing "natives," yet I appreciate SSC members' passion about spreading the Word.

Not wanting to miss the nuances of the prayer circle, I quickly snap my head up, only to notice students sitting in small circles with their heads lowered as they speak softly to each other. Attendees speak in a free-flowing style (reminiscent of free-writing assignments I did in elementary school) and say whatever comes to mind. As one person's voice trails off, another person begins. The group excuses me from the public prayer ritual, which relieves me. Prayers focus on evangelizing and getting people to know Christ. Most pray about the need for God to help the evangelical efforts in Vanuatu. "Because we know You want *all* of them to know You, Lord," one male asserts. Eventually, Christa's voice rings out above the rest during the final prayer. Students reply in unison, "Amen," and quietly return to their seats.

Although prayer circle participants found nothing unusual about their evangelical prayer ritual for the people of Vanuatu, we found it strange. Events of this nature intrigued us and sometimes made us uncomfortable. Just as SSC students' life experiences influence their interpretation of the "exotic" non-Christian Vanuatu culture, our life experiences of this occasionally "exotic" SSC culture influence the ways we observed and interpreted their rituals. Who we are influences what we see and how we interpret what we see. In order to fully understand and evaluate our interpretations of this student organization, readers should understand our life experiences and faith as authors. Peshkin (1986), in his ethnography of a fundamentalist Christian school, discussed researcher subjectivity: "It is clear that no story told about any school can be everyone's story. Obviously, the story in this book is mine. In one way or another, it is about Bethany Baptist Church and its school, about the pseudonymous Pastor Muller and Headmaster McGraw, about my Christian landlady and several other Bethany families, about a school faculty and several hundred students—and unavoidably about me" (p. ix).

Like Peshkin, we realize that to casual readers, these stories appear to be about the SSC—its staff, its students, its programs, and its relationships with peers. Yet ultimately and unavoidably these stories and interpretations are about *us*—the researchers and authors. It is for this reason that we devote the remainder of this chapter to sharing our life stories. We share these stories not as self-indulgent interludes but as a necessary prerequisite to understanding *our* meaning making.

About the Researchers

Kelsey: Finding My Faith

Reinharz (1997) notes that the self-discovery process researchers undertake when conducting a qualitative study is complex because the concept of the "self" tends to change during the inquiry process. She argues, "We not only bring the self into the field. . . . [we also] create the self in the field" (cited in Guba & Lincoln, 2005, p. 210). I knew that studying a personally relevant topic such as religion and faith would likely affect me in multiple ways; however, I did not fully understand the extent to which I would learn about my own beliefs and myself in the process of coming to understand the SSC.

I was raised Catholic. Both of my parents came from Midwestern German Catholic families, and 7:30 a.m. Sunday Mass was nonnegotiable. Sleepy-eyed, my sister and I would pry ourselves out of bed—sometimes willingly, sometimes begrudgingly—to sit in pews in the back section of church; we were two young people in a sea of grey-haired, early-rising regulars. This weekly commitment saved us from the Catholic guilt of disappointing God and our parents but also came with the promise of breakfast afterward in a local diner, something we enjoyed immensely. My family recited a standard Catholic prayer of thanksgiving before dinner each evening, and because I attended public K–12 schools, my parents made certain every Wednesday throughout my childhood that I attended Catechism classes to learn about the sacraments, the need for God to forgive my sins, and what it meant to be "good."

Baptisms, first communions, and confirmation rituals were important extended family gatherings. Thus religious and family traditions were strongly intertwined. Yet my family rarely discussed or debated the significance of these events; rather, we spent time catching up with one another and enjoying the potluck meals, gifts, and cake that always accompanied these major occasions. Similarly, I seldom had discussions with my parents about the religious and faith beliefs embedded in the strong set of moral codes by which they lived, and that they made crystal-clear to my sister and me. "Be responsible." "Work hard." "Be modest." "Be thankful for what you have." "Care for others less fortunate." I am appreciative for these moral codes; they help to form the foundation for my own value system, and I hope to instill these values in my own children one day. However, when I left for college, I had a fuzzy understanding of what it really meant to be Catholic and why religious-based events and morals were so important to our family.

Like many of America's current generation of students, I hoped during my undergraduate career to learn more about my faith and search for meaning and purpose in my life. I expected that a faith-based environment might provide me the opportunity to spend time searching for meaning. I enrolled at St. Norbert College, a small Catholic liberal arts institution in Wisconsin. I found that my values aligned with the college's social justice, service-based mission, and I enjoyed continuing my childhood routine of attending Mass and going to brunch with friends on Sundays. My introductory theology class caused me to think slightly differently about my faith but did not push me to deeply consider my beliefs. We explored several other faith traditions, including Buddhism, Islam, and Judaism, but I never genuinely reflected on how these other traditions compared to my own. In addition, we focused on a Catholic Christian perspective, only touching on Protestant Christianity. My best friend, a Presbyterian, asked me, "Why do you believe what you believe? Why do you go to church every week?" I could never adequately respond to these important questions. Instead, I would automatically reply, "It's what I do and it's important." Academic coursework and student organization activities consumed most of my time, and, regrettably, I never took advantage of opportunities to do what I set out to do—deeply explore my faith with peers.

When Peter and I began the SSC study in 2004, I was concurrently enrolled in a graduate seminar focusing on theories of college student development, including the ways undergraduate students grow in their faith during college. Little did I know I would soon experience the same personal changes, only as a graduate student. At the time, I continued to attend a Catholic church but felt less connected to my faith. I volunteered to study the SSC as part of the research Peter and I were doing that centered on the political actions of college students. Colleagues on the research team seemed hesitant to study the SSC, in light of the stereotypes and baggage that accompanies the label "evangelical Christian." However, my curiosity overruled any reservations I had about the group, and I offered to begin the process of gaining entry.

I had some contact with a few evangelical Christian friends during college but never fully understood their Jesus-centered lifestyle. I should mention that at that point I assumed that Catholicism and Protestantism were really part of "one big happy Christian family," and that I would not encounter anything *too* different from my previous faith-related experiences.

However, as I observed and participated in SSC-sponsored activities, I eventually realized that evangelical Christianity is indeed different from Catholicism. As a result of these pivotal ideological differences, I was more of an outsider than I originally expected. As I got to know SSC students, their behaviors simultaneously confused and pleasantly surprised me. The concepts of salvation, evangelism, deference to the Bible, and a personal relationship with Jesus were foreign—and sometimes uncomfortable—to me. Yet, throughout the project, students' unwavering commitment to their faith and their unquenchable desire to get closer to God struck me. Surprisingly, they were not nearly as "pushy" as I imagined evangelical Christians to be.

During our first year of data collection, scandal and public debates about moral codes and Church doctrine continued to engulf Catholicism. It was a time when Catholics increasingly felt the need to defend their reason for *being* Catholic, and I realized that I could not identify the benefits or truths of my own faith. I began questioning this institution that was an ingrained part of me. During the 2005 summer, Peter and I reviewed literature on evangelical Christianity and Christian college students. Throughout this process, I found myself wanting to learn more about the core ideological beliefs of my faith. Although I am certain SSC students and staff would have been extremely helpful in teaching me about the differences between Catholicism and evangelical Christianity (in fact, they offered to discuss the subject with me several times, not knowing that I was interested in the topic), I decided to direct my questions to other Christian friends. Because the SSC is an evangelical group, and its members feel a strong responsibility to "share the Word" with people who, like me, are spiritually "searching," I avoided sharing this aspect of my life and publicly maintained my Catholic status. I did not want SSC members to evangelize *me*.

Peter and I wanted to minimize the possibility of letting our identities overshadow our interactions with SSC participants; we wanted to focus on enhancing understanding of this subculture and the ways SSC members made meaning of their collegiate experiences. Thus, although I knew it might be possible to deepen relationships with participants by disclosing my faith struggles, my research orientation superseded my desire to use my time in the field to resolve my personal faith conflicts. I found Dewalt and Dewalt's (2002) advice helpful. They recommend striking a balance between disclosing information with participants and maintaining some distance from which to see the culture "as an outsider." I now realize the decision to self-disclose personal information is one of many ethical tensions with which qualitative researchers constantly struggle; it is a challenge to use self-disclosure to develop rapport with participants while simultaneously maintaining an outside perspective. By not seeking SSC members' counsel in personal faith matters, I was able to better achieve this balance. However, I shared much information about other aspects of my personal life that did generate substantial rapport.

Throughout the fieldwork phase and the initial writing of this book, I situated myself as a "questioning Catholic" and spent time exploring other faiths. I reflected on my core beliefs about the nature of God and the purpose of life: Aside from the religious "shell" I inhabited throughout my young life, which was centered on superfluous ceremony, ritual, music and creed, what do I *really believe?* The more I read about Catholicism, the more I realized it did not fully align with my beliefs. Beginning in fall 2005, I attended services at a variety of churches, including some evangelical churches similar in nature to the SSC. I discovered that core Protestant beliefs are a better match to my vision of God and the world than Catholic beliefs. In addition, some of the Protestant churches I visited subscribed to more liberal views on social issues, which appealed to me.

I do believe in God, and I do consider myself "Christian." But I am not an *evangelical* Christian. I find value in aspects of many different faiths, both Christian and non-Christian, and I could never tell another person that he or she was "wrong" about God. My beliefs about God and life represent the best conclusion I have discovered up to this point, but this does not mean that others do not also have equally (or more) plausible conclusions about God and reality. What matters to me is how people conduct themselves and treat others, regardless of the ideology that guides them.

Some Christians may argue that my acceptance of other religions and refusal to overtly "spread the Word" negates my ability to call myself a "true Christian." I understand and respect these arguments. However, I have become comfortable subscribing to Christian beliefs without evangelism. To me, religion and spirituality are very personal quests, and it is healthy to critically analyze one's own religion and hold an individual view of life meaning. The faith community my spouse and I joined—a more liberal, yet mainline Lutheran church—is one that "more or less" describes my beliefs and that is a "better fit" than other options I have explored. In a way, I guess I am surprisingly in agreement with the SSC students who are tentative to label themselves as members of a church and focus instead on finding a supportive community that will allow them to strengthen their personal faith, or what they would call a "personal relationship with Jesus." My church community allows me to worship in a way that is comfortable for me and to continue to explore my own beliefs with individuals roughly in the same frame of thought.

My shift to a new religious community has come only after a turbulent time of personal grief and uncertainty, guilt and confusion. Yet, I am grateful for it and am open to future crisis, epiphanies, and exploration. This research project served as an impetus for my own religious awakening of sorts. One of the greatest personal lessons from this research experience has been that an understanding of faith and one's purpose is an ongoing process of discovery. I am certain I will continue to reevaluate my beliefs, and how I wish to integrate faith into my life. All religions have their contradictions, and it is important to understand the intricacies of one's own faith tradition, as well as those of others'. I hope that readers, as a result of reading this book, will take the time to explore their own faith or sense of meaning in life—whatever that may be. I also hope this book can help debunk some of the negative perceptions of Christian students, which I admit I held at the beginning of the project but have come to see in a new light.

On a professional level, I learned many lessons from this research study. I have gained an enhanced understanding of the ways that religious students' faith so deeply intersects their career and life decision-making. Consequently, I am open to speaking with religious students about the types of careers in which they feel they can best serve God. I also better recognize the importance of Christian organizations in helping students of faith to have positive learning experiences while on campus. These organizations serve as support networks and safe spaces through which students can explore their faith and navigate their collegiate lives. The SSC and other similar organizations promote important life lessons, such as the value of lifelong learning, the importance of collaboration and teaching others, and the ability to define and live by a personal belief system. In the end, these characteristics are valuable lessons we hope all graduates learn before they depart our institutions. Christian organizations are one of many often-overlooked cocurricular sites that provide students with significant learning experiences. I urge readers to search their own institutions for similar "hidden" learning centers, for each has lessons to teach individuals interested in promoting student learning.

Peter: Losing My Religion

I am a "non-Christian" and a "sinner." I confess I had not thought about these descriptors for a while until Kelsey and I began this Students Serving Christ (SSC) ethnographic study in October 2004. These labels troubled me, especially when I listened to Matthew, the SSC director, preach on a Friday evening:

> Jesus was a friend to sinners. We too need to befriend sinners. We all know that we can lead a horse to water, but we can't make it drink. It is not our job, as laborers for Christ, to make them drink; our job is to make them thirsty. . . . Some of my dearest friends reject Jesus. We need to learn how to share our faith with them. We need the right heart, not methods to reach them, and then God will bless all of us.

Matthew's sermon induced a moment of paranoia for me. Was Matthew, who was aware that I am not a Christian, making purposeful eye contact with me as he talked about non-Christian sinners? I immediately flashed back to a scene from the film *Taxi Driver*, where the alienated Travis Bickle stands alone in a room and calls out, "You talkin' to me? You talkin' to me? You talkin' to me? Well, I'm the only one [non-Christian] here." I am curious, suspicious, and skeptical.

Whenever I sense a bout of anger on the horizon, I shift into my analytical mode. In this particular instance, I dissected Matthew's argument. I agree with his advice about befriending and respecting "the other" (in this context, sinners). Matthew appears to respect individuals who view the world differently than he does; I, too, embrace this value. Yet, his implicit pity, resulting from sinners' ignorance about the need to follow Jesus, annoys me. Matthew reminds his congregation that they cannot make proverbial horses drink if they are not ready. As a lifelong learner and professional educator, I concur with Matthew; coercive teaching is futile. Still, I remain wary of people whose calling is to make me (metaphorically) thirsty. Although I enjoy learning about new ideas, I evade solicitors of all sorts—regardless of whether they are teachers, telemarketers, or evangelicals—even if I endorse or need their products. I value persistence—in Matthew's context, if at first you don't succeed in evangelizing, try and try again. I struggle with figuring out the fine line between being persistent and being annoying.

As was the case during many events I observed during this study, SSC core values, embedded in members' commentary and actions, elicited from me wide-ranging reactions. Simultaneous feelings of simpatico and alienation were common. Sorting out these conflicting emotions motivated me in my quest to understand this unique student subculture. If at first you don't succeed in understanding, try and try again.

Weeks later, after discussing the sermon with Matthew, I concluded that my momentary paranoia was unfounded. As a result of several casual debriefings with Matthew, I came to regard him as a genuine, principled, honest, sincere, and respectful human being. As I write this confessional tale,[2] aimed at laying bare my subjectivities, I adhere to the values that Matthew modeled during his sermon—being genuine, principled, honest, sincere, and respectful. Like my reaction to Matthew's sermon, some readers might disagree with the content of my story. This I expect. Minimally, I hope that readers hear my story (not necessarily agree with it), and that the ideas it presents provoke them to think differently.

During a formal interview with an SSC staff member, the dreaded question I knew someone would eventually pose finally arose—"What kind of religious journey have you been on?" The question was sincere and appropriate. Because I was asking SSC members about their religious journeys, it only seemed "right" that I would reciprocate and answer the same question, if asked. Despite having rehearsed a concise response to this question, I froze. Eventually, I offered a meandering, stammered, and woefully inarticulate and inadequate response. Part of the problem was that I no longer conceptualized my life as a religious journey. My frank and straightforward persona usually results in me simply acknowledging this fact and moving on. Yet, in this instance, I could not. Would not being on a religious journey disqualify me from conducting this study?

At the root of this question and my discomfort is legitimacy. I ask myself, "Is it a good idea for non-Christians to study Christians? Can non-Christians really understand Christians? Will anyone take seriously a book about Christian collegians written by a nonbeliever?" Both Kelsey and I continue to ponder these three questions even now, after we have concluded our study.

One strategy to sidestep these questions of legitimacy would be to ignore them by not revealing to the audience our faith-leanings. For instance, Robert Rhoads (1994) in *Coming Out in College,* an ethnographic study of gay men, purposely concealed from his readers that he was a straight researcher studying gay men. Students in my seminars who have read this book inevitably want to know Rhoads' sexual orientation: "Is Rhoads gay?" they never fail to ask. Answering this question mattered; it was a prerequisite to discussing the book.

In personal correspondence, Rhoads revealed that gay men reading *Coming Out in College* have correctly guessed that he was straight based on the ways he described and analyzed the case study.

Kelsey and I suspect that if we were to repress information about our religious upbringings and leanings, evangelical Christian readers, like Rhoads' gay readers, would likely guess correctly that we are nonbelievers, and probably "out" us. Because I have not been on a religious journey, it would be disingenuous for me to fabricate experiences in an attempt to answer religious affiliation questions. Instead, I describe my life journey during the past 52 years and highlight events that have significantly shaped and continue to shape my identity and worldviews. In particular, I discuss the evolution of my views on faith and education, the twin centerpieces of this study, so that readers can determine the legitimacy of this text and me.

During an interview, Steve Earle, a singer–songwriter, commented, "I'm not a Jew, I'm not a Christian, I'm not a Muslim. My spiritual system is retarded. I believe there's a God and it ain't me and that's as far as I've gotten" (Bader & Duxleter, 2003, p. 60). Although I perceive myself to be a bit farther along in my spiritual journey than Steve Earle, I, too, acknowledge that my progress has been slow and that I have a long way to go. I have not seriously explored religion in any depth in my personal and professional lives, and I confess that I am not a religious scholar. These revelations are probably evident to readers. What I have explored in depth, and continue to explore, are the core values that guide me in my professional and personal lives. Recounting my journey is risky and uncomfortable for me, but it is a small price to pay to establish my legitimacy.

I was a Bronx-born baby and a New Jersey resident during my formative years, and my parents and church were the two strongest influences on my identity. As a practicing Catholic (through high school), my parents, brother, sister, and I religiously attended Mass each Sunday. At my parochial school, I served as an altar boy. I sang in the church choir and even served as a church organist for a brief stint.

Even my "secular" elementary school activities had Catholic connections. My Boy Scout troop had an affiliation with the Church. I earned merit badges for reading, camping, and canoeing and was the recipient of the Ad Altare Dei Cross and the Pope Pius XII medal—awards recognizing me as having meritoriously achieved the National and Diocesan regulations and requirements. These seamless uncommon connections served me well as a youth.

My mother and her nun colleagues were no-nonsense teachers at my school. They followed the rules and expected students to do the same. Lessons were black-and-white; there was the Catholic way in life, and the wrong way, with nothing between. Catholic dogma was the foundation for all rules in school and at home. Teachers integrated the topic of religion into every subject of study. A scrapbook that my mother maintained for me includes volumes of evidence of this strong Catholic influence during my formative years. A Christmas letter I wrote to my parents in 1964 read: "Dear Mother and Father. May Baby Jesus bless you and always keep you mear (sic) Him. Happy Christmas. Love, Peter." I recall copying the message from the blackboard onto my card as part of an art assignment. I also possess numerous loose-leaf pages where I had printed 20 times on each sheet the phrase "I love God." My teachers assigned these punitive tasks whenever students violated a Catholic rule.

My family regularly linked family get-togethers with special church rituals such as Christmas and Easter services, First Holy Communions, confirmations, and even funeral Masses. The majority of the keepsakes my mother included in my scrapbook were mementos of religious milestones. One card read: "Dearest Peter: This is to commemorate a very blessed and happy occasion—serving your first Mass on December 8, 1965—St. Luke's Church, Stratford, NJ at 6:00 p.m. Love, Mother."

At an early age, I learned that in order to remain in good standing with my parents and my church, I had to refrain from questioning authority, especially Catholic dogma. Blind faith, not critical reflection, was the foundation upon which my parents organized my world. A negative by-product of this absolute adherence to Catholic dogma was that my family seldom discussed or critiqued the religious rituals in which we engaged. We simply accepted them. My parents' commitment to Catholic doctrine made for an unambiguous childhood.

Like many of my peers during adolescence, I began to question and ultimately rebel against authority. Seldom receiving satisfactory explanations to my incessant "why" questions pertaining to faith, I created some family strife. The absolute nature of Catholicism in my family made it an obvious and easy target of critique for me during this mutinous phase of life (which my father claims lasted a decade). I was a rebel who knew little about his cause—but I was a rebel nonetheless. I rejected most formal institutions with which I was previously affiliated, such as the Boy Scouts, high school, and especially the

Catholic Church. Although I began to disavow these institutions, I credit them today for helping me recognize that one of my raw core values centers on cognitive complexity (i.e., critical and reflective thinking and the integration of cognitive and affective dimensions of my identity). This is a value I continue to nurture 40 years later.

As I gradually established my independence from my parents and the Catholic Church, I abandoned my church organist gigs to play keyboards for a local garage band instead. In my small town, assembling a five-piece combo necessitated that I venture out of my comfort zone and interact with "Protestants," as we called them. This was a risky venture, because all of my elementary school peers were exclusively Catholic.

I recall feeling sorry for these Protestants who attended the local public school, because my parents taught me they were destined to spend an eternity in Hell. As I interacted with non-Catholics, I discovered that many Protestants felt sorry for Catholics, who were en route to Hell because they eschewed reading the Bible. My Protestant friends and I shared many common values. Through these interactions I began to understand and appreciate the lives of other people, many of whom did not fit into tidy categories. Dichotomous categories, such as *Catholic* and *non-Catholic,* that I had employed to organize my worldviews began to crumble. Was I losing my religion?

In high school, I was a moderately motivated student who, surprisingly, succeeded in staying out of trouble. Teachers usually rewarded my good behavior and mediocre academic performance with above-average grades. Reading and listening to music interested me more than sports, which relegated me to the margins of the "in crowd" at my school. I modeled myself after my father, an avid reader. I learned about faraway places and far-out ideas by reading books. Through reading, I developed a curiosity about the "other," something I continue to cultivate 30 years later.

Although I liked to read and learn, I did not really enjoy my experiences at Pope Paul VI High School until I encountered some post-1960s, unconventional priests and lay teachers who appeared less rigid and more flexible than my elementary school nuns. When discussing topics such as religion and faith, I found myself for the first time in my life fully engaged in discussions and debates. Teachers invited me to think and even to disagree with them instead of telling me what to think. I relished the idea of being an independent—though primitive—thinker. Faith and religion became domains of inquiry, worthy of my curiosity. I learned to be a principled dissenter—a rebel who was slowly learning about his causes. My Catholic mentors helped me not only to acquire and value knowledge, but also to critique it.

Teachers also blurred the boundaries of learning. I not only learned in their classrooms, but we also went into the community to practice what we were learning. In conjunction with reading about the poor, and about social responsibility, we visited nearby Camden and cleaned up parks and met with priests who ministered to residents. As a member of the lower middle class, I suddenly realized how my parents had shielded me from the troubles of the world. I became more self-aware and sensitive (a quality my current students might argue I have since lost). Retrospectively making sense of my high school years, I realize that being a Catholic, something that was in the foreground of my identity development as a youth, moved to the background, whereas exploring what it meant to be a moral person moved to the epicenter of my late adolescent identity portrait.

My parents lobbied for me to attend a Catholic college. They were willing to go into debt to pay for private higher education that might bring me back into the fold. I enrolled in a nearby Catholic institution, LaSalle College, for reasons that had little to do with its religious affiliation or the desire to satisfy my parents. The College was one of the few higher education institutions that expressed an interest in me, and it was far enough from my home that I had to live on campus—but close enough that I could continue to regularly interact with family and high school friends. I remained ambivalent about joining another religious community, but the college was kind enough to want me, so I enrolled.

In August 1974, during my first week of college, I joined an organization that booked rock concerts and films on campus. Organizational leaders promised new members they could hang out with the touring bands performing on campus and regularly screen 35-mm films in their residence halls. In light of those perks, I enlisted. In 1976, I became president of this organization. Two months later, I had a showdown with the dean of students, because the organization wanted to screen the film *Fritz the Cat,* the first X-rated feature-length cartoon, on campus. By today's standards, *Fritz the Cat* would be considered too tame for the Cartoon Network, but at the time, it was a highly controversial film, especially on this Catholic campus. Needless to say, the dean banned the viewing of the film.

Despite this stinging defeat, I gained an invaluable education in Catholic college politics and began to realize the benefits of learning opportunities outside the classroom. Booking films, negotiating band contracts, and verbally sparring with the dean were powerful educational opportunities that allowed me to experiment and gain confidence as a leader, orator, debater, ethicist, and collaborator.

Meaningful academic opportunities augmented my educationally rich cocurricular experiences. I remember thinking differently about "bums" after I read James Spradley's (1970) *You Owe Yourself a Drunk: An Ethnography of Urban Nomads,* required reading in a sociology seminar. The book introduced me to issues of class privilege and social justice. In my developmental psychology seminar, we discussed empirical studies that erroneously linked race and ethnicity to intelligence. I altered the way I thought about "facts," "truth," "objectivity," and race as a result of seminar discussions. My experimental psychology instructor taught me what it took to produce high-quality scholarly work. After numerous missteps, I recognized that I needed to spend days (not minutes) in the library if I wanted to learn to be a serious student. My religious studies professor modeled for me ways I could be both a critic and proponent of organized religion. Through his tutelage, I recognized the perils of my dichotomous thinking. These mentors helped me to explore more deeply the many values I developed as a child, including dedication to caring for the less fortunate, to combating discrimination, to working hard, to doing the best I could, and to respecting individuals different from me.

The dean of students, my initial nemesis and eventual mentor, allowed me glimpses into his professional life. Faculty encouraged me to pursue a graduate degree. These interactions influenced me to pursue a graduate degree in higher education administration. I appreciated their tireless efforts to support students. I hoped to do the same after I completed my graduate studies.

As a master's student in 1978, I continued to develop my intellect in the classroom by viewing social problems through a variety of disciplinary lenses. Seminars in student development allowed me to retrospectively make sense of my developmental journey and how I might use this knowledge to help future college students persist in college and achieve academically. Organizational development seminars helped me understand my propensity to distance myself from formal organization while remaining close to members of these organizations. In my graduate assistantships and subsequent full-time work experiences in residence life, student activities, and the dean of students's office, I was able to apply knowledge I gained in the classroom and recognize the struggles associated with espousing an ideal and enacting it.

In 1985, Marcia Baxter (a Protestant, now my spouse of 23 years) and I intended to wed. Preparing for marriage was a crossroads of sorts for me. My lifelong quest to lead a moral life never waned, though my affiliation with organized religion did. My experiences in high school and college were not very religious or Catholic, but members of these institutions taught me how to acquire knowledge, think, serve society, appreciate others, gain practical skills, set life goals, collaborate, be ethical, and maintain integrity. As we planned our wedding, we explored the possibility of getting married in the Catholic Church, a reconciliation of sorts with an institution I abandoned years ago.

Because Marcia had been previously married, if she were to marry in the Catholic Church, she would need to seek an annulment. We consulted a priest, who listened carefully to Marcia's story and then gently suggested ways for her to craft a story that would meet the Church's criteria for granting an annulment. He tried to help Marcia fit her "square peg" story into the Catholic Church's "round hole" ideology. The irony of a priest coaching a non-Catholic to tell a story that contained lies of omission to gain entry into a religious congregation that commands "Thou Shall Not Lie" influenced our decision to abandon this Catholic option for marriage. The priest understood, supported, and respected our intentions; I respected and appreciated his intentions and values. Of grave concern to me was the Church's absolute and unyielding stance, which did not take into consideration Marcia's particular history and context before rendering a decision. The ideological conflict helped me to clarify my values and also illuminated my skepticism toward organizations in general and religious organizations in particular.

As a doctoral student in higher education administration in 1989, I focused my efforts on understanding and appreciating human difference. My many anthropology seminars aided me in this quest. Philosophy and social foundations of inquiry seminars invited me to explore in great depth concepts such as ontology, epistemology, and methodology—ideas I could apply to not only my research but also my life. I reconsidered what it meant to learn.

Since 1993, I have been a faculty member in a graduate program that prepares students interested in pursuing careers in higher education administration (e.g., as a dean of students). As a professor, I try to profess my evolving values. As a lifelong learner, I seek to learn from the students with whom I interact on a daily basis. For the past 25 years, I have resided in college towns and affiliated myself with a variety of public institutions as a graduate student, an administrator, and a faculty member. Assuming these diverse roles at these diverse universities has allowed me, among other things, to teach, learn, revisit, and evaluate my formative foundational beliefs and subsequent worldviews. While on this journey, I may have lost my religion, but I have found meaningful ways to live my life.

Although this tale is hardly as comprehensive and coherent as I had desired, I hope it reveals some of my core values, which influence my stories and interpretations regarding the SSC, as well as my motives for initiating this study. Still two key questions persist: Why would a person who has lost his religion want to study a religious student organization? Does he have an axe to grind?

My stock reason for wanting to study a Christian student organization is that it represents a distinct and understudied student subculture worthy of inquiry. Yet, if this were the only selection criterion, I could have as easily studied hundreds of other student organizations. My motivation for wanting to study the SSC stemmed from my curiosity about this student subculture, whose members' life experiences appeared so different from my upbringing, my peers, and me. I seldom interacted with peers who read the Bible, attended evangelical worship services, sang praise songs on Friday evenings, thought it was "wrong" to challenge authority, or openly talked about their love for Jesus. I base my preference for studying the SSC on studying a group whose interests, life story, and beliefs seemed, at first glance, so foreign and antithetical to my own. Although I have no interest in being like SSC members, I have a sincere interest in understanding them. Peshkin, when discussing his researcher subjectivity, noted,

> My subjectivity is the basis for the story that I am able to tell. It is a strength on which I build. It makes me who I am as a person and as a researcher, equipping me with the perspectives and insights that shape all that I do as a researcher, from the selection of a topic clear through to the emphasis I make in my writing. Seen as a virtue, subjectivity is something to capitalize on rather than exorcise. (Glesne & Peshkin, 1992, p. 104)

Like Peshkin, I acknowledge my subjectivity that was the basis for studying the SSC. I recognize that "we will never be entirely free of our own preferred ways of viewing situations and our own biases. We can, however, be more self-aware" (Ely, Anzul, Friedman, Garner, & Steinmetz, 1991, p. 54). Greater self-awareness and acknowledgment of my biases have been the goals that I hope are reflected in the story of my life journey. As Barley (1983) admits, "the justification for fieldwork, as for all academic endeavors, lies not in one's contribution to the collectivity but rather in some selfish development. Like monastic life, academic research is really all about the perfection of one's own soul" (p. 9). Although I have not perfected my soul as a result of this SSC study, I have learned much about it. While gaining an enriched understanding about the SSC, its members, and evangelicals, I also grew more knowledgeable about the values that guide me, something that is a priceless byproduct of fieldwork. Peacock (1986) quite aptly argues that fieldwork is much like Christian rebirth:

> Fieldwork is a rite of passage, too. The field experience is said to be radically self-transforming; it is like psychoanalysis, like brainwashing, but it is also an initiation ritual that, through ordeals and insights, moves the initiate to a new level of maturity. A parallel is the conversion experience in which, to use a phrase popularized in fundamentalist Christianity, one is "born again." Like Saul on the road to Damascus, like Augustine or Martin Luther, the convert experiences a dramatic transformation; the scales fall from his (sic) eyes, he sees the world anew; in fact, he lives in a new world, for he is born again, a new person. (p. 55)

Although members were not able to achieve their organizational mission by evangelizing me as a nonbeliever, I am thankful to have undergone a "convert-like" transformation through this fieldwork. I now have a deepened appreciation for and understanding of Christian college students.

Summary

Guba and Lincoln (2005) assert that it is of foremost importance that qualitative researchers

> interrogate each of our selves regarding the ways in which research efforts are shaped and staged around the binaries, contradictions, and paradoxes that form our own lives. We must question ourselves, too, regarding how

those binaries and paradoxes shape not only the identities called forth in the field and later in the discovery processes of writing, but also our inter- actions with respondents, in who we become to them in the process of *becoming* to ourselves. (p. 210)

Throughout this research study, our values and biases as researchers came to the forefront of our consciousness, especially when they clashed with SSC members' values. Frequently, we implicitly re-present our biases and assump- tions, which were, and are, ever-changing. A careful reader would likely be able to glean from these stories and analyses the foundational beliefs upon which we build our practice. Our confessional tales (Van Maanen, 1988) reveal our initial subjectivities, as well as the ways these changed as we spent time with SSC members. The tales also reveal some unique struggles we each encountered as we navigated the process of self-disclosure. Peshkin (1986), when discussing the infusion of himself as a Jew into his ethnographic text about a fundamentalist school, noted that

The field researcher assumes the license to gawk and poke about in the name of scholarship. Of course, I hope always that the respectable scholarly ends will emerge in the course of the gawking and poking about in places that, while not necessarily far-flung, may be far-fetched for me to be in. Perhaps it is unseemly to parade in public one's private joy in doing what is supposed to be done for exalted reasons. However, as I increasingly come under conviction (an expression I owe to this study) about the relationship between who I am, what I see, and what I conclude about what I see, I feel increasingly inclined to reveal enough about myself [sic] so that readers can make their own judgments about what I saw, what I missed, and what I misconstrued. (p. 15)

We, like Peshkin, did our fair share of gawking and poking into the world of the SSC participants. We include our abridged life stories because our life experiences influence who we are and who we are not, what we saw and missed during our fieldwork, and what we concluded and misconstrued during the writing of this book.

4

EVOLVING CHRISTIANS

Precollege Evangelical Rituals

Let Us Pray

"Everyone says 'hello.' We are going to pray now. I've got to go. Bye." Aaron clicks shut his cellular phone to conclude the conversation with his fiancée. That act signals the start of this week's Students Serving Christ (SSC) Beacon prayer meeting, during which students devote an hour of their time to communicate with God about ways to reach non-Christians. As the SSC electronic newsletter suggests, "The Beacon is a great way to develop your heart for the lost and to impact others for the Kingdom!"

The SSC director asks Rebecca to lead the group in prayer. Rebecca complies as her 15 peers (8 women and 7 men) bow their heads. "Lord, thank You for gathering us together. . . . Help us open our hearts to all those who are on campus. Lord, we will be faithful. We will follow what You want us to do." As Rebecca concludes, other attendees—all seated in a tight circle on the altar of a campus chapel—raise their heads in unison and resume eye contact with each other while remaining silent. Following a pause, another woman continues: "Thank You, God, for allowing us to form relationships with people in our classes and our professors. Thank You for allowing us time to get involved in their lives."

The solemn tone of these opening prayers is a stark contrast to the lighthearted banter that preceded the service, as students joked about their not-so-coordinated attire, their favorite sports teams, and the ministry road trip they cancelled because of inclement weather. Participants appear unfazed by the program's unusual starting time of 5:30 p.m.—a time when most of their peers are unwinding after a long day of classes or eating dinner. For these students, prayer takes precedence. Their prayer session continues:

> Our non-Christian friends are missing something, but they don't know what it is. We can share them with You and Your love. . . . We pray in our hearts that we will allow our friends to find You and be open to Your Word. We share with others all the love You give us. Let us show Your love to others. We want others to know Your Word.

Bursts of extemporaneous prayers, each lasting 5–10 seconds, commence and continue building on each other: "We pray that You will draw us closer to You and open us to the joys and comfort You give to us." . . . "Lord, be with us and help us make good decisions." . . . "Jesus, we pray for more men to get involved in our ministry." . . . "We pray to remove our doubts". . . . "Help us when we are lost and confused." Leah alters the prayers' staccato cadence by offering a mini *feel-good* evangelical story:

> Lord, for the past few weeks I have been praying for my roommate. I asked her a couple of weeks ago—"If you could ask any question about life, what would you ask?" She was curious about what happens after we die. God worked through me, and we had a conversation about her spiritual background. Since then, girls in my corridor gathered together and prayed two more times.

Rapid-fire improvisational prayers resume. "We pray that You will spend more time in the dorms, through us, with our non-Christian friends. You are working in our lives. Help us open people's hearts." . . . "You have wisdom; give us Your knowledge, and we will seek Your wisdom and truth in every situation we are facing. We rely on You and what You tell us is true." . . . "We depend on You for the words to say. Help us to be respectful of our friends. Pray to keep our spirits going as we make a sincere effort to get to know others." . . . "Jesus, here we are. We humble ourselves before You. We put our faith in You."

A minute of silence fills the air, signaling the conclusion of the 30-minute collective prayer component of the service. Students help each other off the floor and gather their belongings. Without instruction, they divide themselves into single-sex dyads and spread throughout the chapel. From afar the eight pairs of students recite solemn pleas to God, incomprehensible to us at our distance. Resisting the urge to eavesdrop, we remain a safe distance from them, which inhibits our ability to hear the 20 minutes of stream-of-consciousness prayers. Instead, we watch them pray.

Young Evangelicals

Before starting this ethnographic study of Students Serving Christ (SSC), if we had brainstormed activities in which college students at a public university would participate on a weekday evening, we confess that our Top 100 list would not have included gathering together to pray. Yet this is one of many exotic and intriguing events that we observed during our 2-year research study of the SSC.

The Beacon narrative reminds readers of an obvious, yet often overlooked, realization about higher education: numerous diverse, distinct, and competing student subcultures, such as SSC and its non-Christian counterparts, coexist on every college campus, and each has its own definition of what is "normal." The narrative illuminates a unique SSC ritual of faith and reveals a shared set of values that guides SSC students as they attempt to adhere to God's Word, satisfy their faith needs, and encourage non-Christians to understand and embrace their values.

Who are these collegians that join organizations such as the SSC and attend programs such as the Beacon? What counts as normal for these students? What are the origins of their evangelical passions? What do these rituals of faith, such as prayer meetings, mean? This chapter answers these four questions.

We introduce five students' stories that reveal numerous rituals of faith in which they engaged on a daily basis before attending college. Embedded in these rituals are students' established and prescribed beliefs about evangelical Christianity. Understanding these personal values is a prerequisite to understanding their larger SSC organization (which we discuss in later chapters). We extrapolate from these precollege rituals of faith three themes that these five SSC members (as well as many of their peers) share, and we situate these themes within the scholarly literature involving collegiate Christians.

Kiley is a 19-year-old sophomore elementary education major; her vocational aspiration is to teach in a Christian school. Caleb is a 21-year-old senior history major who is also pursuing a minor in comparative religion. Evangelical ministry work is his vocational aspiration. Leslie is a 22-year-old senior English education major who plans to be a high school English teacher. She lives with several SSC women and leads the senior women's Bible study. Dennis, a 21-year-old African American junior English education major, is currently devising a plan with fellow SSC members to live together and evangelize in an urban community after graduation. Timothy is a 19-year-old sophomore marketing major who is also contemplating a career in evangelical ministry.

Kiley: Becoming Born-Again

Kiley was born and raised in a Christian home. She attended church and Sunday school every Sunday with her family. In the evenings she participated in youth group and choir rehearsals. She grew tired of these activities for a while because her parents forced her to participate, and she felt she was not growing or benefiting from these experiences. "I really didn't have any friends there; I was kind of by myself with God, which was the good part. In my freshman year of high school, I made the varsity softball team. I was the only freshman and I was playing with older girls. They were into things I was uncomfortable with—like alcohol and stuff. I prayed about it."

Kiley's parents, unhappy with the public school, sent her to a Christian high school. The principal, who interviewed Kiley, eventually became a significant influence on her life. For the next 3 years, her life was bliss as she grew as a Christian and forged forever-lasting friendships. Friends encouraged Kiley and put her on a "spiritual high" when she was down.

Kiley's [Christian] high school staff required the 420 students to attend weekly chapel, where they sang worship songs and listened to sermons. Students enrolled in a Bible class each year. In her sophomore year, Kiley enrolled in a class called *Christian Thought and Spirituality,* where students learned about the history of Christianity. As juniors, Kiley and her peers read Christian books such as *Mere Christianity*. In her senior year, she completed an ethics course where students talked about big issues such as abortion. She remembers,

> My parents wanted me to go to a Christian college, but I did not want to go. God needed me to spread Christianity here. I visited a Christian college,

but it was too hardcore. They had chapel everyday; I was not ready for that. . . . I wanted to visit a [Christian] school in Illinois, but going to school there would be too far away from my mother. Deep down I did not want to search for colleges. My mom and aunt went here, and this is where I wanted to go to serve God.

Kiley's goal is to become a teacher. She explains that "[t]he Bible says that we are called on this earth to spread Christianity to others. . . . Life on earth is the blink of an eye; eternal life is awesome. My time on earth is important." She intends to share her Christian beliefs with others on campus and to be a good influence to youth. For Kiley, school and her Christianity are intertwined.

Caleb: Developing a Christian Heart and Mind

Caleb's parents raised him as a Christian, but he didn't take religion seriously until high school, when his church hired a new youth pastor who encouraged him to attend church regularly. He had an academic frame of mind, which he developed while being home schooled until fifth grade. During middle and high school, his peers and teachers recognized him for his academic achievement and for being "the nice guy." Yet he did not want to be known as simply the nice guy. He wanted to be the nice Christian guy, so he quickly altered his image. "If I could not be number one in my class, then my goal was to mix categories. I wanted to be the smart Christian, so I wanted to know as much about the Bible as possible. During high school I spent my time gaining as much biblical knowledge as I could. I studied up on everything. I was debating people left and right."

A peer who was leading one of Caleb's Bible studies accused him of being prideful in his pursuit of biblical knowledge. That hurt Caleb, but after thinking about it, he agreed.

I had this attitude that I knew more than anyone else. He [the peer Bible study leader] pointed out to me that it was something that I needed to work on. Even at that time, I realized that I was not that great of a practicing Christian, but I wanted to get better. I eventually learned the difference between becoming a head Christian and a heart Christian. I was definitely heavy on the head side, and I had hardly any heart at all.

Caleb's mentor told him it was better to be all heart and no head than all head and no heart. Ideally, he told Caleb, Christians want to be in the middle and balanced. Caleb realized that knowing about the Bible was necessary, but not sufficient. The most important thing about being a Christian, says Caleb, is to take it to heart and have faith—not out of legalism, but out of love and character.

Leslie: Forging a Christian Identity

Leslie grew up in a Christian family and was heavily involved in her church. In school she described herself as "a goody two-shoes who got straight As." She confessed that she was "the nice, quiet little girl who always did everything right." She did not dispute these descriptors. She attended public school, but her church was the epicenter of her existence. "My church was in a different town from where I lived, so it was kind of hard because all the kids went to school together. I went to that church all the way through sophomore or junior year of high school. Then we switched churches since there were leadership changes and a lot of drama, and our family got pushed out."

Leslie and her family started attending a new, bigger church. Her high school youth group grew from 15 to 100 adolescents, something she described as intimidating and challenging:

> There was also stuff going on with my friends in high school—they did stuff I did not approve of . . . and that's when I really started to figure out who I was, I think. . . . Then I found myself without a group for a while, and so that was a big time in my life.
>
> . . . My sister went [to school] here; I never wanted to do what she did. . . . It surprised me that I came here. . . . I felt like I was supposed to want to go to a Christian college, because that's what good Christians did. So I was kind of torn between those two things, and really I felt like—you know, that's not really where I was supposed to go, and that's okay. I knew I wanted to be a teacher and I knew _____ had a great education program . . . it was also an hour from home—a good distance . . . one night I was laying in bed, thinking about it and praying about it, you know, picturing myself at a Christian school and then here, and I thought, you know, I think I'm going to go to _____. And it was like "okay," and I went to sleep. I don't know exactly how it happened but it did.

Dennis: Becoming a Real Christian

Dennis and his three brothers moved often during their formative years, because their father was in the Navy. His parents raised the boys in a Christian household. Dennis regularly attended church with his parents and remembers accepting Jesus in the first grade.

> We were watching this movie, and the premise was that there were these teenagers riding in this car, and they have a car accident. One of them was Christian and the other ones weren't. They all survive, but the ones that weren't Christians yet have to go through and look at their lives from the perspective of being dead. . . . They saw some not-so-nice things. I realized that "Oh, my gosh, going to church doesn't make you a Christian!" I think maybe one of the characters said that. So, my younger brother and I decided we wanted to become "real Christians" and not just go to church. . . . I kept going to church, and things really started changing, like I really made it my own personal thing when I went to this Christian camp. . . . They had activities and stuff . . . zip wires, hiking, rock climbing, and all that cool stuff. . . . And they'd also have devotions in the morning. We'd wake up in the morning and read our Bible and pray and they'd lead us in lessons and stuff, and it was really like awesome times, and I started to feel really connected to God.

Dennis revealed that his passion waned once he returned home from camp. He would continue to attend church and attend a weekly Bible study meeting, but he lost his "Jesus high." He explains:

> One night I was out taking a walk, and I just stopped and was thinking and was praying and I was still feeling connected, and I realized, *I don't really have to lose this. It's not something I just can get at camp; I can get it wherever I am.* That's when I truly started changing my life—getting into the Bible more on my own and not depending on other people for it. So that's what's shaped a lot of my life in high school and onward, and now here I am in college doing the same thing.

Timothy: Following the Christian Path

Timothy's parents were both Christians, so Timothy attended church every Sunday morning. His father was Catholic. His mother grew up in a church, but was much more rebellious. It wasn't until her mid-20s, when she gave birth first to Timothy and then to his sister, that she found her faith. Since then, his mother has been the spiritual leader of his family. She taught Timothy in Sunday School class and encouraged her children to learn more about the Christian faith. Both of Timothy's parents were proud of his involvement in the church. By age 7, Timothy had a basic sense of the Bible and recognized his sinfulness and the need for Jesus to cleanse him.

> I remember wanting to be baptized so that my sins could be washed away. . . . When I got into the middle school years, I joined an adult Bible study at my church. I even joined a weight-loss accountability/Bible study group, and I would just come for the Bible study half with all adults. I loved absorbing knowledge about the Bible and worked hard at learning as much as I could. I also enjoyed the praise I would get from my parents and adults in our church. I had a pretty good relationship with my pastor, and I liked being recognized for my good morals and the virtues I had learned [partly] from my pastor, but mostly [from] my parents.

During his junior year, Timothy interacted with friends who did not practice the code of morals that he had embraced as a child. He sought recognition by being cool and attractive according to his peers' standards, rather than by impressing adults at church, although he still attended church every week. In essence, Timothy separated his Christian life from his social life. He attended church in hopes of gaining the approval of adults and some peers. In school he interacted with "cool and popular athletes—jocks." Initially, he did not recognize the conflict.

> For 2 years I justified what I was doing. I just shirked off convictions that nagged at me. I became friends with my high school buddies because we were funny and our personalities matched. Back then there were no cool Christians in school. They [Christians] were on the outskirts of the "in" social groups. Looking back now, the kids following the Christian life were cool, but I did not know it at the time.

Timothy and his friends did not have the heart to follow Jesus. Timothy liked to be invited to popular events, where he and his friends could consume alcohol and "go crazy." He felt that if he lived out his Christian morals and faith in front of these peers, he would be ostracized and ridiculed and would have to find new friends. "I was like Jonah—swallowed up by a fish." By the time he graduated high school, Timothy was deeply immersed in the party scene and was trying to shirk the convictions about how he should be living.

Before attending college, Timothy realized that he needed to make a hard decision about his lifestyle. His major catalyst for change was cigarettes. He was "addicted" to smoking, which pleased his "cool" friends. The girls in his Bible studies knew he was smoking, which caused him feelings of shame and confusion. "God was nudging me. I knew I was hypocritical. I eventually changed, but it was not an overnight transformation. I was torn for a few months." Timothy credits Jesus for saving him: "He turned me around." Timothy realized that if he wanted to be Christian, there was no middle ground.

Precollege Evangelical Rituals

Although the life experiences of Kiley, Caleb, Leslie, Dennis, and Timothy are unique, a set of shared core values are embedded in their interview musings. In this section, we examine students' precollege rituals of faith to reveal these core values.

SSC members' weekly rituals such as the Beacon and the church services these five students attended during their youth clearly display a strong sense of purpose and rightness and serve to connect members to the larger community. Kiley's rituals of faith include praying, attending church, participating in Sunday school, singing in the choir, refraining from alcohol consumption, forging friendships with other Christians, studying classic (e.g., the Bible) and contemporary texts about Christianity, and spreading the Word of God. Caleb, too, discussed rituals of faith, which included consulting with his youth pastor, studying the Bible, modeling "good guy" behaviors for peers, debating Scripture with both believers and nonbelievers, and seeking feedback about his Christian life from trusted Christian mentors.

Leslie's rituals of faith included "doing things right" and being a "goody two-shoes" by distancing herself from friends who did not adhere to a Christian life, and seeking counsel from God and her elders (e.g., her sister). Dennis regularly listened to his parents, analyzed popular culture texts (e.g., film) for messages about Christianity, attended Christian camps, and eventually learned to self-monitor his commitment to Christianity—all examples of rituals of faith. Timothy's rituals of faith centered on identifying and adopting a moral Christian lifestyle by giving up smoking and drinking, seeking advice from Christian mentors, staying attuned to God's will for his life, and immersing himself in the study of the Bible.

Throughout these five students' rituals are common symbolic threads that demonstrate their Jesus-centered core values, which include devoting oneself to Christian morals, seeking mentorship, learning more about God and his will, examining one's own life, and making counterculture choices to follow Jesus.

Making it All about Jesus—For a Long Time

For Kiley, Caleb, Leslie, Dennis, and Timothy it's all about Jesus, and it has been for a long time—for at least a decade before attending college. When they left their Christian homes, churches, and youth groups to begin college, they expected to continue following Jesus and strengthening their faith. This is also true of many of their SSC counterparts. As Braskamp (2006) asserts, "Entering college students not only bring their faith to campus with them, they expect to 'grow' in their religious and spiritual lives while in college" (p. 7).

Evangelical Christianity was an integral part of these students' youth, and evangelical ideals seeped into their formal and informal education. Students enacted evangelical ideals, which their parents introduced, when selecting friends and choosing cocurricular activities. These students regularly speak about seeking eternal happiness by establishing and maintaining a personal and ongoing relationship with Jesus. They take faith matters seriously; their relationships with God began at an early age, and these relationships matured as the students developed. Barna (1996) found that 60 percent of evangelical survey respondents reported that they made their decision to accept Christ as their savior before age 18. This is true for most SSC students.

"Walking with Jesus" is a way of life for these students. This philosophy of life is compatible with Lowery and Coomes' (2003) research findings that concluded, " . . . Evangelical students emphasized the importance of a personal relationship with Jesus Christ as a core element of their faith. However, for these evangelical students, simply having a relationship was not sufficient. It was equally important to strive to grow in one's relationship with Christ" (p. 36). As the interview excerpts reveal, however, this life with Jesus is not without moments of doubt and resistance. SSC interviewees confess to lapses in faith (e.g., Kiley's burnout, Caleb's pride, and Timothy's smoking and drinking), as they attempt to enact their espoused Christian beliefs.

A common challenge these SSC students encountered in their youth was blending the sacred with the secular. This tension was most obvious as Kiley and Leslie talked about their college choice options, when they vacillated between attending a Christian college or a public university. Still, they strove to "walk with Jesus" and chose, in fact, to attend a public university because they thought it would challenge their faith and thus make them stronger Christians. Similarly, Timothy talked about his difficulty maintaining "dual personas"—one Christian and one secular—in high school. In the end, he knew he needed his inner Christian beliefs to mesh with his everyday lifestyle choices. Several SSC students mentioned their desire to do *everything* "for God," including their coursework and leisure time—a desire that often conflicts with the accepted norms of their secular peers and the secular institutions they attend.

Religion, spirituality, and the pursuit of meaning in life are topics of interest for these SSC believers—topics they began exploring prior to college and hoped to continue during their collegiate experience. A summary of a recent national survey of 100,000 first-year students at 236 colleges revealed an interest in religion and spirituality resembling the experiences of the SSC interviewees:

> Today's college students are showing a high interest in spirituality (Higher Education Research Institute [HERI], 2005). According to this survey, entering college students are interested in spirituality (80%), searching for meaning in life (76%), using their beliefs for guidance (69%), discussing life philosophies with friends (74%), attending religious services (81%), believing in God (79%), and praying (69%). (Braskamp, Trautvetter, and Ward, 2006, p. 7)

However, SSC students also regularly initiated rituals of faith aimed at encouraging other people to share their beliefs or ideals. It is this evangelical emphasis that distinguishes SSC students from other spiritually oriented survey participants.

As aspiring evangelists, SSC students commit themselves to sharing their religious beliefs with others. Barna's (1996) defining attributes of evangelicals bring clarity to these students' long-standing belief that it's all about Jesus:

> They assert that they have made a personal commitment to Jesus Christ that is important in their life; they say that their religious faith is very important in their life; they believe that they will have eternal life because they have confessed their sins and have accepted Christ as their savior; they have a biblical perception of God, the Father; they believe that the Bible is totally accurate in all it teaches; they acknowledge a personal responsibility to share their faith with nonbelievers; they believe that the only means to spiritual salvation is through the grace of God, provided by the death, resurrection, and ascension of Jesus Christ; they contend that Christ was both God and man, but remained untainted by sin.

Discussing alternative evangelical initiatives, Riley (2005) states, "Serving in soup kitchens, tutoring, building homes, or volunteering in prisons are obvious ways that students can spiritually influence others without handing out pamphlets or proselytizing door to door. Indeed, for many students, service work has all but replaced their more explicit evangelization efforts" (p. 243). These "gentler" and less "in-your-face" kinds of evangelizing are more akin to SSC students' brand of spreading the Word.

Personally, educationally, and vocationally for these students, it is all about Jesus. Being an evangelical is not simply a personality descriptor; it is a way of life. They weave evangelism into the tapestry of their existence.

Seeking Mortal Counsel

As youth, SSC interviewees not only prayed to God for guidance, but also sought the advice of elders including parents, mentors, and siblings. Seeking this "mortal counsel" was a second commonality embedded in SSC students' precollege rituals of faith. Dennis' parents introduced him to Christianity during his formative years and reinforced these values by sending him to a Christian camp. Caleb's parents home schooled him, which accelerated his Christian education. The mothers of Kiley and Leslie encouraged their daughters to select a college based on where they could grow in their faith. Likewise, Caleb's youth pastor and Kiley's high school principal regularly provided them with spiritual guidance.

Unlike past generations of college students who shunned parents and authority figures, Dennis, Leslie, Caleb, Kiley, and Timothy maintain strong relationships with elders and have sought their counsel as youths and throughout adolescence. As SSC students prepared to "leave the nest" and attend college, they expressed little desire to distance themselves from their parents and spiritual mentors. Kiley, Caleb, Leslie, Dennis, and Timothy—all college students of traditional age—are members of the millennial generation (the latest generation/birth cohort, born between 1982 and early 2000). These five individuals and their SSC peers possess many millennial characteristics, including optimism about their ability to improve the world, modesty, acceptance of authority, and a close relationship with protective parental figures (Howe and Strauss, 2000).

Millennials' close relationships with their parents and their acceptance of authority are one of the sharpest departures from past generations. This "closeness to parents" is particularly descriptive of SSC interviewees and proves to be a relationship forged long before they stepped foot on campus. Riley (2005) argued that "life on most college campuses remains defined by the 1960s mantra that college is the time for students to get out from under the thumb of their parents and 'experiment'" (p. 170). SSC interviewees bucked this trend. For example, Kiley recounted a story about her relationship with her residence hall peers:

> I went to a party the first week of my freshman year. I did not want to sit in the dorm by myself. I went with my roommate to a party and she drank. I did not drink. She got sick everywhere. It was a nasty scene. I was asked if I wanted to drink; I said "no" and they respected my wishes and me. It was fine—whatever. I have never been in situations where there was hard-core pressure. They asked me later if I wanted to go out with them, but I would say "no." I just did not want to put myself in situations. It was hard. I ask myself why can't I go out and be normal and stuff. At the end of the day I am a Christian. . . . At the end of the year, every girl in the dorm respected me, and they would come to me. I was the "go-to" girl. I guess it was a struggle to say "no," but at the end of the year, it was a blessing.

Kiley's story illuminates a steadfast commitment to Christian norms and resistance to experimentation during college—values she attributes to her elders' influence during her youth.

As college students, SSC students actively sought elders to assume functions and responsibilities of their parents. This contemporary version of *in loco parentis* is evident in Timothy's story about his relationship with an SSC intern:

> I meet regularly with Aaron. We are never at a loss for topics. For example, I wanted to know what he thought about smoking, since I was addicted to smoking. I was hoping that it was okay, since I did not want to quit. He asked me "What do you think?" That question is a [SSC] favorite answer to any question I ask. Aaron was great in that context by helping me find answers in the Bible, like why is it I can't drink [alcohol] and yet die in a war.

As college students, SSC interviewees expect and intend for their Christianity to grow. They regularly pose questions such as: What is God's will for my life? How would Jesus want me to use this period of my life? They look to and continue to seek out mortal mentors to help them answer these questions, and to interpret and enact God's will. When SSC students begin college, they have high expectations that spiritual mentors will connect them with other people and resources, as well as serve as role models while guiding them on their faith journey. Their spiritual mentors include parents, SSC staff, and upper-class students, as well as the Bible, which serves as the ultimate "final word" for SSC students on how to live their lives while in college.

The Spiritual Life of College Students: A National Study of College Students' Search for Meaning and Purpose (UCLA Higher Education Research Institute, 2005) concluded that new students expect their institutions to influence their emotional and spiritual development. Similarly, SSC interviewees rely on staff of Christian organizations as guides in the collegiate spiritual journeys.

Existing on the Margins

Describing how many Christians perceive contemporary college culture, Miller (2006) states:

> Since secular higher education's relinquishment of the *in loco parentis* role in the late 1960s, many campuses have come to seem increasingly chaotic and dangerous to a number of students and parents, places where men and women share dorm rooms, and where drugs and alcohol are easily available.

Structures, limits and clearly articulated values provide a behavioral exoskeleton for many students who would flounder in a more permissive environment. (p. 6)

Venturing into the worlds of non-Christians' profane lives creates great anxiety for SSC student interviewees. For these students, encounters with the profane occurred frequently during their high school years. Timothy, Leslie, and Kiley encountered challenges from high school peers who acted in ways contrary to their Christian ideals—for example, by consuming alcohol. Dennis, when talking about his first days on campus, expressed a similar sentiment: "College movies make it look like everyone drinks, has sex, and it's a big drugfest. So I was kind of nervous about going here and not finding a solid Christian base. I wanted to, like, hang out with at least a couple people who had similar interests as me and whatnot." These uneasy feelings are compatible with Lowery and Coomes' (2003) research findings that "most of the evangelical students discussed challenges or conflicts between the broader student culture and their own religious beliefs" (p. 34). Developing strategies to navigate the secular and the profane are daily chores for SSC interviewees and form a third common theme among the five SSC students' rituals of faith.

SSC students' sense of estrangement from the mainstream, which for most began in elementary and high school, follows them to college. Lowery and Coomes (2003) and Weingarten (2005) capture SSC students' sense of collegiate marginalization and estrangement from their mainstream peers:

Evangelical students described themselves as living on the margins of the broader residence hall communities in which they lived. They used words such as 'outsider,' 'distanced,' 'foreigner,' and 'not normal' to describe themselves in relation to the broader university community. (Lowery and Coomes, 2003, p. 36)

Similarly, Weingarten (2005) notes:

Christians are often stereotyped, says the Rev. Adam Blons, a member of the University Religious Council at the University of California at Berkeley and head of that city's First Congregational Church. People are quick to assume that all Christians are humorless fundamentalists bent on converting others, he says. "I can confirm that it isn't easy to be 'out' as a Christian." (para. 17)

Christians in the United States in general and in higher education in particular are not minorities, yet their sense of being on the margins is genuine. They view public higher education values such as tolerance and diversity as ideals rooted in the Bible, but they struggle to reconcile them with their other biblical foundations centering on a "right" way to live a Christian life. Particularly on a public college campus, SSC students find themselves on the margins within a dominant campus culture filled with students who demonstrate hedonism, individualism, and materialism—among other "sinful" secular tendencies. Commonly, as SSC students become more involved in the organization, they increasingly see their strict adherence to Christian principles as starkly different from other Christian students who they feel do not live out their faith. Dennis, for example, explained how he realized he needed to become a "real Christian," and that church attendance is not enough. This self-labeled marginalization is a theme to which we return in subsequent chapters.

Prior to attending college, organizations such as churches, youth groups, camps, and Bible studies provided students a haven from the dominant masses; these groups helped students to solve their faith disputes. Once SSC interviewees arrived on campus, they looked to parachurches to support them. Lowery and Coomes (2003), referencing the work of Marsden, connect Christian collegians' need for support with the rise of parachurches such as the SSC:

> While religious-based student organizations continued to exist, religion was effectively marginalized from the academic life of the university. For the past two decades, that void has been filled on many campuses by new evangelical groups. . . . The decline in popularity of mainstream Protestant denominations (e.g., Methodist and Presbyterian) coupled with more contemporary approaches to worship have contributed to the rise in popularity of evangelical parachurch organizations. (p. 31)

Once they arrive on campus, finding like-minded peers with whom to blend faith, fellowship, and fun is of great importance to SSC interviewees. They seek peer niches that blend the sacred and the secular by intertwining Jesus with their formal education, while allowing them the freedom to practice their faith. Prior to college, Dennis found this in his summer camp, and Kiley in her Christian high school. Leslie's story, in which she began attending a bigger church where some peers in her youth group acted in ways contrary to her own values, captures the angst associated with "going it alone."

Kuh, Kinzie, Schuh, and Whitt (2005) concluded, "By becoming involved with people with similar interests inside and outside the classroom, students develop support networks that are instrumental to helping them deal effectively with academic and social challenges" (p. 260). SSC interviewees confirmed these conclusions and acknowledged the importance of the organization in helping them blend the sacred and the secular while providing a supportive home on campus in which to freely explore their faith with others. Several interviewees commented that they would have felt "lost" without the SSC organization, and they attribute much of their collegiate success and satisfaction to their association with the group.

A notable feature of this supportive environment is the organization's overwhelming homogeneity. According to Kim (2006), the homogenous nature of the SSC reflects nationwide demographics for evangelical Christian organizations: "Multiracial congregations are few and far between. According to the National Congregations Survey and Survey of Multiracial Congregations, about 90 percent of American religious congregations are racially homogenous" (p. 10). Three of the five students highlighted in this chapter are White (Caleb is Hispanic and Dennis an African American), but these diverse demographics do not mirror those of the organization as a whole, which is mostly White. Similarly, students' responses were all remarkably similar with regard to using the Bible as their daily guide and unquestioningly following the advice of their spiritual mentors. Although this homogeneity contributes to students' comfort and support, it can be a liability in that the organization becomes insular and is not likely to critically consider its values and practices. Continuing to assemble like-minded people in the organization also makes it even more difficult for students to meet their evangelical goals of interacting with their secular peers on campus.

Summary

Understanding SSC students' rich faith histories provides a backdrop for understanding more about the lives of Christian college students as well as the supportive power of the SSC organization, which brings together like-minded

individuals such as Kiley, Caleb, Leslie, Dennis, and Timothy. Study participants' lives were *all about Jesus* from an early age, and they continued to grow
in their evangelical Christian faith with the guidance of spiritual mentors such
as parents, teachers, youth ministers, and pastors. Students selected a college
based on their ability to find like-minded students and a safe space on campus. Attending a Christian college was not necessary to continue one's walk
with Jesus, and in fact, attending a public university fit better in some ways
with their evangelical mission. Upon arriving at college, SSC students—like
the majority of entering college freshmen—hoped to have the opportunity to
continue to explore their faith and find a sense of life purpose, so they quickly
explored groups such as the SSC. The SSC students are also similar to mainstream college students in many other ways—they struggle with selecting a
college, "fitting in" and finding friends, knowing how to maximize their
college experience, and navigating relationships with their families.

Many SSC students fit the millennial generation profile of optimistic,
forward thinkers who believe they can make a positive influence in the world.
Together in their supportive SSC enclave, and through distinct *rituals of
faith,* Christian students are able to live out their shared values. These values
include following a moral lifestyle that shuns drinking and sex, seeking the
counsel of spiritual mentors, learning more about God, and sharing their
faith with others, with the end goal of making the world a better place. They
describe this faith-sharing process as "building God's Kingdom." They also
widely demonstrate the millennial characteristic of deferring to the authority
of mentors and parents. However, SSC members also have an "ultimate
authority"—in God. God and the Bible serve as powerful compasses for
many SSC members as they defer to God in making major life decisions.

Further, SSC students' exceptional relationship with authority is but one
way they differ from other collegians. SSC students carry an additional duty of
blending the sacred and the secular, whereas other students—and many
Americans—are able to easily compartmentalize their spiritual and work-related
lives. In the Beacon meeting, for example, students prayed that God would help
them in their classroom interactions with professors and other students. Overwhelmingly, embracing an evangelical identity is a full-time, 24/7 way of being;
SSC students strive to follow Jesus in *every* aspect of their lives.

What is considered "normal" for SSC students is different from what is
"normal" for the majority campus culture, which leads SSC members to feel
marginalized. Groups such as the SSC play an important role in connecting

these marginalized Christian students and providing a supportive community in which they can continue to grow in their faith, pursue a moral lifestyle, and seek life purpose. In the coming chapters, however, we question whether SSC students' separation from other student subcultures limits the possibility for genuine dialogue and understanding between groups—an espoused goal of higher education professionals.

In sum, the five students' rituals of faith stories demonstrate three themes, which will also be apparent in the SSC organization rituals: [1] students often bring to college a long history of evangelical influence, [2] students seek moral counsel as an important part of their collegiate experience, and [3] students feel marginalized as they struggle to blend the sacred and the secular in everything they do. In the next chapter, we connect these themes to the wider SSC organization's recruitment strategy, in which the organization seeks out other students wishing to make their lives *all about Jesus.*

5

GOD'S SQUAD

Rituals of Recruitment

We're Not Weird, if That's What You're Thinking

Visible at nearly every intersection are U-Haul trucks or trailers—a sure sign that the end of summer approaches. Like Rip Van Winkle awaking from his 20-year sleep, this sleepy college town is again showing signs of life after its 4-month sabbatical from students. No longer are the local residents guaranteed instant access to checkout cashiers at the local grocery, nor are they confident that convenient parking spaces await them at downtown eateries. Ready or not, the academic year begins in 5 days.

Students Serving Christ (SSC) members dressed in shorts, T-shirts, and sandals greet us as we arrive at a rustic cabin on the outskirts of town. This pastoral setting is a popular retreat site for student organizations; the remote locale minimizes the distractions commonly associated with assembling on campus. For the past few years, the SSC organization has used this cabin for its Servant Leadership Team's (SLT) annual 3-day planning retreat. At this event, these most committed upper-class SSC students who make the SSC the epicenter of their collegiate experience discuss ways to recruit new SSC members, orient these new recruits to college and the SSC, and provide long-term support for new and returning SSC collegians as they "walk with Jesus." The primary purpose of the SLT retreat is to reconnect members with each other, clarify the organization's vision, and as Matthew said, "get on the same page for the coming semester." Planning and recruitment are of secondary importance to the organization but of great interest to us—and thus they are the focus of this chapter.

The previous evening, 22 SLT members and 3 SSC staff prayed in unison, dined together, and then attended an ice cream social at the home of the

SSC regional trainer and his spouse. They also participated in an icebreaker acquaintanceship activity, which hardly seemed necessary since this intact group is already close-knit. In fact, several SLT members participated in SSC-sponsored summer programs in Florida and Colorado. Throughout the evening, participants seamlessly blended following Jesus with fellowship and fun activities as they exchanged stories about their summer experiences and shared future aspirations.

Sitting on the ground in front of the cabin is the 2005–06 Servant Leadership Team (SLT), poised to begin their work. Because we spent the previous academic year with this group, we quickly and quietly assimilate ourselves into this gathering. Our presence causes minimal disruptions, as they are already familiar with our notebooks, laptop computer, and unobtrusive-as-possible observation strategies. Our reunion with SSC members is both relaxed and comfortable.

To begin the gathering, attendees engage in their usual opening prayer ritual. Matthew, the SSC director, calls on Caleb to briefly and extemporaneously speak to God as peers bow their heads. When Caleb concludes, Matthew circulates promotional postcards that highlight eight upcoming SSC events for the fall semester. SLT members peruse the fluorescent cards as Matthew introduces each event and explains its importance. The Friday evening worship service and the weekly Bible study gatherings are familiar events; Matthew briefly alludes to these two offerings. He presents more in-depth information about the remaining programs, which include an ice-cream social to welcome new first-year students, an outdoor concert featuring a popular local Christian band, a road trip to a nearby city to enjoy its Labor Day fireworks, a camping trip in a nearby state park, a paintball outing, and an SSC regional conference. SSC's goal of providing collegians a healthy dose of Jesus, fellowship, and fun is evident in these offerings.

Matthew explicitly encourages attendees to widely promote these events to Christians and nonbelievers, SSC members and nonmembers, and first-year and upper-class students. However, he speaks most passionately about first-year Christian students who aspire to join a Christian student organization, and he implicitly suggests that this group is his primary target audience.

With a new crop of first-year students scheduled to arrive on campus in 2 days, the purpose of this brief session is to help members brush up on their evangelical skills, a cornerstone of the SSC's recruitment strategy. Matthew divides members into dyads and asks them to practice presenting a biblical illustration, which is a 10-minute scripted presentation targeted to their peers that reveals the importance of Christianity.[1] Most attendees first learned how to present this illustration in a 4-week evangelical training program during their first year of involvement with the SSC. Still, these eager evangelists appear a bit rusty during this 30-minute dress rehearsal. Missteps are frequent as participants struggle to gain some fluency in their presentations. "We've got work to do," declares a sophomore woman, and several students dolefully nod in agreement. Matthew urges team members to keep on practicing.

During the next few weeks, sophomore SLT members will set up tables at high-traffic campus locales and invite students to complete a brief, written spiritual interest survey. Two questions read: "Would you be interested in an informal Bible discussion in your dorm?" and "Would you be interested in discussing what the Bible says a genuine Christian is?" SSC members contact those students who respond affirmatively to these questions and ask to meet with them in their residence halls. If the survey respondent agrees to a meeting, the SSC member shares the illustration. The SSC has designed the survey to comply with a university regulation that prohibits solicitation in residence halls, unless invited by the resident. Responding affirmatively to the survey question "Would you like to meet to discuss the Bible?" grants permission to SSC members to enter the residence hall and interact with the resident. The SSC's recruitment strategy—focused on sharing the Bible with potential recruits—reminds us once again that the SSC is all about Jesus, not social or political issues of the day or glitzy advertising promises.

To comfort some anxious sophomores who have yet to share an illustration with peers, Matthew describes a typical exchange between an SLT member and a survey respondent who agrees to a meeting:

> It'll go like this. "Hi, I'm Matthew. Do you remember filling out this survey for an I-pod?" Then start some small talk. Find out where they are from and ask them how their first few days are going, but don't go too long with this or they'll start wondering what you're doing.

> Ask if you can share with them an illustration. If they say "yes," you're in good shape. Sometimes it helps to ask first their spiritual background growing up so you know where they are coming from. Tell them it's okay if they don't know everything or this might be a review of some things for some Christians. Throughout you are trying to observe things. Listen to the words they use—like "Christian-ese" words such as "saving" or "sin." You

don't want to use Christian-ese [words] at all unless they are using Christian terms a lot. Our goal is to form a relationship.

If they are not Christians or practicing Christians, invite them to meet with you to learn about Jesus' life. Tell them you have "no expectations." If they are already Christians, ask if they are involved somewhere. Let them know about Bible study.

Timothy follows this Evangelism 101 refresher course with a question: "What is the best way to contact people?" Matthew replies, "E-mail," as he retrieves a handout from his backpack entitled "How to Lead an Investigative Bible Discussion." An investigative Bible discussion (IBD) is an informal opportunity for SSC members to talk about Christianity with nonbelievers. Matthew encourages others to do the same, and he randomly calls on attendees to read aloud a piece of advice found on the handout:

Learn people's names. Be careful; don't be dogmatic. . . . Use "I believe" or "The Bible says" [phrases]. . . . The spirit has to move people's will; you cannot. . . . Make sure you live up to what you say. If you tell people it is only going to be a half hour, stick to that. . . . Pray for those you invite. . . . Select a specific date, time, and location to meet and advertise.

Once again, the Bible takes center stage in Matthew's exemplar, and we question whether this cookie-cutter evangelism technique actually works with more diverse students on campus who do not share the SSC students' values or remarkably similar backgrounds. "Is anyone nervous about going into the residence halls?" Matthew asks. Several sophomores, in unison, immediately blurt out, "YES." "That's okay," Matthew reassures them. "Tell them you'll find the answers and get back to them. That really helps the relationships, if you say you're learning a lot through this, too."

Although the learning conditions are uncomfortable due to the brutal summer heat—as evidenced by the sweat-drenched T-shirts of several men—attendees appear to muster the energy to remain attentive and involved. Paul, scanning the IBD handout asks, "What are some ways to advertise?" A student replies, "With the Bible, pizza, and beer—root beer that is." His clarification elicits a giggle from a nearby woman. Matthew adds a caveat, "That works well on the guys' floor; ladies, you'd know better than I about what do to on women's floors. Be creative."

Matthew concludes by summarizing key recruitment tips, then returns to a popular theme he frequently discusses with SSC members—the need for them to live a Christian life and seek their own spiritual fulfillment each day:

> Your job description this year is to bring people back to the central issue of Jesus. Issues such as evolution, relativism will come up, but we have to bring them back to Jesus. . . . Yes, we pray for them and want them to become Christians, but we can't be manipulative. Let the Bible do the work. Make sense?

Matthew concludes, "Your first priority has to be *your* walk with God. . . . Now, go hang out with one another as much as possible and build team unity!"

After a short break, we shift our observational focus to a workshop targeting junior SSC members. "Who are we missing?" Matthew asks. A student replies, "Dennis is still in the bathroom." Matthew looks slightly agitated as he says, "Hopefully, he doesn't take long." Tony yells out, "Pray for 'number one!'" Several men chuckle at his quip. Dennis returns from the cabin by crawling through the open window rather than using the door. Matthew tersely instructs Dennis to retrieve his Bible, notebook, and pen and to sit down as he resumes his recruitment discussion. Matthew begins to describe his vision for the year; as usual, the students listen submissively to their spiritual mentor:

> Recruiting has already started. We've e-mailed over 100 incoming freshmen and sent them mail. We used the religious preference cards they filled out during orientation [to get their names]. Also, during the summer, some of you met with incoming freshmen in your area. I'll be anxious to see the impact all this has. We're a few steps ahead of where we normally are. Oh yeah, we have welcome bags, which are new this year, and we have T-shirts for sale.

Matthew explains that for the next few weeks select SSC members will be following up on surveys, meeting new students, and finding first-year students to work with the SSC in the residence halls. Friday, SSC members will help new students move into their residence halls. Saturday, some SSC members will be downtown to distribute and collect surveys. Students nod excitedly as Matthew passes a clipboard around the circle. They sign up for multiple time slots and seem willing to recruit members. Matthew continues:

> Sunday is the ice cream social. Don't forget, Tuesday we'll be in three din-
> ing halls; we need 24 people to help with this. Please don't forget if you sign
> up. That happened last year. It's not fun to be the only person doing it.
> We'll give out additional surveys in the dining halls after school starts if
> needed. . . . Let's be prayerful that He'll provide people to connect us with.

Matthew speculates that recruitment will be a bit easier this year because SSC has hired a Christian band to play after their first Friday worship pro-gram, which will be held on the outdoor patio near the student center if weather permits. This high-visibility program is a deviation from SSC's stan-dard operating practices, which shun the glare of publicity and instead favor low-profile, small-group interactions.

Matthew not only insists that members recruit new members by helping new students move into the residence halls, distributing surveys, and sharing illustrations, but he also mandates that members follow the organization's recruitment protocol:

> Remember, there are other [Christian] organizations on campus also
> expanding the Kingdom. Other [Christian] organizations will have [Bible]
> studies in the same dorms as you. That's fine; there is a place for them. *Do*
> *not* speak negatively of any [Christian] organization. If I hear of that, you'll
> have serious problems. Be proud of the priorities of our organization. We
> will speak about those and not be ashamed of them. There are reasons
> you're in this organization instead of others. We need to communicate
> clearly about who we are and what we're about.

Students are silent for a moment as they contemplate Matthew's stern call to describe the organization to potential recruits as "different" rather than "superior" to other Christian groups. Matthew pauses for a moment and then poses a question to attendees: "What two things does God call *every believer* to?" Lynn shouts out, "Love one another and obedience?" Matthew replies, "Yes; true, but what else? I'm looking for two things that are the *most* impor-tant." Students appear puzzled as they haphazardly brainstorm responses. As the "incorrect" guesses continue to mount and participants lose steam, they look to Matthew, their wise leader, who finally reveals the "correct" answer he had hoped others would propose: "Make disciples and evangelize." He offers a rationale for these choices, as we wonder whether other students' responses could have been equally valid.

> The most important thing to God is that He is glorified. Evangelism and discipleship are moving others toward God's glory. We need to keep in mind that leaders follow God and evangelize and disciple people to build the Kingdom for His glory. . . . God might lead one of you to be a computer programmer, but you must go there as a missionary. . . . Your life looks different as a leader in the Kingdom. . . . God has things for us to do—evangelize and disciple.

As the afternoon comes to a close, Matthew summarizes "tried and true" strategies for evangelizing first-year students and reiterates ideas he has been discussing throughout the afternoon:

> You need to share from your heart. The first 3 weeks will make the difference for the year. You don't have much time to get it on your heart, but spend the time and do it. You'll reap a lot from your investment.

> First we will talk with the Christians who are interested, then share illustrations with other students. Sit down and talk to each person in your Bible study. Remember, *relationships recruit* . . . Love them; remember their names and ask how things are going. . . . During the first week of classes, I'd like all of you to get a meal with a freshman. Yes, it is to recruit and for them to get to know the organization, but also to just love them and show them we care.

> I've heard people don't think SSC is serious about evangelism. That is not true. Our methods are just different. We are living among the lost. We don't use what I call "guerrilla tactics" to hit people with the Gospel. We're really praying for people who have a heart for Jesus.

Warren yells out, "Amen, brother!" Students are proud of their relational style for evangelizing, in which they become friends with non-Christians first before sharing their faith. Matthew concludes with words of encouragement: "As we get started, you might forget things. Don't worry, just muddle your way through it and do the best you can. Think about recruiting and practice your illustration this weekend."

As the workshop adjourns, Timothy jokingly proposes to his peers an opening line for SSC members to recite when meeting non-Christians for the first time—"We're not weird, if that's what you're thinking." This tongue-in-cheek comment appears to resonate with his peers, based on their smiling faces and nodding heads. While SSC students perceive themselves as "relatively normal," we wonder if their evangelical recruitment agenda is strange and unusual, especially to non-Christians.

Recruitment Rituals: Understanding the Strange

"We're not weird, if that's what you're thinking." Timothy's comment, referring to outsiders' stereotypical perceptions of evangelical collegians, becomes the main topic of conversation as we debrief the afternoon recruitment session. "Weird" is exactly what we are thinking as we attempt to make meaning of SSC's recruitment and leadership training session. Compared in particular to other collegiate organizations we have studied, three distinct aspects of the session seem unconventional: recruitment outcomes, organization and leadership structures, and organization recruits.

Recruitment Outcomes

At first glance SSC's rituals of recruitment, like most college student organizations' practices, appear ordinary, predictable, and familiar. SSC's comprehensive and integrated recruitment plan involves the following: [1] contacting prospective students long before they arrive on campus to inform them about the organization; [2] designing eye-catching brochures that promote the organization and its events; [3] seeking prospective members rather than waiting for the members to find the organization; [4] employing grassroots approaches to interact with members on their own turf (e.g., helping new students move into their residence halls); and [5] sponsoring sundry programs that are fun (e.g., paintball), fellowship-oriented (e.g., overnight camping trip), and value-based (e.g., Bible study).

Viewing the SSC recruitment plan through a marketing lens, one would likely conclude that it is neither innovative nor distinctive compared to other "sure-fire" college organization recruitment efforts. Nevertheless, these mundane recruitment strategies get the job done. SSC knows its target audience, understands itself and its mission, and believes in its product—Christianity. Dedicated SLT members invest their time and energy to get the job done. That said, there seems to be something weird amid these seemingly ordinary practices, and it has to do with the group's values embedded in these recruitment rituals.

A more in-depth examination of the SSC recruitment plan and workshop reveals a unique feature of the SSC that distinguishes it from other collegiate organizations and accounts for some of its "weirdness." *SSC members recruit for the Kingdom of God, not for their student organization.* Students Serving Christ, as its organizational name suggests, exists to serve Jesus. For Matthew and veteran SLT members, their ultimate recruitment goal is to bring college students to Jesus. Contacting prospective members, designing promotional materials, and sponsoring welcome programs are conduits to connect students to Christianity, not to a particular Christian organization like the SSC. During one of his recruitment pep talks, Matthew argued that it was the job of SLT members to "bring people back to the central issue of Jesus." Aaron, an SSC intern, explains this emphasis on recruiting for the Kingdom:

> We talk about the art of recruiting, put up flyers in freshmen halls, and have ice-cream socials. Freshmen arrive on campus and check out the options. They go to _____ [high-profile Christian organization] first, since it is on Thursdays. If they feel good, they stay. They have more people going around the dorms. It is harder for us, but we don't try to compete. We have a different view of the Kingdom and how to expand the Kingdom than _____. We tell students these differences and let students make the choice. We try to get the people who are most interested in morally leading. We don't get people who just drop by; we get people who are committed to the Bible and Christianity.

Matthew's stern warning to SLT members to not "trash-talk" other Christian organizations seems counter-intuitive to conventional recruitment techniques, whereby recruiters persuade prospective members that their organization is "the best." But this warning serves as a subtle reminder to SLT members that all Christian organizations are recruiting to expand the Kingdom. He noted, "other [Christian] organizations on campus are also expanding the Kingdom, but in a different way. . . . We need to communicate clearly about who we are and what we're about." SSC's purposeful and unique agenda, which many other Christian organizations share, is all about Jesus and expanding His Kingdom.

Organization and Leadership Structures

SSC's organizational and leadership structures are also "weird," which influences the organization's recruiting efforts. The SSC neither resembles nor operates like a traditional collegiate student organization.

SSC has a president because the university stipulates that in order for a student group to maintain its status as a registered student organization, it must have an individual designated as "president." The SSC president has no special standing within the organization. Instead, that person serves as an equal member of the Servant Leadership Team (SLT), a soldier of God who leads by serving. For the president and the entire SLT, the concept of serving eclipses traditional leadership roles that focus on power and control. Serving others involves simultaneously focusing on others' needs while modeling a Christ-centered lifestyle. For current SSC members, *serving is leading*.

Although the SSC sponsors more than one event per day, the organization seldom explicitly involves itself in administration, such as discussing old or new business, approving minutes, or voting on motions. The full-time staff members manage administrative functions. The only "business" that matters to SSC is God's business—spreading His Word. Rather than conducting bureaucratic committee meetings guided by Robert's Rules of Order, SSC conducts educational seminars (e.g., the illustration practice session) guided by the Bible (the SSC's Constitution of sorts) that center on evangelizing, discipling, and helping members become better followers of Jesus.

During private SLT gatherings such as the SLT retreat, Matthew and SSC interns usually assume primary responsibility for setting the agenda and facilitating the work session. Matthew's leading role as organizer and facilitator in private settings is firm and authoritative; he sets the content and structure for these meetings and often has the "final say" on the team direction. This behavior is a striking contrast to his much lower-profile, traditional advisor role during public, general membership events and programs (e.g., Friday night worship or Bible study). In these contexts, SLT members take center stage. Thus, the SSC leadership strategy uniquely combines the structure of traditional Christian organizations, which often feature a main authoritative figure (e.g., a pastor) with that of many collegiate organizations, which are often led exclusively by students.

Regardless of who is leading, SLT members seldom challenge their elders' decisions or assertions in public. Instead, they act as dutiful disciples eager to implement the elder's plan. If differences arise, members raise their concerns in private. In the recruitment narratives, Matthew follows the Bible, and SSC students follow Matthew. Members' reluctance to challenge authority, which seems "weird" to most college-age students, is not surprising in this evangelical context. The rationale for the SSC's organizational and leadership structures becomes apparent in an excerpt from an interview with Caleb, where he discusses Matthew's leadership style:

> Matthew communicates biblical values and principles to the people he is leading. . . . His goal is to create people who can do what he does. That is a goal of discipleship. Take someone who is not you, and make them as much like you or better. . . . His goal is to focus on a few people and train them as best he can and use "the few" to get to the many.

Evangelizing and discipleship are, in many ways, the means through which the organization cultivates its "leaders" and conducts its administrative business. Through this evangelical mentoring program, students learn to serve God and disciple the next generation of evangelical collegians.

The SSC is interested in recruiting selfless individuals who will direct all their efforts toward building the Kingdom. SLT students explicitly convey to prospective members that a relationship with God comes before the interests of the organization or individual members, and the authority of the Bible clearly defines how members should enhance this relationship with God. Leadership takes on a unique meaning for this group; as leaders, members embrace a quiet, "servant" lifestyle in the name of Jesus.

Recruits

A third and final source of weirdness centers on SSC's Christian recruits. Two questions arose initially during our workshop debriefing session and persisted throughout the study: What kinds of students would be receptive to a stranger asking about their religious beliefs, feelings on spirituality, or faith-leanings? What kinds of students would be receptive to the use of a biblical illustration to get acquainted with a stranger? The short answer, probably, is "Christian students."

Students with a long-standing affiliation with evangelical Christianity—just like current SSC members—tend to be receptive to SSC recruitment strategies such as freely sharing and discussing their religious/faith beliefs and the Bible, even with strangers. In fact, they seek out Christian organizations and friends with whom they can have these discussions. For Christian students, SSC recruitment practices aimed at encouraging them to follow Jesus are anything but "weird."

The SSC's Jesus-centered recruitment strategy stifles its evangelical overtures to diverse non-Christians. Non-Christians' reactions to SSC's recruitment tactics are much different than those of Christians. Frequently, non-Christian students politely resist or rebuke SSC recruitment overtures such as faith-based surveys and biblical illustrations, despite the evangelist's attempts to resist "guerilla evangelizing" tactics. More often, the SSC "soldiers of Jesus" turn to an easier recruiting target: current Christian students. As a result, the organization membership maintains its uniformity, which provides a comfortable environment for current members but severely limits their ability to reach out to and evangelize the "other" on this campus. A strong focus on Jesus makes organizational diversity and true evangelism tough goals to achieve.

The SSC's espoused recruitment "game plan" is to reach out to Christians and non-Christians. In reality, however, their enacted recruitment plan initially targets Christians, who would be predisposed to a Christian organization. With this implicit Christian recruitment focus, much of the "weirdness" surrounding the recruitment process dissipates. The SSC "knows" Christians and keenly understands two of their primary needs: finding a community that shares their values and seamlessly interconnecting the following of Jesus with fellowship and fun. SSC's recruitment strategies directly and substantively address these two needs of the Christian students they hope to recruit.

The SSC's goal of recruiting non-Christians becomes an ongoing project for members, as they seek to slowly build friendships with such individuals over the course of their time in college. They pray that these individuals will eventually reach a point where they will be more open to the SSC's messages. Because these relationships take a long time to mature, it is obvious why the recruitment of more Christian students—to increase the ranks of evangelizers—is the organization's foremost goal. With more Christian students on board, the SSC has more opportunities to share the Word with others.

The Christian Community

Ernest Boyer (1987) argued, "One of the most urgent obligations colleges confront is to build a sense of community among students—a sense of belonging at the institution" (p. 1). "Belonging" is on the minds of most first-year students. This is especially true of Christian first-year students, who expect to address this need of belonging by joining a Christian community soon after they arrive on this public university campus. They desire a Christian community that is compatible with their values and lifestyle.

The theme of Christian students yearning for affiliation emerged during interviews with a first-year SSC member and a senior as they discussed their early days on campus. The first-year member explained:

> I knew about all the Christian groups. . . . I got my student organization directory, and I went through every single one [Christian groups] and high-lighted everything. That first weekend I was here, I looked for anything happening from those groups. I went to one meeting for each. . . . At the SSC table I filled out the survey and signed up for Bible study. I filled out the survey so that I could win a bike; I didn't win it. I got an e-mail [from SSC] that invited me to the Friday [worship] event. I went.

The senior member noted:

> They [the campus's largest Christian organization] are more loud and con-temporary, like they have punk rock bands at their Thursday meetings. SSC is more my style. Picking a student group is like picking a church. The first criterion is: what do they teach? Is it grounded in the Bible? Is it evangeli-cal? Fire and brimstone? How do they encourage you to get involved? . . . I need structure. I get nervous if things are too loose. SSC was organized and had the right message.

The SSC leadership team recognizes the importance of Christian students' need for belonging to a community where they can openly express their Christian beliefs. SSC also recognizes that there are multiple evangelical communities. It tries to make clear to prospective members the unique aspects of the SSC Christian community, which aims to bring students closer to Jesus. SSC recruiters do not pretend that their community is all things to all Christians. As one student noted, "It [SSC] knows what it believes, which

I liked." The SSC recruiters unambiguously clarify the core values of this unique Christian community and seek to recruit Christians who subscribe to those values. Once students with Christian values join the SSC, their faith continues to strengthen, which enhances the organization's overall mission.

Faith, Fellowship, and Fun

Following Christ, fellowship, and fun (the Three Fs) are three desires of new Christian students (again, an attitude that seems somewhat weird to non-Christians). Excerpts from interviews with Kelly illuminate the importance of the Three Fs to Christians, especially as new college students:

> I thought they [SSC members] were really welcoming. The first week they really focused on us. . . . the sophomore girls did. It seemed really sincere the way they wanted to get to know me. They stopped by my room with a goodie bag, just to say hi again . . . I mean, they remembered my name and stuff. And then they'd call and see if I wanted to go to a Bible study, a camp-out or something.

SSC recruitment strategies make clear to prospective members that creating a community that seamlessly integrates following Christ with fellowship and fun is an important aim of the SSC. For example, the illustration dress rehearsal reminds SSC members that following Jesus is what it is all about. Matthew's decision to have dyad partners share the illustration with each other is an opportunity for fellowship. The group's willingness to joke about their rusty and stilted dress rehearsal illustrates how members intertwine fun with following Jesus and fellowship.

These Fs are also evident when SLT members share the illustration with recruits. The content of the illustration conveys the importance of Jesus and the Bible. Sharing the illustration one person at a time symbolically communicates the importance the organization places on fellowship. The SSC integrates these three Fs into its program offerings, and each program emphasizes at least one of the Fs (e.g., Bible study emphasizes following Christ; camping emphasizes fellowship; paintball emphasizes fun). SSC leaders weave the three Fs into the fabric of the organization and create the sense of community and belonging that college students desire. Boyer (1987b) argued, "The first weeks on campus are critically important. This is the time when friendships are formed and attitudes about collegiate life take shape" (p. 43). Based on their recruitment plan, SSC members clearly recognize the potency of the first few weeks of college in the lives of students, and through the three Fs they aspire to make a difference in the lives of new Christian collegians.

Summary

"Weirdness" matters. SSC members proudly embrace the "weirdness" of their recruitment outcomes focused on building God's Kingdom, their leadership structure centered on servant leadership, and their emphasis on recruiting (at least initially) new members who are *already* Christian. It is precisely these characteristics that make SSC stand out as a unique option among Christian organizations on this campus. Members explicitly share with prospective members what exactly makes this organization "weird," which allows students to make an informed decision as they select a Christian organization. The SSC has become very good at recruiting people like them, which creates implications for their sweeping evangelical goals. We explore this issue further in Chapter 9.

Although SSC members are proud of their "weirdness," Timothy's comment that "we're not weird, if that's what you're thinking" demonstrates that SSC members recognize that outsiders on this campus perceive the group as strange and do not always embrace that characteristic. Who determines which groups are "weird?" Why do groups such as the SSC feel the need to defend their "weirdness?" These are two pivotal questions we answer in the following chapter, as we explore how the SSC, as a subculture, opposes the dominant campus groups that determine legitimacy and "weirdness" on this campus. Jesus' opposition to the dominant thinking of His day inspires SSC students to join a Christian organization. They make their lives all about Him, even while being perceived as "weird" by peers.

6

PRAISE JESUS

Rituals of Difference

Thank God It's Friday[1]

From the porch of a modest-size interdenominational Christian church on the edge of campus, we gaze at the swarms of neophyte collegians occupying the manicured green quads that surround the nearby residence halls. Some students dress casually and toss Frisbees. Others, adorned in eye-catching styles, are individuals we suspect are preparing to spend the evening downtown. Deciding what to do on this first official college weekend is no easy task for new students.

Current and prospective members of Student Serving Christ (SSC) have made their decision for the evening. The vestibule of the church is brimming with activity as the organization prepares to host its first Friday night worship program of the academic year. Veteran SSC members chat as they anxiously await the many new first-year students they hope will attend tonight's program. The Servant Leadership Team (SLT) members have been working tirelessly all week to recruit new members and publicize this weekly event, but the fruits of their labor have yet to be harvested.

As we enter the air-conditioned sanctuary and escape the muggy August evening, two SSC members descend upon us. Timothy, after quietly conferring with Tammy about the spelling of K-e-l-s-e-y, prepares our nametags and hands them to us with a gleaming smile. "So glad to see you both. . . . Welcome back!" Matthew, wearing long shorts and a rugby shirt, greets us and then continues his jaunt through the small clusters of students; he welcomes each by name as he works the crowd. Returning students hug and share stories about their summer vacations.

We casually chat with Bethany, a sophomore we met the previous year, and immediately notice that she is eyeing a group of first-year students who arrived moments ago. We quickly finish our conversation as she proceeds to personally meet and welcome the visitors, clad in casual shorts and T-shirts, who continue to file into the room. On this evening, bonding time with old friends is secondary to the SSC's primary goal of becoming acquainted with new students.

The 80 attendees' loud conversations and laughter fill the room as SSC band members stroll up the red-carpeted center aisle toward the small altar. They tune their instruments as they unfold crisp sheets of music. The band's somewhat unusual "come as you are" clothing adds to the SSC's casual and welcoming atmosphere: one singer wears a Hawaiian shirt, two members wear SSC T-shirts, and another displays a T-shirt reading "Daddy's little girl."

The Servant Leadership Team has extended tonight's preworship social to allow upper-class students additional time to interact with prospective members. Current members appear to be making good use of this extra time for meeting and greeting. New members blend easily with the veterans; the collective group creates a sea of mostly White, mostly middle/upper-class students dressed neatly, but not trendily. At 7:15, the band leader clicks on a microphone and signals the percussionist to begin tapping the beat for the first song. SSC members simultaneously begin what appears to be a well-organized, yet organic, scheme. Each member personally asks the first-year students with whom they are speaking to sit next to them for tonight's meeting.

The music signals to current members that they should begin to file into the 20 rows of chairs. A student sitting in the back of the room retrieves PowerPoint slides of Christian song lyrics from his computer and projects them onto the screen at the front of the room, which refocuses students' minds on Jesus. Under the soft yellow lights of the ceiling, the lyrics brightly splash across the screen and invite audience members to fully participate in the singing. The band plays and the attendees sing with gusto. The band has improved since last year, but their performance is still not quite "tight." Nevertheless, the attendees—including the new students—seem to revel in this collective act of solidarity for Jesus.

As the band concludes its first song, a woman jumps up from her seat and scurries to the altar. "Welcome to SSC! I'm Sarah, a senior, and I'm really excited about this year and about you all being here! Let's get started. We're going to have a great night tonight. Let's start with some more worship!" She skips back to her chair in the front row as the band leader leans into his microphone, "All right everyone, praise God with everything you've got!"

A stirring version of *Blessed Be Your Name* (Redman, 2005) follows, which is an SSC favorite. With nearly 100 students present, the unrehearsed singing sounds like not-so-harmonious yelling. After another song about "dancing upon injustice," the band leader passionately closes his eyes and clenches the microphone as he offers a prayer: "Thank you, Lord, for bringing us here today. Bless this time tonight and help us all to have an attitude of prayer and devotion to You. Amen."

"Okay, we're going to play a game!" exclaims Sarah as she returns to the altar. This revelation elicits smiles from the attendees. "Okay, I need one freshman, one sophomore, one junior, and one senior!" No one volunteers, so Sarah, an aspiring elementary school teacher, switches tactics. "Okay, we need one senior—who will it be?" A cluster of men nominate a well-built peer to participate; amid cheers, he saunters to the front of the room. Soon after, two women, one a junior and the other a sophomore, volunteer. Remarkably, a freshman woman boldly proceeds to the front of the room.

"Okay, this is called Flaming Flamingo!" Sarah shouts. "Your goal is to get as many atomic fireball candies in your mouth [as you can] and stand on one foot and say 'flaming flamingo.'" Attendees loudly cheer on their representatives as they predict who will win the competition. "Let's give them some support!" screams Sarah, as she distributes candies to the four contestants. A majority of students appear invested in the event; they sit on the edges of their seats and laugh uncontrollably as contestants fill their cheeks with the fiery treats. Jessica, the SSC intern, runs to the restroom to retrieve paper towels for the drooling contestants. Just as Jessica returns to the altar, the freshman contestant expels the fireballs from her mouth and sits down to rousing applause. "You can do 35!" a group of rowdy sophomores yell to their class representative. The sophomore and junior contestants eventually drop out of the race, and Sarah declares the bulky senior male the victor moments after he wedged a 26th fireball into his mouth.

Contestants receive a round of applause as Sarah returns to the altar for announcements, which are simultaneously projected onto the screen:

> Okay, we have a list here. Look to see if you [your name] are on here and
> if so, see if it's right. If it's not on the list, add your name and then you'll

get our e-mails about what's going on. Bible studies are now forming, and we have them for freshmen, sophomores, juniors, and seniors. Sign up at the back table. Be sure to do that! We also have The Beacon, which is a good thing . . . we get together and pray to lift up the non-Christians on campus. It's at 5:30 on Tuesdays in the campus chapel.

We've also got fireworks on Monday for Labor Day, and that's a great time to get to know each other. We have camping in a few weeks . . . it's an absolutely great time. We sleep in tents and have fellowship all night. We play capture the flag at midnight."

Songs of praise resume as the band plays three more songs, more than the usual standard fare for these Friday night gatherings. Attendees who were laughing and screaming outrageously 10 minutes ago are now hushed as they sing along to a more mellow set of songs. Quiet and passionate, these tunes resemble traditional love songs, only they are about *God*. Again the band leader closes with a prayer: "We pray You'll move our hearts to You every day."

Sarah returns to the altar and introduces Kiley, a sophomore. "I'd like to say something about Kiley. She was one of my first two students in my Bible study. She and Bethany were so much fun together, and Kiley was always faithful with her Bible verse memorization and study. I'm going to pray for Kiley." Sarah puts her arm around Kiley as both bow their heads in prayer. "Lord, we pray that Kiley will share her story with us. Lord, calm her nerves and we thank You and praise You for her."

Kiley pauses nervously and then, taking her turn in a weekly worship ritual, begins her testimony:

I was born and raised in a Christian home, and I went to church all my life. . . . I honestly believed in God and Jesus Christ, but I was never actively pursuing my faith, and I was not a fan of being united in the body of believers. God was definitely working in my life, though. On my 11th birthday, I was baptized and proclaimed my faith in front of the whole congregation. This was an unusual experience because I had never done anything like that before, and I didn't know most of the people, because it was a huge church.

From third grade through the end of the summer before my sophomore year in high school, three of my grandparents had passed away and all of my great grandparents. That was a lot of funerals for me to have to experience at such a young age. I definitely had a lot of trust issues with God. For a long time, I was very bitter and angry and really resented the Lord for taking them from me. And what made it worse is that my grandpa who is still living, I didn't have a good relationship with him, and I still don't to this day. So for years of my life, I wondered why I had no grandparents who cared about me to watch me turn 16, 21, watch me get married, and get to know their great grandchildren. I always had Jesus in my heart, but I definitely pushed him aside for many years.

Kiley further explains that she attended a large high school as a freshman. Her friends knew she was a devoted Christian, so they tried not to cuss around her because they recognized that it bothered her. Despite that indication of respect, Kiley had few close friends who also devoted their lives to Jesus. She describes how she has found a supportive faith environment in college, in the SSC:

> I love these Friday nights, and then there's fun activities afterwards . . . the best one I can remember was when we all played Texas Hold 'em poker and the girls beat the boys . . . I'd encourage you all to get involved with Bible studies. It will help you grow as a person and a Christian. I'll close with sharing a passage: "Seek Him and live." I'd encourage you do to that—seek Him and live. Thanks.

Matthew nods approvingly as he passes Kiley en route to the altar. It makes sense that tonight's featured speaker would be Matthew, the SSC's "second in command" (after Jesus). A moment later he moves a music stand in front of him and neatly arranges his notes on it. He introduces himself and tells a short story about his mission trip to Thailand, when he mistakenly introduced himself as "I urinate Matthew" rather than "I am Matthew." Students laugh as Matthew smiles coyly and admits that he does urinate, but he avoids mentioning it when meeting people for the first time.

"Well, my job is to hang out with college students and help them become closer to Jesus without becoming religious weirdos." Matthew treads lightly and tries to convey to prospective SSC members the group's fellowship and fun dimensions, in addition to their strong commitment to faith. He introduces three themes for his sermon—identity, community, and opportunity—aimed at helping students live successfully in college. Several returning students flip to blank pages in their notebooks and wait expectantly with pens in hand as he begins to speak.

> So how many of you know about this college? One thing—image is important. Twenty percent of students struggle with eating disorders. Also promiscuity is high, but also many people come here and get to know Christ. And some get to know Him better than ever before if they already know Him. We'd love to sit down and talk.
>
> . . . Identity, community, and opportunity are the three keys. I'll start with identity. When I went to college . . . I graduated from here in 2000, just to give you some background. When I came I was nominally a Christian. . . . I was a Christian when it was convenient for me. I was Lord of my life. One thing I liked about college—I could be whatever I wanted to be. In high school, you know, I was already defined. Here I could be anything. But Matthew 16:15 says, "Who do you say I am? Who do you say Jesus is? For me, I say the Son of God and the Lord of my life."
>
> Okay, the second one. Community. A full life is one lived in community with other believers. We let down our masks with one another here. We are real with one another. We want to get to know you so we can minister to each other. I read a study that the loneliest group of people in the United States is college students. Wow. Not widows or the elderly. . . . I thought, "There's no way! College students have people around them all the time; they live in the residence halls." . . . But then it became clear to me that we spend time around people, yet we are not always involved with people. I can remember being lonely after transferring here. Community is so important. With the SSC, that is a priority. We want to get to know you. We want to walk this journey together and help you in your quest for Jesus. Community is what we are all about.
>
> Honestly, I understand most of you are looking at different [Christian] groups. Look for one where you can get involved and have people know you. Look for a place where you can develop. The group you choose will determine how much you grow over the next 4 years. Find a place. We hope it is here because we want to get to know you and we want you to get to know us. If it is here, be patient, wait for the community to develop. It will.

Matthew appears more relaxed and animated than usual as he casually reiterates his key points. His passion is unmistakable, as is his message as to why students should join Christian organizations in general and the SSC in particular. He then introduces his third point:

> Okay, now: Opportunity, my favorite category. What do you want out of your college experience besides an education? God didn't bring us here solely for education. God does not call people to be engineers, teachers, and accountants. There are no biblical examples of that. He calls them to first be in a relationship with Him and to work with Him to build the Kingdom. He brings people to certain careers because He cares about his people. We need people to have different missions to help other people in specific places. There is one unified story throughout the Bible. It starts with Adam and Eve, then there was Abraham, many Egyptians went with the Israelites . . . David and Goliath . . . yadayada . . . Jesus. And now here we are . . . building a part of that Kingdom. God is saying, "I've positioned you here among non-Christians . . . they're in the dorms . . . all around you . . . to share your faith. We must live among the lost."

Matthew alerts the attendees that the SSC does not practice guerilla evangelism by getting charged up, going out and sharing with people, and then feeling good about it. "We don't blast people with Bible verses." Matthew acknowledges that God calls some people to do that work, but he insists it is not a goal of the SSC. "We need to relationally connect with non-Christians. That way, the Kingdom will grow." Students appear captivated by Matthew's message, especially as he explains their mission and the way God has positioned them in the dorms *here*, on campus. Matthew's dual message is clear: there are many acceptable Christian organizations students can join, and SSC is unique in its serious commitment to interactions with campus non-Christians.

He continues:

> One day God will tap Jesus on the shoulder and say, "It's time to come back." But until then, we have work to do. The things we're doing now are no less significant than what those people in the Bible did. I believe that there'll be a book about what we did here. Like Sarah, for example, one of our seniors, she could be in the book. It could talk about how she trusted God and went into the dorms and shared her faith. You will be God's witness. Our measure of success in this ministry is you in 20 years. Are you walking with God in 20 years? Do you have on your heart God's Kingdom?

Matthew reads a passage from Scripture to support his argument. Upper-class students have heard variations of this main point before, but they listen intently anyway. "I am interested in 20 years from now, whether you have a heart for God. We'd be extremely excited if you guys joined us." Matthew bows his head in prayer, and students silently do the same. "Lord Jesus, thank you for your love, and that You want to use us. Hammer home the truths You want us to take home and Your plan for us."

The students remain silent, perhaps contemplating Matthew's message. For current members, he reinforced the mission of the SSC while simultaneously providing for prospective members a clear picture of the organization's core values centered on Jesus, and what would be expected from them if they chose to join. Absent is any mention of the SSC's views on hotly debated cultural issues that dominate exchanges in the media and on campuses.

The musicians reach for their instruments one last time as the band leader reiterates Matthew's message: "Understand what God can do in your life this year. If you embrace that power within you, you'll do great things." After one final song, Sarah skips back up to the stage.

"Tonight we are going over to Oak Street, where two of the guys live. And they just moved in, so it should be clean! We're going to play games and hang out and have fun, so you should all come!" One of the men calls out in response, "We need more games . . . Monopoly, card games, chess . . ." Students laugh when he names chess, which apparently does not fall into the category of a "fun" Friday night game. "What's wrong with chess?" he asks incredulously. The noise level in the room rises again as students conclude their faith-based time together and embark on an evening of fellowship and fun. Thank God it's Friday.

Rituals of Difference: Creating a Unique Community of Interest

Praying, singing, listening to a sermon, and playing chess—these are unlikely images one would conjure up when brainstorming college students' activities on a Friday night. As unusual as these components of the SSC's Friday worship service may seem to outsiders, SSC members purposely and voluntarily participate in these activities to distinguish themselves from their collegiate peers. SSC's unique mission and programs, such as the Friday Worship service, coupled with SSC students' desire to be "different" from other collegians creates a one-of-a-kind SSC *style*—a unique "brand" of getting to know Jesus and spreading His Word. In the remainder of this chapter, we explore the SSC's distinctive style and illuminate ways the SSC distinguishes itself from other campus groups, both secular and Christian. We also explore the implications of this style on the SSC and the larger university community.

Carlson (1994) noted that the dominant conceptualization of community in the United States is that of a normalizing community. Those in power define a cultural center and a "natural order" that become the foundation of this normalizing community. Moreover, those in power render only the dominant group's behaviors and values as acceptable, while situating the other[s] on the margins. Hall (cited in Hebdige, 1979) asserts that dominant cultures control subordinate groups, not by coercion or by the direct imposition of ruling ideas, but by hegemony—"winning and shaping consent so that the power of the dominant classes appears both legitimate and natural" (pp. 15–16). Communities of interest, also known as subcultures, emerge when a single "unified in thought and action" community does not adequately encompass the beliefs and values of all members of a larger social entity (e.g., a college campus).

The SSC is a collegiate student *subculture*, or what Carlson (1994) terms a *community of interest*. SSC views itself as a marginalized group, whose mission is to provide support, kinship, and voice to members of the campus community who want to resist expectations such as hedonism, materialism, and individualism that the dominant cultures have normalized. The SSC subculture formed as a reaction to the normalizing expectations of at least three noteworthy dominant cultures: the secular campus culture, the secular student culture, and other Christian student organizational cultures.

Opposing the Dominant Secular University

The SSC opposes and resists the *natural order* of its public, secular university that typically steers clear of religious teachings. Tensions between the sacred and the secular have a long-standing history in American higher education, the early purpose of which, ironically, was focused on religious training. Religious denominations and churches founded many colonial colleges (Lowery, 2000; Rudolph, 1962). University presidents were often clergy, and church leaders composed boards of trustees. "During the nineteenth century, evangelism, which was the dominant religious force in American Society, exerted substantial control over education . . . evangelism's influence stretched far beyond education into virtually every major sector of American life" (Lowery, 2000, p. 22). But by the end of first quarter of the 20th century, American higher education had all but purged evangelical Protestant influence from the classroom and, in some instances, from the university (Kim, 2006).

Warren Nord (cited in Laurence, 1999) detailed the origins of American higher education's gradual gravitational pull toward a more secular collegiate atmosphere and away from religion:

> If there was an overriding purpose to American colonial education it was to nurture and sustain a Christian civilization, but between the time of the American Revolution and the end of the nineteenth century an educational revolution took place: religion dropped by the wayside as America marched into the modern world. The mantle of high purpose in the schools was passed on to democracy and Americanism, the new faiths of the new nation. At the same time, education became more and more utilitarian, serving whatever purposes individuals might happen to have: in an increasingly commercial society, those purposes were largely vocational; in an increasing modern society, they were almost invariably secular" (p. 63).

Cherry, DeBerg, and Porterfield (2001) expanded on this divide between higher education and religion:

> Until the rise of the modern American university in the late nineteenth and early twentieth centuries, when the traditional divisions of scholarly study began to be transformed into academic disciplines presided over by specialized professionals, religious and moral instruction permeated the entire curriculum of many colleges. Educators often assumed that religious principles and biblical knowledge were coextensive with science, history, and languages. And they believed that a thorough grounding in religious principles and biblical knowledge supported advances across the educational spectrum. (p. 2)

Practical knowledge and modern science replaced the influence of religion on college campuses and created new ways of interpreting the world. Evolution, for example, supplanted creationism as a better explanation of the development of the human species. U.S. Supreme Court rulings also contributed to this secularization of higher education. Several Court cases defined the role of religion in public higher education, which ultimately mandated that colleges and universities act more "neutral" in matters of religion. Higher education became more tentative as it heeded the Court's advice and tried to be receptive to all types of religions and to provide space for those wanting to embrace religion, as well as those individuals interested in purging religion from campus. Achieving an appropriate balance of religious expression has been a murky and formidable task for decades, which has led to both religious and nonreligious marginalized subcultures.

Since colonial times, American higher education has supported religious extracurricular and cocurricular organizations. In the early 20th century, the Young Men's Christian Association (YMCA) and Young Women's Christian Association (YWCA) were campus outlets for students wishing to mix religion with their college education (Butler, cited in Lowery, 2000). In the mid-20th century, when religion moved from the epicenter of American higher education to an "incidental periphery" (Marsden, 1992, p. 33), the role of religion in the cocurriculum (i.e., life outside the classroom) increased as its influence within the larger university decreased.

While student affairs staffs grappled with ways to meet the religious and spiritual needs of students and uphold the law, evangelical Christian organizations that were not directly affiliated with colleges and universities began to appear on campuses to address the spiritual and religious needs of some students. Lowery (2000) explains:

> This secularization paved the way for new evangelical groups such as Campus Crusade for Christ and InterVarsity Christian Fellowship to enter the campus and flourish. As mainstream denominations (e.g., Methodist and Presbyterian) began to play less central roles on public college campuses, new religious groups formed and quickly gained a parity of prestige and power on campus with more established religious groups. (p. 24)

In 1975 two recent graduates formed the campus chapter of SSC, after finding Christ during their college years. They recognized and responded to a perceived biblical void in public higher education and on the campus. SSC's DNA, so to speak, has been *passion* (i.e., following Jesus with passion, truth, and sincerity by focusing on prayer, witnessing, fellowship, and discipleship), *people* (e.g., by truly loving God, one loves people), and *purpose* (i.e., aligning one's values and priorities with the values and priorities the Bible espouses).

Since then, the SSC's implicit agenda has been to oppose the dominant secular university. Unlike its university, the SSC celebrates religious instruction and moral education. The SSC tries, through its programs and initiatives, to reassert the Bible as the definitive source of knowledge. Unlike American public higher education, the SSC eschews the illusions of neutrality, balance, and the desire to be all things to all people. Although SSC members seldom engage in public debate with secularists about religion and higher education, they convey a strong sense of pity for the students and faculty who have not yet "seen the light," and they lament their limited ability to share their faith in the classroom. As is apparent in the Friday night program, SSC celebrates its unique brand of religious expression that provides safe space for Christians who perceive themselves on the margins on this college campus.

Opposing the Dominant Secular Student Culture

In addition to the SSC's resistance to secular public *institutions'* long-standing aversion to religion, SSC students also oppose the dominant *secular student culture* of this university. The SSC's university is known for enrolling a disproportionate number of image-conscious, affluent, competitive, high-achieving, highly involved, and academically successful students. Frequently, SSC's Christ-centered values clash with materialism, hedonism, and individualism—dominant values of the larger student culture, according to SSC members. Leslie, an SSC senior, elaborates on the values of the larger student culture and their influence on her college experience:

> I guess it's feeling like I have to do everything perfectly and be in control, doing everything. Even people in other organizations are committed to so many things here, and it's a very "we're smart . . . we're on top of things . . . we're leaders . . . we're in control of what's going on." . . . everybody appears like they have it together, and they're cute . . . and just realizing that it's okay that some days I'm not all together on the inside and it's okay if that shows on the outside, and to be able to be open with those people and say "You know, I'm really having a rough time." So that's something I've grown in, and it's hard. Even in classes, I know in my mind that these people probably have problems, too, but I've never seen them. They don't talk about it, so it's hard for me to be the first one to say, "Yeah, I'm having a really rough time."

Although many SSC students describe themselves as high achievers and mirror the mostly Caucasian, traditional-age demographics of the campus, they otherwise do not fit the dominant profile. Instead, they have created their own subculture and have their own SSC "dominant profile."

The SSC opposes the dominant student cultural norms through mostly gentle, subtle means. SSC-sponsored programs such as their Friday worship service—replete with spiritual songs, evangelical advocacy, *born again* testimonies, prayer, and wholesome activities (e.g., playing board games)—oppose the dominant culture. Influenced by popular culture, the dominant culture focuses on tradition (i.e., the way it has always been done), reasoning (i.e., it is logical), and emotion (i.e., it feels right) (Warren, 2002).

Jablonski (2001) noted that college students' antiestablishment stance in the 1960s and early 1970s and materialist leanings during the 1980s contributed to contemporary expressions of hostility and ambivalence toward religion. This is perhaps the most salient point of divergence between the SSC and the dominant secular student culture; many students on this campus shun religious teaching in their everyday lives. This attitude differs sharply from SSC members' Christ-based lifestyle.

On the nationwide level, a survey the Higher Education Research Institute conducted in 2004 found that "most college freshmen believe in God, but fewer than half follow religious teaching in their daily lives" (Bartlett, 2005, A-1, A-40). On the SSC's campus, the overwhelming majority of students *do* classify themselves as Christian; however, SSC students strongly distinguish their brand of Christianity from that of the mainstream students. Caleb, a senior, commented, "Legitimate Christians on campus are clearly the minority." Leslie further clarified this distinction:

> What's hard is that, like, a lot of freshmen and a lot of people feel like they already know all about Christianity and all about Jesus, so it's harder for them to take a fresh look and look at things in new ways. Whatever misconceptions they've had from their parents or their churches throughout their lives, they don't realize they need to take a second look, but we need to do that. Everyone needs to do that. . . . this is going to sound weird—but to get them to look at it with their heart rather than just with their mind. Because . . . for me in college, and I think a lot of Christians in college, it moves from your head to your heart. You really know it and it becomes a part of you . . . instead of just doing it, it means something to you.

Unlike mainstream Christian college students, SSC members' interests lie in moving from "head" to "heart" Christianity and living a "clean," seamless life for God. Therefore, they purposely situate themselves as different from the dominant "Christian" culture on this university campus.

While opposing the dominant secular student culture, SSC concurrently acts to transform it. Matthew, in his sermon, purposely leveraged this campus's image-conscious reputation to portray the dominant culture as "sinful" (e.g., engaging in promiscuous sexual behavior). He invoked this image of the normalizing culture to further propagate the SSC's transformative agenda, which is rooted in their evangelical mission. Transformation is fundamental to the Protestant theology of evangelism. While many American Protestant groups seldom talk about transforming or structurally changing society, evangelical groups often envision the transformation of society (or in this context, the university) through the lifestyle changes individuals must make as they turn their lives over to Christ (Riley, 2005).

SSC members embrace a Christ-centered lifestyle and hope to persuade others on campus to do the same. As one student said in a prayer session, "We pray that Christ would have greater presence than academics or alcohol on campus—all the things people are obsessed with here." Therefore, the SSC subculture is not only a site of resistance but also a site of transformation, where students hope to change the dominant secular campus culture. They insist on changing students' minds to have a new obsession: Jesus. SSC students continue to pray for and be friendly toward students unwilling to adopt their Christ-centered lifestyle, but they harbor pity and disapproval of their sinful ways.

On the surface, SSC students appear to emulate many of the characteristics of the current generation of college students known as the "millennial" generation (Howe and Strauss, 2000), but they manifest these qualities quite differently from the majority student culture on this campus. For instance, like their peers, SSC students are busy, yet their style of "busy" contrasts sharply with the busy nature of their classmates, many of whom are involved in multiple extracurricular activities. Stacey discusses the way SSC became her focus in college:

> SSC is really the only cocurricular I'm involved in. Freshman year I was thinking about joining other organizations, but I didn't really feel drawn to many and school was taking up more time than I really wanted it to. I decided SSC should be my focus—it's not just SSC, it's building the Kingdom of God, which is what I want my life to be about, especially this

semester. I'm taking more hours than I normally do, and I just feel like my life is just schoolwork and SSC, but at this point, that's really what I want it to be . . . SSC is definitely the primary focus.

And Kelly explains how her definition of "busy" changed between high school and college:

SSC is the primary thing I'm involved in. In high school I was involved in everything and never had a free moment, which was fun, but it's harder to give 100 percent to anything. So it's cool now to be able to do that. Last semester I worked 8 hours a week to get some extra money, too . . . but I do like being able to focus a lot on God.

Whereas other students on campus involve themselves in multiple student organizations and activities, SSC students are busy because they exclusively devote the bulk of their time outside of coursework to SSC activities. Many students commented that they had "SSC stuff" every night of the week—prayer sessions on Mondays, Bible study on Tuesdays, discipleship meeting on Wednesdays, Servant Leadership Team training on Thursdays, and the Friday night program and SSC social activities over the weekend. Additionally, SSC students actively try to live a balanced life by spending daily quiet time meditating, reading the Bible, or praying. Most of the first-year students with whom we spoke were involved in one to two other activities such as music ensembles, Christian sororities/fraternities, community volunteering, and sometimes other Christian organizations in addition to the SSC. However, as they became more involved in the SSC as upper-class students, they often dropped other activities to devote their time to "God's work." The SSC became their only cocurricular pursuit.

SSC students also differ in the ways in which they view achievement and pressure to succeed. Howe and Strauss (2000) contextualize millennials' achievement mostly in terms of their focus on academics and "getting As" in their courses. However, Kelly comments on the way SSC students focus on achieving for God, rather than in the classroom:

I think my mom's worried about my schoolwork—she keeps saying that that's the reason I'm in college. I think to myself "not really," but I can't tell her that because they're paying for it. . . . I'm here to do God's work, that's why God put me here.

Further, SSC students manifest their conventional values much differently from the wider student population. Howe and Strauss (2000) comment that millennials are more conventional in their attitudes than the Boomer generation because they have stronger relationships with parents and seem to support tougher standards regarding deviant behavior in society. SSC students seem to take this concept of convention to the extreme in the arenas of dating, drinking, and entertainment. SSC members engage in serious dating only; the end goal of dating is to find one's God-selected life mate, and relationships must remain "pure" until marriage. Members adopt various standards on drinking, but drunkenness is widely scorned. On several occasions we heard students deploring popular TV shows such as *Desperate Housewives* and *Sex and the City*. According to SSC students, they felt most isolated from their peers on campus as a result of their strikingly different conventional values.

Opposing Dominant Christian Organizations

Whereas SSC's resistance to the dominant secular campus culture and its peers is obvious, SSC also distinguishes itself from a third cultural force—the higher-profile and more powerful campus-based Christian organizations. SSC, a mid-size student organization, has a much lower campus profile and a considerably smaller membership than the organization featured in Chapter 1, whose membership exceeds 1,000 students and 30 staff members. These higher-profile and larger organizations attract students by employing glossy advertising blitzes and sophisticated and unyielding recruitment strategies. They sustain and satisfy their membership by producing flashy, high-tech video promotions, showcasing trendy skits replete with popular culture references, and designing worship services that are more akin to a rock concert than a religious worship gathering. Such powerful entities influence Christians' opinions about what constitutes contemporary Christianity to such an extent that these conceptualizations appear both legitimate and natural. Two SSC members elaborate on how they position their organization in relation to the largest Christian campus organization:

> SSC has 2 full-time staff; _____ has 20. Members breed members. They have that many more people talking about their organization. The basis of their organization is number-focused. For better or worse, they are bigger

and more social-based than us. _____ has vast levels of commitment . . . For those who want simply a weekly fill of God, _____ is an easy place to go and get nourishment and hide. In SSC, we are not pushy; we notice new faces and know our membership. We are a tight-knit group; our focus is not as social. We do it differently.

In terms of what we [SSC] have to do, our job is to reproduce and reach new non-Christians. _____ is structured to reach quotas. Every week/month you have to share the gospel with a set number of people. Years ago SSC did that, but we stopped that practice. It was contributing to competition among ministries and also it was competition within staff. It got to be "I shared Christ with xx many people; how many did you get?"

The SSC recognizes and respectfully distinguishes itself from its more powerful Christian competitors that favor breadth versus depth and style over substance. The Friday worship program does not feature slick rock-band music or videos; rather, SSC positions the Word of God and students' faith commitment front and center. SSC resists urges to "give the congregation what they want" and thus situates the Friday worship program not as "the place to be" for Christians, but rather as the place Christians "need to be"— especially individuals who are serious about serving Christ. In his sermon, Matthew clearly defined the niche of the SSC organization: its small size allows students to create *community* in which to grow as Christians and individuals while doing God's work. SSC founders established this ministry to fill voids created by the dominant cultures of which Christians are expected to be a part.

SSC has a distinctive style. The SLT purposely schedules its weekly worship meetings on Friday nights to offer Christian students a sacred alternative to the dominant culture's profane Friday night activities. Essentially, the SLT redefines what "Friday night" means to college students. Staff members encourage general members to use Friday night to build community within the organization and to use Saturday nights to interact with non-Christian friends. The SSC members communally celebrate their faith and love of Jesus rather than expend their energies on drugs, sex, and rock and roll.

The students' down-to-earth, casual, and conservative dress of shorts and T-shirts at public events such as the Friday night services conveys the notion that members define themselves by their genuine relationship with Christ and their desire to live a moral life, not by their attire or appearance. This style is antithetical to the dominant secular college culture, which endorses materialism and affluence.

This unique style not only distinguishes this community of interest from its secular peers, but it also directly distinguishes the group from other Christian organizations. The SSC favors substantive interaction on a more human scale. The not-so-polished Friday night worship meeting is in stark contrast to the more stylized Christian worship service we featured in Chapter 1. SSC's homemade nametags and student-led activities reflect the organization's preference for sincere substance rather than excess and extravagance. Apart from the weekly fun event such as the Flaming Flamingo game, the Friday worship program is serious in tone and simple in its construction. It differs from the larger Christian organization's program, which is mostly a social gathering. The ambiance and delivery of the SSC service is less important than the content, which consists of unambiguous messages that foster students' inward thinking about their faith. Earnest SSC members take notes during services and seldom worry about being hip. The staff and worship facilitators are not usually charismatic; instead, they embrace the Bible's charismatic message.

Students reach out to Christians and non-Christians by spreading the Word to "one individual at a time" in a deliberate and personal way, avoiding "righteous" or "holier than thou" interactions with non-Christian peers. Matthew's comment that group members need to "relationally connect with non-Christians" rather than practice "guerrilla evangelism" exemplifies the SSC's distinctive style. SSC students go into residence halls throughout the year and casually speak with interested students in hopes of forming in-depth and lasting relationships within which they can eventually share their faith.

The 80-member organization prides itself on substantively and warmly greeting and getting to know all new members, while comprehensively attending to long-term members' spiritual needs. The particular focus of the group is on the new, first-year members.

Other Christian and non-Christian organizations often recruit numerous first-year students with the knowledge that many will likely leave the organization as they become upper-class students. However, SSC's style centers on creating strong relationships with first-year students from the start; through this process, they aspire to accomplish their goal of sustained student involvement. Whereas larger Christian groups do not have the luxury of ensuring that everyone knows each other, SSC's smaller-scale discipleship approach to mentoring members while spreading the Word of Christ fosters intimate relationships that encourage in-depth faith development.

The organization's philosophy focuses on quality, rather than on the number of members. SSC does not degrade other Christian organizations, but instead labels the dominant organization as "different," rather than "wrong." Matthew encourages all new attendees to get involved *somewhere* (i.e., with any of the Christian student organizations on campus), so they can come to know Christ better during their college years. SSC creates a unique, cohesive style that focuses on the simple life and on personal relationships with Jesus, which contrasts with the dominant cultures the organization opposes.

The SSC Friday night worship meeting is a gateway for new members to sample the subculture's distinctive style. Once members join the SSC, leaders strongly encourage them to make their lives *all about Jesus*. For example, Matthew's sermon stressed the importance of knowing one's own identity and knowing Christ while in college. In the next chapter, we reveal ways in which the SSC continues to enact its unique style while educating future evangelizers through Bible study.

GETTING TO REALLY KNOW JESUS

Teaching and Learning Rituals

Biblical Brethren: Men's Bible Study

The starless sky does little to assist me (Peter) in navigating the pitch-black parking lot of the Christian Fellowship Church on the edge of campus. As I cautiously ascend the handicap-accessible ramp leading to the front door of the church, I squint to read a billboardlike sign near the entrance:

Sunday Worship Schedule
9:30–11:15 a.m.
Welcome Students
An Evangelical Free Church

I stand alone in the unlit vestibule and ponder the meaning of the phrase, "An Evangelical Free Church." Does this mean "free of evangelism"? Or perhaps, "free to evangelize"? The faint sounds of a praise band from another Christian organization practicing in the main sanctuary of the church are barely audible. Numerous Christian organizations use this off-campus facility each day, but the level of activity appears low this Wednesday night in April, likely because of impending final exams.

Uncertain as to the location of the lobby's light switches, I feel my way down the stairwell to the lower level of the church. The emergency exit signs provide minimal sight guidance as I tentatively walk down the winding hallway toward one of the multipurpose rooms located in the bowels of the church. I silently ask myself, "Has this evening's men's Bible study gathering been cancelled?"

This area, part kindergarten classroom and part warehouse, has a 1960s feel to it. The brightly painted chartreuse and orange walls and the children's artwork do little to brighten the drab cinderblock walls. I peruse the construction paper "masterpieces" that read: "Smile, Jesus loves you"; "Only use kind words"; "Give the speaker your full attention"; and "Happy Valentine's Day." A few minutes later, I hear sounds like a stampede in the distance, disturbing the building's serenity. Rowdy men race down the stairway and linoleum-clad hallways. Their long, stomping strides echo throughout the lower level. One by one, each member of the entourage enters the multipurpose room, roughly grabs a chair on the periphery, and relocates it to form a loose circle in the middle of the room. With brief greetings of "Hi" or "How's it going," the men acknowledge my existence.

Timothy, wearing a baggy T-shirt and an even baggier pair of shorts, appears to have an abundance of energy for a 9:00 p.m. midweek study session. Warren's baseball cap does little to hide his shortly cropped, yet wild hair. He appears more subdued than usual this evening. Hal's clothes look crumpled, as if he just awoke from a nap, but his infectious smile looks fresh. Unlike many of their peers, these first-year men have all donned no-name clothes; there is not a designer clothing label in sight.

Once seated, these mostly 18-year-old White men begin to circulate beef jerky, trail mix, sweet tarts, peanut butter cups, and breath mints. These late night junk-food snacks are a dietitian's worst nightmare and a dream come true for dentists. The nonstop passing of food around the circle does little to slow the conversations. Of the SSC's three "Fs"—following Jesus, fellowship, and fun—the men temporarily put on hold the "following Jesus" goal as they goof around and enjoy each other's company.

Aaron, an SSC intern and this group's Bible study leader, finally arrives. His presence brings a sense of order to this rag-tag entourage. Aaron asks about the lone missing Bible study group member: "Where's Bobby?" Timothy, without verbally responding, whips out his cell phone, pushes a speed-dial number, and calls Bobby. "He's on his way," Timothy calls out. This intact group is tight; the daily SSC offerings—prayer sessions, evangelical outings, and dinners—provide opportunities for these men to interact often. Three of them have already agreed to be off-campus apartment mates next year, and two plan to attend SSC summer internship programs in Florida and Kentucky.

Aaron promotes a regional SSC gathering taking place in 3 weeks, soon after the academic year concludes. "Joe _____ [one of the organizers and keynote presenters] is a wise speaker. He knows God's Word. . . . It is a great time to spend time with Christian guys from other schools, pray, and listen to great speakers. . . . It's only 35 dollars. Pray about it." Aaron nods to Warren, who understands the nonverbal gesture. He removes a stick of beef jerky from his mouth long enough to offer a prayer. "Help us to stay with You, Lord. Help us to reach out to the lost . . . and survive our exams. Thank You for bringing us together, and we praise You and seek Your love. . . . In Your name, we pray."

Throughout the semester, this Bible study group has been reading and discussing Paul's epistle to the Ephesians, a New Testament book of the Bible. To refresh my memory, I scan bits and pieces from my past field notes, which serve as an essential cheat-sheet for me in this context. "Book of Ephesians, written during the first century AD . . . Letter written by Paul while in prison to the Ephesian church . . . the letter highlights Paul's commitment to the church. . . . Paul's letter advocates strict adherence to Christian teachings. . . . interesting stuff about marriage, slaves, and gender relations."

During a previous gathering, the group carefully studied Paul's opening greeting, Paul's prayer for spiritual enrichment, and Paul's discipleship of the Gentiles. For this evening, which marks the final meeting of the year, the agenda centers on tying up loose ends related to this semester-long Ephesians discussion and brainstorming strategies to continue individual Bible study during students' summer hiatus from campus.

Aaron, as always, takes the lead and begins with an icebreaker question: "Based on your reading so far, if you could retitle the Book of Ephesians, what would it be?" A steady stream of replies is forthcoming: "Gifts . . . Duty . . . Responsibility . . . Life . . . An outline of Christian living." Apparently satisfied with the responses to his question, Aaron continues, "Let's look closer at Ephesians 6:21–24. Any thoughts?" I crack open my loaner Bible and locate the passage as Timothy reads the verse aloud.

Warren raises his hand to offer the first interpretation of the passage. Aaron reminds him that it is not necessary to raise his hand before speaking. "Oh yeah," Warren replies, then continues, "Paul is concerned about their well being. . . . Paul is spreading the Word." Subsequent interpretations follow. A few minutes later, Aaron asks, "What do we know about Paul's relationship with the Ephesians?"

During a lull in the conversation, I study the men's Bibles. They come in all shapes and sizes, ranging from jumbo to pocket size. A few are leatherbound, but most are soft, paper versions. The only commonality is that all the books appear to be dog-eared and tattered, something I would not have expected from a group of first-year college men at the outset of this study. Aaron asks an emphatic question, "Paul has a special relationship with his people; what is it?" that refocuses my attention on the dialogue.

More members of the Praise Band, practicing upstairs, appear to have arrived. The loud drum beats and guitar chords make it more difficult for me to concentrate on the conversation, which eventually drifts to another Ephesians passage about Paul's imprisonment. Hal notes, "Paul is in prison. This is powerful stuff. He is in chains and still in charge. . . . His ministry is not dying; in fact, it is flourishing." Aaron nods in agreement as he offers a follow-up question: "Is he [Paul] boastful? Is he doing it for God?"

Attendees do not directly answer Aaron's question; instead, they use it as a springboard to launch a mini-discussion about the proverbial chains that restrict their efforts to minister to their collegiate peers. Aaron, as he has in the past, vacillates between providing students maximum degrees of freedom to explore interesting tangents and briskly reigning in the discussion: "Any questions about these four verses?" Warren offers a summative comment rather than a question: "What is going on here is a basic outline of Christian living. It is about unity, living with God." Timothy adds: "It's about relationships between members, from member to member. . . . By His grace, we are saved. . . . It is about the things you do and the reason you do them." Aaron offers a smile and a nod of approval as the discussion continues.

The cohort's hearty appetite for spiritual nourishment is as strong as their junk food cravings. Several members take notes as they munch on trail mix. Aaron thanks Jeff and Timothy for their comments and then inquires, "Did anyone do the summary?" Only two students raise their hands to acknowledge that they completed their biblical homework, which Aaron had assigned the previous week. Hal offers half-hearted excuses about being exhausted by the end-of-the-term chaos.

Aaron appears momentarily annoyed because the men did not complete their homework, but his disappointment quickly dissipates as he raises a new topic. "Obedience is not a bad word. In our culture, to obey is a bad word, but it is not in Christian life. What is the opposite of obeying?" Warren obeys Aaron by offering a quick-witted response—"disobedience"—which elicits some laugher. A brief interlude of male bantering ensues. Aaron instructs Bobby to read from Ephesians 6:1–9 as a vehicle to explore the Bible's views on obedience—seemingly a hot-button topic. The verse commands Christian children to obey their parents and slaves to obey their masters, while also suggesting that parents and masters treat their children and slaves well, for the Lord is master of all.

A string of comments and questions follows: "Why did Paul write this?" . . . "This has everything you need to know to grow as a Christian." . . . "Paul had intent, God's plan—What was it?" . . . "Put your critical thinking hats on." . . . "We are asking for His wisdom and understanding."

I confess that observing a group of college men discussing obedience, parents, children, masters, and slaves at 10:00 p.m. on a Wednesday evening appears unusual. Equally odd is that as the evening grows later, the energy level of these men and their capacity to focus on their biblical interpretations appears to increase. With gusto, they tackle the idea of a "good slave." Aaron casually yet purposefully guides the conversation as provocative ideas ricochet around the room like balls on a racquetball court. Attendees appear determined to ascertain the "correct," or at least the best, interpretation possible. They look to Aaron to offer the "real truth," based on his privileged interpretation of the Bible.

At about 10:20 p.m., I expect the discussion to soon wind down and for the men to call it a night. Determined to complete his Ephesians tutorial, Aaron opens up Pandora's box as he broaches the topic of the Bible's teaching about the relationship between husbands and wives, a topic explicitly discussed in Ephesians. Aaron asks Bobby to read Ephesians 6:22–33:

> Wives, submit to your husbands as to the Lord. For the husband is the head of the wife as Christ is the head of the church, his body, of which he is the Savior. Now as the church submits to Christ, so also wives should submit to their husbands in everything.

Bobby is unable to finish reading this verse as pandemonium erupts. Predictably, sophomoric jokes about being the head of the household commence. Aaron redirects the conversation so that these brief jokes become a gateway to a more serious discussion. The few men who share their views on this topic, not surprisingly, endorse Paul's views in Ephesians. I confess that their endorsement of this seemingly unequal relationship sounds Neanderthal, even though their use of God's Word seems to elevate the legitimacy of their arguments. I cannot help but wonder how SSC women would interpret and evaluate this passage. Headshakes of disbelief are as common as bobbing heads of affirmation as most men remain silent during the exchanges.

The discussion becomes more heated as the men speculate on what it means to behave properly in marriage and for wives to be subject to husbands. The topic of women submitting to men gets more airtime than the implicit message that husbands submit to their wives. When confused, or when conflicting perspectives arise, the men regularly look to Aaron for guidance and the final word. Such is the case this evening, but in an unusual move, Aaron resists answering their tough questions. Instead, he poses some questions of his own: "What is the relationship between submission and obedience?" . . . "What does a submitting wife look like?" . . . "When you get ready to marry, is a submissive wife important?" . . . "Why marry?"

It is difficult to ascertain if this pedagogy (continually turning the question back on the students) is an attempt to get them to critically think about this topic or an effort to avoid offering "the answer" because he does not immediately know it. The awkward interlude of silence following this intense discussion prompts Aaron to summarize key points about authority figures and God's relationship with His church. It is hard to tell if it is Aaron's rambling and sometimes unconvincing arguments or my fatigued state at 11:10 p.m. that prohibits me from fully comprehending his message. He talks around the topics of authority figures in the Bible as the men listen attentively and record his commentary in their notebooks. The ease at which he recites memorized Bible verses adds credibility to his stream-of-consciousness arguments, which seem to satisfy the men.

Abruptly, Aaron shifts gears and urges the men to read and discuss the Bible throughout the summer. "We never have the time to fully talk about these ideas, but take your own time to do it the best you can. . . . This summer, try to read the Bible 30 minutes a day. . . . Memorize passages and pray. Let's close with some prayer requests." Men instantaneously offer extemporaneous and simultaneous prayers. Sorting out the specific requests to God is a nearly impossible task. I concentrate to hear the men call out "surgery," "exams," "pain," "cancer," "nonbelievers." After 8 minutes the requests taper off, and Aaron finishes with a resolute "Amen."

The moment of silence following his "Amen" prompts Aaron to call on Graham to offer the final prayer of the night and the academic year. Graham complies with the wishes of his Bible study mentor. Graham's prayer signals the end of this year-long Bible study and their evangelical apprenticeship, and thus marks the beginning of their new roles as disciples of Jesus. Like

Paul, the men leave tonight's meeting prepared to *sacrifice* some of their summer fun in order to follow Jesus.

Women Warriors for God: Women's Bible Study[1]

"Hi, Kelsey! How are you? I'm so glad you came!" exclaims Sarah in her usual
spirited tone. I've come to know Sarah as one of the most highly involved
women in SSC. "I'm doing well, how about you?" I inquire. "Oh . . . good,
but tired. It's another busy week," she responds wearily, as she attempts to
maintain her upbeat tone. We crossed paths the evening before as we both
attended the weekly meeting of the Servant Leadership Team, of which Sarah
is a member. Tonight, she is the Bible study leader. In addition to these two
major SSC responsibilities, Sarah meets weekly with two first-year women to
disciple them, and she regularly attends the Friday night worship meetings.
Given her daily involvement with SSC in addition to her collegiate studies,
it is no wonder she is fatigued.

The jingle of Sarah's keys refocuses my thoughts as she unlocks the
church office door and locates the light switch to rescue us from the darkness
of the evening. "It is getting to be the end of the semester, so there are a lot
of end-of-year projects, you know," she adds with a sigh and a half-smile. I
nod in agreement as I follow her down the hallway to a small conference
room.

After flicking on a light switch and pausing to let the ceiling's fluorescent
panels buzz to life, Sarah arranges the old wooden chairs and heavy plastic
tables to form a square. "How many are you expecting?" I ask, aiming to be
helpful. "Oh, probably about ten freshmen girls," she asserts, as she counts
chairs. I help arrange a few of the worn chairs and then select a corner seat.
As Sarah neatly arranges her notebook, Bible, and workbooks on the table in
front of her, I gaze out the window at the quiet April night and breathe in
the room's faint odor of dust mixed with stale candle smoke.

"Hey! Sarah!" shrieks a vivacious woman with red hair who enters the
room as the clock tolls nine o'clock. "You'll never believe what happened
today!" she shouts excitedly. "What, Claire?" Sarah asks impatiently. As we
wait for the story, Sarah abruptly turns to welcome six other women—all
White, with long hair of varying shades and dressed casually in jeans and T-
shirts—who enter the room with bubbly greetings. A few, whom I've
already met, offer "hellos," and others approach me to introduce themselves.

They settle quickly into their seats, then lean into the table to begin sharing the day's news. One woman tosses a bag of potato chips into the center of the table, which indicates that everyone is free to indulge. As three more women arrive, the noise level rises, and I quickly find myself amid the hubbub of gossip and giggling. I learn about the upcoming fall class scheduling, dinner recaps, the whereabouts of a regular attendee who will arrive late because she is taking a shower, and a guy named Adam whom one woman declares is cute.

"O . . . kay . . ." Sarah gently speaks out in an effort to corral the members' attention. As in the past, she takes charge by starting a prayer list and passing it to the woman sitting next to her. One by one, attendees eagerly write their prayer requests for the week. The woman sitting next to me calls her friend to determine if she has finished showering. As Sarah makes eye contact with the women, they quickly finish their conversations and arrange their books in front of them—looking like schoolchildren preparing to learn.

"Okay, then." Sarah begins again with an enthusiastic tone only an elementary schoolteacher-in-training could possess. "Let's hear some Scripture verses." "Ooh! I've got one!" declares Katie, as she waves her hand wildly in the air. Katie perfectly recites the Scripture verse she recently memorized for this study session, and the recitation wins affirmation from Sarah. "Excellent! Anyone else?" Sarah asks. Claire, who appears disconcerted, looks down for a moment and then offers a confession: "I haven't been good about memorizing the verses. I'm sorry." Before Sarah has a chance to answer, Katie instantly swivels in her chair to face Claire and says eagerly, "That's okay, how 'bout you and I work together this week? I'll help you." "That's a deal!" Claire replies.

"How did study go this week?" Sarah asks. I quickly surmise that Sarah is referring to homework assignments as I watch the women retrieve from their knapsacks completed workbook pages full of ink scribbles and Bible verse notations. The high volume of Bible study preparation these students complete each week, in addition to their academic coursework, stuns me. "Oh, one more thing," Claire interrupts. "I've decided that next year during Lent I want to do an extra 10 minutes of quiet time with God per week instead of giving up something like junk food." "That is just excellent!" replies Sarah. "Well, why wait until next year?" counters Kiley. "Couldn't you do that now?" Claire's face lights up. "That's an awesome idea!" she replies.

Sarah asks Katie to offer a prayer. The women bow their heads as Katie thanks God for bringing them together to learn. "All right—Ephesians 6:10–20. What do you think this means?" questions Sarah. The women scurry to open their Bibles and flip through their workbook pages. After locating the page, a few women begin passing around the bag of chips, but they never take more than a small handful of snacks. "I think it is talking about temptation," Kiley states confidently. A few of the women slowly nod; judging by their furrowed brows, they, too, appear to be thinking.

A woman abruptly enters and apologizes for disturbing the serene moment. She slides into the chair next to me, tosses her keys on the table, and then introduces herself as Angela. Immediately I notice her keychain, which displays the message, "I (heart) Jesus." The women momentarily abandon their discussion about tonight's homework as Claire randomly starts talking about the new Pope.

As the women continue to chat excitedly about tangential topics for a few minutes, I realize that I have become accustomed to their scattered conversation style. Although they spend most of their time during these weekly meetings digging deeply into the meaning of Scripture, they see spending time together in fellowship as an equally important goal . . . and for these women, fellowship is synonymous with giddy chatter.

"O. . . kay . . . ," Sarah says again, this time in a firmer voice. "Oh! We're getting yelled at!" chirps Claire. The group members stifle their giggles and again direct their attention to Sarah. "Close your eyes; we are going to do an imagination activity," Sarah explains. She reads a biblical passage about Jesus in temptation and then follows with two questions to encourage reflection. "Think about if *you* were so hungry from not eating lunch or dinner. What is the Devil trying to tempt *you* with? . . . Maybe he's trying to get you to date a non-Christian just so you can feel loved?" I wonder how to reconcile the contradictory implicit messages—avoid dating relationships with non-Christians while also adhering to the group's mission to spread Christ's Word by befriending non-Christians.

The women open their eyes, and Sarah invites them to talk about temptation. "I usually want to give into temptation when I am lonely, like Jesus was in the desert," replies Bethany. Most women nod in agreement. "I decided to fast last week since a few friends were really on my heart. My roommates ordered food, and I knew God was testing me!" adds Angela. "Yes! Good!" Sarah affirms excitedly, again in her warm, yet genuine, elementary schoolteacher tone.

"To me, temptation is right and wrong; there is no gray area in it," Kiley states pensively. Following a moment of silence, I conclude that the women are tapped out of ideas. Sarah then asks everyone to retrieve their workbooks, and she begins going through the pages question by question. Today's workbook lesson asks students to respond to short-answer questions about selected verses from Ephesians regarding being a "warrior for God." Half of the questions simply reinforce students' comprehension, such as "What does the *breastplate of peace* mean in this verse?" Other questions encourage application and reflection, such as "When is a time you used the breastplate of peace in your own life?"

Fresh ideas continually blossom across the room as the women connect this ancient text to their struggles with living a Christian lifestyle at a modern public university. The students' level of engagement in the discussion easily surpasses that of students enrolled in most first-year seminars. Sarah initially poses questions and solicits clarification, but the women eagerly probe and disagree with one another.

Today's topic, the extended metaphor about being a warrior for God, is particularly challenging. "I think the breastplate means the Gospel of Peace—it's what makes Christianity so cool! The joy after you accept the peace and knowing you are going to heaven," exclaims Angela. "What is peace?" another woman asks. "Assurance you know death is a passageway to heaven," Kiley responds. Spontaneously, three women break out into a children's song about peace, apparently reliving their Sunday School days. Commotion ensues as the women's energy level soars, and they dance in their chairs while simultaneously high-fiving each other across the tables. They seamlessly transition between serious scholarly debate and fun fellowship, but never lose sight of the importance of their faith.

Sarah refocuses the conversation to the task at hand—coming to a better understanding of Jesus. "Peace is like no eternal worries, like about Hell. But what did you make of faith being a shield? I personally didn't fully get that part," she admits. I am unsure whether she actually does not understand the passage or whether she is simply trying to provoke participation. Either way, it has the desired outcome as the women jump at the chance to "teach the teacher." "I think it's so you can be more confident against adversity," asserts Katie. Bethany interjects, "You can be sure what you hope for, certain of things you don't see, like God, salvation, miracles, his love." "Well, I think faith is like a fire extinguisher," states Kiley. Amid a sea of giggles, she explains her metaphor; one by one, the women acknowledge her remarkably keen insight.

"Satan is always firing arrows at us," Sarah says in a grave voice. "Like that we won't be acceptable, lovable, or usable for God." "Or like right here on campus," confides Claire, "how all the girls are so pretty and smart. I am always tempted to think that I'm not good enough." Bethany shouts, "We just have to use our sword to puncture Satan's lies!"

The degree to which these students are willing to wrestle with this extended metaphor surprises me. It is disorienting to observe these seemingly innocent Christian women, wearing cross necklaces and bracelets with Christian symbols, talking excitedly about armor for war. I suppress a yawn, glance at my watch, and note that it is 10:10 p.m. Only one woman's eyelids appear to be drooping; the remaining attendees appear prepared to take the session into the wee hours of the night, if necessary, to gain clarity about this important topic. As I ponder an exit plan, Kiley asks whether we should "be on the offensive or defensive for God, and how that affects what parts of the armor we'd use." My brain is swirling as Sarah recaps the group's conversation and provides a definitive and biblically based "big picture" message about the day's topic. My mind drifts for a few moments; I am intrigued by the unique way the students debated Scripture, only to have Sarah provide the "correct answers" at the end of the meeting.

I snap out of my drifting thoughts as Sarah concludes her mini-sermon and congratulates the women on their preparation for today's gathering. I straighten up in my chair to stretch my body, which has settled into the worn wood. Sarah says, "Close your eyes again and listen to this prayer. It's a prayer Jesus said for you even before you were born!" Angela gasps and exclaims, "We should totally do that! We should start praying now for our future husbands and children!" Sarah laughs quietly and shakes her head as she lowers her gaze playfully. "Maybe you should start with your husband, then worry about children later," she suggests, which elicits smiles and more giggles around the table. Following the prayer, Katie starts packing up her Bible and notebooks, which begins a domino effect of rustling papers.

"Wait, I have one more question," says Kiley. "If Satan cannot hear our thoughts, then how does he know how to tempt you? Where does it say in the Bible he cannot hear our thoughts?" "That is a good question . . . I'm just not sure," replies Sarah with a frown. After a moment, Kiley dejectedly slides back in her chair and realizes she has asked an unanswerable question. "We'll explore that next week," Sarah replies.

"All right—who has time to do the prayer request list tonight?" asks Sarah, as she scans the room. She waits for a volunteer to take the list and pray for each individual the women listed as being in need of prayer. I scan the sheet as it passes by; women have listed family members and friends who are ill or in need of support, and students on campus who they hope will come to Christ. Claire responds that she will do it, because she only has a small paper to write this evening for her political science course. I wonder why someone must do the prayer list *tonight*, since it is already past 10:30 p.m.!

Shepherds: Senior Bible Workshop

Inside the University's rustic off-campus retreat cabin, members of the senior committee gather around a primitive table while trying to get comfortable sitting on rickety folding chairs. Don (the SSC Regional Trainer), Jessica and Aaron (the two SSC interns), and six students constitute this afternoon's workshop. Although the dank cabin provides a refuge from the blistering sun, the room's musty and stagnant air is taking its toll on attendees.

Unlike SSC-sponsored Bible study sessions, which are single-sex gatherings that require students to prepare in advance, SSC workshops are co-ed, and the facilitator does not share the content with attendees in advance. This afternoon Caleb pushes his chair against the wall and tries to get closer to the open window as he opens his notebook. Leslie rustles through her tan knapsack to locate her Bible, which shows years of wear and tear. Tony, with his surferlike bleach-blond hair and toned physique, flashes a smile as he leans back in his chair and fans himself with a notebook. Despite the rising temperature, the students' eyes appear hungry, ready to devour the Christian delicacies that Don will likely serve them as celebrity guest chef.

Although Don's primary responsibilities include overseeing SSC campus staff and organizations throughout the Midwest, he is a mentor for this SSC enclave because his home is in close proximity to campus. He smiles as he introduces the biblical topic de jour, "a shepherd's responsibility." Students offer nods of approval as they open their notebooks to a fresh page. Most of these traditional-age college seniors are beginning their fourth year of affiliation with the SSC.

Don, a seasoned storyteller and facilitator, begins by recounting a story about his past missionary experiences in Romania. He starts with a tale describing the joys and challenges he experienced as a missionary "behind the Iron Curtain." He describes his clandestine activities aimed at spreading God's word and circumventing the Romanian government's anti-Christian policies. He laments having had to destroy numerous printed Christian artifacts shortly before departing the country, but he feared reprisal if he did otherwise. The story neither conceals Don's fervor for spreading the Word of Jesus to non-Christians nor obscures his disdain for Communism.

The students, too, appear eager to pronounce their pride in Jesus. Religious icons are evident on nearly every attendee's casual attire. Tony is wearing his "Got Jesus?" T-shirt. Aaron proudly displays a bold silver cross on a heavy silver chain. Liz and Leslie wear bracelets displaying the Christian fish sign. These fashion accessories are intentional symbols that make public their evangelical affiliation.

In keeping with the shepherding theme of today's session, Don reminds attendees that they are both shepherds and sheep. As shepherds for Jesus, Don expects students to know what is best for their flock and to guide them according to the Gospel, as he did with the Romanian nonbelievers he encountered. As the proverbial sheep in God's flock, he expects them to follow God's knowledgeable and understanding shepherds, as he followed his own mentor. Implicit in these stories is the invitation for seniors to act as one of God's shepherds on earth, which is both a challenging and a rewarding vocation. Simultaneously, students must remain open to following God's designated shepherds.

Don instructs seniors to open their Bibles to Psalm 23 and memorize the passage. Understanding the nuances of shepherding is the apparent goal. Students retrieve their Bibles and immediately turn to the passage, sitting in solitude as they begin to memorize. Caleb whispers to Don that he already knows Psalm 23 by heart. In a soft voice, Don replies, "Memorize Peter 5:2–4."

Conversely, I try to mask my biblical ignorance by casually perusing my loaner Bible in hopes of serendipitously stumbling upon the Book of Psalms. I eventually locate Psalm 23 and study its contents. As students complete their 15-minute memorization task, they quietly recite the verse to each other—an impressive feat in this repressive heat.

Don reconvenes the group and distributes to each attendee a handout entitled "A Shepherd's Responsibilities." I scan the guide, which contains seven Bible passages that explicitly mention the responsibilities of the shepherd and a series of discussion questions. The quiet memorization session slowly morphs into a more interactive session as Don asks Tony to read aloud Psalm 28: 70–72, the first passage listed on the handout.

Without encouragement from Don, students offer brief insights they gleaned from the passage. "The responsibility of the shepherd is to listen to God," Caleb asserts. "Start small," says Liz. Jessica adds, "A shepherd needs integrity and skills." Aaron follows, "A shepherd's job is to keep up on his own skills; God will recognize our goodness." Leslie chimes in, "Our Lord is our ultimate shepherd. He sees our needs and helps us." Don listens patiently and makes direct eye contact with each contributor. As the unsolicited interpretations dwindle, Don poses a series of questions to prod students to sharpen their analytical skills. He begins, "How does one develop integrity of the heart?" Liz makes clear that she does not intend to answer this question by picking up her pen and preparing to write down whatever answers her peers propose. Other students not-so-deftly dodge the question by initially remaining silent. Slowly the group picks up steam and the responses, though tentative, eventually begin to flow: "praying," "reading the Bible," "sharing with nonbelievers," "listening to your shepherd."

Leslie explains the importance of listening to Jessica, the SSC intern who disciples her and serves as her shepherd of sorts. Leslie smoothly connects her commentary to the shepherding theme. Through her discipleship relationship with Jessica, Leslie asserts she is developing "integrity of the heart." Jessica smiles at Leslie and silently mouths "thank you" as a response to the compliment.

Don asks Sarah to read aloud Jeremiah 3:14–15, the second biblical passage listed on the handout. Sarah complies: "Return, faithless people, declares the Lord, for I am your husband. I will choose you—one from a town and two from a clan—and bring you to Zion. Then I will give you shepherds after my own heart, who will lead you with knowledge and understanding." This arcane passage momentarily perplexes students. Aaron grasps onto the shepherd reference and connects it to the previous Psalm 78:70–72 discussion. This buys his peers some precious time to decipher the cryptic references to "faithless people," a "husband," and "Zion." The strategy works. Students mentally decipher the passage, then follow Aaron's lead and offer their interpretations in rapid fire. "The shepherd needs to go to where the flock is; they won't come to us." . . . "Knowledge and understanding are good qualities for shepherds." . . . "We need to be on the same page as God." . . . "Remember, it's God's flock, not our flock; we are just taking care of it for Him."

Don prods students to think more deeply about the passage. He inquires, "What does this passage say about God's compassion?" After the all-too-familiar interlude of silence, interpretations resume as these aspiring biblical scholars blend knowing with wondering. Don concludes the discussion of Psalm 78 with his interpretation, which clearly carries weight with several seniors who frantically scribble Don's privileged interpretation in their notebooks. Like sheep, they follow their shepherd.

A familiar discussion formula reemerges. First, Don asks a student to read a biblical passage. After a student complies, Don solicits multiple and competing interpretations, then responds with a series of probing and provocative follow-up questions. Temporarily bewildered workshop participants, who are not expected to prepare for the session, offer half-formed and tentative perspectives that occasionally blossom into important insights. Students extrapolate from these commentaries lessons they should apply to their own lives as collegiate evangelicals. Finally, Don offers the "final word" on the topic. Seniors "religiously" adhere to this discussion formula as they explore the meaning of the remaining passages listed on the handout: "Ezekiel 34:1–24 . . . John: 10:11–15 . . . Acts 20:28 . . . Hebrews 13:20–21."

I struggle to comprehend the antiquated biblical terminology: "Thessalonians . . . Not for shameful gain, but for the Glory of God . . . Psalms . . . We are not hirelings . . . Daily be with Him." All these ideas whiz by me. I also struggle to comprehend the passages and their connection to shepherding. I learn that "shepherding takes time and patience." At the moment, I have neither. My confidence continues to erode. I ache for a break, but one does not appear forthcoming. At best I record snippets of the discussion:

> Should not shepherds take care of the flock? . . . Look at Matthew 9:36–38. Why does he have compassion on them and where does it come from? . . . As you study Ezekiel 36:1–24, what does this tell you about your heart? . . . What are the critical issues involved in your heart from John 15:1–11? . . . You have not brought back the strays or searched for the lost . . . We need to restore and heal the flock. Why lay down your life for sheep? I'll tell you why—because we are giving our lives to Jesus.

Unlike me, the seniors—familiar with the Bible and this workshop format—revel in the discussion and come alive. They truly understand the importance of shepherding. After a short pause, Don concludes by offering extemporaneous closing comments, which does little to slow the pace of the session.

> God cares about you as a shepherd. You will mess up, but over time you will get better. . . . If you fail, it is because you believe you no longer have a shepherd. . . . Remember, there is always a shepherd above you. No matter how far you go in the Christian hierarchy, you are never the top dog. Jesus is the top dog. . . . Who are their shepherds? *You* are their shepherds. We need to take seriously the role of shepherd. . . . You need to set pace as shepherd. Not what you say—what you do. . . . Do you get the idea behind shepherding? It is a big responsibility. . . . Trust God and let Him guide and continually change your heart. . . . You need a chunk of humility. . . . if you think you are on top, be ready for a big fall. . . . You are the cream of the crop. . . . You are the Senior Committee—top dogs. You only have to be one step ahead and you are. Let us pray.

The senior shepherds, who have taken advantage of all major SSC training and ministering opportunities, bow their heads and close their eyes as they pray for God's strength and guidance in the coming year. The weight of responsibility settles onto the group; they recognize God's call for them to lead others in the SSC while also remaining open to continual training from their SSC shepherds. For these highly invested seniors, it's all about both *listening* to and *emulating* Jesus.

Studying Bible Study

Matthew often concludes his weekly e-mails to the SSC membership with a Scripture verse that reads: "And the things you have heard me say in the presence of many witnesses entrust to reliable men who will also be qualified to teach others" (2 Timothy 2:2). This biblical passage is one of many ways Matthew encourages his aspiring evangelicals to become biblical scholars, by participating in an in-depth and sustained Bible study. Whereas the Friday night program provides a low-obligation entryway to the organization, Bible study— the organization's second level of involvement—requires a substantial commitment on the part of the approximately 60 students who participate each week.

The three Bible study exemplars reveal dynamics evident in most of the single-sex Bible groups we observed. Bible study facilitators are the unmistakable leaders of their respective groups. They assign required readings and expect students to read, study, and memorize select Bible passages. Students dutifully respect their Bible study mentors. During these gatherings, students' roles are substantive, yet subservient. They lead prayers, participate in discussions, listen to peers, adhere to the advice of elders, and brainstorm ways to apply the Bible's unambiguous lessons to their own lives.

The key feature of this level of involvement is in-depth learning and personal edification. SSC views personal learning as an important requirement of evangelical faith. As Grahmann (2001) asserts: "Evangelicals not only hold to the authority and trustworthiness of the Bible, they place great emphasis on the ability for lay people to study the Bible on their own and not depend on preachers, teachers, and other experts (Dyck 1996, 7–9; Milne 1982, 50). Thus the relationship of evangelical Christian students to the Bible is an important one" (p. 1). The goals of facilitators are to ensure that students understand the authority of the Bible and evangelical elders; transform participants from dependent Bible study students to independent biblical scholars; and model Jesus-friendly cocurricular activities rooted in Christian ideals. In the remainder of this chapter we introduce and discuss five distinctive aspects of the SSC Bible study that reveal its commitment to learning, as well as its unique contribution to meaningful cocurricular involvement.

A Personalized and Unified Organization That Systematically Facilitates Learning

The three Bible study narratives remind readers that the SSC is more than a cocurricular social organization; it is a unique learning organization. Teaching and learning are important to the SSC as it remains true to and focused on its distinctive educational mission—first learning about Jesus, and then disseminating His Word.

Peter Senge (1990) identified five characteristics of a learning organization, which the Bible study narratives exemplify. *Systemic thinking*, the first characteristic, is the ability to recognize the interrelationship between individual events and actions that are part of a more complex pattern, and often difficult to discern. Those outside SSC might erroneously conclude that programs such as the Friday night worship program and Bible study meetings are merely discrete programmatic offerings. SSC insiders would argue that the organization's purposeful agenda is to sponsor interrelated programs to carry out its mission in a methodical and organized manner. Although all programs blend faith, fellowship, and fun, Bible study programs, for example, place a greater emphasis on clarifying participants' knowledge of their faith. Because each discrete program offering places one of the three Fs at the forefront, the organization acts systematically to meet all students' needs as they move through the integrated SSC curriculum.

Personal mastery, Senge's (1990) second learning organization characteristic, is a commitment to lifelong learning, whereby one continually clarifies and deepens one's personal vision, focuses one's energies, and develops one's patience. Although fellowship and fun are interspersed throughout Bible study gatherings, the two primary goals of this event are for attendees to develop a mastery of the Bible and deepen their understanding of themselves, in order to establish deeper relationships with God. Implicit in these Bible study discussions is the message that becoming biblical scholars is a lifelong quest. Sarah, Aaron, and Don, though upheld in the organization as advanced biblical scholars, admit that they do not have all the answers and continue to expand their own knowledge of the Bible.

Senge's (1990) third learning organization characteristic centers on *mental models,* which involve the ability to discover and modify the assumptions, generalizations, and visual images that affect how organization members behave. The Bible study discussions provide attendees space to discover and reflect upon their assumptions about Christian life and assess how well their behaviors align with God's Word. Bible study leaders encourage participants to use the Bible as a guide to align their everyday actions with God's intentions.

Shared vision, Senge's (1990) fourth learning organization characteristic, is an ability to unite people around a common sense of purpose and commitment. Living a Christian life is the vision that SSC Bible study participants share. Using this shared vision and the Bible as their guide, these Christian collegians create a sense of solidarity that contributes to their success on this secular public university.

Team learning, Senge's (1990) fifth and final learning organization characteristic, is the ability to contribute to collaborative problem solving with co-workers and students, which produces accelerated results. Grahmann (2001) found that evangelical students participated in Bible studies to learn and analyze the Bible together *in community,* and this characteristic permeates the three Bible study stories. Participants freely share their life struggles and work collaboratively to optimally understand God's instructions to remedy these struggles. Being with like-minded individuals who encounter common challenges makes the learning process during Bible study discussions meaningful and important.

The SSC learning mission, based on Senge's principles, likely resembles the mission of many other evangelical Christian collegiate organizations. However, SSC members enact this mission using their unique subcultural style (Hebdige, 1979). Like SSC's unpretentious and no-frills style during their Friday night worship program, SSC Bible studies reflect a *back-to-basics* approach that emphasizes personal relationships that support students as they come to know Jesus. Participants, adhering to teachings of the Bible and their elders, voluntarily complete homework assignments and collectively use the Bible and elders' wisdom as guides to arbitrate real-world quandaries. Such actions are in keeping with the organization's style—simple, and seriously concerned with Jesus.

A Single-Sex Environment That Facilitates Learning

SSC purposely sponsors single-sex educational programs, such as Bible study, to optimize learning. The senior men and women meet together for fellowship a few times a year, but single-sex sessions are more common. Why would SSC separate women and men during Bible study? SSC women report they are more comfortable talking about women's issues, many of which center on men, in single-sex contexts. Angela suggests that the women "pray for their future husbands," a suggestion less likely misinterpreted in a gathering of women. In other women's Bible studies, discussion topics ranged from praying about ways to resolve issues with boyfriends, how to maintain "pure" relationships with men, and ways to avoid lust. During men's Bible studies, attendees struggled with male issues centering on lust, whether to assume a dominant leadership role in heterosexual relationships, and the role of women in marriage. Kelly summarized SSC's views about single-sex programs:

> At least for me, and for most girls, in Bible study you can get really deep, personal, and open. Girls are a lot more comfortable sharing things about themselves with other girls. And if we get into gender issues or dating, it's

easier to be open and honest, and you don't have to worry about impressing guys or not sounding stupid.

SSC students' views align with Bryant's (2007b) research concluding that
evangelical students' ability to focus on their relationship with God was
enhanced in same-sex groups. In addition, women in particular developed
strong relationships with one another, which helped them gain independence
apart from dating relationships. Astin (1993) also concluded that first-year
students' ability to solidify same-gender relationships is integral to their college success. "Students tend to form same-sex friendships and same-sex clubs
and organizations during the undergraduate years. As a consequence, women
are more likely to be influenced by the values and behavior of other women,
and men are more likely to be influenced by the values and behavior of other
men" (para. 20). This type of peer interaction, Astin argues, provides a "safe
space" for students to explore their personal values.

A Serious and Structured Cocurriculum That Facilitates Learning

In higher education, one way scholars separate collegians' experiences is to
divide them into two categories: what happens in the classroom, often referred
to as the curriculum, and what happens outside of the classroom, often known
as the cocurriculum. The latter concept, the cocurriculum, has replaced traditional notions of extracurricular activities, which narrowly and stereotypically
focused on social activities. Contemporary conceptualizations of the cocurriculum, like those of the curriculum, focus on education and learning. These
nonclassroom environments are what Kuh et al. (2005) refer to as *catalytic
spaces*—"places where learning and development are integrated" (p. 134). Still,
whereas many cocurricular activities emphasize learning, SSC cocurricular
activities such as Bible study are educationally distinctive to the degree that
they emphasize a serious, structured curriculum.

If SSC outsiders were to watch a videotape of the three Bible study exemplars, they would likely conclude that the gatherings more closely resemble
traditional classroom educational experiences than *traditional* cocurricular
activities. The most obvious clue that these gatherings are cocurricular in
nature is the absence of older, seasoned professors. Despite the presence of
snacks and the occasional moments of levity, a sense of serious learning and
a genuine intellectual curiosity are pervasive throughout these voluntary gath-

erings. Bible study leaders expect attendees to memorize Bible passages, complete homework assignments, and engage in serious discourse, which is atypical of cocurricular activities.

In the story of the men's Bible study, participants arrived with Bibles and their thoughts about the material, and they spent hours debating the intricacies of a single passage from Ephesians. Women's Bible study participants applied biblical teachings to their everyday experiences in the dating scene as they compared Jesus' temptation to their everyday temptations to "date someone who is non-Christian, just to feel loved." These aspiring biblical scholars arrived with completed worksheet pages in hand and Bible verses memorized. Participants spent the majority of their Bible study meetings vigorously offering interpretations of passages and thus improving their analytical skills and familiarity with the Good Book.

Similar dynamics are evident in the story of the senior workshop. The dynamic dialogue that took place in the coeducational senior Bible study showcased the depth of learning and the critical thinking skills students have amassed since arriving in college. Traina (cited in Grahmann, 2001) highlights the critical thinking skills Bible study students use as they examine biblical texts when he compares Bible study to detective work:

> A good detective must be skilled in certain techniques, such as knowing where to look for clues and how to go about finding them . . . And having found evidence, he must be able to interpret it properly . . . and to draw valid conclusions from it. And in all this a good detective must be systematic. He follows insofar as he is able an orderly process. . . . The effective Bible student follows much the same course. He too must be adept at knowing what to look for and how to discover those facts which are necessary for understanding particular passages. He must be able to ascertain the relations between the clues, to interpret them and to assess their worth accurately, and to make legitimate deductions. And in carrying out these steps it is just as important that the Bible study be methodical as (with) a detective. (p. 3)

SSC Bible study gatherings also showcase students' strong academic work ethic and commitment. Attendees concern themselves with exploring in-depth provocative questions more than with concluding their weekly 2-hour study session on time. Their activity aligns with Grahmann's (2001) assertion that "Bible study implies a serious approach to the Scriptures to ascertain meaning and application from them" (p. 7).

Two of the most valuable benefits of the SSC Bible study, according to students, are to better understand the Bible and to form strong friendships with like-minded peers. Within these tight-knit peer groups, students motivate and support each other in their learning. For example, in the women's Bible study, Kiley encourages Claire to start devoting more quiet time to prayer and Bible study every day.

Jessica, an SSC intern, best describes this blend: "Bible studies are the next level of commitment. That's where they really get to develop deep friendships and study the Bible pretty intensely. We hope they get a lot out of that." Men's Bible study participants with whom we spoke referred to the weekly Bible study ritual as something "fun" they looked forward to each week. Senior SSC members smiled as they recalled their first-year Bible study; many of them formed their strongest collegiate friendships with other study members during their first semester on campus. These friendship bonds among SSC members often contribute to students' interest and sustained involvement in the organization throughout their time in college.

A Collaborative, Yet Authoritative Pedagogy That Facilitates Learning

In the narratives, the Bible study facilitators are clearly in charge and employ a traditional instructional pedagogy. Aaron favors posing Socratic questions followed by answers and additional questions. Sarah employs a supportive "team" approach to teaching students about Jesus and His way. Don follows a tightly scripted learning agenda and assumes the role of biblical sage. Encouraging students to collaborate with each other to enhance their learning, while strictly adhering to nonnegotiable biblical edicts are two commonalities that transcend the three facilitators' unique styles of teaching. Astin (1993) argued:

> My best hunch about cooperative learning is that it works because at least two things happen during the process. First, students are held accountable by their peers for achieving certain learning outcomes. Second, students assume a certain degree of responsibility for assisting their peers in achieving the same learning goals. These two peer group phenomena may well serve to motivate students to invest additional time and energy in the learning process. (para. 13)

SSC students hold themselves and their peers accountable to biblical teaching and to their elders' expectations (e.g., homework). They assume responsibility for their own learning, yet it is their elders who set the learning agenda. In the Bible study meetings we observed, their elders encouraged students to spend considerable time debating the meaning of biblical passages. This pedagogy disoriented us initially, because it seemed inefficient and disingenuous. If the "right" answer exists (i.e., is rooted in the Bible), we wondered, why spend hours facilitating discussions aimed at bringing multiple interpretations to the surface? Over time, however, the value of Bible study discussions became clear. We learned that facilitators do not intend these discussions to surface multiple biblical interpretations. Instead, facilitators encourage discussions so that participants can become intimately familiar with the Bible, which leads to greater clarity and firmer adherence to these absolute teachings. This pedagogy aligns with the SSC ideology.

Human scale contexts augment this collaborative learning pedagogy. SSC's emphasis on small-scale interactions encourages participants to collaboratively learn with and from peers. Kuh, Kinzie, Schuh, and Whitt (2005) note that effective active and collaborative learning includes the following:

> (1) asking questions in class or contributing to class discussions, or both; (2) making class presentations; (3) working with other students on class projects inside or outside of class; (4) tutoring other students; (5) participating in a community-based project as part of a course; or (6) discussing ideas from readings or classes with other students, family members, or others outside of class. (p. 193)

With approximately one mentor for eight students, Bible study meetings provide a fertile environment for in-depth and collaborative learning. Facilitators provide attendees safe and intimate space in which to interact with others, pose questions, and collectively glean biblical lessons. SSC Bible study participants report that they benefit from substantive interaction with Bible study mentors and peers, who understand the issues with which they struggle.

These small-scale gatherings provide participants with a high level of support during the learning process—a higher level of support and friendship than students normally achieve in the classroom setting at this medium-sized public university. Dalton (1999) states: "Students' experiences with a supportive sense of community in an educational setting can contribute substantially to the development of their values. A community support system makes it easier for students to experiment and take risks" (p. 54). Within the SSC Bible study, students feel safe sharing their struggles with one another and asking for advice. Leslie commented, "For discipleship and Bible studies, one of the main things is just establishing accountability with each other . . . we really know what's going on in each other's lives. It's deep fellowship and getting to know each other on a really deep level."

The SSC pedagogy allows students the opportunity to learn *the* teachings of their faith while remaining part of a supportive, human-scale community. In interviews, several SSC students labeled an SSC activity as their "most powerful learning experience in college."

An Engaging, But Unequal Partnership That Facilitates Learning

The SSC's unique Bible study pedagogy, involving partnerships of sorts between students and their facilitator, starkly contrasts with contemporary higher education learning partnerships. For example, Baxter Magolda (2004a) advocates a learning partnership between teachers and learners whereby college students become the center of their learning experiences, and in which both teacher and student are equally valid sources of knowledge. Such a partnership contributes to students' personal development. Specifically, students who come to see themselves as a credible source of knowledge are better able to reach *self-authorship,* a primary aim of higher education.

Baxter Magolda (2004a) defines self-authorship as

> The capacity to internally define a coherent belief system and identity that coordinates engagement in mutual relations with the larger world. This internal foundation yields the capacity to actively listen to multiple perspectives, critically interpret those perspectives in light of relevant evidence and the internal foundation, and make judgments accordingly. (p. xxii)

Educators who work to foster self-authorship among students intend to help students learn to construct their own beliefs, values, and identities internally, rather than encourage students to adhere to existing beliefs.

Baxter Magolda (1992) offers educators three principles that teachers and leaders can employ to support students in learning partnerships: [1] situate learning in students' own experiences, [2] validate students as knowers, and [3] define learning as mutually constructing meaning. Baxter Magolda's principle of situating learning in the student's own experience demands that the more powerful individual (e.g., the teacher) welcome the less-powerful individuals' "real-life" experiences into the learning process, rather than dismissing such experiences as irrelevant. Validating students as knowers, the second principle, necessitates that those in power (e.g., teachers) relinquish some power by inviting the less powerful (e.g., students) to participate in learning contexts. Concurrently, students must realize that they, too, have valid ideas and permission to express their views. Allowing participants to shape the agenda symbolically communicates that all members of the learning community are knowers. Baxter Magolda's third principle—*learning as mutually constructing meaning*—suggests that learning will result from a dialogue whereby those in power consider all stakeholders' voices. It also means that learners eventually come to construct their own perspectives from this process.

SSC's pedagogy adheres to the first principle, but not to the second or third. During the weekly Bible study gatherings, facilitators regularly situated learning in the attendees' experiences and encouraged participants to share their experiences of being vulnerable, finding Jesus, and coping with the human struggles to live a Christian life. Students' experiences are essential. We attribute the success of these learning situations to the facilitators' desire to use real-life experiences as gateways to learning.

Still, SSC facilitators rarely explicitly validate students as knowers, despite the collaborative spirit they foster. Adhering to this principle would, for example, necessitate that facilitators relinquish power by inviting participants to offer input into the learning agenda. It also means that both facilitators and Bible study participants would have to recognize and validate participants' biblical knowledge and interpretations. Bible study participants seldom shaped the Bible study learning agendas; instead, they deferred to their mentors' foci and situated themselves as eager learners, rather than knowers.

In addition, SSC facilitators seldom explicitly enact Baxter Magolda's third principle—*learning as mutually constructing meaning*. This principle does not require the more seasoned participants to abdicate their expertise or knowledge. In order to mutually construct meaning, however, these seasoned professionals would need to bring their views to the dialogue but not impose them unilaterally. The SSC does not embrace this third principle because of the group's Bible-based ideology. Specifically, the SSC's emphasis on the Bible as *the* authority contributes to the leaders' needs to impose knowledge based on Scripture. Malley (2004) elaborates on American evangelicals' beliefs about the authority of the Bible.

> [T]he Bible is a divinely inspired book—the word of God. As they see it, the Bible is God's message of salvation and guidance to a suffering and confused humanity, and a special conduit by which God convicts, encourages, and illuminates them in their pursuit of him. American evangelicals regard the Bible as one certain truth—a book, many say, completely without error—in a world preoccupied with things of merely temporal value. Thus, evangelicals return to their Bibles frequently, seeking to lead "biblical" lives. (p. 1)

Students believe that the Bible's messages are objective "Truth," and thus Bible study sessions are not sites for mutually constructing meaning; they are more like exercises in finding information. As a result, the more powerful Bible study leaders maintain their roles as omnipotent interpreters of the Bible.

Although the SSC Bible studies do not resemble Baxter Magolda's (2004b) Learning Partnership Model, the organization's approach provides numerous opportunities for students to learn by listening to and debating multiple perspectives and building their own value and belief systems. In an interview, Stacey explains the importance of the Bible study pedagogy to her learning:

> If we had questions we just brought them up and our Bible study leaders were really great. They didn't have all the answers, but they wanted to help us learn things for ourselves, instead of telling us. That really represents the way that SSC is based on a smaller group setting and you developing your own faith, rather than someone telling you.

Leslie, a senior, reflected on what she has learned through participating in Bible study for 4 years. The peer support provided her with a sense of confidence in her own skills and abilities, which she believes will allow her to continue to grow in her faith after she graduates.

> When I graduate it won't be nearly as structured as now with Bible studies . . . but the main thing I get out of Bible study is the preparation I do before I go. Just being able to open to a chapter and learning. Just feeling confident and being able to read the Word and get something out of it,

instead of waiting for someone to tell me or waiting for the preacher to tell me something on Sunday to get me through the whole week. It's being able to have that relationship—just me and God [sic].

SSC's Bible study pedagogy also has liabilities. Although Bible study leaders' pedagogical technique of first encouraging robust debate and discussion and then concluding by providing the "final word of truth" enhances their goals of knowing and following the Bible, it hinders students' strides toward self-authorship. In the three Bible study examples, there were several moments when the participants looked to mentors to "enlighten them" with the "correct" response to their query. When the participants could not determine what they thought to be a sufficient answer, they turned to their elders. This was a common theme, not only throughout the Bible studies but also in all aspects of the SSC and among SSC leaders of all levels of experience and expertise. The authority of the Bible as God's Word is the key issue that drives the group's inability to fully capitalize upon learning partnership opportunities.

Summary

The SSC offers a unique learning pedagogy that centers on absolute adherence to the Bible, student support, and personal development. Bible study participants collaborate and learn in a supportive, yet regimented environment. The intentionally small size of each Bible study group provides opportunities for deep learning and a fertile atmosphere in which students can develop. Still, students' reliance on the Bible and their spiritual mentors may cut short opportunities for development as they focus on the "right answer" rather than exploring multiple interpretations—especially their own. SSC organization leaders hope that Bible study participants have sufficient knowledge of the Bible to begin sharing the Word with others. Thus, in the next level of involvement, the organization builds upon students' personal development by teaching them how to share their passion for Jesus and their knowledge of the Bible with others.

BRIDGING THE GAP BETWEEN EVANGELICALS AND NONBELIEVERS

Outreach Rituals

Hey: Just a reminder that Bridge Building begins TONIGHT @ 8:30. Everyone is welcome. . . . This is a necessary tool to anyone interested in joining the Servant Leadership Team next year!

Not sure what Bridge Building is? It's a time to learn a great illustration to help you communicate your faith in a relevant, clear, and nonthreatening way. This is a tool you can use the rest of your life! Don't miss it! Bridge Building will be held every other Tuesday for four weeks. If you have questions shoot me an e-mail. Laboring with You.

—Matthew [e-mail message to SSC members]

Building Evangelical Bridges

Students Serving Christ (SSC) offers numerous faith development opportunities for its members. Bridge Building training is of particular importance (and the focus of this chapter) because it represents on the part of members a more serious time commitment to the SSC and to Jesus than Bible study or the Friday worship service. This four-session, 8-week program extends members' biblical knowledge and is the gateway to SSC leadership opportunities. More importantly, the training prepares members to move outside the SSC organizational cocoon and spread the Gospel of Jesus to their non-Christian collegiate peers.

The Training Begins: Discovering the Gap Between God and Man

It's 8:30 p.m., and ten students and two SSC staff members are already present. Heidi offers a silent nod of approval as she passes. She removes her hat, coat, and scarf, and then joins Erica at an adjacent table. Following an exchange of greetings, they alternately recite Bible quotes they have memorized and plan to showcase during their women's Bible study session scheduled for the following evening. Hand-slapping and heaps of mutual praise follow the flawless recitations. At 9:05, two stragglers enter and find the last two vacant seats, predictably located at the table in the front of the room, closest to the facilitators. Awaiting the start of the meeting, the 14 attendees chat.

SSC staff members Aaron and Jessica, both casually dressed in jeans and wool sweaters, stand in the front of the class and quietly converse. Around 9:10, they make eye contact with attendees to signal the start of the meeting. The conversations and noise level gradually diminish as the attendees listen respectfully to their wise evangelical elders. Jessica begins, "We're excited about this program and the illustration. We're going to talk about the purpose of Bridge illustrations and teach you to do it. Has anyone seen it?" Three women and one man raise their hands. Jessica continues after offering a nod of approval:

> We use the illustration to describe the relationship between God and us. . . . The Bridge is a powerful tool; it allows us to share mega-themes from the Bible. It invites people to change. . . . It is not just reciting verses from the Bible. It is so much more. . . . We use it [the illustration] to share our faith and harvest or bring new people toward Christ. . . . Mark your calendars. We will meet three more times. . . . Questions?

Aaron poses a question, "Why do an illustration?" After a prolonged pause, a student replies to what we had assumed was a rhetorical question. "Because it's interactive." Aaron replies, "Good. . . . Who's comfortable sharing their faith?" Three students raise their hands. Aaron continues, "Okay, who is *maybe* comfortable?" Four students raise their hands. Aaron concludes his verbal survey with the question, "Who's uncomfortable?" Four additional students respond. Aaron follows with an evangelizing confession:

> My freshman year, I didn't know what to say when I ran into non-Christians. Now, I do. We need to convey some of the main teachings of the Bible. The world thinks negatively about evangelizing. Lots of people don't like it. . . . We have to remember, evangelizing is a slow building process. It begins with friendship and eventually leads to faith. Friendship and faith build on each other. We just don't go up to someone and start spewing our faith. We have

to show we care before we share the Word. . . . Evangelizing is a lifestyle. We have to live the lifestyle. It is interactive. . . . It's about outreach. We have to convey we care and that God is showing His love through us.

A woman raises her hand and waits for Jessica's nod before talking:

My freshman year, I lived with a non-Christian. I invited her to our meetings, and I prayed for her. She didn't seem interested. I even planted Bible verses around the room. Nothing was working. By October, I was not doing enough. . . . God's message was not getting through. I hijacked one of our conversations and told her why she needed to be like me. This made her uncomfortable and she insulted me. I had a good heart but not good tools to share God's Word.

Aaron interconnects the two evangelical stories to the purpose of this training:

The illustration is a good tool. . . . It is not just about conversion. . . . We need to take it seriously. . . . We'll learn to share and you can go out and teach it to other Christians and non-Christians for the Kingdom's sake. . . . Ask questions; there are no dumb questions. This is what we do on the Servant Leadership Team.

The advantage of having two staff people present for this training becomes apparent as the illustration simulation begins. Jessica assumes the evangelist role while Aaron assumes the non-Christian role. Jessica clears her throat and begins. "In the beginning God created man. Do you have any idea why God created man?" Aaron, stealing a quick glance at the audience, coyly replies, "Because he was bored?" Laughter ensues, which adds a moment of levity to this mostly serious gathering. "Not exactly," Jessica replies, and then continues, "The Bible says that God created man so he would have a relationship with Him. Now, have you ever heard of Adam and Eve? What do you know about them?" Assuming a more serious demeanor, Aaron replies, "They were the first two people on earth." Jessica nods her head in an exaggerated fashion to affirm Aaron's response and then continues:

Good. That's right. They were the first two people on earth. God placed them in the Garden of Eden. He said they could do anything they wanted except eat of the fruit of knowledge. They did [eat the fruit], and that created a separation between man and God, and now we're separated from

God because of their sin. Isaiah 59:2 says, "But your iniquities have separated you from your God; your sins have hidden his face from you, so that
he will not hear." Do you have any questions?

Aaron replies, "Not at this time." Students scramble to speedily find this
Isaiah passage in their Bibles, a ritual we have witnessed numerous times
throughout our fieldwork. Jessica, to engage Aaron in more substantive dialogue, poses a follow-up question. "Do you know what 'iniquities' means? It's
a pretty big word." Aaron, following his non-Christian script, replies, "Not
exactly." Jessica clarifies the term. "Iniquities means it is your sin; your sin
hides Him from you. Okay?"

On the blackboard, Jessica draws a visual representation of her commentary. She scribbles the word "man" on one side of the board and "God" on
the other. Between the two words, she draws a line and writes "sin" above it.
Below the line she writes the Scripture passage she cited—Isaiah 59:2.

The audience appears attentive to this performance. The deliberate and
slow pace of the simulation allows members to take extensive notes at a
leisurely pace. Jessica poses the question, "How would you describe God?"
Aaron replies, "All knowing, divine, and supreme? . . . He is confusing at
times. He is all good, but lets bad things happen." Jessica records Aaron's
descriptors of God on the blackboard (under the "God" heading on the continuum) and then poses another question to redirect and further focus the
conversation. "Would you say God is perfect?" Aaron replies, "I guess so."
Jessica quickly asserts, "The *Bible* says he is perfect," and writes "perfect" on
the "God" side of the diagram. "Now, how would you describe man?" I wonder to myself, "What about woman?" Jessica stands at the blackboard as she
awaits Aaron's response, which is "imperfect or flawed?"

So far, the illustration is not as intrusive, threatening, or heavy-handed
as I (Peter) expected. As the evangelist, Jessica exhibits a sense of respect for
non-Christians. She approaches her evangelizing duties respectfully, not as if
she is "crossing enemy lines." Predictably, the Bible is the centerpiece of the
illustration and the final authority and arbitrator of human actions. Aaron's
brief "yes," "no," or "I guess so" responses appear authentic, and Jessica's
patient approach to initiating and sustaining a conversation is an asset. The
sincerity and seriousness of both facilitators and participants impress me, yet
the simple plan for salvation and the deliberate pace provoke me to wonder
about its effectiveness in a college context. Is the illustration *too* scripted to

facilitate a thoughtful exchange between a Christian and a non-Christian? Fifteen minutes into this illustration, I have a more complex understanding and deeper appreciation for why approximately 66 percent of the SSC students in attendance expressed some reservations about evangelizing—it is a risky, yet necessary, task.

Students take copious notes, which I suspect they will intensely study before the next session. Jessica writes "FLAWED" in big letters on the board (underneath the word "man") and then adds, "Would you say he is imperfect?" "Yeah, that is a better word than flawed," replies Aaron. Jessica continues:

> Okay, Romans 3:23 says, "For all have sinned and fall short of the glory of God." Romans 6:23 also says, "For the wages of sin is death, but the gift of God is eternal life in Christ Jesus our Lord." Man does not measure up to God's character. God is holy and man is a sinner. Do you know what a wage is?

Aaron sheepishly replies, "Something you earn?" Jessica indicates that it is something a human earns, and the Bible says, "for the wages of sin is death." I surmise that sin equals death and humans receive death, or hell, for their sins. Jessica concludes, "Any questions?" Aaron temporarily assumes a new role—that of the engaged and inquisitive non-Christian—when he replies, "Tell me more about [Romans] 3:23." Jessica relishes the opportunity to extemporaneously elaborate. She adds the two Romans verses to the blackboard and then responds, "Basically, our sins are what have caused the bridge that separates man from God. Man realizes he is estranged from God. What does he do? What do you think we can do to *bridge* the gap between God and man?"

Aaron remains quiet for a moment, then replies, "Reflect on what we do? Maybe go to church?" Jessica, apparently not fully satisfied with Aaron's response, gently tweaks it without overtly suggesting that the response is incomplete or incorrect. "Would you say it has to do with having good morals?" Aaron nods affirmatively. Jessica continues, "Anything else?" Aaron's only response is, "I don't know." Jessica follows with a series of leading questions: "How about morals? . . . Religion? . . . Reading the Bible? . . . Being a good person?" Aaron nods his head up and down as Jessica's list continues to grow.

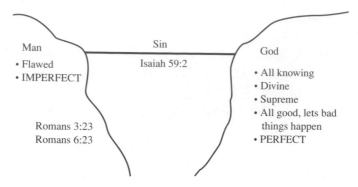

Figure 8.1. Phase 1 of the Bridge-building Illustration

Jessica turns toward the audience and declares the first segment of the illustration complete (see Fig. 8.1). She explains that in 2 weeks, the group will learn the second half. Jessica shifts her attention away from Aaron and toward the audience as she continues.

> If someone comes up and asks you how to become a Christian, you say three things: First, confess your sins. Second, accept Jesus as your Lord and Savior, and third, begin to live for Him, which is the gift of salvation. . . . Let's think about these ideas this week. E-mail or call me if you have questions. Start to practice the illustration. It'll get better over time if you practice.

Aaron solicits attendees' feedback about the simulation segment. Students' comments include the following: "There're lots of Bible verses to remember." "Is it manipulation? You take the person's words and redirect them?" "It seems to work." "I like how you [Jessica] kept asking if he [Aaron] had questions."

The two facilitators continue their tag-team facilitation duties by introducing the SSC's six principles of evangelizing. Aaron introduces the first principle—*get permission.* "We always ask permission to share the illustration before we begin. We *don't* want to force it on them. Find out if they are willing to try to accept the Lord. Be respectful; don't be pushy or aggressive."

Jessica follows with the second principle—*be interactive.* "Make them feel comfortable. It gets them involved and listening. Talk to them; avoid preaching." She encourages attendees to ask numerous questions to get the person involved in the illustration and to convey a sense of care. This practice aligns closely with the SSC's relational style, which emphasizes getting to know the other person, rather than just transmitting the message of Jesus. Ironically, this segment of the training is far less interactive than I expected. I suspect that the late hour has contributed to the students' preference to simply record these principles in their notes, rather than discuss or debate them. Aaron's comment interrupts my reflective interlude. "If you follow these two principles, we'll break down stereotypes [of evangelicals]. This is really important. We don't want to reinforce bad stereotypes."

Aaron pauses and then introduces the third principle—*use and write out* [Bible] *verses*. He reminds attendees that they need to memorize Bible verses in order to use them. "During the illustration, it is important to write out the verse references on a piece of a paper, like we did on the blackboard. I have even done the illustration on a napkin. If the moment arises and one is ready to hear God's word, I'm ready." Jessica introduces the fourth principle—*ask several times, "Do you understand?" and "Do you have questions?"* She continues, "This is important. Ask these two questions often. This is the way you get to know them."

The fifth principle—*make it clear there is a decision to be made*—follows immediately. Jessica explains, "Once you learn the illustration you will realize there are many decisions we want the person to think about and make, like do they want to follow the Bible or give their life to Jesus. This is the *most* important step or principle." Aaron reveals the sixth and final principle— *leave contact information and your Bridge illustration drawing*. "This is important. It will allow them to get back to you. . . . They might reference the Bridge if they have a handout. . . . Any questions? In 2 weeks, you will need to know these six principles. We are about halfway through the illustration."

It is 10:15, and the end of the meeting is not in sight. Jessica instructs the students to divide into pairs and practice the first segment of the illustration, and they form same-sex dyads. I observe two women rehearsing the illustration. The level of detail contained in their notes rivals my field notes. The women wordsmith their scripts and fine-tune each sentence in the presentation. "Sincere," "serious," and "tentative" are three descriptors I record in my field notes. The formative evaluation that I scribble in the margin of my notes suggests that their exchanges are genuine, yet mechanical.

At 10:40, Aaron and Jessica reconvene the attendees to thank them for their involvement and investment. Jessica asks Heidi to offer a prayer to conclude the meeting, and she complies: "Lord, we thank You for bringing us together and teaching us to spread Your Word. . . . We are indebted to You for Your love and compassion. . . . We hope to share Your love with those we meet. In Your name, Amen."

The Training Continues: Learning How to Reconnect with God

One week later, instead of beginning at 9:00 p.m. sharp, Jessica and Aaron encourage students to continue to socialize until their peers arrive. There appear to be more students present this evening than during the initial training session. One unfamiliar and energetic student approaches us (Kelsey and Peter) and introduces himself: "My name is Kyle, and I understand you are writing a book about us." After we introduce ourselves and acknowledge that he is correct, he responds, "Cool!" and heads toward his seat. As Aaron moves to the front of the classroom, he reminds the students—who have begun to settle down—about the purpose of building bridges. "It's *not* about harvesting. . . . If someone says they are willing to learn more about the Bible or Jesus, we can contact them and share the Word with them." It is all about relationships.

Implicit in this brief statement is a rationale for the survey the SSC administers during the opening week of the academic year. More importantly, this statement answers a long-standing question we had harbored for months: "How can SSC members evangelize in the residence halls when the University prohibits solicitations in these campus buildings?" Aaron's comments reveal the way the SSC accomplishes its recruitment and evangelical aims without violating University policy. If a residence hall student completes the survey, expresses an interest in meeting with an SSC member to discuss the Bible, and includes her/his name and residence hall address, the SSC has the right to visit that student's room. The University does not make it easy for Christians to "harvest" students, but the SSC has devised a way to accomplish its evangelical aim while adhering to policy.

Jessica asks the 11 women and 7 men who are present tonight to write as much as they can remember about the first training session. Students appear less focused and more rambunctious compared to their demeanor during the initial evangelical training meeting. Aaron and Jessica wander around the room and occasionally look over students' shoulders as they complete the assignment. From our seats at the back of the room, we hear and write down snippets of conversations: "What's that called?" . . . "I can't remember principle 6" . . . "I know that."

The volume of side conversations increases, which signals the facilitators that most participants have completed the assignment. Aaron inquires as to which Bible verses the students had forgotten, and Bobby rattles off the few he forgot. Jessica pleads with the students to memorize all of the passages—reminding them of the centrality of the Bible in the SSC's evangelism strategy. Aaron asks students if they have shared the Bridge illustration with peers. Four individuals raise their hands.

Next, Aaron asks for a volunteer to perform the first segment of the Bridge illustration. The room remains silent for approximately 30 seconds, and we sense the students' discomfort based on their level of collective squirming. Kiley breaks the silence and agrees to be the "guinea pig." She proceeds to the front of the classroom to perform and visually represent the Bridge illustration on the blackboard, as her peers quietly observe and take notes about her performance. Kiley's allegiance to the Almighty is unmistakable. Her writing closely resembles the script modeled at the previous gathering, and she mimics many of Jessica's comments and mannerisms during the exchange. Her near-flawless performance suggests that she invested numerous hours memorizing Bible verses and the Bridge script. As the abbreviated Bridge illustration concludes, Jessica solicits feedback from the attendees.

Following a long stretch of silence, Kiley's peers cite numerous positive aspects of her mini-illustration. Students call out: "Kiley knew and wrote out the Scripture verses." "She was interactive." "She did it in the correct order." "She has good handwriting." Negative feedback is less forthcoming. Jessica tries to solicit students' criticisms, and they respectfully decline her invitation. "Plan B" involves Aaron sharing his reactions. He recommends that Kiley elaborate more on the biblical verses after she recites them. He also reminds the group that Kiley did not explicitly ask if it is okay to share the illustration, which violated the SSC's first principle of evangelizing.

Aaron insists that students follow Kiley's lead by closely adhering to the illustration content and sequence. He then shifts his critical eye to the blackboard visual: "Draw the arrows here. . . . Make sure to explain Romans when you write it down." Kiley readily acknowledges that she has work to do, despite the mostly positive feedback she received and her near-perfect performance. Jessica and Aaron offer thanks and encouragement to Kiley, and her peers follow up with polite applause and a few cheers.

As the demonstration of the second segment of the illustration commences, the staff facilitators reverse roles. This week, Aaron is the evangelist and Jessica plays the non-Christian. During the opening minute of the illustration, Aaron becomes temporarily disoriented and can't remember a Bible verse. Jessica swiftly suspends her role as the non-Christian and rescues him. She correctly recites the verse and then abruptly resumes her non-Christian role. Howls, especially from the men, are loud and boisterous. Aaron smiles and suspends his evangelist role as he faces the audience to offer advice. "You will occasionally mess up and not say things correctly. This will happen, but God makes amends for your blunders. It can happen to anyone."

As the demonstration resumes, students continue to take furious notes to make certain that what Aaron verbalizes and draws on the blackboard appears verbatim in their notebooks. A collective routine emerges—in unison, the students look up, look down, record comments . . . look up, look down, record comments . . . look up. . .

Aaron gets back on track by recalling the list he and Jessica developed during the last session—ways in which man tries to get closer to God, including morals, religion, and good behavior. Then he refutes that list by correctly reciting Proverbs 14:12: "There is a way that seems right to a man, but in the end it leads to death." He follows by offering a clarification. "So, whatever we do and enjoy will lead to death without God. Make sense?" Jessica nods as Aaron scrawls "religion," "morals," and "good works" on the "man" side of the board and draws a line for each one that extends only halfway across the continuum toward God. We surmise that we are about to receive the "punch line"—what will "bridge" humans to God.

Aaron continues, "Are you a sports fan?" Jessica shrugs her shoulders. "Have you ever seen a baseball game where you see someone holding up a sign that says John 3:16? That verse says: "For God so loved the world that He gave His one and only Son, that whoever believes in Him shall not perish, but have eternal life." Aaron proceeds, "And His son is Jesus Christ. And Jesus died for our sins. Do you have any questions?" Jessica replies, "No." Aaron resumes the illustration script without asking probing questions to encourage Jessica to offer more expansive responses beyond one-word "yes" or "no" replies. "Okay," he continues, "basically Jesus connects God with man." Aaron pauses to draw a cross, connecting man and God, and writes "Jesus Christ" above it. "Okay, now how would you define belief?" Jessica replies, "Something true to the people. . . . Something that I have thought about and tested and come to a conclusion that is true."

Aaron nods his head and launches into an extended true story about a man who went to Niagara Falls in the late 1800s. The attendees learn that the man stretched a long tightrope across the falls and gathered a large crowd. He asked, "Does anyone believe I can walk across this tightrope, up and back, in my bare feet?" As the story goes, everyone was cheering for him and telling him, "You can do it." So, he walked across the tightrope and back unharmed, and the people cheered. Aaron continues the story and reveals that the man got a wheelbarrow and asked, "Does anyone think I can wheel this wheelbarrow all the way across the tightrope and back, unharmed?" And everyone was cheering, "Yes, you can do it!" So he did it and came back. Aaron describes the crowd as ecstatic and impressed. The man continued, "Does anyone think I can put someone in the wheelbarrow and take them across the falls on a tightrope with me?" And the crowd yelled, "Yeah, you can do it!" So, then the man asked, "Who wants to be the first person to get into the wheelbarrow?" And the crowd fell silent. Aaron concludes by making the moral of the story explicit. "So no one actually wanted to take an action to show what they believe. So, belief is trusting something is true, but also [being] willing to take an action. Belief equals trust plus action."

Aaron draws an arching arrow above the illustration. It connects man to God and reads "Belief = Trust + Action." Jessica's response to the protracted story is, "That makes sense." Aaron follows by reciting a biblical quote, providing a summary, and posing a question: "So basically, Jesus died for our sins, and He rose by being alive by the spirit, bridging this gap between God and man so we are able to love God and be on the righteous side with God. Do you have any questions?" Jessica shakes her head. For her and all the students in the room, the idea of salvation through the Cross, a cornerstone of the Christian faith, is likely so ingrained at this point that they may not realize what types of questions non-Christians may raise about this tenet of faith.

After a brief pause, Aaron poses a follow-up question. "Where would you put yourself in this illustration?" Jessica replies, "Probably somewhere over here [pointing to the middle of the continuum]." Aaron replies, "Why would you put yourself there?" She answers, "Because I am closer to being imperfect than perfect." In response, Aaron recites two biblical quotations and continues, "So maybe I didn't explain it well, because you have to be on one side or the other. Because you are either with God, or you're without him. So now, where would you place yourself?" Jessica, after listening attentively, alters her response and concludes that she wants to be on the side "with God."

Aaron temporarily halts the performance to talk with the attendees. He asserts that the latter half of the illustration is more challenging than the first segment and encourages them to be more conversational and interactive. Jessica offers her response to students who situate themselves on the "man" side of the continuum. "That response is fine. . . . It might be because these students don't have enough God in their lives. That's okay. God makes it possible for the student to cross over to Jesus Christ, when the student is ready." Not only is the Bridge illustration about Jesus, but students also rely on Jesus to help them convey their message. Aaron returns his attention to Jessica and resumes the illustration, highlighting three "nonnegotiables" in the process of becoming a Christian: [1] confess your sins; [2] accept Jesus as your Lord and Savior; and [3] live your life for Him. On the "God" side of the visual illustration, Aaron adds these three items in numerical order (see Fig. 8.2).

"So," Aaron asks with a smile, "do you have any other questions?" Jessica shakes her head. " . . . Okay, in Corinthians 5:17 it says: 'Therefore, if anyone is in Christ, he is a new creation; the old has gone, the new has come!' And that is the Bridge." Jessica asks Aaron to clarify his final statement by asking, "What does that last quote mean?" Aaron replies, "For me it means when you accept God, it is a whole new way of living. With him you can be a whole new creation. Does that make sense?"

Aaron models a way for attendees to find out whether the student wants to meet again, and then he exchanges contact information with Jessica. The attendees applaud as the demonstration concludes. Jessica asks them to form pairs and continue to practice the illustration. Students turn to nearby peers and immediately dig into the exercise.

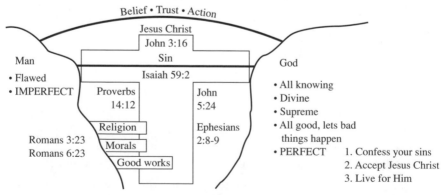

Figure 8.2. Phase 2 of the Bridge-building Illustration

As they practice, we attempt to summarize our understanding of the main arguments of the Bridge illustration:

- God is perfect and humans are imperfect.
- Sin has caused a separation between humans and God.
- Humans will be judged after they die.
- Dying with sin results in the eternal separation of humans from God.
- Humans should accept Christ as their savior. *He is the bridge.*
- Humans should believe in Him and live their lives for Him (e.g., following Jesus' teachings).
- Once humans accept Christ, they will cross over from death to eternal life with God.

This session concludes, like the previous one, with a prayer and a plea from the facilitator for students to memorize the verses and practice the illustration.

The Training Concludes: Perfecting the Delivery of the Good News

Tonight the classroom configuration is different. The tables are at a v-shaped angle, yet they still face the board. The mood also differs from that of the previous training sessions. Three days remain until the start of spring break, and the students are boisterous and energized. Aaron, with a finger in his ear and a strong arm on a male student's shoulder, tries to engage in a serious conversation. Two women prance around the room and distribute cookies as several attendees at a nearby table discuss plans for the SSC spring break trip to New Orleans, where they will spend time assisting with the cleanup from Hurricane Katrina.

Breaking with the two previous sessions, which featured segregated seating, Heidi crosses over and sits with the men tonight. Engrossed in raucous conversation, the men hardly notice. Aaron moves near the blackboard at the front of the room and poses a question unrelated to the third evangelical training session: "Who's ready for spring break?" Most students raise their hands, and the noise level in the room reaches a feverish pitch. Unlike the majority of university students who venture south for some fun in the sun, most SSC students plan to either participate in a mission trip or return home to relax with family.

After a few failed attempts to restore order, Aaron settles the group down by announcing a pop quiz. "Okay, what are the six [evangelizing] principles?" The mood quickly shifts from excitement to fright. Students look forward silently; most avoid looking directly at Aaron. Despite the cohesive nature of SSC students, they are generally slow to participate in nonsocial large-group activities. They almost always gain momentum as these events unfold. Bobby raises his hand, stands, and—sounding as if he were reciting the Pledge of Allegiance—declares, "One, get permission. Two, be interactive. Three, use and write out verses. Four, ask 'Do you understand?' and 'Do you have any questions?' Five, make clear there is a decision to be made. And six, leave your contact information and your handout." The crowd erupts in applause to acknowledge that Bobby passed the quiz with flying colors.

Aaron asks for a second volunteer, this time to demonstrate the entire Bridge illustration. Again, no volunteers are forthcoming. He faces the women's side of the room and inquires as to why the "girls" are not volunteering. He shares the recollection that his female peers, with whom he student-taught the previous year, liked writing on the blackboard. Neither the women nor the men appear to take offense at Aaron's borderline sexist reference, and not a single woman "takes the bait." Instead, they remain silent. Jessica, attempting to break the impasse, stands and warns in a schoolmarm voice, "Don't make me call on you."

Eventually Warren, a sophomore, grins broadly and reluctantly agrees to model the illustration. Jessica plays the role of the soon-to-be evangelized student. Warren often assumes the role of joker in the SSC organization, and we wonder if he will use his humor to offset any public faux pas during the demonstration.

Timidly, Warren begins by asking Jessica if he can share an illustration with her. Her exaggerated nonverbal cues suggest that Warren's question puzzles her. She replies, "What's an illustration?" Warren looks like the proverbial deer in the headlights as he swings his lanky limbs, shuffles his feet, and looks toward the ground. Clearly, he expected a smoother opening exchange. His nervous laughter quiets the room. After two failed attempts to define the term, he blurts out, "Oh, it's just a story about the Bible." Jessica, not wanting to further derail the demonstration, replies, "Okay." Having accomplished the organization's first evangelistic principle—getting permission—Warren proceeds.

"In the beginning, God created man. Do you know why God created man?" Jessica remains silent. Warren continues, "The Bible says that God created man so that he would have a relationship with Him." For the next minute, the illustration unfolds without a hitch. Warren mostly follows the script that Aaron and Jessica presented during the previous two meetings. His style is tentative and mechanical, but it is obvious that he has devoted a significant amount of time to memorizing the Bible passages. Warren's handwriting on the blackboard is difficult to decipher, resembling an elementary school student's printing. The drawing is very primitive and sloppy; the man–God continuum slopes upward. A few of Warren's male peers, sitting nearby, make jokes under their breath about his poor handwriting.

Warren jumbles a Bible verse. His not-so-discreet male peers try to get his attention so they can feed him the correct sequencing of the verse. Unfortunately, Warren remains focused on Jessica and the blackboard and tries unsuccessfully to regain his composure. He asks, "How would you describe God?" Jessica uses the same response she offered the previous week when she role-played the non-Christian student. This familiar response helps Warren navigate this segment of the illustration more smoothly. Matthew, the SSC director, sits in the back of the room and observes the role-play. As is his role during Friday night worship programs, he remains ever present, ever influential, but usually off-stage. It is difficult to interpret his nonverbal reactions to the turbulent performance.

Warren asks, "Do you know what *iniquities* means?" and Jessica says, "No." Warren appears a bit more prepared to define this term than he was to define "an illustration." He appears more comfortable with the scripted components of the illustration, which he delivers in a stiff manner. The women onlookers resemble stenographers as they take copious notes, and most of the men seem more like spectators at a sporting event. Side conversations are more frequent this evening. Warren begins to recite the "barrel over Niagara Falls" story. For the most part the story is understandable, but unfortunately he rushes through the final few sentences, and the moral of the story remains murky. As the not-so-smooth demonstration concludes, the applause—especially from men—is loud and enthusiastic.

During the feedback segment, students struggle to offer positive comments: "He made eye contact." "He wrote out everything." "He asked if she understood." Eventually, Warren's peers gingerly offer constructive criticism: "Warren could spread out the drawing more." "His handwriting is hard to read." Aaron reminds attendees to make sure to preface their comments with, "The Bible says . . ." He continues, "We don't want people thinking we are making this stuff up. . . . Don't say 'you're wrong' to the person; say, 'in the Bible it says . . .'" As Aaron summarizes his feedback, Warren retrieves his notebook and jots down some notes. Jessica's critique follows. "Use all the knowledge up to this point to know how to end it. This is the 'fluidity' of the Bridge. It's the most difficult part." Warren defends his awkward ending by pointing to another male and exclaiming, "He messed me up. He told me the wrong thing before I started."

The students seem content to fidget in their seats and allow the staff to control the training agenda. Finally, a woman raises her hand and asks, "What if a person accepts Jesus Christ but says he cannot put himself with God [on the continuum]?" Jessica replies, "Good question. I will come back to that [question]. If I forget, remind me."

Jessica, though an intern, commands the respect of most students. Her extensive familiarity with the Bible is remarkable, and her moral convictions are unswerving. She does well with both the scripted and the extemporaneous components of the illustration. Students, especially women, describe her as a positive role model and seldom challenge her authority, despite her mild-mannered personality. Aaron, the more extroverted personality of the two, has forged a strong bond with the men. He leads a section of the men's Bible study and organizes portions of the Friday worship service. These contexts allow him to support the male members of SSC while occasionally challenging them when they showcase a "boys will be boys" attitude. The men respect Aaron and seem to recognize when they step out of bounds. This staff duo—Aaron and Jessica—appear to work well together as role models, educators, and Bible authorities.

A male student asks a follow-up question about what to do once the person places him or herself on the continuum. Aaron encourages attendees not to be afraid and to explore what is preventing the person from reaching God. "If the person is relying on the things that aren't enough like religion and good works, be sure to use Ephesians 2:8–9 or John 5:24 to explain salvation. . . . You can't be in the middle; you must be with God or without." Although on the surface this strategy—which aims to establish a relationship with nonbelievers—seems respectful of the other's viewpoints, it is clear that SSC students are drawing a line between the "right" and "wrong" ends of the continuum.

Jessica shifts gears to discuss the skeptic, and she urges attendees to use verses to refute. "If a person seems disinterested, like if he rolls his eyes or acts like he wants to get out of there, close up quickly. Ask if they have questions.

Give them your contact info and just go. Just end the session." Matthew recites a Bible verse that students can use with skeptics and then adds, "Help them to see that Jesus Christ will give them strength to live a life that's different."

Jessica follows up: "If a person is ready to accept Christ, if the spirit is moving them, then ask what is holding them back from taking those steps. You could do it [convert them] right then; pray with them as they accept Christ." Jessica reminds students that a conversion-like experience is very rare. "Most students typically are not at the point during the illustration to accept Jesus, but don't close yourself off to that possibility. . . . The in-between people are more likely the ones you will encounter. If they are tracking along with you, ask if they want to arrange a meeting to get more info. Let one of the staff know."

Another male offers a suggestion: "I know it helps if you ask if you can pray for them, right there." Jessica offers a nod of approval and then interjects a caution. "Be careful—not everyone will respond well to this [praying] . . . it may scare them. . . . A better option, if possible, is to schedule a follow-up meeting." Aaron adds, "We don't want to reinforce evangelical stereotypes."

Matthew commands students' attention as he reminds them that they are an invaluable source of knowledge for their non-Christian peers. "We can't come off as being manipulating. . . . Be careful when inviting them to our Friday program. It may be kind of weird to them—too much like church. . . . Establish a relationship; that is the first step. . . . We don't want them to think our sole purpose was to get them to join our organization."

Practice makes perfect. As was the case during the previous two meetings, attendees break into dyads and continue to practice the illustration for 20 minutes. Some small talk and laughing resound around the room, but most students remain on task. Matthew, Jessica, and Aaron fan out and visit the dyads to calm the group, offer constructive feedback, and answer lingering questions.

The meeting concludes with a prayer—which focuses on everyone having a safe spring break—and a closing comment by Aaron. "Share the illustration with friends, preferably people unfamiliar with the illustration. . . . Maybe share it with a friend from home over spring break? Think about it."

En route to our car, we encounter Kiley. We pose two questions to her: "What are desirable outcomes of the Bridge?" and "What counts as a good

evangelical exchange?" Kiley replies, "Someone who listens and pays attention and wants to learn more. That is what we are called on earth to do—to
bring people to Christ." We follow up, "What do you want non-Christians
to know?" Kiley answers:

> For me personally, if I am talking to a non-Christian, I want to show them
> how happy the Spirit makes me, and they can live their life like that. That
> actually happened. It is an amazing feeling. You know that you helped
> bring someone closer to God. I can understand how some non-Christians
> would be unsure since there are some things I will never understand about
> Christianity.

Like Kiley, students enrolled in the Bridge training program feel they
have benefited from being all about Jesus and want others to have the same
experience.

From Novice Evangelical to Servant Leader[1]

"Let us pray." The 25 attendees fall silent. The designated prayer initiator
thanks the Lord for the recent rain, all SSC members' safe return from spring
break, and the clear thinking of this evening's participants. A chorus of amens
follows this hodgepodge communication with God.

Unlike in the previous meetings, Matthew, the SSC director, leads this
session, while Aaron and Jessica assist. SSC students who attended the previous three evangelical training sessions and are present for this final meeting
are preparing to begin their journey as campus evangelists. They are joined
by several upper-class SSC members. Tonight, the agenda expands to include
the exploration of leadership opportunities within the SSC.

Wasting no time, Matthew poses a question: "What is leadership?" Several
of the 9 men and 16 women make eye contact with each other before Tim nods
and responds, "Being in charge?" His tentative and not-so-comprehensive reply
evokes a second response from a nearby woman: "A position of honor, setting
an example, how to serve." Tim immediately retorts, "I like her answer better;
I change my answer to that," which elicits a burst of laughter.

Matthew acts to immediately refocus the group's attention. "I would
define it as influence." He asserts that all attendees are leaders and have
influence. After a long pause, he inquires if attendees are leaders who serve

or servants who lead. Several individuals offer their rationales. As responses wane, Matthew refers once again to the Bible as he instructs the group to turn to John 13:2–17. Joan reads the passage aloud, which describes Jesus washing the feet of his disciples. Matthew asks the students to interpret the passage, reminding them that they don't have to have "mind-blowing answers." Collectively, the group concludes that "servants who lead" is the ideal response to Matthew's initial query.

Matthew follows with a mini-lecture about the biblical context of slaves and washing others' feet. Abruptly, then, he switches to student lingo and concludes, "Wow, Jesus Christ is really serious about this servant stuff." Matthew's message is unambiguous. SSC members need to be "a slave to Christ" and put His priorities first. Matthew uses this comment as a segue to begin discussing the meeting's primary agenda item—the 2005–06 Servant Leadership Team application and selection process.

He acknowledges that there are parts of being on the team that require sacrifice. "There are not a certain number of people we have in mind to serve on the team. We need people who have a heart to serve and are willing to pay the price to do it. . . . If you don't feel God is leading you to be a member of the team, don't worry; you won't be a second-class citizen. . . . We don't want a community of snobs."

Everyone receives a handout with 23 bullet points explaining the objectives of the Servant Leadership Team, such as "become a ministry community that emphasizes grace, discipline, acceptance, and authenticity in our relationships with one another and to our friends who don't know Christ." The handout also includes expectations, including intentionally sharing their life with others and helping others come to know Christ and grow as His disciples. Finally, the list includes the benefits of joining the SLT, such as growing in understanding of God's Word and His plan for one's life.

Each attendee, in turn, recites 1 of these 23 points. At the conclusion of the public reading, Matthew entertains comments or questions. "How do you divide the groups?" is the first question asked. Matthew explains that there are three teams: an Evangelism Team (E-Team), a Discipleship Team (D-Team), and a Senior Team. A male student follows up: "Is there a hierarchy in heaven for people who do more serving than others?" Matthew contemplates the question for a few moments, then replies, "We don't know what heaven looks like. I don't think there'll be jealousy, but we will be rewarded according to how we live our lives."

Satisfied with the response, attendees continue with their interrogation—"What do you do on the teams?" A current SLT member fields this question. "You learn more effective ways of sharing the faith. We do worksheets, read books and talk about them, learn to share the Lord's Word in dorms, and we meet new people and build relationships with them." Matthew augments this comprehensive response: "My goal for the E-Team is to become equipped in heart, vision, and skill in reaching all types of people. We want you to be prepared to work for God beyond this campus." Another question immediately follows: "What about when [SSC] meetings conflict with other things, like a big test the next day?" Matthew offers students a jolt of sobriety. In a stern and unyielding tone, he replies, "I expect you to be there [at the meeting]. It is all about planning." Matthew offers examples of students who stayed up all night a few times just to attend the SLT meetings and study. He softens his tone and responds, "I wouldn't kick you off the team, but we'd talk about your priorities." There appears to be no end in sight to the barrage of questions. "How strict [are you] on attending the Friday night worship sessions?" Matthew prefaces his response with "Good question," and then follows up:

> I don't take attendance. We want you to have a heart to be there. . . . You devalue me as a leader and the team in general when you skip. You have to commit and set an example. . . . There must be a legitimate reason you have to miss, and you have to let me know ahead of time. Setting an example and making sacrifices are part of what it means to be a leader in the Kingdom.

A senior member of the SLT attempts to soften Matthew's intense response: "Remember, it's not SSC stuff, but God's stuff. It's all about expanding the Kingdom." Current SLT members chime in with upbeat testimonies about how much they have grown and how much they love the experience. We suspect that students are mentally running through their already tightly packed schedules. Most of them are currently involved in the Friday night program, prayer sessions, and a Bible study; the SLT will add 4 to 6 hours a week to their schedule. Finally, a student poses a question that I would ask if I (Peter) were contemplating joining the SLT: "What do you mean by the expectation that Servant Leaders need to support *all* decisions made by the SSC staff?" Matthew jokes, "All you need to do is nod and say I'm the greatest after I say anything. . . . Just kidding." This moment of humor relieves the tension that has been building in the room since the start of the discussion.

Matthew then explains that there are times when SLT members come together and make decisions that will impact the entire ministry. Even if someone is not happy with a decision, that person needs to present a united front to the rest of the ministry. "There's lots of room for voices to be heard, though," He adds. As questions finally cease, Matthew quickly proposes, "Let me pray for us. Lord, thank You for helping people around the room come to peace with their decisions." As Matthew distributes the applications, he offers a reminder: "Don't feel compelled to take one. After you turn them in, there will be interviews; we're not looking for the perfect person, just those who are ready."

Collegiate Evangelism: A Closer Look

SSC collegians' interest in evangelism is part of a larger evangelical movement that has been growing in the United States for decades. As increasing numbers of evangelical students enroll at public universities, faculty and staff encounter new challenges including the "appropriate" role of campus missionary work and the "appropriate" role of religion in the curriculum and cocurriculum. This section addresses these two issues.

The Rise of the Missionary Generation

The ever-growing and prominent evangelical movement in America influences how contemporary Christian collegians spend their time on campus. These students have grown up as part of a missionary generation that seeks to "enhance the ethical core of American life, combating the tendencies toward individualism and materialism" (Riley 2005, p. 262). For Christian collegians, following the Bible, which is their external authority for life, and preaching the Word of God to peers appear to be "right" and necessary, though at times challenging and uncomfortable.

Generally speaking, SSC students subscribe to these missionary generation goals, but their Christian lifestyle and brand of evangelizing defies easy categorization. Like their parents, SSC students position religion as a cornerstone of their existence, but SSC students' brand of religion hardly resembles that of their parents. Unlike previous generations of Christians, they seldom describe themselves as "religious" and seldom affiliate with mainstream religious denominations or local churches. Adler (2005) noted a

1,120-percent increase in self-identified nondenominational Christians from 1990 to 2001.

SSC students not only distance themselves from the "religious" descriptor label and formal religious institutions, but they also eschew affiliation with the spirituality bandwagon movement, which is experiencing a trendy revival on college campuses (UCLA study, 2003; Jablonski, 2001). Braskamp (2006) best described SSC students' concerns with spirituality movements when he wrote that people following this spirituality trend "are attracted to free-floating spiritual ideas and practices they can assemble together into their own personal bricolage of faith" (p. 2). For SSC students, the Bible contains the *one* and only path that allows Christians to walk with Jesus, and they describe themselves as "filled by the Spirit." Establishing and maintaining a personal relationship with Jesus by strictly adhering to the Bible is the epicenter of SSC students' "religious" existence.

The SSC organization shares core beliefs about evangelism with other Christian organizations. McMurtrie (2001) reveals the origins of common and distinctive evangelical components:

> the British historian David Bebbington has identified the key ingredients of evangelicalism as conversionism (an emphasis on the "new birth" as a life-changing religious experience), biblicism (a reliance on the Bible as ultimate religious authority), activism (a concern for sharing the faith), and crucicentrism (a focus on Christ's redeeming work on the Cross). But these evangelical impulses have never by themselves yielded cohesive, institutionally compact, easily definable, well-coordinated, or clearly demarcated groups of Christians. Rather, the history of these evangelical impulses has always been marked by shifts in which groups, leaders, institutions, goals, concerns, opponents, and aspirations become more or less visible and more or less influential over time. (p. 8)

Although SSC religious beliefs align with those of many other Christian organizations, the SSC's religious practices are unconventional. As one of Leland's research interviewees puts it, evangelical Christians whose views parallel those of SSC members "don't want to show up on Sunday, sing two hymns, hear a sermon, and go home" (2004, p. 2). SSC students seldom attend traditional once-a-week worship services and then "go home." Instead, students continually weave their relationship with Jesus into the fabric of their collegiate lifestyles. SSC students pray and evangelize each day.

They worship in unison, attend Bible study sessions, participate in evangelical enrichment programs, and plan seasonal mission outings. For SSC students, simply declaring themselves to be "Christians" is insufficient. Living a Christian life, every day of their time on earth, is a nonnegotiable aspect of the SSC ministry.

Riley (2005) noted, "Some evangelical students take a similar approach to Mormons, separating their school lives from their missionary lives. They spend their summers or vacations in missionary activities abroad, for example, but don't explicitly proselytize during the school year" (p. 209). For SSC students, however, attending college represents a calling from Jesus to spread His word each and every day. One SSC student commented, "I look to the Scripture, do everything for the glory of God. I believe God has called me here to come to [this university]. My purpose is to get an education, so I definitely put that time and effort into it since He has called me to do it." Walking with Jesus and spreading His Word are not seasonal or occasional activities. SSC staff members affirm that remaining close to Jesus is a daily agenda item that takes priority over traditional academic pursuits.

The heart of the Bridge illustration is for the SSC evangelist to help non-Christians realize that walking with Jesus is the ultimate purpose of life. This philosophy aligns with Dalton's (2001) research, in which he stated, "For most students, the college years are a time of questioning and spiritual searching in which there is particular emphasis upon two dimensions of spirituality: making connection with ultimate life purpose and finding an inward home" (p. 17). The SSC staff recognizes that college is a critical time to shape students' lives, and evangelizing is an effective way to shape the spiritual lives of both Christians and non-Christians. SSC does not want to squander this opportunity to influence others and reshape their character. SSC students view themselves as aspiring Christian accountants or aspiring Christian physicians, not simply aspiring accountants or physicians who happen to be Christian. Learning the Bridge illustration and teaching it to others blends their roles as Christians and students.

SSC staff members have designed the four-session Bridge Building training to involve intentional, ongoing, and in-depth character development activities that shape the lives of SSC members, with the expectation that these students will, in turn, shape the lives of their peers. The SSC recognizes, as do Kuh and Umbach (2004), that "character cannot be 'taught' in a single course, or developed as part of an orientation program or capstone experience. Rather, the multiple dimensions of character are cultivated through a variety of experiences that take place over an extended period of time in the company of others who are undergoing similar experiences" (p. 51).

This philosophy applies not only to the SSC's Bridge Building training program, but also to the ways in which SSC students evangelize other students. SSC's modus operandi is to shun in-your-face, confrontational proselytizing techniques when meeting individually with peers. Instead, SSC evangelists use surveys to identify interested students and then politely ask peers' permission to initiate a brief Bible discussion. If granted permission, these aspiring evangelists introduce their peers to the Bible with the hope of strengthening their relationships with Jesus.

Nancy, an SSC staff member, said, "One thing that is helpful is our survey of spiritual interest. It is low-key and asks questions on your opinion, like, 'Is this something you would be interested in?' Our faithfulness is to follow up on these surveys as a door to a relationship." Through these nonconfrontational, one-on-one brief presentations of the Bridge illustration, SSC students hope to forge a longer-term and more substantive relationship with non-Christian peers that will eventually allow SSC members to showcase their evangelical lifestyle and encourage peers to make their lives *all about Jesus*.

Historical Roots

The historical secularization of higher education has influenced collegiate organizations such as the SSC to make evangelizing a centerpiece of their organizational mission. Wolfe's (1997) utopian vision of the academy illuminates the voids evangelicals encounter and try to fill on secular college campuses:

> Professors would talk openly about how their religious beliefs influence their work. They would apply for academic jobs without fear that making their religious views public would destroy their chances of being hired. Students would be encouraged to speak more in class about their beliefs and to bring a religious voice to their extracurricular activities, including athletics and student newspapers. In general, the academic culture would become more amenable to religion. (p. 1)

Like most public university campuses, SSC's secular campus is far from Wolfe's (1997) ideal academy. The SSC members act to resist and alter the dominant secular campus culture. One of the main ways they accomplish this task is through evangelism. McMurtrie (2001) traces the historical roots of evangelicals and the ever-changing tactics that national collegiate Christian organizations often use to return religion to academia.

> When Campus Crusade began, evangelicalism—which holds that salvation comes through faith in Jesus alone—was roaring back from an early 20th-century decline. The four largest nondenominational campus Christian organizations today—Campus Crusade, InterVarsity Christian Fellowship/USA, The Navigators, and Fellowship of Christian Athletes—all formed during the 1940s and 50s. In contrast to the starchy fundamentalism of their predecessors, they packaged their message in a positive, worldly form. (p. A-42)

McMurtrie argues that in the 1970s and 1980s large-scale rallies and "blunt proselytizing" became the norm, but in this new millennium, one-on-one, nonconfrontational evangelizing is in vogue. SSC staff members' mission is to teach and encourage students to learn about topics that have been, from their perspective, essentially banned from college classrooms. SSC's personal and gentle brand of evangelizing is ever-evolving and responds to the unique needs of contemporary college students.

Teaching and Learning

Student learning—in the sense of intellectual, personal, and relational growth, gaining content knowledge, and more effectively imitating spiritual leaders—is at the heart of the SSC and its evangelical training. The SSC evangelical training builds on biblical knowledge skills that participants gain through their Bible studies and weekly worship services. Aspiring SSC evangelists learn to apply their Bible study knowledge with the hope of "saving" peers. The intention of the illustration is to harvest students for Jesus and grow the ministry.

The SSC staff expects evangelical trainees to become Christian scholars, teachers, and ambassadors. Most students who participate in the Bridge training program intend to join the Servant Leadership Teams, serve as Bible study leaders, and disciple younger recruits. Grahmann (2001) asserted, "The main methodologies used by Christian students at secular universities were: digging deep into the text and analyzing it; love for the Bible and for Jesus;

community; generating questions; and putting oneself into the story" (p. 513). The Bridge Building facilitators encourage participants to dig deep into the Bible and analyze (and ultimately love) it, forge and expand their Christian community, and generate and answer "importance of life" questions. The ultimate goal of the evangelical training is for SSC students to "Christianize" the campus.

Although other campus Christian organizations permit first-year students to engage in activities such as facilitating Bible study sessions or evangelizing, SSC resists these practices until students demonstrate deep learning about themselves and Christianity (i.e., regularly partake in Bible study and complete the Bridge training). SSC purposely provides its students with the requisite biblical knowledge and a "foolproof" evangelical pedagogy to eventually teach others about Jesus.

Although the Bridge Building illustration is neither as in-depth nor substantive as we expected, it is an initial opportunity for members to establish relationships with nonbelievers. The long-term goal is for non-Christians to embrace the Bible and enact its lessons in their everyday lives. Through the Bridge training session, the SSC equips students with knowledge of one effective way to evangelize their peers. Several SSC students commented on what they learned about the effectiveness of the one-on-one approach. Aaron, during an interview, elaborated on the SSC's evangelical strategy of forging long-term relationships with non-Christians:

> Evangelizing is spreading the Word of Christ. Building bridges is a form of evangelizing. . . . Get the Word out to non-Christians. . . . We try to relate to someone and get to know them; then talk with them about the Word of Christ. Once we establish a friendship with them, we share the Word of God. If they are not receptive, we still are friends with them, and we pray for them. If the spirit moves them—someone who is capable of walking the Christian life—we stay with them and get them to the point of them spreading the Word. We train them to pray, study the Bible, relate to other people, fellowship, training and working with others.

Gaining lessons from the Bible and learning about effective outreach strategies form the basis for SSC's evangelism efforts. In addition to encouraging in-depth learning about the Bible and faith, the SSC Bridge training augments members' passions, which sustain and grow the ministry. Throughout the Bridge illustration training, the SSC's overarching goal is for students to *develop their hearts* for God. Students focus on developing a personal relationship with Jesus that extends beyond the Bible's teachings. Through this relationship, students grasp God's meaning for their lives and discover their call to evangelize. Matthew elaborates:

> We want to know that your heart beats with the SSC heart—that you're passionate for God, for the Lost, and for multiplication. Our niche is developing students, and I would say that speaking from the personal perspective, other ministries use students . . . we develop them. . . . We challenge people with things that are obtainable for them and things that will keep them motivated.

SSC, therefore, focuses on developing in students a passion for their faith and for being in a lifelong relationship with Jesus. This passion spurs students to become more involved in the organization's evangelism and leadership activities.

Like other evangelicals, SSC members accept the Bible as God's authority without critiquing His messages. The SSC staff encourages students to engage non-Christians in in-depth discussions of Bible verses and Christian faith; they are not to "gloss over" these important issues or oversimplify them. In addition, the SSC staff invites students to complete Bible study, advanced evangelical training, and personal reflection to ensure their ability to clearly describe their faith when evangelizing. The SSC leadership prefers depth rather than breadth; it emphasizes combining members' knowledge about their faith with their burning passion to spread the Word.

Challenges and Critiques

> Most evangelical students experienced teasing and joking in varying degrees of severity as a result of their religious beliefs. . . . Evangelical students described themselves as living on the margins of the broader residence hall communities in which they lived. They used words such as 'outsider,' 'distanced,' 'foreigner,' and 'not normal' to describe themselves in relation to the broader university community. (Lowery and Coomes, 2003, p. 34)

The potential for having to endure teasing, joking, and marginalization contributes to SSC students' reluctance or fear when it comes to evangelizing. Aaron's informal survey during the initial Bridge Building session revealed that two-thirds of the attendees expressed some apprehension about evangelizing their peers. During an interview, Kiley illuminated the origins of these uneasy feelings:

> I know the Bridge really well, but don't really like sharing it. It was really difficult for me. I feel people do need to hear about God, especially on this campus, where people do things like drink. We got paired up with seniors to share the Bridge with people on campus. . . . I was uncomfortable and awkward. It is a great illustration, but for me, it is not how I would go about things. . . . It is important for you to let them know who you are and to always be a good role model, and it is important for you to invest your time into them. When something naturally comes up, tell them what you think . . . get them more involved. God is working through me to reach them. It will happen when it is meant to happen.

Miller (2003) noted two challenges that evangelicals regularly experience that contribute to their uneasiness, both of which are evident in Kiley's commentary:

> The problem with Christian belief—I mean real Christian belief, the belief that there is a God and a devil and a heaven and a hell—is that it is not a fashionable thing to believe. I had this idea once that if I could make Christianity cool, I could change the world, because if Christianity were cool then everybody would want to deal with their sinful nature, and if everybody dealt with their sin nature then most of the world's problems would be solved. (p. 107)

Miller continues:

> My friends who aren't Christians think that Christians are insistent and demanding and intruding, but that isn't the case. Those folks are the squeaky wheels. Most Christians have enormous respect for the space and freedom of others; it is only that they have found a joy in Jesus they want to share. There is the tension. (p. 114)

Because of their belief that non-Christians are *sinners who must be saved,* evangelicals appear rigid and intolerant of other faiths. SSC staff members customize their Bridge illustration to avoid the perception that if students do not follow, they are on the inevitable "highway to hell." Still, tension remains.

Balancing respect for non-Christian views with sharing one's passion for Jesus is easier said than done, and the Bridge illustration exemplifies the SSC's contradictory evangelical strategy that appears to solicit others' viewpoints—but in reality does not. Students initiate a friendly conversation and ask, "Do you have questions?" but they do not ask about the individual's religious background or learn much about them. SSC students want to recruit new members for the organization, yet they are reluctant to solicit and accept others' ideas because they believe that the Bible is the Truth. This tension prohibits mutual interaction with non-Christians, as well as contributes to the group's insularity and homogeneity.

McMurtrie's (2001) critique of a national collegiate Christian organization reveals further political tensions between evangelicals and non-Christians that contribute to SSC evangelizing struggles.

> Abortion, communism, evolution, feminism, and homosexuality are antithetical to Campus Crusade's vision, angering those who hold a more inclusive definition of Christianity. Its focus on evangelism, the zealous effort to spread the Gospel, has come under attack from those who feel that true Christians should also aid the poor and fight for social justice. (p. A-42)

Although SSC members share conservative social and political views with those in other campus Christian organizations, they purposely avoid discussing these views when evangelizing. What matters most to SSC students is developing a personal relationship with Jesus and reading the Bible in order to understand the type of "servant" lifestyle that God intends them to lead. However, their peers' perceptions stem from stereotypes of pushy evangelical Christians and the views associated with the political right. Thus, when sharing the Bridge, SSC students engage in the difficult work of setting themselves apart from "other Christians" through their gentle, polite, Bible-based (not social or political issues-based) approach.

Publicly expressing one's belief in God and subscribing to the Christian life as a collegian is neither in vogue nor hip, and SSC students are keenly aware of their peers' longstanding perceptions of evangelicals as intolerant, pushy, righteous, and zealot-like. These widespread perceptions complicate and impede SSC's efforts to share the Word, yet members persist in carrying out their evangelical mission.

Summary

The SSC staff hope that students involved in the Bridge training program will later become organizational elders and invest in other SSC teaching and learning opportunities, including participating in advanced evangelism training, being disciples to other members, leading retreats/workshops, and perhaps becoming a full-time missionary after graduation. Nevertheless, SSC leaders support students who decide not to increase their involvement.

By continually developing students' evangelical leadership skills as first and second-year students, SSC hopes to have qualified members who will carry out the mission to spread God's Word. The Bridge training not only teaches students how to share the biblical Bridge illustration, but it also serves as a "bridge" of sorts for SSC students. They are able to extend their biblical and personal knowledge while beginning to explore the outward faith activities of evangelism and Christian leadership. The completion of the Bridge training is a crucial gateway for SSC participants who must decide which type of Christian they wish to become. The Servant Leadership Teams, the subject of the next chapter, require an additional time commitment and the additional challenges of spreading God's Word on a secular campus. But for those students who advance to the next level, the Servant Leadership Teams provide an opportunity to further cultivate relationships with like-minded Christian peers and Jesus, in order to fulfill God's will.

LEADING BY FOLLOWING JESUS

Servant Leadership Rituals

"Jesus Freaks"

As students become increasingly dedicated to the SSC mission, they fully embrace their outsider status as "Jesus Freaks" on this public university campus. This shared identity motivates sophomore, junior, and senior students on the SSC's Servant Leadership Teams to mobilize to implement a two-pronged outreach agenda—extending their SSC colleagues' understanding of evangelism and spreading God's word to campus peers.

The Evangelism Team: Gentle Messengers of God's Word

I (Kelsey) glance in the rear-view mirror and notice a parade of headlights bouncing behind me as I roll through a series of new subdivisions at the edge of town. It is obvious that I have left the ramshackle student rental neighborhoods and am now entering the world of "the locals" as I journey to the 8:45 p.m. Evangelism Team (E-Team) meeting at the SSC regional director's home. Spotting Don's driveway, I park along the curb as the stream of cars behind me maneuvers smoothly to the shoulder in one synchronized motion. Car doors slam one by one and SSC members, wearing jeans and T-shirts and carrying small backpacks, cut across the neatly trimmed lawn, careful not to step into the flowerbeds lining the walkway. I use the driveway and fall in behind the students as they enter without knocking.

Once inside, I follow the premeeting rituals of removing my shoes, hanging up my jacket, and acknowledging Don and Nancy's golden retriever with a quick pat before following the drifting sound of students' laughter into the living room. The students sit comfortably on the couches and form a circle around the room. "Okay, tonight we're going to talk about the reliability of the Bible," Matthew calls out, as students finish their conversations. The 4 men and 11 women members of the E-Team face forward, locate their Bibles, and giggle quietly with one another.

"But first, we need to check in about Friday night program attendance. How are you all feeling about the requirement to be there?" Matthew asks in a direct, no-nonsense tone. Without waiting for a response, he continues, "I remind you that when events are going on on-campus, such as last week's big concert, these are not good reasons to miss. You must check with me before committing to something else." Students avoid eye contact with Matthew, but they appear to be intently listening. Last week's major concert on campus was a chart-topping Christian group. Matthew's unyielding adherence to the rules reminds me that the SSC is serious about its leaders' commitment to the organization.

After an uncomfortably long pause, Kelly cautiously squeaks, "Well, it's hard to discern when it's okay to miss. Could we instead have it be up to us, to pray about it and decide, without necessarily going to you first?" Predictably, other students immediately feel comfortable chiming in with additional concerns. "What about things with family?" "What about if we want to meet with a non-Christian and that's the only time they can meet?" Matthew unfolds his arms and softens his expression. "I can see there's been confusion," he says, "and I want to make sure you know that legitimate things are okay to miss. I would be okay with trying again having you thinking and praying over what conflicts and then coming to ask me if it's okay. I trust your decision-making and your commitment. You've made a choice to commit yourself to the SLT. I don't want to be your parent; I just want you to take seriously your participation in this ministry. Are there questions? How do you feel about that?" The tension in the air seems to dissipate as students' smiles return and they reply with 'okay' and 'good.'"

Matthew adds "Oh, one more thing. It's important to spend time with non-Christians. In my previous position, I would always spend one night a week with a guy, and eventually over time, he became a Christian. Sometimes I had to rearrange other ministry stuff to do it. You will just need to work with those schedules and make sure you're committing to this, too, okay?" Students nod in agreement.

"Now, on to talking about the Bible," Matthew continues, as he passes around a handout with a two-column table and a series of questions. The columns compare the Bible as a historical document to the *Iliad* and other ancient texts in terms of when it was written, the number of copies we have found, and external versus internal evidence. Matthew asks students to read aloud from the handout, taking turns around the circle. They discuss Scripture passages as they are read, and Matthew has to help students as they stumble over ancient names and words. "God doesn't always approve of all the Bible records, especially in the Old Testament. For example, think about David's infidelity with Bathsheba or the subsequent murder of Uriah. Even though these stories are in the Bible, that doesn't mean God approves of them," states Matthew. Looks of curiosity cross several students' faces, and I admit that I am also intrigued by Matthew's discussion of the Bible as a complex document—authoritative, but not always easy to decipher. "Non-Christian texts are significant—those which verify and talk about the Bible," he adds, and he launches into a discussion about internal and external evidence that proves the credibility of the Bible as a historical text.

Matthew's discussion of the credibility of sources intrigues me, but the ancient language seems to confuse some students. Perhaps they are too fatigued by the end of the semester to be enthusiastic. I wonder whether they would actually use historical information to defend their views about the Bible in conversations with non-Christians. I suppose such an argument could be powerful for non-Christians in a secular university environment, because it emphasizes "fact" rather than "faith." Because the Bible forms the foundation for all of the SSC's values and activities, I wish Matthew would go into even more specifics. Students remain attentive, but they whisper to each other to gain clarification.

The sound of pages flipping brings me back from my ponderings. On the flip side of the handout is a section on Greek letters. Matthew instructs the students to "put an apostrophe above the first *iota*." A collective "*What?*" rises from the crowd as students await clarification. After several failed attempts to get students to follow his verbal instructions about rearranging markings and letters in Greek words, Matthew takes charge and aborts the activity. He explains his main point: that something as simple as forgetting an apostrophe could have changed entirely the meaning of certain verses in the Bible. Still, the main messages are the same in different translations, and much external evidence that verifies the Bible exists in other texts.

"Oh, I see!" exclaims Kevin, as several women giggle. Matthew continues, "I got all this info from [J. McDowell's] *Evidence That Demands a Verdict;* it's a great book. Basically, the way we look at the Bible, God is sovereign—He put it in there. All of this can help with non-Christians who ask how we know the Bible is true. It stands out above all historical texts." Students around the circle take brief notes in their journals. "This can really help us when we go out in dorms," cites Warren. Matthew nods in approval.

Matthew switches gears, "Let's talk about and process the year on the E-Team. Let's start with successes." Immediately, the excited students offer comments. "I liked going to the SSC regional conference." "I like how you actually made us go into the dorms. Once I was there [evangelizing] I really liked it." "We did a good job of getting freshmen to join." "We created new activities for fellowship, like Women's Hikes." Matthew nods and adds, "I was so encouraged by how you all took initiative."

"I now understand the motivation for evangelism, and I know Scripture better," offers Timothy. "I'm also more confident when talking with non-Christians and answering questions," he adds. "Yay for our team!" shouts Kevin as he pumps his fist in the air, which draws a round of giggles and cheering from the women in the room. "The support here is good," Rebecca asserts. "People have the same heart, so we have the same frustrations and can bounce ideas off each other."

Matthew smiles and asks, "Okay, so what are some of the things God has done this year?" The students continue their rapid responses: "He gave us a strong freshman class." "He put [His] trust in us." "He helped us grow our community." "He gave us confidence to tell our testimonies at the Friday night program." "We grew as a community of grace. . . . Like I knew I could go into an E-Team meeting with a bad attitude, but they would turn me around and have good insight."

Glancing at his watch and noticing it is almost 10:00 p.m., Matthew thanks the team for their work. "I appreciate you. I am impressed with you and I am really happy everyone has been here. God is moving in all of you, and I've seen a lot of growth. . . . I look forward to things God will do through you in the next few years, so thank you." He adds, "I will be sending evaluations home this summer; please fill them out and give us feedback." Students do not seem to notice that the group did not brainstorm *weaknesses or failures* for the year. Even if Matthew had pressed students to consider weaknesses, I wonder whether they would have obliged. The similarity and cohesion between group members often makes it difficult for them to critique their own organization. After members list all the group's successes, a strong sense of camaraderie and collective achievement permeates the room. Will these upbeat feelings motivate next year's D-Team (i.e., Discipleship Team for juniors and seniors)?

Matthew signals to Jessica, and she asks the group to begin praying together. Instantly, all students close their eyes and bow their heads as students randomly enter the conversation-style prayer. "Inscribe truth in our hearts, Lord" . . . "Work in us to reach out to others" . . . "Thank You for this time to reflect on the year and all You've done" . . . "Thank You for letting us be a part of Your mission" . . . "We ask You to prepare the hearts of people who will be on this team next year, and help us as we decide whether to join the D-Team." . . . "Help us apply what we learned in the E-Team in the summer."

As students' voices trail off, Matthew concludes: "We pray that You will help everyone put You first on their schedule this summer. Amen." Students begin packing up their books as one woman yells out, "We need a big SSC group hug!" After the hug, they retrieve Don and Nancy from the other room to sing happy birthday to Nancy, and then dash to the kitchen to eat cookies and celebrate the end to a successful year of evangelizing together for Jesus.

The Discipleship Team (D-Team): Serious and Scholarly Messengers of God's Word[1]

As the E-Team members finish the last few cookies and prepare to leave, D-Team members start arriving at Don's home for their 10:00 p.m. weekly meeting. When I (Kelsey) return to the living room, three women from the D-Team are already seated on one couch, and two begin to get settled on another. "Why don't you take my seat on the couch and I'll sit on the floor?" offers Samantha. I spend a few minutes graciously declining her repeated offers and opt instead for an overstuffed cushion situated near the fireplace, which provides me the best view of the meeting.

As I settle into my cushion, I listen to the students' conversations. I learn that two women attended the stage production of *Peter Pan* last weekend; they giggle uncontrollably as they recount their quest for autographs from the actors and their plans to see *Little Women*. These students' outward innocence never ceases to amaze me. I am relieved that they know little about my passion for slightly less-innocent forms of entertainment, such as *Sex and the City* reruns or *Grey's Anatomy* episodes.

"So how is your semester going?" I ask Samantha. She reveals that upon graduation, she is contemplating applying for an SSC-sponsored internship. This is her natural "next step" after being so highly involved in the SSC as a senior, where she disciples other women; leads a Bible study; evangelizes in the residence halls; and attends prayer services, SLT meetings, and Friday night sessions each week. She then offers humorous stories from the recent SSC-sponsored spring break service trip to New Orleans. Before I am able to learn more about the trip, Dennis, the final D-team member and one of only two non-White students in the SLT, enters the room breathlessly and scans the crowded room intently as he searches for a place to sit. Dressed in gym shorts, an old T-shirt, and a bright green bandana, he is a bit disheveled and apologizes for his tardiness. In return, Matthew nods and asks him to open the meeting with a prayer. Dennis releases a loud sigh as students bow their heads and he begins, "Lord help us learn more about You, how to be an impact. Prepare us to see Your wisdom Lord, Amen."

"Great. Thank you," Matthew says, a bit abruptly. "Who has tonight's spiritual illustration?" he inquires. These students learned a set of standard illustrations the previous year when they served on the E-team, but this year they have the opportunity as D-team members to generate an original illustration compatible with their own style and personality.

"It's my turn!" one woman responds enthusiastically. "And, I have visual aids!" She smiles playfully as she retrieves from her bag two light bulbs with elaborate hand-painted designs on them. She explains her extended metaphor, whereby the light bulbs represent our desire to be lights for God, even though all of us are different on the outside. "And we can be screwed or not . . . *as a light bulb,*" she adds, which generates raucous laughter from around the room. She pauses to giggle and then reminds everyone to "shine your own unique light that God has given you."

"Good. Good job," says Matthew. "Okay, let's get started then. Remember tonight's question? When you are discipling someone who is doing some-thing wrong, but they don't agree that it is wrong, what do you do?" Except for the constant ticking of the cuckoo clock, the room falls silent again as students ponder this difficult query. Just as the silence begins to feel uncom-fortable, Josh suggests using the Bible as a guide and telling such students that "Lordship means giving everything to God." The woman next to me bites her lip nervously and comments, "But that might not work." "We need to pray that God works in their heart and get them to pray about it," asserts Sarah. The students scoot forward in their seats. Their creased foreheads suggest to me that they are in deep thought. Finally one woman exclaims, "You just can't give up on the issue!" The students search one another's eyes. No one seems to know what to say as they look down at their laps and momentarily shrink back into their chairs.

Matthew nudges the group along by discussing guilt by association. "For example," he says, "I have chosen to not drink at local bars. Some Christians don't think drinking alcohol is proper, especially since I work with students. Or, what about a student having a boy or girlfriend in their room overnight with them, even if they say they're not doing anything?"

Josh again rifles off two appropriate Bible quotations so quickly that I can't comprehend them. The woman next to me, Ann, sighs and shakes her head. I tentatively conclude that she is trying desperately to compose her thoughts. "How far should we be willing to go with this person, when something is not pleasing to God?" she finally asks. I cannot ascertain whether the group comprehends her concern before she launches into a complex argument about faith and God's will. In an effort to validate Ann's commentary, another woman adds, "If your conscience is right with God . . . maybe a sin to one person is not to another." Suddenly, the room falls silent again.

Matthew continues to recite Scripture verses that address the issues at hand. "There are four types of believers: first, mature believers; second, non-Christians; third, new believers; and finally, weak believers. Numbers two and three are priority for us to try to reach," Matthew adds. As he delivers multiple Scripture verses, several students struggle to keep up as they quickly page through their Bibles to locate the verses. The argument that "weak believers may not be worth pursuing" intrigues me. As a restless Catholic considering Protestant Christianity, I wonder if I might qualify as a weak believer.

One woman pulls her long hair into a ponytail as Matthew continues discussing gray areas. "The gray areas move as the culture moves. The spiritual leader decides, and you must ask if it's worth fighting it or to have self-control . . . authority issues are bound to come up." I assume he is talking about moral issues. I can't help but wonder whether these students, who seem to be passively absorbing his words, would actually rebel against the will of their spiritual leaders. In the SSC enclave, they are certainly unwilling to rebel against Matthew as their spiritual elder. He continues:

> Always use Scripture as a means of defense. For example, I can defend my having a beer because there's nothing against drinking in the Bible. You all are spiritual leaders for the people you disciple. Just like . . . for anyone on the SLT teams doing something known to be wrong, they would not be allowed to participate. Our reputation as a ministry, but more importantly as God's ambassadors, is on the line. For example, a former SSC student slept with his girlfriend and did not find anything wrong with it. . . . Following the Bible, we didn't treat him as a Christian anymore.

Tensions are rising during this discussion. Students are silent and motionless, but their expressions suggest great interest in Matthew's discussion about moral decisions in college. I wish I had access to their inner thoughts during this conversation. Although I have conclusively ascertained through multiple conversations that these students believe strongly in Christian morals, I ponder how difficult it must be in the college environment to "stay on the right side" of Christianity's gray areas.

"Okay, chapter 12 for today . . . our final chapter in [L. Eims] *The Lost Art of Disciple Making*. How does Eims say we should bring a young believer to maturity?" Matthew queries. The woman next to me scans pages upon pages filled with diligent notes from each chapter. Most of the women have binders full of notes, decorated with colorful labels that read "SLT" and "D-team." The men seem less organized. Two of them sheepishly acknowledge that they forgot their books, while most others stare at their notebooks.

"Um, teach them how to teach themselves?" asks Jen. Her dark eyes study Matthew's face for affirmation. "I agree, but what does the book say about that?" he responds. Jen reads aloud a passage from Eims's book, as Matthew continues. "What are some of the traps in teaching others?"

Student replies include "not making it personalized to people" and "focusing on some people more than others." The conversation tempo quickens considerably as these exchanges appear to energize students. "That's right about not wanting them to take your beliefs," Matthew interjects. "A disciple shouldn't take my word for it. I need to back everything up with Scripture. What does God reveal about Himself? Young believers may look to you for answers, but they should be looking to the *Word*," he asserts firmly. Students thoughtfully jot notes as Matthew continues his mini-sermon.

After a brief moment of silence, Samantha jumps in and poses a final question. "So . . . what about some women in my freshmen Bible study . . . some get discipled, and some don't. Will they have a better chance of making it [i.e., getting closer to becoming "true Christians"] with discipleship, or is it all God's decision?" A weighty silence fills the air. With this question, Samantha seeks clarity about SSC's disciple-based mission.

Participants patiently wait for Matthew's response, which is a familiar one of "trust God." Students remain completely quiet, but their luminous faces suggest they understand Matthew's biblical interpretation. The nearby dog's snoring reminds me it is past 11:00 p.m. Still, the conclusion of this gathering is nowhere in sight. Finally, Brian breaks the silence. "Is that why selection is so important? To make sure that it is God's plan for us to meet that person to disciple?"

"Good questions. What three things are involved in discipleship?" asks Matthew in an instructive tone. The students reply eagerly: character development, fun and games, and life/ministry skills. They readily identify "character development" as the element that is most often omitted. "Character development needs one-on-one time. For example, you wouldn't want to point out someone's pride in front of a group," comments one woman. "Right," says Matthew, approvingly. He continues, "If you can't see what's going on in their life, you can't effectively disciple. Yet, people try to do it. In the Christian world, discipleship gets thrown around without people understanding it." Students quietly take notes as Matthew continues to quote a series of Bible verses to support his argument. Glancing at his watch, Matthew moves to adjourn. "Questions? Okay, here's the worksheet for next time," he says, sounding much more relaxed. Students start shifting in their seats and putting their books back into their bags; they pause during the closing prayer. "All right. Nice job, everyone. See you next week," says Matthew with a smile.

Mobilizing to Spread God's Word

Almost every student organization provides opportunities for its members to improve themselves. A soccer club helps members become better athletes. A sorority's philanthropy committee teaches members to become effective fund raisers. Student government associations are places where members develop leadership skills. The SSC is no exception; programs such as Bible studies and the Bridge program help members become better Christians and knowledge-able biblical scholars.

But some student organizations aim not only to provide enrichment opportunities for members, but also to achieve a greater good by mobilizing members to serve and/or influence a larger constituency group. Unlike a soccer club whose sole aim is to provide members an outlet for their athletic interests and physical abilities, the sorority's philanthropy committee benefits members and serves a greater good by raising money for worthy causes. Involvement in student government benefits elected leaders and the constituents they serve by influencing and shaping policy to benefit the greater good.

Similarly, both its Evangelism and Discipleship teams reveal how SSC defines the *greater good* and the ways it educates, energizes, and organizes members to implement its political agenda to "build God's Kingdom." For SSC, the greater good involves spreading the Word of God and teaching others to "live with Christ." At this fourth and final level of involvement, the organization continues to use the Bible—God's Word—as *the* authority to influence, educate, and motivate members to live with Christ. But what separates this level of involvement from the others is a stronger focus on *outreach rituals* to achieve the organization's core mission. Through involve-ment with the Bible study and the completion of Bridge training (i.e., the second and third levels of involvement), SSC leaders encourage students to share their personal knowledge with others as they contribute to the organi-zation's political mission, which centers on spreading God's Word.

SSC employs a strategic, two-part approach to outreach and likewise divides its outreach activities between two teams: the E-Team and the D-Team. These teams constitute the SSC's "Servant Leadership Team (SLT)," and they work hand-in-hand to bring others closer to God. The E-Team spreads the Word of God to others with the hope of gaining "converts." D-Team mem-bers participate in one-on-one discipleship mentoring relationships with stu-dents to help them strengthen their faith.

The E- and D-Team members' beliefs align with those of collegiate evan-gelical Christians, which Lowery and Coomes (2003) identified as follows:

> All of the evangelical students emphasized the importance of a personal relationship with Jesus Christ as a core element of their faith. However, for

these evangelical students, simply having a relationship was not sufficient. It was equally important to strive to grow in one's relationship with Christ. . . . The evangelical students often spoke of a desire or even obligation to share their faith with others on campus. It was clear that evangelism was a fundamental element of how these students understood their faith and how it should be expressed in their lives. (p. 36)

The SSC, although it finds evangelism highly important philosophically, does not consider evangelism to be the organization's ultimate goal. Rather, evangelism is a necessary prerequisite to the organization's central mission of building God's Kingdom through discipleship. SSC members evangelize to identify believers, and then they encourage these students to remain SSC members and *grow into true Christians* through the discipleship process.

The SSC's brand of evangelism differs from other campus Christian organizations. Whereas "recent campus evangelical groups have emerged by abandoning their traditional isolationism in favor of a more active role in campus life" (Lowery and Coomes, 2003, p. 32), SSC students maintain a low profile as they quietly carry out their evangelical mission within the confines of this public, secular campus. SSC is hypersensitive to the school's and the general public's resistance to evangelical initiatives, and it responds accordingly to "gently" spread its spiritual message.

Active and Passive Evangelism Outreach

As "gentle" evangelists, the SSC uses both *active* and *passive* outreach strategies to spread God's Word. Entering residence halls and sharing the Bridge and other Gospel illustrations with residents represents an active evangelical strategy. E-Team students also sponsor "Investigative Bible Study" in residence halls, whereby they invite students to an open discussion about questions such as "Who is Jesus, and what does He want from me?" During these encounters, SSC students avoid quoting Scripture or using "Christian language." Instead, they share the "gist" of the message in a nonthreatening manner and use their biblical knowledge to answer students' questions.

During weekly E-Team meetings, students exchange and learn additional biblical illustrations, as well as brainstorm strategies to actively spread God's Word. Two common components of E-Team meetings are learning more about the Bible, as in the narrative when Matthew discussed the validity of the text, and collectively constructing answers to challenging questions that non-Christian students frequently pose during residence hall interactions. Kelly, a sophomore E-Team member, offers her rationale for E-Team training:

> I was a little confused about what the E-team actually was for a while. I was like, 'Are we just reading Bible verses about evangelism? Or is it just the recruiting team of SSC, that we went out and got more people?' So I was so confused, but by talking to people on the team, I learned it was more about practical ways to talk to people about your faith. I'm really glad that I did it.

As SSC members befriend other students on campus, they first get to know the other person, share their faith, and offer to read the Bible with them. If they determine that the other student seems open to Christianity (or is already a Christian), they may invite their new friend to SSC's Friday night worship program. This welcoming and supportive program acts as an entry-way to the Christian life. If new members enjoy meeting new friends and listening to the messages espoused during Friday programs, they often join the organization. The success of this strategy resonates with Lee's (2002) research, which found that students' attendance at religious services

> leads to stronger personal religious beliefs and convictions (i.e., stronger personal faith). This study also found that attending an institution with peers who frequently attend religious services strengthens one's personal beliefs, confirming past research on the powerful influence of peer groups. (p. 382)

Thus, while the SSC's "gentle" evangelism strategies may seem surprisingly timid in light of stereotypical conceptualizations of evangelism that advocate stern calls to "spread the Word," SSC members are actually quite deliberate and often productive in their unique approach to evangelizing.

In addition to the E-Team's active efforts to follow up on surveys, hold investigative Bible study in residence halls, and invite friends to the Friday night program, *passive strategies* are also important components of their out-reach program. SSC students pray during E-Team meetings for students who they hope will one day become Christians, and they sponsor weekly meetings in the campus chapel, where they pray for non-Christians on campus and in the world. Besides prayer, SSC leaders encourage members to silently "model" Christian behaviors for others on campus with the hope that others will ask about the origin of SSC's members' motivations and positive outlook on life. This strategy resembles a larger movement on the part of collegiate Christians termed "lifestyle evangelism." Riley (2005) elaborates: "Indeed, this idea of evangelizing by living a particular kind of life and waiting for people to ask you about your faith (sometimes known as "lifestyle evangelism") rather than proclaiming the faith aggressively is prevalent at evangelical schools" (p. 209). In the D-team narrative, Matthew expects students to "sacrifice" and live a Christian lifestyle that exemplifies SSC's constant mindfulness of the way they present themselves to the outside world. Ideally, they want to be visibly serving Jesus.

Organizational Sustainability

Besides recruiting new members to join the organization, perhaps an equally important function of the E-Team is *organizational sustainability*. The ongoing E-Team training helps students develop the ability to articulate clearly the mission and core values of the organization, which helps them to portray clearly the character and beliefs of the SSC and to recruit students who align themselves with their unique subculture. The E-team also provides a forum for students to use the skills they developed during the Bridge training sessions. Thus, E-Team students receive a "new challenge" and are encouraged to join this more progressive level of involvement.

E-Team members accept additional organizational responsibilities. For example, because students on the E-Team are completing the core organizational mission to "spread God's Word," they understand that they need to make a greater commitment of time and energy to the team. In return, Matthew told students in the final Bridge meeting that they "will be rewarded with both earthly and heavenly benefits according to how we live our lives." These motivated and ultra-involved students on the SLT form the foundation and lifeblood for the organization.

The structure of the SLT promotes organizational sustainability because it allows for increased and structured in-depth interaction between seasoned and novice members. Veteran D-Team members encourage new SSC members who complete the Bridge training to join the E-Team. In the final Bridge meeting, D-Team members (i.e., older students) attended the recruitment information meeting to extol the benefits of participation and encourage their younger colleagues to join the E-Team. Matthew commented, "One of the goals of the E-Team is to reach out to freshmen. The D-Team leads Bible studies and identifies people who are most ready for one-on-one training."

The E-Team meetings contribute to organizational sustainability by cultivating in students a desire not only to bring people into the group, but also to "move them along" on their faith journey. Since the centerpiece of their active evangelism efforts is becoming friends with a non-Christian and slowly helping that person move closer to God, evangelism efforts dovetail nicely with one-on-one discipleship. In the Discipleship Team text, *The Lost Art of Disciplemaking,* Eims (1978) urges readers to consider the next point: "Let's say you've had the joy of leading a person to Jesus Christ. Are you happy? Of course you are. . . . But are you satisfied? No, not yet. Your objective now is to help this new Christian progress to the point where he is a fruitful, mature, and dedicated disciple" (p. 61). SSC leaders encourage E-Team members to become fully integrated into the organization and join the D-Team the following year, to "continue God's work."

Servant Leadership Rituals

Discipleship, a more intense and personal faith experience, is a natural corollary to the evangelism initiatives designed to recruit new members to the organization. The primary goal of the D-Team and the SSC is *multiplication.* Based on the way Jesus used his disciples to reach out to the masses, the SSC believes that if one disciple mentors another disciple, then there are two people building God's Kingdom in the world. Over time, with more disciples working in the world, the number of people brought closer to God will increase. However, multiplication efforts will falter if disciples are not properly trained or committed to God. Thus the D-Team's discipleship program is both intensive and personal. Matthew and his interns invite students to commit to their weekly D-Team meetings, meet with at least one disciple, lead a Bible study for first-year students, and attend the Friday night worship programs.

The key distinction between evangelism and discipleship is that whereas evangelism can be more of a large-scale effort directed at both Christians and non-Christians, discipleship focuses exclusively on Christians and is

intentionally small in scale. D-Team members choose discipleship participants (all of whom are already members of the SSC) very carefully, based on
their level of commitment, motivation, and faith. Team members spend considerable time in discernment and prayer to be certain that God is leading
them to select a particular disciple. Sarah commented on the importance of
prayer and discernment from the beginning of the disciple-selection process:

> Sometimes they come to you, or mostly it's girls from our Bible studies. . . .
> That's how we connect with a group of freshman girls. . . . You look for
> someone who is faithful, available, takes initiative, teachable, and has a
> heart for God and other people. Basically, you just want somebody that
> follows those things, and that's through Scriptures—like how Jesus chose
> the disciples. So that's kind of how we choose, but it's totally God.

This discernment process is especially important, considering the high
expectations for what D-Team members hope to accomplish with their disciples. Eims (1978) comments on the mindset Christians must adopt if they
are to disciple other Christians:

> [T]hree things are a must for the person who would help others become
> stalwart, loyal, productive disciples in the ministry of Jesus Christ. [1] He
> must have clearly in mind what he wants them to know and understand of
> the things of God; he must know what are the basic ingredients in a life of
> discipleship. [2] He must have a clear picture of what he wants these disci-
> ples to become. He must know what bedrock elements of Christian char-
> acter must be theirs and what kind of people they should be. [3] He must
> have a vivid vision of what he wants them to learn to do and a workable
> plan to help them accomplish it. (p. 36)

The SSC D-Team members attempt to meet Eims's (1978) objectives
through a process that is purposely deliberate and personal. Pairs meet at least
once a week at a time of their choosing. D-Team members often identify
Scripture verses to help them discuss selected faith and personal issues with
their disciple. D-Team students integrate *character development* (i.e., discussing how to become like Christ, not just understanding what Jesus would
do), *fun and games* (i.e., holding the meeting at an ice cream parlor), *and
life/ministry skills* (e.g., learning how to manage money and learning new

illustrations) into their weekly one-on-one meetings. D-Team members have a loose curriculum to follow, but they are free to select topics that will meet the unique needs of their disciple.

In addition to meeting with their disciples, D-Team members also meet weekly, and as the D-team narrative reveals, they "troubleshoot" discipleship challenges and enhance their Scriptural knowledge. Sarah explained some of the challenges associated with discipling peers that are common topics at D-team meetings: "Just having no idea what they need . . . It's been a struggle for me to explain something and know if she understands it . . . and if she can apply it to her life. . . . I can't change her actions. All I can do is teach her and know that that's not my job or responsibility."

In addition to discussing discipleship dyads' progress during weekly meetings, Matthew advises disciples to study selected Scripture verses, spend "quiet time" pondering the topics from the previous week, and lead a Christian lifestyle. He also recommends texts students might wish to explore with their students and techniques they can use to enhance the effectiveness of the relationship.

These intensely personal and complex topics make this mentoring relationship unusual in comparison to those of other organizations. But perhaps the most unique element of the SSC mentorship program is the amount of *training and support* the organization provides mentors to tackle these difficult character issues with their mentees. Unlike other student organizations, the SSC maximizes this level of involvement as a vehicle for student learning. Therefore, individual mentor relationships between D-Team students and their disciples are often quite powerful in helping younger students learn about and live according to their faith.

Leadership Rituals

When designing D-Team training sessions, Matthew seeks to enhance SLT members' faith, as well as the faith of those they serve. The D-Team infrastructure incorporates Eims' (1978) four essential components of a strong discipleship-making team: *prayer, Bible study, fun and games,* and *witness.* The first three components are an obvious extension of previous levels of involvement. First, D-Team students recognize that because God *uses them* to implement His will, they must include a healthy dose of *prayer* into their daily routines to better understand His plan. In the D-Team narrative, Sarah said of a disciple who does not seem to listen to a D-Team member's advice: "I think we need to pray that God works in their heart, and get them to pray about it." D-Team members integrate prayer into their everyday lives to strengthen their discipleship efforts as well as become stronger Christian individuals.

The D-Team also has an obvious *Bible study* component that assists students in strengthening their relationship with God. Founded on the SSC's Bible-based ideology, D-Team members defer difficult discipleship questions to God's will. In the narrative, Matthew commented that students should not be sharing their own personal opinions with their disciples; rather, they need to base all their advice on the Bible. Thus, an organizational goal is for D-Team students to become advanced biblical scholars. Sarah describes how she integrates Bible study into her weekly discipleship meetings: "I come up with a couple of key passages of Scripture and then talk about how it worked in my life . . . I try to build people up to a point where they're actively learning and seeking answers for themselves . . . so they can have their own walk [with God]." Because disciples are often quite young in their faith, D-Team members' knowledge of the Bible is an essential prerequisite to "coaxing them along" on the path closer to God.

As a result of the SSC's commitment to the three Fs (i.e., faith, fun, and fellowship), it makes sense that *fun and social times* would be a third essential component of the D-Team experience. During D-Team meetings, students allocate time for joking and laughing together and sharing their recent experiences. Fun and games, such as spring break service trips, serve an important purpose. Because they spend significant amounts of time together, D-Team members develop an in-group bond that makes the group tighter and allows them to better identify and further refine their common value system. Students take pride in their organization and consequently assume leadership roles within the organization. Although the SLT is an advanced, intense level of commitment, fun is a mainstay for this organization and contributes to students' satisfaction and retention. The most intense level of commitment is for students to be discipled by a staff person.

The fourth of Eims' essential components of a D-Team is *witness*. He describes witness as sharing one's faith with others on the team. During D-Team meetings, students discuss their personal faith struggles and remind each other of their responsibility to live a Christian life and "be a witness" in all their actions. D-Team peers seek to hold one another *accountable* for their actions. A student interviewee in Kim's (2006) study of evangelical collegians said, "Accountability is working with one another, supporting one another, following out what you believe in as a Christian together. It means I have other Christians keeping me in check, asking me questions, examining my life . . . to see if I am living in Christ . . . An older person or partner keeps you in check and will be candid with you" (p. 75). SSC students, particularly D-Team members who are fully invested in the organization and their faith journey, likewise seek accountability relationships with their peers so they can be strong role models for their disciples.

Because they are the most highly committed and invested students in the organization, D-Team members evolve into responsible *witnesses* of Christian morality. Matthew's comment that a former SSC member who slept with his girlfriend was "not treated like a Christian anymore" symbolizes the SSC's high morality expectations for D-Team students. And the fact that the D-Team's common moral code is *religious* in nature contributes to students' increased adherence to the code. Hoekema (1994) elaborates:

> Religious organizations . . . are likely to uphold explicit moral as well as theological views. Their meetings and activities, too, shape students' sense of moral responsibility, of what is acceptable behavior . . . these groups make an indispensable contribution to the formation of moral maturity in students. . . . Surely, any institution, public or private, ought to encourage students to participate actively in those groups that, on the whole, model responsible decision making in personal, political, and institutional contexts. (p. 158)

SSC members base their moral code strictly on the Bible. Since students establish a personal relationship with Jesus, they follow His law. According to a national survey conducted by Adler (2005), 30% of college students say they practice religion to become a better person and live a moral life—a response that was second only to developing a better relationship with God (39%). D-Team members, too, follow a strict moral code to become "better people" and enhance their ability to influence others to do the same.

The D-Team structure aligns closely with Berkowitz and Fekula's (1999) *Five Elements of Postsecondary Character Education*:

1. *Teaching about character* (e.g., SSC leaders instruct students about the "proper" Christian moral lifestyle, invite students to reflect upon their values, and decide whether they need to better align their actions with their beliefs).

2. *Displaying character* (e.g., Matthew comments on his decision to avoid drinking at local bars).
3. *Demanding character* (e.g., Team members confront peers who do not conform to the organization's accepted moral code).
4. *Apprenticeship, or practicing character* (e.g., During their weekly meetings with
   their disciples, students teach SSC values and act *as witnesses* to emulate the
   SSC's moral code).
5. *Reflecting on character* (e.g., Matthew encourages D-Team students to continually question the "gray areas" of proper Christian behavior and reflect on
   whether they have achieved their desired level of morality).

Benefits and Liabilities of a Righteous Moral Community

Despite the benefits of a strong focus on morals, the D-Team's strict adherence to moral codes within a tightly knit community has negative consequences when, for example, it leads to a sense of righteousness. Because
D-Team members follow a strict moral code, they commonly identify themselves as "real Christians" and distinguish themselves from "other Christians"
on campus. C. S. Lewis (1945), who wrote one of the SSC's favorite books,
Mere Christianity, elaborates on this separation between "real" and "wannabe"
Christians: "We have all departed from that total plan in different ways, and
each of us wants to make out that his own modification of the original plan
is the plan itself. You will find this again and again about anything that is
really Christian: everyone is attracted by bits of it and wants to pick out those
bits and leave the rest" (p. 66). Dennis, during an interview, comments on
this "a la carte style" of Christianity: "With some Christians, they do things
just because they feel like it's a good idea, not because it's the actual teaching
and stuff, so people get misconceptions from that."

This sense of righteousness can be positive when it helps D-Team
members rally around the organization's mission as well as inspire younger
members to remain in the organization. As the organization leaders at the
pinnacle who personally disciple younger members, D-Team members are
the strongest contributors to the *cultural reproduction* of the SSC. Giddens
(1997) defines cultural reproduction as

> the mechanisms by which continuity of cultural experience is sustained
> across time. The processes of schooling in modern societies are among the

main mechanisms of cultural reproduction, and do not operate solely through what is taught in courses of formal instruction. Cultural reproduction occurs in a more profound way through the hidden curriculum— aspects of behavior, which individuals learn in an informal way while at school. (p. 581)

During discipleship meetings, D-Team members (i.e., the organization's teachers) transfer not only content knowledge, but also cultural knowledge about "what it means to be in the SSC," such as accepted SSC behaviors, values, and language that are rooted in the Bible. After new students enter the organization, D-Team students take it upon themselves to *develop and equip* these future leaders. According to Kim (2006), in her study of Korean American campus ministries, pairing older students with younger students in Christian organizations bolsters the group's ability to recreate itself. This reproduction can be beneficial, in that the group maintains a strong and consistent focus from year to year. That allows the group to recruit students who align with the mission and thereby maintain its subcultural identity on campus.

Thus, year after year, the D-Team members as leaders of the SSC's reproductive process "build up" and teach younger members how to be "truer Christians." There are liabilities associated with SSC's cultural reproduction, however. As D-Team members reproduce their sense of righteousness, the SSC becomes less willing or able to clearly recognize shortcomings of their culture. One SSC student commented that the goal of discipleship was to "make the disciple as good as or better than you." Because everyone shares a similar worldview, it becomes difficult over time to view the organization with fresh eyes and to reevaluate and improve beliefs and practices. Eims (1978) cautions against what he calls the "rose-colored glasses" danger:

> As you see disciples develop, you realize how far they have come, and watch their growing effectiveness for Christ, it is easy to become blind to their weaknesses. . . . So you miss whole areas of need in their lives with which you should deal. Again, exposing them to the influence and scrutiny of other godly men will help you evaluate their strengths and weaknesses objectively. (p. 106)

Although Matthew and the D-Team students monitor the group's shortcomings, their efforts are flawed because the SSC conducts these self-audits in isolation. The homogeneous membership exacerbates the SSC members' inability to self-audit their organization. Cross-organizational communication may help them discover their biases. Tierney (1993) suggests that campus groups participate in *dialogues across difference* to come to a richer understanding and appreciation of their commonalities and differences, as well as to see an unfiltered picture of their own organization. If SSC members were to break out of their isolated team structure and dialogue with other Christian and non-Christian organizations on campus in a nonthreatening *and* non-evangelizing way, they might learn more about themselves and be able to make improvements to their organization.

McMurtrie (1999) notes the rise in multifaith chapels being built at U.S. colleges and universities and the growing religious diversity on many campuses. She quotes Rabbi Susan Laemmle, dean of religious life at the University of Southern California, as saying, "The more students from different religious backgrounds can come together and interact, the more they're prepared for the so-called real world out there" (para. 16). McMurtrie speculates that isolated communities founded on righteousness, such as the SSC Servant Leadership Teams, may find themselves increasingly isolated from the campus community as more universities recognize the importance of preparing students to interact with others in the diverse world. Groups such as the SSC may be doing a disservice to the students whom they hope will go out and be agents of change after graduation. Tierney's (1993) call for dialogues across difference does not require students to lose their own faith identity or values; rather, the desired outcome is *enriched understanding*—which would certainly help the SSC better target their evangelism and discipleship efforts and achieve their mission to spread God's Word.

Summary

The SSC engages in a two-part outreach program comprising evangelism and discipleship. Evangelism builds upon the Bridge training and includes active outreach strategies to spread God's Word to larger groups of both Christian and non-Christian students. It also includes passive strategies in which students model a Christian lifestyle and pray for non-Christians to be receptive to God's Word. Evangelism works hand-in-hand with discipleship, which is a core value of the SSC. D-Team members work one-on-one with Christians to help them better understand and appreciate their faith. Although similar to other collegiate mentoring programs, discipleship meetings are more in-depth and personal. Both teams have a strong positive influence on students' learning about their own faith, developing their character and leadership skills, and contributing to the organization's retention of members; however, a potential liability of this level of involvement is the development of righteous attitudes among participants. Rather than viewing non-evangelical Christian students with "pity" because they are not "on the path to salvation," SSC participants could engage in dialogues with other organizations aimed at developing a deeper understanding and appreciation of their differences.

Despite their hesitations about engaging in substantive interactions with "the other" on campus, by the time SSC students reach their senior year, they begin to feel comfortable and skilled at sharing the Word with others through evangelism and discipleship. Yet, as graduation approaches, students' anxieties increase as they consider what life will be like outside the confines of their insular, supportive SSC environment. In the next chapter, we explore the ways SSC leaders provide students with the tools they believe will help them make their lives *all about Jesus* in the secular world through a unique, 4-week training program.

FROM COLLEGE SENIORS TO
REAL-WORLD EVANGELICALS

Transition Rituals

That's Life!—With Jesus

"Lord, we look forward to seeing what Matthew has to teach us as we prepare for the real world. Amen." As Brad concludes his prayer, Matthew clears his throat and declares, "We have 6 weeks of the semester left. Living a Lifetime with Christ (LLC) will help you make a transition from campus to the community." The seven seniors—three men and four women—listen carefully as Matthew describes the origin of this 4-week LLC seminar.

> After college I participated in the SSC internship program. My close friend . . . couldn't decide between applying for the [SSC] internship program or becoming a computer programmer. He prayed and God called him to become a computer programmer—to be a light for God. . . . His first 2 years after college he was a wreck. He didn't understand what being out of college looked like, especially in what his walk with God would be like. He was equipped to serve God when he was here, but no one helped him apply his Christian beliefs to his work and community.

Matthew explains how numerous Christian friends recounted similar stories, which prompted him to distribute a questionnaire to SSC alumni that asked what they wish they would have known about the "real world" before entering it. He assured participants that the 4-week seminar would be contemporary and relevant, and that he would solicit their input after they graduated.

These seven seniors, all of whom are Caucasian and all of whom have been active SSC members for at least 3 years, represent the organization's depth and uniformity. Tony looks more like a surfer than a stereotypical evangelical. His uncombed, dirty blond hair and unshaven face look perfect with his frayed shorts, flip-flops, and tattered T-shirt that reads "Jesus Lives." His attire dramatically contrasts with Caleb's, who showcases his recently buzz-cut hairstyle and wears a neatly pressed striped shirt, khaki shorts, and deck shoes. The four women's attire is nondescript and more similar to each other's than the men's. Their sundresses, mismatched sweat pants and shirts, or simple T-shirt-and-shorts ensembles augment their pulled-back hairdos and faces without makeup. Generally speaking, attendance is more important than attire. A similar argument could be made for the seminar location, which is the same as that of the Women's Bible study—an off-campus church conference room. The room's threadbare, colorless carpet, an aging conference table, and mismatched chairs convey that meeting in a Christian center is more important than gathering in one of the more chic on-campus accommodations.

Matthew appears somber and serious on this unseasonably warm March evening as he distributes a one-page summary of this SSC senior seminar and reads aloud the topics with which he intends to nourish this usually spiritually hungry cohort: "March 22: Introduction and Culture . . . March 29: Daily Walk and Schedule . . . April 12: Money Management and Stewardship . . . April 19: Relationships (Singlehood and Marriage)/Work and Ministry." Matthew asks Sarah to read aloud an extended quotation from a 1999–2000 SSC graduate that is printed on the bottom of the handout. With a warm smile, Sarah complies:

> I think in some naïve fashion or another, I believed life after college would be just as richly blessed with believers as life in college had been. I had no idea that fellowship would be so few and far between. . . . I expected to find a support network and large groups of friends like I had in school. I realize I was unrealistic, as my group of SSC friends was unique and could never be replaced. I am still in touch with about everyone, and I wish we could see each other as frequently as we did in school. Our reunions are even more joyful, however, and always incredibly deep and impactful, as we catch up in such a short amount of time. I . . . had to learn that my expectations were very naïve for what would be true in the "real world"— especially in . . . corporate America, where I find myself now.

As Sarah concludes, Matthew slowly surveys the faces of the attendees before asking, "What do you hear in this quote?" Tony replies, "Obviously, fellowship." Leslie adds, "Expectations are not always met." Matthew nods and replies, "Good. We can help you set expectations so that they are reasonable, and help you adjust to life after college. Expectations are good to have, but they can be difficult to set."

Edward enters with a swagger in his step and a hint of sweat on his forehead. He apologizes for being late and then takes a seat. The noise he creates as he retrieves his Bible and water bottle from his knapsack distracts the attendees as Matthew asks Liz to read a second SSC alumni quote:

> So you're about to graduate! If you are anything like me, your years in college have flown by. . . . Chances are your college experience has dramatically changed who you are. But guess what? The way you handle this next transition will mold the way you live your day-to-day life for the next forty years! I want to help you successfully make this transition, so that you can live the life of fulfillment and influence that God desires for you.

As Liz reads, Sarah highlights text on her handout. Edward plays with the tape holding his eyeglasses together as Molly kicks her spindly legs. Tony hoists his water bottle and sips water loudly, which draws attention away from Liz, who stares intently at the handout as she reads aloud. As Liz concludes, Matthew nods to Brad to read from a second handout a brief essay that discusses culture.

The anonymous essay predicts that graduates will be ill-prepared as they shift from college to their new work and home settings. Forecasts of stress and isolation are inevitable. As new professionals settle into their careers, larger life questions will emerge: "Who should I be in this world? What is God calling me to do? How can I make God real to my non-Christian friends? Where can I connect with other people my age who love God and know how to have fun?" The essay suggests that life experiences will help new professionals find answers to these difficult and important questions, but notes that it is essential for the new professionals to intentionally connect with like-hearted friends and to follow Christ.

Matthew interjects, "How do you get beyond college and live an integrated life with a compelling sense of purpose and meaning?" Without waiting for a reply, he explains that the goal of this class is to help prepare seniors to find answers to that question. He also promises to examine the major transition issues from college life to work life and propose ways to navigate them successfully.

Matthew allocates 5 minutes for the seniors to answer three questions: "[1] As you think about the transition, what are some feelings you have? [2] What are some issues you expect to face? [3] On a scale from 1 to 10, how difficult do you think this transition will be?"

Conversations and laughing accompany the completion of the task. "Is a '10' good or bad?" asks Leslie. Tony jokingly proposes that Matthew separate Sarah and Leslie because of their nonstop chatter; his comment does little to stifle the women's conversation. As students complete the written assignment, we peruse the handout, which includes a sidebar that an SSC alumnus wrote to provide three snippets of advice for the seniors: [1] Establish consistent quiet time before you graduate—it only gets more difficult; [2] Get your priorities in life set now, so you won't allow yourself to be swayed by Satan in the future; [3] Don't be afraid to take risks. It's a great way to depend fully on God rather than yourself.

Matthew's voice, which arches across the room, cuts the side conversations short. As all eyes focus on Matthew, he calls out, "What did you come up with for number 1?" One by one, the students produce a string of stiletto responses: "Uncertainty and anxiety." "No opportunity for intense growth." "I don't want to move away." "Excited and worried." "Getting out of the dorms." Matthew's head bobs nonstop as students share their responses.

When silence momentarily refills the room, Matthew exclaims, "Excellent! You are doing great." He follows with a second question: "What do *you* expect to face?" This question, like the others, elicits a series of brief responses: "Poverty." "Being exhausted." "No fellowship." "A loss of my identity as a student." "Accountability." Liz's response, "Living again with my parents," elicits the most chuckles, which continue as she adds, "I could last about 7 months with them; then I'd get kicked out." Pessimistic responses about the future are more plentiful than optimistic ones, but Molly asserts that she expects the transition to be different, but not necessarily harder.

Matthew asks Sarah to read John 17:13–18. In unison, the students retrieve Bibles from their backpacks and quickly locate the verse as Sarah reads aloud. Matthew then poses a series of questions: "Why does Jesus pray for the disciples? What does He think they need or want them to have? Why do you think Jesus sees things as necessary?" Tony's shuffling feet disturb the quiet of the room that, as usual, initially follows Matthew's barrage of questions. Responses to the question regarding the needs of the disciples include:

"Protection." . . . "Joy." . . . "Sanctification." . . . "Truth." Matthew follows with, "Why is joy important in this transition?" Tony replies, "To keep them going when things are up in the air." Matthew augments Tony's brief response: "Joy energizes us when we enter rough waters." He continues, "What about protection? Why protection?" Brad replies, "Satan comes after us when we are going through rough times. We are susceptible."

Matthew warns that SSC graduates at times get involved in cults because they are starved for fellowship. They also get involved with non-Christians and fall in with evil. He argues that Christians are susceptible when they are hurting or going through hard times. The links that Matthew establishes between cults and non-Christians and non-Christians and evil seem contrived and overstated, but the seniors appear to be unfazed by these juxtapositions. Caleb asks Matthew if Christian students are not "susceptible" while in college. Before Matthew can reply, Molly interjects, "In college, we're surrounded by Christian friends, and we have Jesus with us. We have intense growth, fellowship, and guidance. All of a sudden, disciples are thrown into the world without Jesus." Clutching his Bible with two hands, Matthew affirms Molly's thesis:

> College with a Christian organization is easier. In the real world, you go where you do not know people, and you might be [the] youngest, like at work. You don't always have interaction with people in your Christian walk at work. You might be close to some Christians, but you are further along than them on your journey. It is an eternal battle to decide what to do. . . . It is easy to fall and do stupid things when our support system goes away. We will see the habits of non-Christians.

Sarah, a student teacher, offers a real-world example. "Teachers gossiped during lunch. That was a daily struggle, and it made me uncomfortable." Matthew nods in agreement and argues that when Christians try to get out of uncomfortable situations they either allow themselves to get absorbed into the non-Christian world or they insulate themselves from the world. These individuals, for example, do good things at their church, but they do not evangelize. Matthew cites John 17 as he argues that students must stay focused on Jesus, no matter what. "This is a tension you will feel," he says. "You may have felt it here, but it will be magnified once you leave. You don't get to have influence on who you will work with and rub shoulders with. . . .

You need not be surrounded only by Christians. You need to stand out with non-Christians and be with God."

Molly gets up to open a few windows, but this effort does little to relieve the staleness of the room. The seniors appear energized and invested in the discussion, despite the stagnant air. Matthew's address to his loving community of believers reminds them that they have been in a cocoon of sorts while in college, and SSC has been their safe haven. But soon, he predicts, they will be marching into the belly of the beast, and seniors need to prepare for it. Matthew's dualistic and divisive rhetoric—Christians versus non-Christians; God versus Satan; college versus the real world; Christians versus real Christians—is troubling. The students neither notice nor challenge these "black or white" dichotomies and the absence of gray areas. Instead, they cling to his message and diligently record his advice in their notebooks.

Matthew introduces three principles to which students will adhere when they depart college. First, he argues, the attendees need to know what is coming and remember that God is with them throughout the transition. Matthew predicts that after graduation, students will experience a loss of spiritual motivation, become lethargic, and refrain from sharing the Gospel. "Keep memorizing Scripture," he charges. "These changes are natural; don't freak out." Second, Matthew predicts a grieving process after graduation. "You'll be getting up early, not staying up late, not being able to cut work like you cut classes, not easily getting your friends together, spending more time alone, and only staying in touch with two or three college friends." Following each of Matthew's "adult world" predictions, the seniors' collective anxieties seem to grow stronger. Matthew adds, "That's life! I keep in contact with one person from college each week. I also get together once a year with another group of friends. When we get together, there is a bond, but it is very different."

Matthew introduces his third point—that students will lose their naïveté. Immediately, Liz raises her hand and asks, "Is *naïveté* a word? How do you spell it?" Quietly, some peers snicker as Caleb defines and spells aloud "n-a-i-v-e-t-e," so Liz can record it in her notes. "Work is overrated," Matthew asserts. He continues, "People are not as happy as they thought they would be. Grads get ensnarled in the 'grass is always greener over there' syndrome. They have unrealistic expectations. . . . There's a lot of change. Don't be freaked out; it's normal."

Fear gradually appears on the faces of students wedged along the perimeter of the table as Matthew demands, "Know the culture." He systematically

TABLE 10.1
"College Life vs. Real Life" Handout

Campus Culture	Community Culture
All one age group	All different age groups
Conceptual environment	Concrete environment
One language	Many languages
Same purpose	Different purposes
More time	Less time

discusses the Culture Shock Cycle visual that appears on one of the handouts and warns students to be careful with the decisions they make, especially during the 8 months following graduation.

Matthew seems to be describing a utopian college as he compares it to his vision of the real world. "College is a fantasy where everyone is your age. It is easier to relate to people here." Matthew stands and approaches the blackboard to recreate a table as it appears in the handout (see Table 10.1).

This description of the campus culture (when compared to his community culture) is very different from the previous descriptions he has conveyed to the SSC flock. In this new framework, the within-campus student subcultures appear more homogeneous. When discussing the campus culture, Matthew emphasizes similarities, not differences. That is a dramatic change from his views expressed in previous training sessions and sermons. Matthew's campus–community dualism sends jolts of sobriety through the attendees. Around the room, the students' moods have shifted dramatically from stress-free, relaxed, and interested to troubled. Matthew describes numerous work scenarios; each one is less flattering than the previous one. I think to myself, "unemployment seems more appealing than work," as Matthew's pessimistic list grows. He then poses a rhetorical question: "If I am here to honor God and others do not, are we going to bump heads? How are you going to deal with this next year?"

Matthew draws a quiz on the blackboard to make certain that students remember the three principles and aspects of transition: [1] Know what's _____! [2] Know the _____! And [3] Tensions between the _____ and the _____. When students have called out the correct responses, Matthew places the chalk on the blackboard ledge and quietly sits down. He reminds the students, "All Christians are called to be

ministers of the Gospel." He instructs the seniors to turn to Acts 1:8 and
Romans 1:14–15, two passages that provide biblical support for his request for
students to spread the Word of God in work settings. Matthew reminds students that when Christ gives gifts to Christians, they must share them. "We
are indebted or obliged to spread God's love and increase the Kingdom."

Matthew stares at Liz, an art student, and asks the attendees, "Does God
want Liz to be a graphic designer?" When Liz responds "Yes," Matthew asks
her for a Scripture passage to back up her conclusion. Liz wrinkles her brow
and ignores Matthew's biblical citation challenge. Instead, she offers a passionate extemporaneous rationale for her decision: "God cares about me, and
He has planned out my life that includes being a graphic designer. He cares
about what I do, how I do it." Matthew chimes in, "God has uses for teachers, graphic designers, and administrators. Yet His ultimate goal is for us to
know Him. How does this relate to the secular and the sacred?" Sarah
responds, "As a student teacher I was a missionary disguised as a teacher."
Matthew nods his head to affirm Sarah's comment and then continues:

> Too many Christians divide their life into secular and sacred worlds. If you
> divide your life between secular (have to do) and sacred (what God wants
> you to do), you will be unhappy. If Liz is drawing [designer], her colleagues
> are not growing close to Christ. Likewise, if Sarah is teaching about Romeo
> and Juliet, God does not care if kids know about Romeo and Juliet. When
> you divide, you are missing what God is calling you to. God may be call-
> ing you, but not to teach or design graphics. He is sending you because He
> cares about the people there. He wants you to draw them to the Kingdom.
> When we draw our lives in that way, there is no sacred or secular divide; it
> is integrated. Does that make sense? That will challenge you, especially
> when you are disillusioned.

Tony reads the final advice sidebar from a 1998–99 SSC graduate: "My
prayer life is more meaningful and my connection in the vine is better . . .
because the trials of life necessitate that it be." Matthew immediately follows
with a handout titled "Thoughts on Launching." He proposes that students
answer the questions printed on the handout: [1] Reflect on your years at
_____. What did you learn about yourself? Get real with this and
think broadly . . . Extra credit for identifying things that are really cool about
you. [2] Conviction and foundation ideas—What are the one or two things
you want to keep in mind as you step out into the world? [3] Where do you

want to go after college? What does your heart say? [4] Begin a list of 100 things you want to do in your lifetime.

When Matthew allows them to share their responses, the students have numerous responses about what they have learned: "I did positive things." "I like things to go my way." "I can't survive without my family, but they can survive without me." "It is not good to label things." "Drunk people and high people are still people." "I can't do anything by myself." "If I go for personal achievement without God, I am miserable."

Approximately 2 hours after the seminar commenced, Edward offers a closing prayer: "Thank you for teaching us what is coming up. We take to heart what Matthew imparts on us. We pray to encourage and support others as we head toward bumpy roads. We will make the most of our life and glorify You. We will depend on You to give us open hearts. Bless our weekends and nights. Amen."

Walking with Jesus Every Day

By 7:15, nine seniors have arrived—five men and four women. As always, the meeting begins with a prayer: "Heavenly Father, thank You for this chance to come together and learn more about You and our lives as we come closer to graduation. Thank You, Lord Jesus, for the lessons Matthew bestows on us. Amen." "Any lingering questions?" Matthew asks. Andy, who missed the previous seminar, inquires, "What did you do last week?" Tony offers a humorous summary while remaining deadpan serious: "We'll be busy, lonely, have no free time. Don't join a cult, and don't date a non-Christian. Basically, life will bite. Oh yeah, and make a list of 100 things you want to do." After the rowdy laughter subsides, Matthew responds, "Not a bad summary. You missed a good week." The atmosphere appears mostly upbeat as the seniors settle themselves around the conference table for round two of their senior seminar. Tonight's topic is "Schedule and Daily Walk."

"Schedule dictates walk!" Matthew declares, as he instructs students to turn to the second page of his handout entitled "Time and Life Management." Andy reads aloud the opening paragraph, which acknowledges the obvious—all humans manage life demands. The handout asserts that Christians need bedrock foundations that will withstand life and time demands in order to achieve a sense of harmony with God as they progress through life toward death.

Matthew asks Edward to read aloud Ephesians 5:15–17 and John 5:19. The students' interpretations of these two passages sounds like a hodgepodge of biblical clichés: "Sin is all around us." "Remember the evils of the day." "Avoid temptations." "There is so much more we should be doing." Matthew offers a hyper-condensed summary of the students' comments: "Christians have limited time on earth, and they need to use it wisely." Liz returns to the temptation theme and claims that Christians get sucked into things, which sometimes compromises their faith. Matthew cites an Ephesians passage to support the biblical claim that world systems are under Satan's control and the world is moving away from God. Although sincere and serious, this biblical claim sounds part conspiracy theory, part doomsday prediction. Still, Matthew continues as he highlights Christians' struggles in a secular world:

> Bucking societal norms is hard work. If we relax our Christian faith, we will be seduced by evil societal mores. Christians need to be careful how they live and must continually try to understand God's will. If seniors are to live a godly life, they must intentionally allocate their time to God and must be mindful of the decisions they make.

Matthew momentarily shifts from the topic of *time* to the topic of *order*, as he quotes Richard Halverson:

> Order is the first law of heaven. Order is fundamental to life. Its alternative is chaos! Planets move in their courses according to divine order . . . if they did not, they would destroy one another. If they did not, there would be no space for science. . . . In fact there would be no science at all. . . . For science is dependent upon observable order. God who ordained physical order also ordained moral and spiritual order! Violation of the moral and spiritual order is as totally destructive as violation of the physical order. We ignore that fact to our doom!

In most corners of the university, Matthew's analysis, which entangles science with religion, would spark a hotly contested debate—but here with these SSC students, a desire to critically analyze the message is not evident. "Why is this passage relevant?" Matthew asks. This follow-up question generates an eclectic mosaic of responses: "If there is no order, we are doomed." "We need an organized life if we are to get the most out of it."

Matthew uses the students' responses to interconnect time with order. He reads a passage from the handout that argues, "Time is precious; we are fragile and life is short."

Matthew warns that Christians should be neither too ordered nor too disorganized; if the former, they miss fun and spontaneity, and if the latter, they may fall into chaos. He offers practical time management tips: If a person adds something to his or her life that takes time, that person has to take away something that takes the same amount of time. He advocates that his Christians eliminate frivolous activities such as surfing the Internet. Such sacrifices will allow them to invest more of their time in Christian endeavors. Andy's question, "Is it right to get upset with people close to you who demand your time?" focuses his peers' attention. He elaborates that he refers to "people who call on you when they need you. What do we do to be a good servant?" Immediately, Matthew declares, "Good question. Early on, I'd help them. If a pattern of dysfunction emerges, I'd confront the person. You have to confront them when people make bad decisions against God." Molly offers a kinder and gentler addendum to Matthew's confrontational and hard-line advice. "Remember, there are different relationships—parents, sisters, friends, and acquaintances. For close people, we have different standards."

Matthew quickly shifts gears as he holds up the handout, like a lawyer offering evidence to a jury. On the handout are six steps Christians can take to ensure that there is enough time for Christian activity in their lives. As Matthew continues, I (Peter) review the printed list: [1] Learn to expect the unexpected. Because most everything takes longer than anticipated, build margin into your planning. [2] Learn to say no. Contrary to your perception, you are not indispensable. [3] Cut down on activities, as they have a way of self-perpetuating and multiplying. [4] Practice simplicity and contentment. Choose to live with less. [5] Get less done, but do the right things. Assess all your activities. [6] Decide to live the life of Jesus—whatever the cost.

Matthew emphatically states that the seniors should *"choose the important over the urgent!"* His advice keeps on coming: "Determine what is fixed, you know, the things we must do and what is discretionary. Spending time with God is mandatory." The students struggle to reach a consensus about what is important versus what they perceive as urgent. Matthew draws a diagram on the board to show them what God considers urgent (see Figure 10.1).

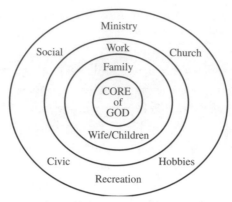

Figure 10.1. SSC Post-college Priorities

Matthew explains that all humans manage time, and there are competing demands. In order for Christians to reach equilibrium, they must identify bedrock foundations that will guide their decisions when inevitable
competing demands arise. Matthew carefully discusses each ring of the hub
in his visual; he begins with the core, which (predictably) is God. He states
emphatically that "God has to be in the forefront, the center. . . . The man
of God must maintain this core, even as things like work, money, and pleas-
ure vie for this core position." As always, Matthew accompanies his assertions
and recommendations with biblical evidence. He cites Mark 12:29–33,
Corinthians 6:19–20, and Matthew 6:33 as the final words on this topic. Students casually search their Bibles and locate the passages Matthew mentions,
recording the citations in their notebooks.

Matthew acknowledges the multitude of demands in Christian's lives as
he discusses the second priority ring. He argues that if "man" is married, the
family is his second-highest priority. I (Peter) expect the women in attendance to question why the visual and Matthew's commentary exclusively
mention and seemingly privilege men, while ignoring women. Neither men
nor women raise a stir regarding these seemingly exclusionary assertions.
Instead, students locate the biblical passages—Ephesians 5:23–33 and Titus 1:
6–9—that support this claim and review them.

As the seniors focus on the third circle in the concentric circle hub,
Matthew reads the handout and asserts: "God gives authority and responsibility to all *men* to work. . . . Work is an important part of life, but we have
to keep our work and profession in perspective." He warns that work can

eclipse God and family, which is contrary to the Bible's teachings. He offers a barrage of biblical passages to support this claim.

"Every man has the task of sorting through many options for his discretionary times." Matthew uses this quote to discuss the final ring in his concentric circle visual. He mentions activities such as church, ministry, social life, civic action, recreation, and hobbies. The relative position of these activities on his diagram reminds seniors that these important and valuable aspects of one's life should never overpower the other three priorities of God, family, and work. Matthew asserts that too much time devoted to work and friends pulls Christians outward—away from God, the hub of the schema.

Matthew argues that if seniors remember the relative importance of these three competing domains on their time, strength will follow. If Christians invest their energies too heavily in outer rim activities, they will be ineffective tools for God. Matthew generates a series of questions: "How will your daily schedule impact your walk with God? How will you ensure each day you have quiet time with God, prayer, Bible study, Scripture memory, witnessing, and fellowship?" His answers follow: "Be intentional. . . . Don't let your life with God suffer, because your life will suffer. . . . Connect with God each day. . . . I have worked with you for 4 years to be freaks. When you get out of here you will struggle to find folks like yourself."

Money and Jesus

I (Peter) expect tonight's seminar, "Asset Management," to focus on seniors' spiritual assets as they depart college. But as Matthew introduces his father, John, as the guest lecturer, I suddenly realize that the focus is on managing fiscal, not spiritual, assets. I take my seat at the far end of the table and launch my computer's word processing application to record my field notes. This evening Matthew sets aside one topic that I know little about—the Bible— and substitutes finance, a topic about which I am equally uninformed. Although estranged from this evening's seminar topic, I experience a superficial sense of camaraderie with John, who appears to be close to my age. For once, I might not be the oldest person attending an SSC event. I settle into my chair and prepare for what the 14-page handout suggests will be an ambitious agenda.

The regulars are in attendance. Caleb stands tall and stretches his lanky body before settling into his seat. Liz and Sarah slap hands; the origin of their enthusiasm escapes me. Personable Tony caucuses with Brad in one corner of the room; from afar, it sounds like sports talk. Molly, forcing a smile, appears exhausted and a bit disengaged; she sits alone and organizes her Bible, water bottle, and notebook. Sarah navigates around the umbrellas and fluorescent rain slickers that students have haphazardly strewn throughout the room. Liz circulates a package of store-bought cookies. Andy, as always, assumes the role of observer.

Following Matthew's brief introduction of his father, John prays aloud and then acknowledges his gratitude for the invitation to speak. He confesses from the outset that he did not make a lot of money while working: "I'm a middle-class, conservative, hardworking father." His sincerity compensates for his monotone presentation style. Students appear fascinated with John's introductory comments, which center on Matthew's upbringing. Instead of their usual note taking, their eyes are on John as they listen attentively.

The students learn that Matthew's mother did not work, and that the presenter attended a nearby rival university and majored in accounting. John's mention of the rival college draws a few whispered "boos" from the men. Students also learn that after college, John worked for several companies, mostly on budgets and finance issues. He proudly announces that he retired when he was 46 years old—a goal he had set as a young adult.

John's goal for the evening is to share his wisdom about asset management. His opening advice resembles a checklist that is simple, straightforward, and sounds intuitively "right"—even to finance-phobic people like me. "Common sense is all you need. . . . Set goals and priorities, and plan to achieve these goals. . . . Stay on course. . . . Ask questions; the only dumb question is the one you don't ask. . . . I hope this information makes a difference in your life."

John invites students to share their career aspirations. Sarah and Caleb proudly proclaim that they have been selected as SSC interns and will be working on college campuses in the fall. Other seniors' job aspirations include teacher, graphic designer, sales representative, and computer programmer/consultant. John introduces and defines the concepts of assets and liabilities, then concludes his opening primer with a statement that affirms my naïve understanding of finance: "Having more assets than liabilities is good."

John allows the seniors to briefly discuss money—a topic I suddenly realize that SSC students seldom raise. SSC staff and students appear to live modestly within their fiscal means. They have sufficient funds to attend programs such as post-Friday worship program outings, spring break trips, camping outings, SSC-sponsored off-campus seminars at nearby colleges, and worldwide missionary trips. SSC staff members or students seldom complain about their short-term needs of making ends meet each week, or their long-term college debt realities. Caleb and Sarah joke about how their upcoming SSC internships are not like the fast track to getting rich (at least financially). Liz worries about securing a job as a graphic designer. The two aspiring women teachers—Molly and Leslie—express concerns about making ends meet. Andy appears the most confident about earning money as a computer programmer and immediately repaying his college debt.

This "Accounting 101 seminar" takes a surprising turn when John asks students to open their Bibles and turn to Luke 16:11–13. Once I realized the business focus of this evening's seminar, I did not expect to make use of my loaner Bible. Once again, however, the SSC "reality" confronts my preconceived notions, and my preconceived notions lose as the Bible takes its place at center stage. John continues, "How will you manage the assets that have been entrusted to you by God?" Students exchange interpretations about the Luke verse and readily generate a list of the potential evils of money. A discussion of money and priorities follows. John keeps refocusing the students' attention on God, rather than on the accounting or finance-related issues that students raise. "Remember," he says, "assets are given to us by God. He is loaning them to us. He is entrusting us to do good. . . . It is hard to serve two masters; too often we get caught up with money and forget God."

John continues to assemble an unusual (at least for me) collage of accounting and biblical principles. He instructs students to review passages from Proverbs, Malachi, and Romans prior to discussing the topics of saving and giving money. Students conclude that the Malachi passage, which centers on tithing, is an appropriate reminder as they prepare to exit the SSC organization. It demonstrates that they recognize the SSC's need for external funding in order to sustain its existence. The Proverbs verse reminds students of their privilege and their need to give alms to the poor. The Romans passage instructs students to give to other Christians. In total, the emphasis favors giving, not receiving.

John sandwiches his sage advice between students' comments and their interpretations of the biblical quotations: "Be careful to avoid 'get rich quick' schemes. . . . Remember, God is testing you. . . . Your tithe should be 10 percent. . . . God says 'test me and I will take care of you.' . . . God represents the poor; if you give your assets to the poor, you are giving to God." He warns students that their current priorities will change over time, which leads him to make one final recommendation—continually reevaluate your priorities. "Once a year, sit down with your wife and see where you want to go."

As I frequently do during these presentations, I bridle my tongue and silently wonder about student anomalies, outliers, or outsiders. In this instance, I wonder if *all* attendees expect to marry so that they can eventually sit down with their spouse and reevaluate priorities. I struggle to discern if John's "spouse" reference is an expectation, or a result of his sloppy oratorical style. As usual, the students do not react, and they seem oblivious to the power of language as a means to shape culture.

John effortlessly blends accounting and biblical discourses into his commentary. Thirty minutes into this seminar, I have an epiphany of sorts—the Bible has much to say about money. "How do you accumulate assets?" John asks. Responses to his question are short and predictable: "By praying." "Working." "Borrowing." John asks students to turn to their handout, locate the Bible passages he listed, and review them. One book—Proverbs—I immediately recognize. The Philippians and Thessalonians books are unfamiliar to me, because SSC students and staff seldom mention them.

When referring to Philippians, John asserts that if Christians are down to their last dollar, God will respond. He continues, "Don't worry about money. . . . It works out; we are still here. . . . Trust me. We get assets through hard work, gifts, and also through wise asset management." John uses the Thessalonians passage to focus on gaining assets through labor. The three Proverbs passages help students discern Bible-wise approaches to asset management.

John mimics his son's pedagogy. Both individuals are knowledgeable about the topics they profess. Their detailed handouts are useful guides during presentations and invaluable artifacts long after the sessions conclude. The sequencing of the handouts suggests that both individuals have clear goals, as well as unambiguous and ambitious action plans. Both John and Matthew have a command of the Bible and couple these truths with everyday common sense to offer guidance about life's challenges. Both men attempt to induce a Socratic dialogue with their students. Typically, they pose a question or dilemma, invite students to respond, probe by critiquing the students' arguments, probe some more, and then declare what is "right." During sessions that they are leading, they both tend to talk more than listen. Teaching the Bible trumps collecting students' views.

Students' responses to John are similar to their reactions to Matthew's approach to teaching: They are polite; they ask good questions; they seldom challenge their elders; they almost always defer if conflict or dissent arises; and they are grateful for the knowledge their elders impart. As a professor, there are aspects of the pedagogy that appeal to me, especially Matthew and John's knowledge, organizational skills, passion for teaching, and genuine concern for students. Less desirable aspects include their preference for a Socratic dialogue that sometimes resembles a lecture.

After establishing a biblical foundation for gaining assets and discussing the mechanics of acquiring it, John explicitly introduces four purposes of money. Not surprisingly, he uses the Bible as the final authority. He mentions Matthew 6:26, 28–30 to introduce the idea that a primary purpose of money is to provide basic needs. He cites passages from Psalms and James to make the biblical case that Christians should use money to confirm direction (i.e., God's will). The topic of Christians giving money to Christians, the church, widows, the poor, and missionaries dominates this segment of the lecture. Romans 12:13 and Corinthians 8:14 are John's biblical foundation for his mandates. Matthew smiles at Caleb and Sarah as John uses the two soon-to-be SSC staff members as an example of the need for Christians to donate to Christian missionaries.

John clarifies the fourth purpose of money—to illustrate God's power—by having students read Psalm 50:15 and Acts 5:12–14. He packages his advice into short phrases that are easily digestible by students: "God did not heal these people because they were rich, but rather because they were faithful. . . . Remember, there's a link between life priorities and establishing a balanced budget." John encourages attendees to identify their priorities. One by one, students offer their one-word responses. Some responses are practical, and others are faith-based: "Family." . . . "You stole mine; I was going to say family; Okay, faith." . . . "Health." . . . "Getting a job and maintaining it." . . . "God." John affirms each response and connects the students' ideas to the importance of compromise with one's spouse.

Brad and Sarah sit together; they scribble notes on their handout as John shifts his focus to discuss the inexact science of budgeting. Students brainstorm a predictable list of exemplars that includes food, housing, healthcare, education, and haircuts. John follows up: "If expenses are more than income, that's a problem." He uses one of his cousins as an example to bring abstract, budget-related concepts to life. John advises students to create weekly, monthly, and annual budgets that include conservative estimates of income and conservative estimates of spending. The ultimate goal, students learn, is a balanced budget in which income equals or exceeds spending.

Up to this point, John's presentation has mostly made the obvious obvious and the familiar familiar to the attendees, even novices like me. During John's next segment, I contract a headache and a sudden case of carpal tunnel syndrome as I frantically attempt to type the key points of his obtuse mini-lecture. Purchase-price averaging, 401K plans, diversifying investments, asset leveraging—I, along with the students, struggle to record key points of this informative, yet rapidly paced presentation.

Temporarily oblivious to the speed of his presentation and the not-so-knowledgeable attendees, John charges on. "Get a financial advisor. . . . Avoid short-term debt, because it usually has high interest. . . . Get a 401(k) account; you never see the money, so you never miss it. . . . Buy low and sell high. . . . Stay in the stock market for the long term or don't get in it at all. . . . Diversify investments: get land, stocks, bonds. . . . Monitor your portfolio. . . . Consult with your financial advisor. . . . Know your risk tolerance." Students struggle to dig themselves out of the avalanche of information. Brad shakes his writing hand to get his blood recirculating. I suspect that the presentation speed and the dense content are contributing to the dearth of questions.

"Avoid short-term debt. What does that mean? Like credit cards. They will charge you a 21-percent fee. Over time, you'll pay more on interest than the original loan." Liz and Brad look like they have been caught with their hands in the proverbial cookie jar as John's credit card lecture unfolds. Their smirks are a dead giveaway that they understand firsthand the concept of short-term debt. Students gain a brief respite from the fast-paced lecture as they reverse roles with John. For a few minutes, the seniors act as teachers and John as the student. They discuss the "unethical" strategies that credit cards companies use to lure students into accepting their cards and the woes associated with not paying on time. These usually trusting and optimistic seniors exhibit a degree of skepticism and cynicism that I seldom observe. Using all caps, I type the word "REFRESHING" into my field notes.

The landslide of information and definitions continues: "cash, savings accounts . . . checking accounts . . . money market funds . . . certificates of deposit . . . stocks and bonds . . . mutual funds . . . rental property . . . life insurance . . . fine art and land investments." Students remain prayerfully silent as John unpacks the terms. The attendees have heard many of them, but they publicly confess they know little about them. Caleb scratches his head as he tries to discern the most relevant information to include in his notes. John's comments are thorough and logically sequenced, yet dense. He regularly asks the students if they have questions, and their collective response is silence. Nevertheless, they seem to welcome John's extended real-life examples.

Typically, I feel like a stranger in a strange land as students recite and translate Bible passages, but my usual biblical confusion pales in comparison to my confusion with the content of this retirement planning seminar. Suddenly, I long for a Corinthians verse to chew on. Tony, with a smirk about to hatch on his face, leans toward me and whispers, "If you don't have any money, this stuff really doesn't matter."

After a long hiatus, the Bible as a money management guide reappears in the lecture when John presents his closing arguments. "Pray to God for guidance. . . . Establish godly goals and priorities. . . . Plan actions to meet your goals and priorities. . . . Employ effective asset management techniques, such as regular investing. . . . Stay invested and diversify your investments. . . . Regularly consult with financial advisors and, if possible, Christian advisors."

In unison, the students thank John. Leslie then offers the closing prayer: "Thank You, Father, for helping us to understand the resources You give. We pray You will give us wisdom and insights as we juggle more than usual. We pray You will give us patience and understanding. Thanks for blessing us. In the name of Jesus, Amen." Matthew embraces his father as the prayer concludes, and the students wish God's blessing on one another before they depart. Money and Jesus—a provocative duo and unlikely bedfellows, I think to myself, as I exit the Christian church into the rainy night.

Ministering in the Name of Jesus

I conduct a mental roll call as the opening prayer commences. "Heavenly Father, we thank You for the beautiful day, Your awesome creation, and pray we can have open hearts and minds and learn from each other, Matthew, and

You. In Your name, Amen." I quietly conclude, "Hail, hail the gang's all here." Andy, Brad, Molly, Caleb, Tony, Sarah, Liz, Leslie, and Edward are present and accounted for.

T-shirts, shorts, and sandals appear to be the attire of choice this evening as attendees prepare for the final Living a Lifetime with Christ (LLC) seminar. Matthew rallies the troops in his quiet and no-nonsense manner. "This is our last meeting, and we have our senior outing on Saturday. We have a lot to cover. It is going to be full." Matthew reminds students that this evening's seminar will cover two topics. The first centers on godly relationships, and the second on work and ministry. Matthew acknowledges that originally he envisioned this senior seminar as a 5-week program, but scheduling snafus condensed it to 4. That necessitates combining today's topics. "It'll work," he assures the seniors.

Matthew distributes a handout entitled "Godly Relationships" and reveals that he will not be discussing it in depth this evening. Instead, he encourages attendees to read the entire document later in the week and e-mail him if questions arise. Matthew begins tonight's lecture with an assertion that he made in the previous three sessions: that feelings of isolation and loneliness will likely accompany graduates as they transition from college to their respective communities. This evening he adds a new twist to this familiar message—marriage.

> Up until this point in your life you may have always considered marriage to be something far off in the distance, but now it becomes more of a real possibility. Soon, you'll be on your own and making money. Why not consider marriage? . . . You need to trust God for a spouse. *You* do not need to control it. Don't go on a mate hunt just to relieve the loneliness and isolation you might feel, and don't despair. I was married when I was 28. What does it look like? Here I am. . . . Listen to what God is calling you to do. Sometimes when you get to be 25 or so, you start feeling like you should not trust God. . . . Some Christians join a dating service or a singles group. What this packet talks about is that God wants us to focus on Him and His purpose in our lives. Searching is a waste of time. Wait for God. He uses loneliness to increase our desire for Him. If you respond to His wishes, this can be a time of growing intimacy with Him, as long as you honestly face the realities of your experience and take them to Him in prayer. God knows what is best. If you have questions, ask God.

Matthew briefly discusses appropriate ways to relate to the opposite sex by citing guidance included in multiple verses from Corinthians. Unlike his usual pedagogy, which asks students to interpret biblical passages and grapple with the embedded meaning, today he cuts to the quick and reveals the morals of the stories. "The right way to live is in undivided devotion to the Lord, whether single or married . . . the commitment to obeying God must be foundational in our lives if we are to walk with God." Matthew recites an Ephesians verse and then reads from the handout: "A husband is commanded to love his wife, since her primary need is love. The wife is commanded to respect her husband, since his primary need is respect." I regret not having the opportunity to listen to students discuss this topic and to learn more about Matthew's interpretation of Ephesians, and how students should enact these lessons in their everyday actions.

Matthew, obviously on a mission to efficiently conclude this godly relationship mini-lecture, introduces multiple purposes of marriage. I follow along as Matthew synthesizes the handout's key arguments and offers preparation-for-marriage tips. He briskly sketches out the roles of the husband and wife in marriage and offers some practical tips for singles. I skim the handout suggestions as Matthew wraps up this segment:

1. Don't make marriage your top priority. Serving God and others comes first. Focus on building friendship. Don't jump ahead in your mind and quickly decide if he or she "is the one." It is not wrong to desire and plan for marriage, but it can't be the central focus of your life.

2. Don't put your life on hold thinking you will get married soon. Pursue grad school and other career options. Take advantage of training opportunities, explore short-term mission opportunities . . . Be adventurous!

3. Acknowledge the dilemma of modern society. The age of puberty is getting younger and the age of marriage is getting older. In big cities, the average age of women getting married is 26 and men is 29. It requires vigilance and self-control to remain pure.

4. Learn to resolve conflicts. It is easy as singles to avoid relationships where there is tension. If a relationship goes bad, it is tempting to walk away and not deal with underlying issues or work it through to biblical forgiveness.

5. . . . It is not wrong to desire certain qualities or have some standards for the person you're looking for, but be aware of the danger of so idealizing the list that no flesh-and-blood person could ever measure up. Your

preconceived notions can protect you from risking the disappointment that comes in every relationship, and they can prevent your heart from maturing.

6. Another danger of the checklist is falling for someone who seems perfect, but discovering that person doesn't feel the same. You are then left dismayed and discouraged by God's withholding of something you believe is so good for you.

As I continue to ponder these tips, Matthew introduces the evening's second seminar topic—ministry in work contexts. He offers some brief opening remarks: "God gave us jobs to do, like Adam and Eve. . . . We work to get money. . . . We need money to buy things. . . . Money is a source of evil. When we work, we work for *Him,* not ourselves." Sarah recites verbatim a Scripture verse suggesting that humans work to glorify God. Matthew poses the question: "What is the purpose of work in God's Kingdom?" Brad responds, "Spread your witness of the Lord." Matthew entertains a few additional student insights and then boldly proclaims, "Work is ministry." He continues, "If there are no Christians in graphic design, who will minister to them? God puts us in different places to minister to other people. . . . He takes advantage of an opportunity to get us around people." Tony asks if Christians need to have a job in order to minister. Edward quickly reminds his peers that housewives minister. Caleb argues that Paul in the Bible worked not to be a burden to others. He follows with a more contemporary conclusion: "So we are not sponging off of other people all the time. We should work, so we can eat."

Matthew reminds the students that Christians work to gain money to give to the Kingdom. An Ephesians verse (4:28) supports his claim. He abruptly shifts to sloth—one of the deadly sins. "God created us to work; we are fulfilling His will. . . . We should find a sense of satisfaction in that." Matthew asserts, "Work is important, but it should not distract you from your relationship with God (i.e., the core of the concentric circles illustration) and your family."

Matthew appears to be preaching to the choir. I have come to know that these students all possess a good old-fashioned work ethic. On the proverbial showhorse-to-workhorse continuum, these students are definitely workhorses. Their allegiance to the Almighty and to their families suggests that they are revved up and ready to "hit the ground running" as their careers commence. They will not struggle with the sloth-related concerns that Matthew raises in this segment of his presentation.

Matthew ratchets up the volume of his voice as he announces, "Let's move into ministry. . . . When you leave here, your ministry will be one of three places: work, home, or play. Focus your ministry in at least one of these places." Matthew tells the story of a friend who worked with older colleagues, which hindered his ability to minister to them. He shifted gears and discovered that his neighbors were more receptive to his ministering invitations. "Wherever you are, pray and identify a place of witness."

Matthew shifts to a new teaching technique—the hypothetical situation survey—to which students respond favorably:

> Okay, you're at work. Let's take Andy. He's got a job and works on computers and programming and stuff. He goes to work every day and meets people. He meets one guy and learns there is a Bible study group meeting next Tuesday. Andy tells the guy that he will think about it. Next Tuesday, do you go to the Bible study? Who is going?

A show of hands reveals that the group is almost evenly split. Attendees' rationales follow. "If they are already Christians, why minister to them?" "I agree; they are not the ones who need help. They are not on my target list." Liz reveals that she would rather reach out to nonbelievers. Edward argues that if he were not affiliated with a church, he would attend the Bible study to be with other Christians. "What's the right answer?" asks Brad. Matthew, sidestepping the request, recommends that students pray to find out God's plan for them—a familiar response, I have noticed, to many questions. He follows up, however, with a more definitive answer.

Matthew reveals that he based this scenario on the real-life experiences of a friend. Matthew's advice is for students to research workplace politics before affiliating with a Christian subculture. "Walls will go up. Be careful not to be lumped into a broad category of Christians, because those people may have a negative reputation at that particular workplace." Caleb inquires, "Should you deny being a Christian [if asked]?" Resisting a simple "yes" or "no" response, Matthew launches into a mini-sermon on religion and politics. "On campus, ministering happens fast. In the working world, it could take up to 5 years for your colleagues to trust you. The culture here is different. *Understand* the politics of your workplace." Then, to directly respond to Caleb's question, Matthew replies, "I would not tell them I am Christian. Tell them 'I follow Jesus, without being weird.'" Tony replies, "Cool answer."

Brad asks, "Is there a biblical justification?" Matthew replies, "Yes," and rattles off Colossians 4:5–6. He then warns, "We need to be wise when we talk. We don't have the option of saying 'I am not a Christian.' We have to be honest. . . . Remember, Paul communicates the Gospel differently in different places.

"What are the advantages of being new [i.e., in a work setting]?" Matthew asks. Liz replies, "You have a clean slate." "What else?" Matthew probes. Brad responds, "Everyone will talk to you." Sarah follows, "You don't have enemies." Matthew expands on these brainstormed ideas:

> What other advantages? You are ignorant. You aren't expected to know anything. You have an opportunity to ask questions of everyone. When you ask questions and converse, you let them know about your life, and you learn about others. You learn about politics. Make it a priority to ask questions; you will be far ahead and learn the politics—who will help you and who will not. You will endear yourself to others. Ask others what you should know. As a new person, there is a brief opportunity. Listen. Keep your mouth shut; occasionally ask. Don't jump in before you understand the politics.

Like all organizations, especially collegiate student organizations, the SSC is a political entity, though SSC staff members seldom use the "P-word." With God on their side, these Christians don't think in terms of political assessments; instead, they follow the teachings of the Bible. The SSC is also a very strategic organization, but because of its unswerving commitment to following the Bible, SSC members initially mask, to the casual observer, their politics and strategic maneuvering. In this instance, Matthew lays bare the organization's political strategy:

> Once you know your work politics, how do you minister? How do we meet them on campus? We use a survey. That would be a weird idea in an office or school. Get to know people, invite them to lunch or to Tupperware parties. Avoid surveys. Any way you can get next to people in small groups is a good idea. The methods we use on campus that serve us well here won't work there. We need to understand the principles underneath the methods used here and apply them in the workplace.

Matthew prods the students to brainstorm implicit and explicit practices that the SSC employs to reach non-Christians. A cavalcade of predictable responses follows: "Ask questions." . . . "Find out what they do." . . . "Use your basic people skills." . . . "Interact with them on their turf, then they will come to your turf." . . . "Pay attention to details and read between the lines." . . . "Get to know people during your first weeks on the job and learn names. That will endear you to them—and know their kids' names." Matthew adds the final word by stressing the need to pray and apply what students have been taught to new settings.

Ministry in the community is Matthew's next topic for discussion. "At home, people know who you are. Getting to know people and neighbors is important. . . . You have to take the initiative, if you want something to happen. If not, relationships do not happen. People sit in their apartments wishing they knew someone. Invite someone to dinner; do it the first month. If you wait, it'll get progressively more awkward." Matthew asks students to discern differences between ministering at work and in the community. After a few moments of silence, he uses Don (the SSC regional trainer) as an example to clarify these differences.

"Don is a handyman and uses that in his neighborhood. What Don does well is, he serves—no matter if a handyman or a missionary. Look for ways to serve those around you—take in neighbors' trashcans. Get to know them. People skills are important. Initiate contact, or it won't get done. They won't come to you." Matthew posits that it is easier to build ministry momentum in a community than at work. He recommends that attendees invite neighbors with good relational standing to informal readings of the Bible. "To us it sounds hard and scary, but we [i.e., SSC] have community staff who do this, and they say people are generally open."

Matthew turns the group's attention toward Church ministry as he serves up another hypothetical situation. "You live in a new city. You don't know anybody. You find a church. You tell your pastor about your SSC experience. The pastor lets you know the church has a need for someone to lead an adult service. He asks you. What would you do?" As it was before, the group is split. Proponents argue that if they had time, they would do it; it's the Christian thing to do. Matthew emerges as an opponent:

> I would ask questions. Is it a good church? I would find out more about the curriculum. I might wait for a while. If you are the new guy and automatically become a new leader, you could offend some people. Remember, you don't have to have a [formal] position to minister. Pray about it.

Matthew then raises additional concerns, which dampens proponents' desire to satisfy their new hypothetical pastor. He extends the hypothetical situation and adds new issues for students to consider: "Seven months out, you decide to lead it. It goes great, and the pastor wants you to do more with the church. What do you notice about this situation?" Sarah refers back to the concentric circles diagram and notes that the church, the outer band, is far removed from the core, which is God. She suggests, "If we get too involved in the church, it might pull us away from God." To a nonbeliever like me, the argument appears ironic. Involving oneself in the church seems like the ultimate way to be close to God—but to the Christian seniors and Matthew, Sarah's argument "makes sense." Matthew adds:

> The centrifugal force [i.e., of the church] will pull you away from your core. You are equipped and you can help out. . . . Be careful; they will ask for more and more of your time. It is not wrong, but wise for them. But before you know it, you're at the church all the time and your ministry with non-Christians is gone. *Be aware.* You are *freaks* in the majority of churches. They will want you to do as much as you can. You might have to say, "No," so you can hang out with non-Christians. Pastors will support your decisions. The reality is that you need to reach out to non-Christians. Be aware [that] churches will suck you in, even pretty good churches.

Matthew's commentary affirms our suspicions about the SSC's lukewarm endorsement of formal and mainstream religious organizations. Although not hostile, the SSC remains respectfully skeptical. Caleb asks, "If they are your spiritual leaders, do you have to follow them?" Matthew indirectly answers the question by replying, "You will have more than one spiritual leader. To me, we have to follow God, but it is easy to deceive ourselves. There is wisdom in gaining many counselors' input. We don't want to be renegades, but we need to be wise and follow God. . . . Our alumni have a hard time finding a good church. One graduate said it was like winning a lottery." Matthew details his qualities of a "good" church by posing a series of questions and following up with his editorial commentary:

> Do they preach the truth? Do they preach the Word of God? What is their mission? What are their goals and priorities? Do they have an inward or

outward focus? Do they develop people? Are there discipleship opportunities? These questions so far are about what the church can do for you. You need to ask what you can do to serve the church. How can you be involved? Too often we look for churches to serve us. We need to find out how you can serve the church. Pray for these decisions. . . . Good churches are few and far between. Remember, church is luxury, not a necessity.

Matthew pleads with the students to continue their discipleship relationships after they graduate. He encourages them to be discipled and to disciple others. "If it stops, I have failed in my job. The most important question is, 'Do I have an active ministry to both Christians and non-Christians?' Hopefully, you will answer 'Yes' to both."

Matthew gathers his belongings as he prepares his closing comments. He assures these seniors that he will remain in touch, and he hopes that they will do the same. He also assures them that he will be sending them surveys, and that their stories will likely become a part of future senior programs. He asks students to keep him up to date on their lives.

Although money and the funding of the SSC ministry have seldom been topics of discussion during their gatherings, Matthew closes the seminar with a rare request for these soon-to-be alums to lend financial support to the SSC ministry. He distributes fundraising postcards and envelopes that the national SSC office has prepared, and he encourages them to give to the SSC once a year:

> Hopefully, you have seen the work Jessica and I do with our hearts. We are not sitting around living a comfortable life. Pray and listen to where God tells you to give. We all [i.e., staff] have envelopes. Regardless of whether you give, we are with you and care for you deeply. When you leave, pray for us. We will pray for you. Keep in touch. Call us. We are there for you. We will do our best to keep up with you—and remember the senior outing on Saturday.

Leslie concludes with a prayer: "Lord thank You for the opportunities You made available to us for the past 4 years. Thank You for Jessica and Matthew's guidance. Pray for us during our transitions and tough times. Be with us and keep us close to You. Thank You, Lord, for the opportunity to be in this class and know what is ahead. Pray for us. Lord, we love You. Amen."

Understanding Transitions: Living a Lifetime with Jesus

> Students' fundamental moral commitments are largely in place before they matriculate. Yet their moral and political views are affected by their experiences on campus. And it is the smaller communities in which students participate that most decisively affect their personal codes of morals and of behavior. (Hoekma, 1994, p. 157)

The SSC is an intimate and potent collegiate community that encourages students to hone their values, solidify their political views, and develop habits that will guide them for the remainder of their lives. Components of the SSC cocurriculum—including the Learning to Live with Christ (LLC) senior seminar, Friday night worship services, Bible study cohorts, evangelical training, servant leadership gatherings, and one-on-one discipleship meetings—individually and collectively influence Christian members' behaviors, morals, political leanings, and faith development.

Kiley, along with the majority of SSC members whom we interviewed, reported that her meaningful and sustained involvement in the SSC helped her feel a unique connection to the university. The majority of interviewees reported that their meaningful and sustained involvement in the SSC contributed to their retention in college, their overall collegiate satisfaction, and their financial support of the SSC upon graduation. These outcomes align with Blimling and Whitt's (1999) research, which concluded, "Graduation rates, student satisfaction, alumni support, critical thinking, interpersonal skills, and functionally transferable skills are either developed or enhanced through activities outside the classroom that involve students in meaningful ways" (p. 14). The LLC seminar helps seniors, who are immersed in a complex rite of passage, recreate a close-knit SSC collegiate experience in their post-college worlds—an experience that resembles the smaller communities Hoekma describes. The seminar also helps seniors to achieve some of Blimling and Whitt's outcomes, and most important, to attain Hoekma's outcome centering on the refinement of their morals and behaviors based on Christian ideals.

According to van Gennep (1960), *rites of passage* are "ceremonies whose essential purpose is to enable the individual to pass from one defined position to another which is equally well-defined" (p. 3). His rites of passage schema includes three distinct stages: separation, transition, and incorporation. During *separation* (e.g., graduation), the individual or group is symbolically or physically set free from their present situation. *Transition* is a time of flux between the here-and-now and the future. *Incorporation* occurs when the individual or group acquires a new position of status (e.g., securing a job). The LLC seminar addresses all three stages, though it concentrates most heavily on supporting seniors through the separation and transition phases.

Matthew's challenging LLC seminar centers on students' understanding of themselves, with the hope that this understanding will assist seniors with their separation and transition anxieties—such as being alone in the secular world, encountering temptation, and abandoning one's Christian identity. Matthew recognizes this complex rite of passage and attempts to temper the seniors' post-college Pollyanna aspirations of the perfect job, the perfect life, and the perfect partner (Main, 2003). Throughout the 4-week seminar, he shares strategies with seniors to navigate this complex separation and transition process. The goal is to help them locate or form smaller supportive Christian communities at work, at home, and in the community, which will both further their Christian development and grow God's Kingdom. He hopes that students will translate their SSC learning to life as Christian adults. Matthew's primary impetus for sponsoring the LLC seminar is to remind students of their Christian responsibility and thus prevent SSC alumni from abandoning the evangelical identities they cultivated during college.

Analyzing the LLC seminar as a campus exit ritual (Magolda 2003) reveals the SSC's implicit and explicit values, priorities, political leanings, and the most important moral guidance the SSC staff hopes to impart to seniors before they graduate. To accomplish this aim, we scrutinize three specific seminar domains: the LLC staging, the LLC script, and the LLC performance.

The Evangelical Staging: Meager, yet Meaningful

Physical artifacts provide people "with the immediate sensory stimuli as they carry out culturally expressive activities" (Kuh and Whitt, 1988, p. 19). The physical design and space of campus institutions is complex, and, their importance cannot be overstated (Strange and Banning, 2001). An examination of the staging of the LLC seminar (i.e., the site, physical layout, costumes, and physical artifacts) reveals some influences that the physical environment and accompanying physical artifacts have on the behaviors and beliefs of participants.

Scheduling the LLC seminar at the off-campus Christian church is a purposeful decision on Matthew's part. The SSC organization shares the center with other Christian groups, which facilitates a sense of solidarity among Christian collegians. This faith-based locale also affirms the organization's allegiance to Christian ideals and symbolically celebrates the importance of a safe haven for Christians in a not-so-friendly secular university.

The sparse, not-so-stylish, and low-tech conference room—with an aging table, mismatched chairs, and traditional blackboard—symbolically represents the modest lifestyle that SSC staff members endorse. For the SSC members, being humble, unassuming, and tempered trumps showcasing excess, elegance, and stylishness. The no-frills physical environment augments Matthew's counsel to seniors—shun materialism and embrace a simple life that involves God, first and foremost.

The manner in which Matthew makes use of the conference room's *physical layout* also provides insight into the SSC's epicenter of power and knowledge. Matthew (and John, during session three), with a Bible within arm's reach, sits at the head of the table, thereby creating a patriarchal epicenter of sorts. Throughout the 4-week seminar, he is the fountain of knowledge, the conduit that connects God's Word to the seniors. Remaining seats are positioned around the table, very close to one other, which creates a sense of parity and intimacy for participants. This arrangement is ideal for attendees to listen to their elders' lectures and occasionally engage in small group discussions. The physical arrangement of the conference room supports this pedagogy.

LLC participants' no-frills "costumes" buck dominant student culture norms that use clothing and fashion accessories to convey wealth and trendiness. Instead, the makeup-less women and "designer-phobic" men use their clothes and fashion accessories (e.g., "Got Jesus?" T-shirts, crucifix pendants, and fish bracelets) to showcase their core values (e.g., being modest and humble) and allegiance to Jesus. This "come as you are" expectation reinforces one's commitment over one's appearance.

LLC props are meager, yet meaningful. The students' tattered Bibles silently communicate the regularity with which they consult their "guide for life." Likewise, the hefty weekly handouts provide attendees with keepsakes that are aesthetically ordinary, yet extraordinarily rich in content. In total, the subtleties embedded in the LLC locale, room arrangement, participants' costumes, and props support the more overt agenda embedded in the LLC script.

The Evangelical Script: Transfer Faith, Fun, and Fellowship to Your Work, Home, and Community

SSC seniors expect to continue their relationship with God as they join new communities and establish friendships with like-minded peers. They desire persecution-free work contexts as well as home and community environments that will allow them to acknowledge and celebrate their Christian identity. They desire the familiar and similar, but they recognize that locating a Christian world that is familiar and similar [to the SSC] likely will be the exception, rather than the rule. The LLC seminar script recognizes these aspirations and accompanying concerns and attempts to respond to them.

Quebedeaux's (1974) basic truths of contemporary evangelicalism include three core principles, which are the three primary foundations for the LLC script and the key for seniors to enact their espoused aspirations. Quebedeaux's principles are

(1) [t]he complete reliability and final authority of Scripture in matters of faith and practice; (2) the necessity of a *personal* faith in Jesus Christ as Savior from sin, and consequently commitment to Him as Lord; and (3) the urgency of seeking actively the conversion of sinners to Christ. (p. 4)

The LLC seminar helps seniors conceptualize and begin to build an SSC-like experience that will sustain these truths in home, work, and community contexts. The SSC collegiate experience emphasizes faith, fellowship, and fun. The LLC script offers recommendations for seniors to sustain their faith as they create new opportunities for fun and fellowship. Although the fellowship and fun aspects of the SSC's three Fs will likely change in the months following graduation, Matthew hopes that the faith component will remain unchanged and that the Bible remains *the* faith guide for seniors' post-college Christian life. The LLC script includes four meta-themes: valuing the Bible, maintaining a personal faith in Jesus as Savior, converting sinners to Christ, and preparing for the next generation of evangelicals.

Valuing the Bible

> A belief in the veracity of the Bible and a desire to obey its precepts is a
> foundational value of evangelical Christianity (Marsden 1980, 3; Paulson
> 2000, 23). Evangelicals not only hold to the authority and trustworthiness
> of the Bible, they place great emphasis on the ability of lay people to study
> the Bible on their own and not depend on preachers, teachers, and other
> experts (Dyck 1996, 7–9; Milne 1982, 50). (Grahmann, 2001, p. 1)

Evangelical Christians' reliance on the Bible for post-college guidance is
a meta-theme of the LLC script. Throughout the LLC seminar, the Bible is
the source for seniors as they contemplate action, and Scripture is the final
authority should dilemmas or arbitration experiences arise. An SSC alumnus
recommended that graduates: [1] spend time alone with God in personal
worship, [2] avoid Satan, and [3] depend on God. Predictably, Matthew touts
the Bible as the source to attain these three aims.

The Bible is the metaphorical Swiss Army knife for these Christian seniors. This essential, multipurpose tool can be used for praying and avoiding
temptation; establishing and maintaining Christian relationships; evangelizing; searching for jobs; earning, saving, and donating money; managing time;
prioritizing philanthropies; and even selecting a spouse. During the weekly
seminar sessions, Matthew regularly recited Scripture to support his recommendations and frequently insisted that biblical evidence accompany students' claims or recommendations. Although post-college separation and
transition challenges are inevitable, the utility of the Bible can ease these
struggles.

Seniors recognize that the SSC infrastructure will soon vanish, which
will complicate their daily Christian routines such as Bible study and evangelizing. An SSC alumnus confirms this assertion: "Use the Bible. At times it
(my relationship with God) feels very strained because I am not living the
"typical" Christian life. I am not going to ministry events/activities, leading
Bible study, leading prayer meetings, sharing the Gospel daily, or even having a good 1-hour time with God daily."

The LLC script asserts that individual young evangelicals are primarily
responsible for their own spiritual development, and that these individuals
must continually try to understand God's will. For Matthew, the Bible is "an
island of clarity in a sea of ambiguity" (Martin, 1992).

Maintaining a Personal Faith in Jesus Christ as Savior   The second major theme of the LLC script focuses on the need for participants to maintain a personal relationship with Jesus. Throughout the seminar, Matthew emphasized the need for students to sustain a personal relationship with and commitment to Jesus, despite numerous barriers such as bosses, television and movies, cults, loneliness, non-Christian colleagues, money, and even church pastors. A relationship with God was the core of Matthew's concentric circle diagram, which illustrated Christian priorities. Matthew argued that maintaining a personal relationship with Jesus (i.e., the core) was a higher priority than family, work, recreation, ministry, social activities, civic involvement, and church.

Matthew warned seniors not to compartmentalize their lives into Christian and non-Christian components, and he advised the students to allow Jesus to permeate all aspects of their world. For seniors, their time with Jesus should not be just quiet time before work and prior to retiring each evening. Instead, they should integrate Jesus into work, play, family life, civic initiatives, hobbies, and church.

A second threat to seniors' relationships with Jesus, according to Matthew, is time. Throughout the LLC seminar, seniors grappled with the question, "How will you manage the assets that have been entrusted to you by God?" The LLC script includes a laundry list of practical suggestions that will minimize the clutter in Christians' lives and allow them to spend quality time with Jesus. If seniors are to live a godly life, they must intentionally allocate their time to God and must be mindful of the decisions they make.

Converting Sinners to Christ   Adhering to the Bible and establishing a personal relationship with Jesus are necessary, but insufficient criteria for "good" evangelicals. One must also actively convert sinners to Christ. As Matthew put it, "When you leave here, your ministry will be one of three places: work, home, or play." His assertion illuminates the third dominant theme implicit in the LLC script—the need for SSC alumni to evangelize. Throughout the LLC seminar, Matthew acknowledged that for most seniors, the SSC has been a cocoon of sorts for them. The organization provided them on-going support, especially when engaging in the challenging work of spreading the Word of Jesus. Soon after the seniors graduate, they will be "swimming upstream," alone as they evangelize. Matthew warned them about de-emphasizing their evangelical duties and thus becoming too insular:

"These people do good things at their church, but do not evangelize." Numerous Bible quotations that Matthew interjected into his mini-lectures reinforced the theme that all Christians must be ministers of the Gospel. His recipe for evangelical outreach in work and community settings blends a hearty heaping of biblical mandates with a dollop of political reality.

Every cultural script, including the LLC script and the scripts for all SSC initiatives, is political. In SSC narratives presented in earlier chapters, the organization's sacred and biblical agenda has eclipsed its political agenda. Linking the SSC agenda to the Bible and God—the supreme authorities— yields unquestioning faith and subsequently depoliticizes the agenda, which stunts questions or challenges. Oddly, during the LLC seminar focusing on workplace ministry, the obscured but ever-present political agenda appears "front and center" and on par with the Bible and God. Despite the acknowledgment of political action, seniors' questions and challenges remain infrequent. Being godly and a good evangelical requires one to be strategic and political, which is an unexpected plot twist in this evangelical performance.

Matthew makes clear the purpose of work in God's Kingdom. The LLC script privileged the evangelical goal of harvesting members rather than conventional Christian criteria, such as remaining close to God by attending weekly church services. He tells the seniors, "Work is ministry. . . . God puts us in different places to minister to other people. . . . He takes advantage of an opportunity to get us around people."

The politics of SSC evangelizing become clear as Matthew gently distances the SSC from traditional or mainstream religious organizations. He favors individual, one-on-one evangelizing instead of evangelizing that might be one of many expectations an organized church has for its congregation. His tepid support of many religious organizations is a striking contrast to his enthusiastic grassroots evangelical agenda. For Matthew, reading and following the Bible, establishing a personal relationship with Jesus, and evangelizing are more important than advocating for students' participation in denominational enclaves. SSC's concept of an evangelical is one who works for God, not a religious organization or entity. That aligns with Barna's (2003) findings that "Christians in their 20s were 70 percent more likely than older adults to say if they cannot find a local church that will help them become more like Christ, then they will find people and groups that will, and connect with them instead of a local church" (cited in Wolly, 2006, para. 18).

Preparing for the Next Generation of Evangelicals   Although the LLC script focuses primarily on the importance of the Bible, Christians' relationship with God, and evangelizing, one additional theme emerged: regenerativity. For the SSC, its seniors represent "the best of the best." Matthew regularly praised their long-term involvement in the SSC and short-term participation in the LLC seminar. As the seniors contemplate a new beginning, Matthew, too, looks ahead to regrow and rebuild the SSC organization. Cultivating loyal SSC alumni is a key to achieving this aim. Matthew (during his mini-lectures) and alumni (in their testimonies included in handouts) reminded seniors that loyal SSC alumni's support—both spiritual and financial—will aid in the organization's regenerativity goal.

The Evangelical Performance: Centered on Authentic and Conservative Content

"To understand the systemic significance of ritual, one must take note of who interacts with whom and of the regular habitual order, duration, and temporal distribution of their actions with respect to one another" (Burnett, 1976, p. 318). There are many different kinds of evangelical performance, and in this final section, we explicitly discuss our interpretations of them. Miller (2006) offered two divergent evangelical performances:

> Dobson's radio show, which reaches 220 million people worldwide, evoked what he hoped would be a dark and scary vision for his fellow evangelical Christians: a nation filled with married gay couples. With same-sex marriage initiatives on the ballots in eight states, Dobson told his flock in a taped broadcast that they could not afford to stay home on Election Day. If they did, he said, "we could . . . begin to have same-sex marriage in places all over the country."

> Meanwhile in Leawood, Kansas . . . a 42-year old evangelical pastor named Adam Hamilton was preaching an entirely different message. He was helping his 14,000 members parse the parables in Matthew 13 . . . our task is not to go around judging people—Jesus didn't do that. (p. 32)

Matthew is keenly aware of the wide range of evangelical performers and the baggage associated with their evangelical ideologies. He situates himself and his ministry midway between Dobson and Hamilton, and thus identifies himself as an evangelical centrist or pragmatist. In the LLC context, performers include Matthew, John, and the seniors. Matthew's LLC performance is far less overtly political, radical, scary, polarizing, or hardcore than Dobson's performance, but it is more judgmental, edgy, and righteous than Hamilton's presentation. Matthew preaches a firm, middle-of-the-road brand of evangelism that is hardly militant and hardly unconditionally inclusive. Unlike Dobson, SSC's style is not to reach the millions through high-tech means. Instead, Matthew's performance embraces grassroots, one-at-a-time evangelizing that focuses on one-on-one human contact. He hopes that his congregation will emulate this performance in their future evangelical venues.

Although SSC members position themselves ideologically as evangelical centrists (on the Dobson–Hamilton continuum), the authority of the Bible results in a more conservative role for senior women. They seldom challenge male-dominated language and gender role expectations (e.g., marriage). Bryant (2006), summarizing gender and the construction of roles for men and women evangelicals, noted a contentious divide within the evangelical community. This rift is evident within the SSC:

> Representing the majority perspective, conservative Protestants tend to believe that the proper roles for women and men are shaped by their innate differences from one another. As such, a married woman's primary responsibility rests in caring for the home and family, while her husband serves as the household 'breadwinner' (Groothuis, 1994). In adhering to scriptural mandates, some (perhaps many) evangelicals believe women ought to submit to the authority of men, both in the home and in church settings (Smith, 2000). . . . On the other hand, not all evangelicals are content with the current status of women in their churches. Indeed, according to Smith there exists a vocal minority who take scriptural passages to 'stand as clear endorsements of gender equality and mutual submission in marriage as God's highest calling.' (2000, p. 616)

SSC participants situate themselves at various points on this continuum, but most men and women gravitate toward the more conservative and traditional views of women. Bryant's research concluded that many conservative evangelicals support and accept restrictive gender roles for women in marriage and church. Bryant's conservative view seems compatible with SSC women in general and LLC women participants in particular. Bryant's caveats seem to illuminate the paradoxes that SSC women experience:

> Manning's interviews with women in an evangelical church led her to postulate that 'women want to have equality and authority at work and in politics, but they are willing to give up on those things in church . . . Evangelical women say a wife must submit to her husband, but almost none of them do' (1999, p. 150). The paradoxical positions taken by the women in these studies are reminiscent of Smith's (2000) findings, in which evangelical couples agreed with notions of female submission/male headship in marriage, but on a practical level spoke of 'equal partnership' and functioned more as egalitarians than traditionalists. While the majority of evangelicals may harbor suspicions of feminism (Manning, 1999; Smith, 2000), the inconsistencies that prevail in their communities and homes with respect to gender roles attest to the challenge they face in maintaining their doctrinal beliefs and also keeping up with the modern world. (Bryant, 2006, p. 616)

SSC women in the LLC seminar, who aspire to be teachers, graphic designers, and missionaries, struggle with their performances in Christian and secular settings and grapple with balancing biblical truths with modern-day realities.

Pedagogically, the LLC performers acted more conservative than progressive. In the LLC context, Matthew's (and his father's) pedagogy was more content-centered than student-centered. Matthew and John performed as scholarly, well-prepared, and caring teachers, whereas the seniors performed as dutiful, respectful, seasoned, and serious students. In this performance, biblical content, concrete recommendations, and efficiency were higher priorities than cultivating students' views, which would be more characteristic of a student-centered pedagogy. The SSC's content-centered pedagogy appeared to work in this context because of authentic performances by both the presenters and the attendees, as well as the fact that attendees conveyed that they knew little about these topics. Matthew and John believed and understood what they preached, which contributed to the students' receptiveness. The students, too, were authentic. They arrived each week ready to learn, not simply to put in face time. They *wanted* to attend the weekly sessions, which was an asset to the learning process.

Summary

With the LLC's purposeful staging, script, and performance, Matthew communicates that seniors need to focus their lives on the SSC core values they have followed throughout their time at the institution. These values include using the Bible as a guide for daily life, evangelizing non-Christians, maintaining a personal relationship with Jesus, and subscribing to a centrist evangelical viewpoint. Most important, Jesus needs to come first—before work and family, and even before the church.

However, instead of simply reminding students of the centrality of these core values, Matthew advises students to be cautious when bringing their faith into the political environments of work and community. He is keenly aware that the SSC's dualistic viewpoint of sinners vs. saved and Christian vs. non-Christian may deter students' success as evangelicals in secular society. By acknowledging these challenges and suggesting strategies to overcome them, the SSC maximizes learning during this anxiety-ridden, ritualized transition of graduation. Matthew helps seniors anticipate the challenges that lie ahead, while attempting to give them the tools that will hopefully assist them in continuing their walk with Jesus after they leave the safe confines of this Christian student organization (Hansen, 2005).

Nevertheless, we wonder whether this LLC seminar really prepares students for the "real world." Because students are so dependent on the SSC's structure and guidance, they will undoubtedly find it difficult to go it alone and navigate the secular world. Although Matthew's seminar sensitizes students to issues that they might encounter, he paints a bleak portrait of the realities they will face and refrains from engaging students in discussions of how they would resolve real-life struggles. Students will need to take what they've learned and do their best to maintain a life that is *all about Jesus,* despite the fact that their "weirdness" will be magnified in the "real" world.

In this senior seminar and throughout each level of involvement, it is obvious that the organization relies heavily on more advanced leaders and advisors such as Matthew, Don, and the SSC interns for both moral and practical guidance. In the next chapter, we examine the lives of four of the SSC's six leaders and learn more about their decisions to dedicate their lives to Jesus and the SSC mission.

11

THE CHOSEN

Rituals of Vocation

Leading by Example[1]

Students Serving Christ (SSC) members sit silently in the pews of the campus chapel as their 20-something spiritual leader paces in front of the altar. Matthew divides his attention between his Bible, which fits snugly into the palm of his hand, and his weekly Friday night congregation, which this week numbers around 60 traditional-age college students, most of whom are women. Psychedelic and disco attire suggests to us that attendees took this week's "Retro-mission" theme seriously. The solemn image of Matthew clutching his Bible juxtaposed with his comically dressed congregation wearing outlandish '60s, '70s, and '80s attire temporarily disorients and amuses me (Peter).

Matthew commands the students' attention as he flips open his Bible to the desired page and immediately reads a passage, using a serious and formal oratory style. "John 14:6—Jesus answered, 'I am the way and the truth and the life. No one comes to the Father except through Me.'" He repeats the passage aloud while staring directly at the students, waits, and then shifts to a more casual and informal conversation style as he interprets the passage. "Seeking *the* way, seeking *the* truth, and getting into heaven—sounds like hard work. I have a better idea; let's forget about these ideas." He then rips the page from his Bible and dramatically flings it onto the floor. Looks of uncertainty and confusion appear on the faces of the students as they quizzically glance at each other and try to comprehend the bizarre scene.

After a purposeful pause, Matthew returns to his more proper oratorical style of Bible recitation. "Psalms 119:9–11 'How can a young man keep his way pure? By living according to Your word.'" Another long pause ensues.

"Staying pure—in college? . . . That's a long shot. . . . I don't think so. Let's just get rid of that passage as well." Matthew again tears a page from his Bible and nonchalantly tosses it over his shoulder. "Let's just make it even easier and get rid of the entire Book of Psalms." He then clutches a bunch of pages and struggles to remove them from his Bible; eventually, he prevails and tosses the pages into the air as attendees gawk with horror-struck facial expressions.

Matthew resumes his strolling sermon as the drama subsides. The moral of the sermon, which he methodically uncovers, takes center stage for the attendees—Christians need to adhere to *all* of the Bible's teachings, not just those passages that suit their lifestyles or whims. He urges students to use the Bible as a guide for their lives. As the sermon concludes, Matthew bows his head and calls out—"Let's pray."

Students Serving Christ Lifers

This chapter focuses on the lives of Matthew and the five other full-time SSC staff members who support students in the attainment of two foundational Christian goals: adhering to the Bible's teachings and growing the Kingdom. Depending on the type of SSC event, the SSC staff conducts specific leadership rituals that display the organization's core values. Because the SSC values student learning, leaders sometimes encourage students to organize events such as the Friday night worship meetings. In other instances, because the SSC values the wisdom of "learned elders," staff members share their Christian knowledge and take "center stage" in activities such as Bible study, evangelical training, and Servant Leadership Team meetings. In the foregoing narrative, Matthew serves as the keynote speaker and instructor during a Friday night worship meeting in which he dramatically illustrates the importance of obeying all the Bible's teachings. In addition to serving as keynote speakers and instructors, staff members act as role models, trainers, mentors, and facilitators.

In addition to their public rituals, leaders also share many private rituals regarding personal faith development, administration of the organization, and the development of passion for their work. The stories that follow explore these private SSC leadership rituals and the events in staff members' lives that motivate them to set organizational priorities, establish and monitor policies and procedures, and engage in ongoing relationships with students. Staff musings coupled with our analysis further illuminate the SSC's core values that inspire the staff in their work and influence students to follow their SSC leaders—and likewise live their lives for Jesus.

The size of the SSC staff ranged from four to six individuals during our fieldwork. Matthew, Don, Nancy, and Jessica were SSC staff members throughout the study, whereas Aaron and Sarah were SSC students during the first portion of the study. Upon graduation, they applied to the SSC national headquarters to serve as full-time campus interns, and eventually they joined the staff at their alma mater.

Matthew and Jessica

Matthew joined the SSC organization as a sophomore in college and remained active in the organization until his graduation. In 2000, he earned a Bachelor of Arts in comparative religion and creative writing, and then applied to the SSC staff internship program. After the national office hired him, he served on a traveling evangelical team whose primary goal was to start up campus ministries in Texas. In 2002 Matthew returned to his alma mater and accepted the position as campus director for SSC.

Jessica is Matthew's wife. In 2004 she graduated *summa cum laude* with a degree in public administration. While a collegian, Jessica was an active SSC member and served on the leadership team for numerous years. Since joining the SSC staff, her primary responsibility has been to minister to the unique needs of women. She and Matthew married after Jessica was on staff for 18 months. Jessica and Matthew's long-term career aspiration is to reside in Southeast Asia and minister to Buddhists.

Aaron and Sarah

Former SSC student leaders, recent newlyweds, and now full-time staff, Aaron and Sarah are the newest SSC staff members. Aaron graduated in 2005 with a degree in math education. As an undergraduate, he was a dedicated SSC member and served as organizational president in 2004. Aaron's primary staff responsibilities have been membership training, discipling SSC men, and coordinating evangelical efforts in the residence halls. Sarah earned her college degree in education in 2006. She, too, involved herself in the SSC for 4 years and then returned to her alma mater months after graduation to "be on staff." Sarah devotes the majority of her time to disci-pling SSC women.

Don and Nancy

Don and Nancy are 25-year SSC veterans. Currently, Don serves as the regional trainer for the SSC's Midwest campus division. Don mentors younger SSC staff in the Midwest and develops resources for campus staffs. Nancy currently holds no official position in the local or national SSC organ-izations, but maintains her quarter-century of volunteer affiliation with SSC. Because Don and Nancy reside near campus, they are active with the SSC chapter. Nancy and Don lead Bible studies, disciple students, and mentor staff. They also host weekly SSC meetings and socials in their home. Prior to this 12-year assignment, they oversaw ministries in Michigan, California, Ohio, and Tennessee.

Rites of Passage: From Collegiate Evangelicals to Collegiate Missionaries

All six staff people considered themselves Christians prior to attending col-lege, though initially their concepts of a "good" Christian varied. Because of their affiliation with SSC chapters at their respective colleges, these individ-uals developed an evangelical appetite, and eventually concluded that a mis-sionary vocation was their calling.

Coming of Age as Christian Collegians

Nancy grew up in a home where her mother was a believer. Through church and youth group involvement, Nancy maintained a Christian way of life. During her adolescent years, she realized that she did not possess a personal relationship with God. Nancy discussed her evolution as a believer and fac-tors that influenced her decision to involve herself in a Christian organiza-tion as a collegian in the mid-1970s:

> In high school I went to church and knew a lot [about religion], but some-thing was missing. . . . One day a girl shared with me a truth from the Bible—what it means to be a believer. She shared John 14:6—"I am the way

and the truth and the life. No one comes to the Father except through Me." That was my need at that time. I needed to know God personally. I said a feeble prayer to God before leaving for college: "God, put me with people who will allow me to get to know You better."

Nancy attended a large state university in Michigan. During [new student] orientation, she encountered a group of SSC students who were greeting people and sharing a spiritual interest survey. She completed the survey and then promptly forgot about the experience. She recalled the evangelical encounter a week later when a member of the organization contacted her:

> The first week at school, some of the girls in my dorm who were in SSC followed up on that survey and invited me to a Bible study. . . . At first I did not remember filling out the survey, and when I recalled doing it . . . I didn't think anyone would follow up. These girls really cared about me. They kept inviting me and kept coming to talk with me. They won my heart. I recognized their sincerity and got involved in Christian things. I enjoyed my involvement and I learned so much.

During a junior high church retreat, Sarah asked God to come into her life. It was then she learned that she could have a relationship with Him, and she dedicated her life to living for and with Him.

> I was put in the position to lead the junior high group of Fellowship of Christian Athletes. As I was leading, I thought, maybe I should do these things—like praying and reading the Bible—before I ask others to do them. That is when I really started to see that there was a point to all of this.

At the conclusion of Sarah's senior year in high school, she reconnected with a friend who told her that his goal for the summer was to read the entire New Testament. She exclaimed, "*Wow*, that's crazy." She confessed that she did not know anyone who had such a goal. The friend encouraged Sarah to improve her relationship with Jesus and make Him a part of her life. Sarah heeded the friend's advice.

Arriving on campus in 2002, Sarah attended numerous welcome programs sponsored by Christian organizations. She attended an SSC program and liked the women she met, and she eventually joined the organization. "We hung out together and started to form a tight community that was new to me. Then I got involved in Bible study and so much more."

Jessica's story is similar to Sarah's tale. Attending high school in Indiana, Jessica involved herself in an outreach program for high school students who did not attend church or shunned Christian organizations. She explained:

> So, it's really fun and it tries to draw them in—in ways that traditional Christian groups do not do. . . . I was a leader during my senior year, and the woman who was my director told me I had to find some kind of Christian group to get involved with during the first week in college.

In her senior year, Jessica sent away for admission packets from the universities that a career counselor recommended to her. "I really was just praying that God would show me where to go and what would be the best place for me. I narrowed my choices to two colleges and had a pretty bad experience at the other school I was seriously considering, so I came here. God answered my calling."

Like Sarah, Jessica visited several Christian organizations during her first week of college. From her perspective, each group had a "different feel." She eliminated a large Christian organization because she feared she would get lost in the crowd. One mid-size Christian group comprising "artsy people and dreamers" was "nice," but Jessica feared she would not fit in. She also visited a tiny Christian organization and felt she "stuck out." The SSC organization was the right size, and members were passionate about God. Relational aspects of SSC appealed to Jessica. "They sent welcome goody bags to new people to thank them for coming. . . . That was a nice touch. I guess the goals were to help them feel involved, make friends, and remind them they have a place and can fit in here."

Don attended a public university in Michigan in the 1970s. Prior to college, he was a Christian in name only and intended to denounce his Christian upbringing during college.

> When I went to college, my goal was to never darken the door of another church. I had been raised in the church, so when I went away to college, I wanted to get away from it. It was the time of the Jesus movement. I called my mom my first weekend on campus and told her I had a "Jesus freak" as a roommate. This guy read his Bible every day and prayed before meals in the cafeteria, and he went to church on Sundays. I was always hung over on Sundays.

Over time, Don, like his spouse Nancy, came of age in a Christian sense and became a serious follower of Christ. Toward the end of his freshman year, a friend of his roommate approached Don and indicated he wanted to share something with him. Don replied, "I'm too busy; maybe tomorrow night." The student returned the following evening and shared with Don the same biblical illustration he had encountered the week before when interacting with another Christian. During this encounter, Don realized he was one of those guys who were "going to spend eternity in hell." The peer evangelist asked, "Is there any reason why you would not want to come over to God's side?" Befuddled, Don confessed he had no reason to resist the invitation to come over to God's side—so he did.

> Toward the end of my freshman year, he was involved in SSC, and he got me involved in a Bible study. It was weird, since I never read or studied the Bible. They wanted me to do an assignment and read ahead of time. I said, "I can't do that." The student replied, "Sure you can." . . . And so, my Christian journey began.

Aaron's Christian revival took place 30 years after Don's Jesus-awakening, yet the two stories are remarkably similar.

> Sarah and I grew up five miles apart. . . . We were both raised in the church. It is what you did when you were young. In junior high, I called myself a Christian, but I didn't know what to do with my faith. . . . No one was there to teach me to read the Bible. Where do you start? How do you pray? How does prayer become meaningful? I didn't know the answers, but I still would say I was a Christian and condemn others for their actions. But inside, I wasn't any different from them.

Aaron began his college career at a large public university in a nearby state, but he transferred after completing his first year of study. Intellectually, he understood Christianity, but it was, as he said, "not in his heart." He involved himself in the party scene. Aaron described those days:

> I was a typical freshman in college. By the end of the first term, I felt a sense of emptiness. Is this what God has planned for me? Then I felt God saying, "*No, no* it's not." A couple of guys reached out and befriended me. I got a sense that these guys were living for something different. I wondered,

"What do they know that I don't know?" They had a relationship with God. They knew Christ with their heart. That was an experience that I had not had, and I wanted it.

Weeks later, Aaron joined his university's SSC chapter and began an earnest walk with Jesus.

─────────────

As a first-year student, Matthew attended a college on the East coast, but transferred before the start of his second year. As a sophomore, he had a single room in a remote residence hall at this unfamiliar school. He knew only two people on campus—an older woman and younger guy. He revealed his adjustment struggles:

> I had trouble meeting people and socializing. I was not very adept at all. I was highly introverted that year. . . . I met a girl in my English class who I really liked [not Jessica]. She invited me to an SSC program. I did not think much about SSC, but I knew I wanted to go where she was. . . . I went for all the wrong reasons, but I went and liked it. I felt like it was a place where people are real and not trying to put up a front of having it all together. That was in April my sophomore year. I went a few times until the end of the year. The following year I made a decision that I was going to get involved. A lot of weeks I did not want to go, but I went, and my relationship with God strengthened.

In the men's stories, serendipitous encounters with Christians awakened them to a more complex understanding of and commitment to Christianity. The men's ongoing affiliations with their respective mentors and SSC organizations gradually redefined their concepts of what it means to be "good" Christians and transformed them from Christians in name only to what they call "real Christians."

The women's stories are a striking contrast to the men's tales. Nancy, Sarah, and Jessica adhered to Christian ideals prior to attending college. Once on campus, they sought like-minded people who shared their Christian values and could teach them to become better Christians. Unlike their male peers who discovered the need to make major changes in their lives, these women simply wanted to grow closer to God.

Swidey (2003) catalogues Christians into three categories: "those who came with it, those who came with something else, and those who wanted nothing to do with it" (para. 12). During their early days in college, these future missionaries represented each of these three evangelical "types."

The influence of an SSC "evangelical stranger" who took the time to establish a relationship with the student not only led these six individuals to join their respective SSC campus chapters, but also helped these students further define what it meant to be Christian. These evangelical strangers followed a predictable recruitment strategy in terms of seeking students "who are vulnerable at the moment and overpowering them with friendship, community, and acceptance" (Hunt, 1993, p. 49). Effective recruitment strategies included highlighting the human scale of the SSC organization; offering unconditional acceptance; sponsoring wholesome structured activities; and conveying the perception of serious, sincere, and genuine peers. Years later, the power of these chance recruitment encounters with strangers fuels these missionaries' passion for evangelizing.

Crossing Over to God's Side: Redefining College

Several collegiate experiences influenced these six collegians' decisions to pursue full-time missionary work with the SSC. Their in-depth and sustained affiliation with the SSC helped these students clarify their priorities and allegiances.

When Aaron transferred after his first year of college, he joined the SSC organization and met Matthew, who immediately began to disciple him. These one-on-one meetings stoked his involvement in the organization and offered him reasons for wanting to be "on God's side."

> I was doing a few things here and there, but I never had an older and wiser [i.e., Matthew] Christian looking into my life. I realized there were a lot of areas of my life that were contrary to what the Bible says, and I knew that was not good. Matthew encouraged me to turn to these areas. Each time I did, it has been good. . . . Matthew developed the learner within me. Like I had to give up drinking a 12-pack [of beer] on the weekend. . . . By being involved and knowing my Christian faith better, I had a focus for life.

Aaron used his discipleship meetings with Matthew to explore unanswered self-identity questions about his faith, such as "How do I study God's word?" "How do I pull out meaning from my daily devotions?" "How do I make meaning?" Aaron and Matthew began to collectively explore and answer these questions. Over time, Christianity went from Aaron's head to his heart. He learned to be a laborer who could impact and change peers' lives.

Nancy's Christian involvement with like-minded peers redefined her college years:

> There were 50,000 students at my university, and I liked the opportunity to tap into smaller fellowship groups like SSC. It was good spiritually and gave me an identity niche. My nursing program was intense, so the time I spent outside of the classes socially was limited. I felt like I was with good people, involved in healthy and fun things. We had weekly big meetings, and we would go to staff people's houses and pack in 100 people.

Nancy accompanied her Christian peers on a spring break trip to Florida. The experience clarified her reasons for "being on God's side."

> I did not do much camping while growing up, so it was new. We all had a job, and we worked together. We went to the beach and had fun and used those opportunities to strike up conversations with people and see where they were spiritually. If we had a chance to share more deeply about our relationship with God, we would.

During the trip, Nancy and her peers ate breakfast together each morning and then went to their respective jobs during the day. Bible studies followed a community dinner each evening. Occasionally, staff sponsored workshops about faith or character topics. Elders encouraged Nancy and her peers to relate to people while on the job by building relationships and sharing the Gospel with them. "It was a time of intense input spiritually. I learned to develop a heart for God."

Upon returning to campus, Nancy immersed herself in Christian activities and joined the SSC leadership team. The following summer she returned to Florida as a team leader and assumed additional leadership responsibilities. She had a group of women she shepherded by leading Bible study, helping them memorize verses, and sharing her faith.

Don, when recounting stories about his college years, talked about the influence of his newfound Christian peers on his Christian development:

> I was a business major and I was going to make a million dollars by age 30. Once I became a follower of Christ, I realized that my neighbor, the

millionaire with whom I was going to work, was a little unethical—although he did not do anything illegal. There was a guy who led me to Christ while in college and helped me see things I couldn't see on my own. My time with him changed my plans and outlook on life. Instead, I went into both the ministry and construction, which were my real passions.

Discussing contemporary student culture within higher education, Miller (2006) explained, "Since higher education's relinquishment of the *in loco parentis* role in the late 1960s, many campuses have come to be seen as increasingly chaotic and dangerous to a number of students and parents . . . places where men and women share dorm rooms and where drugs and alcohol are easily available" (p. 6). These six students recognized the potential chaos and dangers of the college environment for Christians who wish to "remain pure," and they sought structures and limits that would counter the pervasive permissive environment.

Miller and Ryan (2001) argued, "As students explore aspects of self-identity, they also wrestle with questions of significance and meaning. The study of religion and participation in religious groups are two frameworks within which students may ask themselves questions about what matters to them and to what they are willing to devote their lives" (p. 41). During college, these six students explored the intersection of faith and identity as they sought significance and meaning in their lives. Their SSC experiences invited them to redefine college and re-conceptualize their notion of being on God's side. These revelations, in turn, laid the groundwork for their eventual decision to pursue missionary work as a profession and helped determine the kind of mission work they would ultimately undertake.

Aaron's discipleship interactions with Matthew greatly influenced him as a collegian, but more importantly, these interactions influence the way he disciples the next generation of SSC members in his SSC staff member role. Don's one-on-one collegiate experiences with his mentor also influenced how he currently interacts with college students. His 25 years of ministry experiences taught him that establishing in-depth and multicontext relationships with students is essential. Don described how he forges these relationships with undergraduate men:

> The guys said that if you are going to lead our Bible study, you have to be on our hockey team, so I have been on a team for 4 years now. Once these

guys graduated, non-Christians joined the team and I played hockey for outreach. I try to develop relationships with guys—both believers and non-believers. I play on two teams. I blend exercise with doing God's work. It's hockey for ministry purposes.

Nancy's academic year and summer involvement activities in the 1970s—leadership teams, summer enrichment programs, subtle evangelizing during work, single-sex Bible studies, large group worship programs, whole-some fellowship activities, and spiritual development workshops—are nearly identical to the program offerings for SSC students in 2007. Staff members sustain these evangelical traditions over the years, which provides students with opportunities to ratchet up their involvement.

In total, these stories reveal how SSC staff spent their time in college and engaged in the long-standing SSC evangelical traditions and rituals. More importantly, these stories suggest that sustained evangelical mentorship pow-erfully influenced these individuals' decisions to devote their vocational life to Jesus.

The Calling

Matthew expected to pursue a ministry vocation during his college career, though he had not given much thought to the specifics. The other five staff members had varying interests in areas such as education, business, public administration, and nursing. Despite their different initial career aspirations, all six SSC staff members answered God's calling. Matthew traced the roots of his missionary aspirations:

> I started meeting for discipleship with William, the guy that used to have my job. The end of my sophomore year, I decided that I did not want to be in vocational ministry. I felt I was being called to be a pastor of a church or something. Junior year, first semester I visited seminaries. It was okay. At the same time, William asked me to go to Russia the following summer for a missionary trip. I told him I would pray about it and I did. I prayed about it and started to feel a calling about overseas travel, but not to Russia. Russia was not on my heart. Instead, I went to Thailand.

Matthew traveled to Thailand, which dramatically altered his perspective about overseas mission work. After returning, he made plans to work in

Thailand for 3 years as an SSC intern. In the midst of Matthew's planning, the wife of the missionary with whom he intended to work had a cancer relapse, so the couple returned to the United States. Matthew interpreted these dynamics as God closing that overseas door for a while. Instead, he applied to be an SSC traveling team intern, whose mission was to evangelize on college campuses in Texas. He intended to apply what he learned in Texas to his future overseas experiences. Matthew participated in the team for the predetermined 2 years and then went on to a new work setting.

> I prayed about it and talked to some older guys in the SSC and asked them for advice. Some old SSC guys who had overseas experiences—their counsel was to get a few more years in the States and expand my ministry experience and to build up some donors. This was pretty good advice, so I started to pray and God put Ivy League Schools in front of me. It was on my heart. At Christmas break I came back here and talked to Don. I considered him a friend, and he was my Bible study guide when I was an undergraduate. He offered me the opportunity to come back here or go to a larger nearby school and work under someone for a year and then take over that ministry. Neither option interested me.

In February Matthew submitted his preference, which God put on his heart. He decided to return to his alma mater as campus director for SSC.

Initially, Jessica's post-college aspiration was to return to her home state of Indiana and use her public administration degree to work for a nonprofit organization, or in politics. Midway through her senior year, she started to think seriously about the ministry as a vocation. Because of her political passion, she applied for a few political internships in state government, but ultimately she balked at these opportunities. Jessica prayed to God for guidance:

> It [i.e., politics] was not in my heart. . . . It was not the most important thing to me. Following God and helping students follow God was most important. This seemed like a perfect place for me to be. This is where God was leading me.

> Still, I was really confused about what I wanted to do. I got to the end of the application for the SSC internship, and one question was, "Why do you feel God is calling you to do this?" I had to stop and think. Is this really where God

is calling me? Is this what I need to be doing? I prayed and I really felt I wouldn't be fulfilled or satisfied doing anything else. I started to develop a vision for my life and how God wanted to use me. I started to realize that the promises in the Bible are not just for other people, but they apply to me as well.

Sarah's student teaching experience influenced her decision to continue to educate, but instead of becoming a teacher, she opted to pursue a vocation in the ministry. She explained:

I loved my student teaching. I had adorable 4th-grade kids. It was a great time. I had a good cooperating teacher, and I did well. It went perfectly. It was something I loved, but it was not where my heart was. I couldn't stand in front of this 4th-grade class and say things like, "None of this is going to matter by the time you are 40. What matters is what you are living your life for." I felt like there are many people who can be good teachers. But because I have this craving and because I feel like God is in my heart, I can do something that a lot of people can't—show people a bigger view of life than learning and academics. There is something bigger out there. God has put people in your life for reasons. I prayed about it. I don't fully understand it, so it is hard for me to explain it.

Up until Aaron's senior year, he was "100 percent sure" that God wanted him to teach in the public schools. He says God wanted him to teach, and he could feel it. He, like Sarah, had a highly satisfying student teaching experience and concluded that he could have a happy life teaching. But Aaron abruptly upended his vocation plan shortly after a trip to the SSC national headquarters during spring break. While there, he felt God "tugging" at him. Over time, he felt God urging him to change course because, as a teacher, he would not be able to expand the Kingdom the way God wanted him to do. He decided to "enlist" as an intern for 2 years and see what would happen. Aaron retrospectively made sense of his deliberations:

It was a test to my faith. Not having a regular paycheck would be challenging. It took a lot of prayer. I convinced myself this was right. I was being discipled by Matthew this afternoon, and we were talking. He said he knew midway through my junior year I would be called to accept an SSC internship. He knew I would be on staff. He had this vision for me and thought God was calling me.

Nancy graduated from college with a nursing degree. She wanted to get some professional experience but be somewhere that had a community of Christian fellowship. Her college years taught her that she wanted to be around believers. The national SSC headquarters was starting a community ministry across the state. She prayed about accepting that invitation while simultaneously working as a nurse. She accepted the challenge and worked for 3 years in that capacity.

> Right after college, we met some people in apartment complexes and had some activities. We encouraged singles to attend Bible studies. There were some girls I got to know, and I discipled them. This was after my 7:00 to 3:00 nursing job, so it was a stretch. I was doing it because I loved doing it. Having a job and being responsible financially in an everyday world helped me to relate to people on a bigger picture. . . . [W]e used our abilities to help people, not just spiritually but in practical ways, to make contributions to our worlds.

Nancy continued doing part-time missionary work before moving with her mentors to California, to start up a new ministry with college students.

> I was praying about going back to my alma mater and get more training to minister to people, but God shut the door on that. I ended up going to California and still worked full-time as a nurse. . . . At that time God was increasing my heart to want to be involved in ministering to people. I loved nursing, but I realized that people have more than physical needs. We can heal and help spiritually as well. If we don't tend to spiritual and emotional issues, it can all be for naught.

As Don wrapped up his college career, he knew that he needed more help in his Christian life, so he explored post-college career ministry options. After graduation he merged the two passions he had cultivated during college— ministering to students and construction. He moved across the state and accepted jobs as a construction foreman by day and a community/collegiate minister by night.

> It was hard work, but it had benefits. I was working [construction] and giving myself to people on campus. I was growing up. I would work 8 hours

a day and travel 45 miles to one campus one night and 35 miles to the other college the next night. It was hard getting up at 6:00 a.m. and going to bed at 1:00 a.m. I did that for 2 years. It was a lot of fun, but at times I would drive home and not remember driving home.

Parents' reactions to these six missionaries' decisions to answer God's call were predictable and remarkably similar. When Don informed his father that he was going on staff with SSC, his father expressed disappointment. He had expected Don to pursue a career in business. Don's father likened his involvement in SSC to a fraternity—something he did for 4 years and then "got over it." His father's reaction was predictable—if he had wanted his son to be a missionary, he would have sent him to the seminary. Over the past 26 years, however, his father has become a supporter of Don's career—something Don could not have imagined in the 1970s.

Nancy's parents worried that their investment of money and Nancy's investment of time would be wasted if she did not make use of her nursing education. She desired to blend her two passions by traveling overseas, where she could use both her ministry and her nursing expertise. This compromise satisfied both Nancy and her parents.

Jessica's family "sort of accepted" her vocational decision, but she says they were not "super-supportive" initially because the decision was "outside of their paradigm of a college graduate job." Over the course of the 3 years Jessica has been on the SSC staff, her parents have attended SSC meetings and met SSC students, and they now understand the decision better. Jessica's parents understand the kind of impact she has with students, and they value the work that she and Matthew do.

Sarah explained that her mother worried at first but has grown a lot since then. "She is less scared. Now, she asks about it and gets excited because she understands what we are doing. She is a Christian, so she sees the bigger picture. She is proud and sees the impact we are making. She has met many students and visited." Sarah's father passed away during her senior year of college, but she speculated that he would have been both pleased and worried.

Matthew's parents were less stressed and more pragmatic about his vocational decision. Matthew explained, "I majored in comparative religion and creative writing, so there were not a lot of people banging down my door to give me a job. . . . My father figured I would be going to the seminary, so my decision was not much of a stretch."

The decision to pursue a missionary vocation necessitated that these six individuals abandon their old ways and live for God, as well as model a Christian life for others. Initially, this commitment frightened both those who had been called and their families. Still, these aspiring missionaries continued to march on. For SSC staff, living one's life according to *all* of the Bible's teachings—as Matthew advised students in the beginning narrative—even if it means discomfort or hardship, is a necessary prerequisite to becoming a true follower of Jesus. Staff members recognize that "Christianity is not a religion or a philosophy, but a relationship and a lifestyle. The core of that lifestyle is thinking of others, as Jesus did, instead of ourselves. . . . This kind of thinking is unnatural, counter-culture, rare, and difficult" (Warren, 2002, p. 183).

Vocational Transitions

The application process to become an SSC missionary has changed over the decades. In the 1970s, the internship application process was much simpler than it is today. Don compared the SSC internship application process then and now:

> Back in the day, all I gave them was my social security number and that was it. Now, the [SSC] application is very extensive. They fill out an extensive application. Headquarters compiles extensive applicant profiles; I guess they want to make certain the person is not an ax murderer. They ask many questions, and the resource team follows up on red flags.

The SSC internship experience is, in essence, a full-time, entry-level SSC staff position. It is the gateway to other staff opportunities with progressive ministry responsibilities. Each spring, interested individuals submit their application materials to the national headquarters. The written application not only solicits demographic information, but it also poses numerous Christian questions focusing on evangelical leadership positions, past ministry experiences, spiritual maturity questions (e.g., Who is the Holy Spirit?), doctrine questions (e.g., How does a person obtain salvation?), and character questions.

Applicants also complete and submit a "moral questionnaire." Headquarters staff of the applicant's same gender evaluate the application. This questionnaire includes sundry questions, including some perfunctory ones such as [1] "Do you currently use illegal drugs and/or controlled substances?" [2] "Have you ever engaged in or been the subject of an investigation concerning sexual harassment, rape, date rape?" [3] "Have you ever engaged in or been the subject of an investigation concerning theft, embezzlement, or misuse of money?" Among the more "unusual" application questions directed toward idiosyncrasies are [1] "Have you ever engaged in or been the subject of an investigation concerning violence?" [2] "Have you had a relationship in the past twelve months, which would not be considered above reproach (i.e., petting, sexual intercourse, oral sex, extramarital involvement)?" [3] "Have you ever had a homosexual experience?" [4] "Are there any areas in your life [where] you had or are having difficulty applying your guidelines or convictions (i.e., thought life, sexual purity, pornography, gambling, credit card spending, etc.)?"

If, after interviews and extensive review, the national headquarters staff deems the candidate acceptable and the candidate accepts the internship offer, the intern then travels to the national headquarters during the summer to participate in a 10-day training institute. The interns spend the remainder of the summer fundraising, which we discuss in the following section. Provided they meet their fundraising goals, the new interns begin their campus assignments at the start of the college's academic year.

The SSC internship program provides individuals with missionary aspirations an opportunity to join a campus staff and gain invaluable experience sharing their faith, leading Bible studies, and mentoring college students. Approximately 60 percent of interns continue on with SSC (many in a full-time staff capacity), after their 1- or 2-year internship contract concludes.

Missionary Sustainability

The SSC fundraising expectations for interns are even more elaborate and rigorous than the applicants' review process. Because the SSC national organization is a faith-based ministry, it requires staff members to raise enough money to pay for their salaries and expenses. For many of these dedicated SSC leaders, it is the most stressful part of their jobs. Matthew explained the biblical roots of this fundraising practice: "It's based on Christ. He was a carpenter. Paul was a tentmaker. They asked people who were interested in them to fund them. . . . Once you understood biblically the basis for it, it was okay. . . . When you think about churches, most congregations support their pastors. People put pastors' salaries in the [collection] plate each week."

Every SSC staff member sends hundreds of letters to potential donors who, as Matthew says, "provide the power for what goes on here." The national office works with each staff member to set an annual budget that includes salary, health care benefits, travel expenses, and supplies. Donors send their contributions directly to the national office, and the office establishes an account for each staff member. Each month the national office sends the staff member a stipend. As Jessica reminded us, "The process is stressful, but a good thing. It forces us to trust God for our provisions." Matthew explained some of the inherent struggles:

> It takes humility to go to people who are at various points in their spiritual journey and ask them for money. . . . Some people have a hard time understanding what we are doing. I had one couple supporting me for 250 dollars each month for 2 years. Then, they cut off my funding. They said that they thought it was time for me to get a "real job." It forced me to be humble and got me involved with more people.

Most collegiate staff members, including interns, devote a part of their summers to fundraising. Sarah, a novice SSC fundraiser, described her experiences and philosophy related to fundraising:

> We [i.e., Sarah and Aaron] have about 400 people we send letters to. About 100 are supporting us—some a lot, some not so much. The majority stays connected to our work. They realize we are going to change some students' lives. They are trusting Christ and it [a donation] will have an impact. . . . Our business is spiritual development. As Christians, we have to believe that God has a bigger plan. We are sacrificing finances and possessions and respect and lay it down and serve the Lord. We are doing what God wants us to do. We have to trust He is going to make that work, but it is hard sometimes.

For Sarah and Aaron, fundraising was and continues to be a challenge. Aaron elaborated on the challenges they have encountered as the result of an uncertain salary:

> In math education, I could get a signing bonus because schools are in such dire need of math teachers. I decided to trust where God is leading me.

There are lots of other people doing ministry work, and they are being taken care of by God. We have to be frugal for the duration, but that's not a problem. We don't go out to eat as much. We buy used cars and live in a small place. In the whole realm, these are not high costs to pay for what we are doing and seeing lives changed for the better. I look back on the past 2 years and there is nothing I would rather do. Through faithful people who want to change lives by funding us, I see God providing for us. It is hard to ask for money. Both of my parents are supportive. Some of my aunts and uncles think I am a beggar. They say, "What are you wasting your college education for?" They don't see the impact that I see.

The national headquarters sends interns like Aaron and Sarah to fundraising school as part of their SSC training. Don summarized the advice the national office shares with interns:

Talk to people face-to-face—about 50 percent will give. . . . Sit down with people and communicate what you are about. . . . Tell donors how you are going to impact people. People want to know what God has excited you about; tell them. . . . Press through the awkwardness. . . . Come up with names: family, cousins, janitors, church people, anybody. . . . Don't check people off your [donor] list; let them check themselves off the list. Lots of times people are looking for something to support but don't know there is a need.

Don talked about the long-term effects of this fundraising model on his family's quality of life and the struggles that new missionaries encounter:

Finances have never been a big issue for the two of us. God has provided. We have never not eaten, although we don't eat steak. God has provided in the sense of how to talk to people to support us. We did not have a dazzling slide show—we just told them we were talking to college students. They would say, I'd really like to support you—you are doing what?

SSC staff estimate that an SSC intern needs to raise approximately $40,000 each year, which includes a salary, daily expenses, overseas travel, and trips to national headquarters. The national office expects interns to have 75 percent of their budget before they come to campus and 100 percent of it by the end of the first semester.

Day-to-Day Workings of a Collegiate Missionary

The life of a collegiate missionary is neither glamorous nor lucrative, yet staff members report that the intangible, gratifying aspects of their jobs offset their hectic schedules and modest lifestyles. One-on-one discipleship/ mentorship situations are nearly universal. So too are the staff's commitments to studying the Bible and evangelizing. Jessica described her day-to-day workings while on staff: "There is not a typical day, but there are patterns to the week. A good thing about this job is that you set your own schedule."

During the week, Jessica meets with four different women; three meetings are for discipleship. She also accompanies a student who visits the residence halls and follows up on surveys. She leads two Bible studies and manages many administrative tasks related to the Friday night worship service. She attends staff meetings and weekend events, such as parties and campouts. In essence, SSC staff members continue the busy schedule of personal Bible study, evangelism, and discipleship activities they began in college. Jessica continues,

> Coming back here [to my alma mater] is good in a lot of ways, but it's hard to figure out where I fit in. Even within the organization . . . I am not a student anymore. . . . In the beginning that was really hard for me, and I kind of came through a bit of an identity crisis and realized I was getting a lot of fulfillment out of my grades and having professors pat me on the back, and there's really not much of that in this job. People might say "you're doing a good job," but if you don't see people's lives instantly changing, it's hard to know if you're making a difference.

Matthew's weekly routine includes discipleship meetings with five men once a week. He also facilitates weekly meetings of the evangelical team, discipleship team, and senior team. On average, he has one or two crisis-related meetings with students each week. Like his peers, Matthew attends staff meetings every other week and manages routine administrative tasks. Matthew and Jessica publish a fundraising newsletter four times a year, which they distribute to more than 500 individuals. Their nonautomated process includes writing the articles, preparing envelopes, and signing letters. Matthew estimates that he invests approximately 55 to 60 hours per week in his work.

As a newly appointed regional trainer, Don spends less time on the road and more time on the campus near his home, which allows him to interact with nearby collegians. Don begins each day with quiet time with the Lord, or what he calls the "typical Christian thing." After he and Nancy get their three boys to school, he meets with students at a local eatery. Many patrons are Don's acquaintances, and they frequently tease him about not having a "real job." By mid-morning, Don is corresponding with donors or developing training resources or manuals. He describes the behind-the-scenes work associated with his daily routines and the routines of his staff colleagues:

> When you meet one-on-one, it takes 1 to 2 hours of prep time. The same is true with Bible study; I will prep for 4 or 5 hours. On average, I spend about 20 to 25 hours a week on campus. . . . I meet with the regional leadership team each month and do three to four Bible studies each week, as well as staff training. Preparation is a big part of what I do. I want to have a fresh relationship with God, not recycle things I did 20 years ago.

Nancy begins most days at 6:00 a.m. She makes her three boys breakfast and sends them off to school. She then spends time, as she puts it, "in the Word." Her responsibilities as a mother mitigate her ministry duties:

> Even after we were married I worked, but not as much. My wise husband said to follow what God had for us, not the money. He was responsible, as the head of our family, to decide what we would be and do. It came to a point that we wanted to have a family. . . . Even as a mother, I have been able to stay involved in the ministry. I lead Bible study and disciple women. They need a woman to speak to the issues of their life. Don wants me to be available to the women. He makes himself available to our kids, which enables me to be able to have that time.

For Nancy, each day is different. On Monday nights, she and Don invite two of the three SSC teams over to their house for meetings. Nancy meets with the two women staff. She observes their Bible study regularly, accompanies them into the residence halls to evangelize, and plans activities with them. She also reviews her disciples' presentations and provides them feedback. She conducts a weekly Bible study with seniors. Nancy's oldest son is preparing to attend college, so his college exploration process has consumed much of her time this year. For Nancy, family, faith, and finding time to support SSC women are her daily passions.

SSC staff members blur the distinctions between work time and personal time, as well as between work space and home space. They relish their flexible hours, but their irregular daily and weekly routines are occasional strains. Finding "personal time" with Jesus, regardless of the hectic pace, is nonnegotiable. "Capacity" is an SSC staff buzzword—"We have to monitor our capacity—if we go beyond it, we become mediocre," says Matthew.

Missionary Challenges

Embedded in these on-the-job priorities and routines are numerous challenges that SSC staff people encounter. In this section we introduce and briefly discuss two challenges centering on organizational change and leadership, and on mentoring students.

Membership Resistance to Organizational Change   Prior to Matthew's return to campus as SSC's director in 2002, he served as a guest speaker at a Friday night worship program. He distributed a survey to ascertain attendees' level of satisfaction with the organization and their recommendations for change. The dwindling size of the organization surprised and alarmed him. As director, he used the survey feedback to begin to address students' desires and devise strategies to harvest new SSC members. One problem Matthew noted was a lack of opportunities for members to grow beyond Bible study. William [Matthew's predecessor] preferred Bible study and meeting individually with students. Matthew valued these strategies too, but he concluded that his predecessor's vision was too narrow. He decided to expand SLT training, which became the organization's new epicenter. Aaron described the members' initial resistance:

> When Matthew came, his first year we switched things around. Juniors and seniors, who were not committed, did not like the changes. We prayed a lot about these changes and felt we needed to move forward and grow. It cost us some numbers initially, but when the new students arrived, they adjusted, since it was all they knew.

Peter, a graduate student and SSC veteran member who had observed Matthew's, William's, and Ned's leadership styles, worried about Matthew's new direction.

> I knew Matthew as a student and as director. William was before him, and Ned before him. My freshman year Ned was still here, but not leading. The

move from Ned to William was smooth; nothing changed in terms of structure. Although one thing that did change was that we had more of a laid-back atmosphere. We would sometimes get started on time; sometimes we did not. William left to start another ministry and Matthew came in. He was a staff-in-training, and he came back as director. At first, it looked like things were going to be the same, but then gradually things changed. It became a lot more structured and formal.

When William was leading, there was leadership training. Whoever wanted to be there would go. It was at 6:30 in the morning on Tuesdays. It was a test to see if you were committed, but it was laid back. Each week we would talk about things and it was worthwhile, but there was not much structure.

Matthew instituted a three-tier leadership team, with separate levels for sophomores, juniors, and seniors. These groups, not the larger organization, took center stage, which troubled many old-timers. Peter found Matthew unreceptive to input unless members were on one of the teams. Peter and his allies, though unhappy, joined Matthew's new discipleship team. Peter notes that their investment quickly waned:

I was turned off. I'm not badmouthing. He [i.e., Matthew] was strict in what he wanted. The people on the team followed him. There are verses in the Bible that talk about spiritual authority. Matthew is established by God. He wants order. You don't have to agree with it, but you need to support it. He had us sign a contract. That was something that we clashed about. He was making me and others do things I did not like. I did not respect his authority, and I didn't want anything else to do with it. I backed away and said, "No thank you."

Peter and his allies wanted to maintain a small, informal, and not-so-hierarchical SSC organization, which differed from Matthew's vision. These organizational growing pains, commonly associated with new leadership, eventually subsided, but contested issues of organization scale, level of formality, and limits to authority persisted. Don, Matthew's supervisor at the time, supported and counseled him during his early days:

Matthew did things differently. This is common. He moved the weekly worship program from Wednesdays to Fridays, and students resisted change. . . . Matthew is very capable, and I let him run with it. We meet at the start of the year and we talk about objectives, and then he runs with it.

The Bible says, in Matthew 9:37, "The harvest is plentiful, but the laborers are few." Spreading God's Word, a centerpiece of Matthew's vision, takes laborers. A tension that the SSC staff members encounter is remaining true to their beliefs and visions while constantly creating and recreating a student organization that will attract a multitude of Christ followers who are willing to commit their lives to Him. Blending progressive change with decade-old traditions is an issue that the SSC staff members have learned to grapple with each day. The SSC staff struggles to blend the needs of students with biblical mandates to be spiritual authorities. Although students view staff members as spiritual mentors and authority figures, staff members hope that students view Jesus as their ultimate authority and guide, and that they live according to His mandate.

Helping Students Remain True to Jesus   A second staff challenge is helping students to continually gain depth of knowledge about God, the Bible, and the Christian lifestyle. Most SSC members recognize the importance of God's Word, but persuading them to follow the Bible is a formidable task and a constant challenge. Aaron elaborated:

> We believe that the Bible's words are living and active. We have to focus on the Bible because it is the basis of our faith. That is where Christians get themselves in trouble. They do what feels good to them, and not necessarily what the Bible says, or God's Word. We want students to interweave the Bible and God into their everyday lives—into their minds *and* hearts.

Aaron discussed the importance of developing students' interpersonal skills, as well as cultivating their appreciation for and adherence to the Bible. He described many SSC first-year students as "socially awkward" and "bad conversationalists." Sarah described these dynamics as the "freshman interview" and lamented students' underdeveloped listening skills. She asserted that most new SSC students did not listen carefully when their peers spoke. Instead, they preached, which she considered to be a problem.

> You learn more about a person and their struggles and their hurt by listening. We need to ask thought-provoking questions. . . . We need to understand

people and how they respond and what they want. They want relationships and someone to share their life with. . . . God makes the transformation and He affects the heart. He is the real facilitator of all of this.

SSC training provides students with ample opportunities to refine their interpersonal styles and improve the mechanics of their interviews, yet hot-button ideological topics often challenge students more than their awkward interpersonal quirks. Potentially volatile ideological differences between SSC students and nonbelievers simmer as these groups gently interact. The SSC staff hopes that differences do not result in conflict, or in SSC students abandoning their biblical foundation. Aaron explained:

> When it comes to controversial issues like abortion and homosexuality—the Bible is contrary to what the majority of our society believes. So, at times, it's hard to get our students to stand up for the Bible. Too often, Christians let go. They want to make peace or want to be liked. We need to stand firm with what we believe and not let external forces be a stronger force. . . . It [i.e., exchanges with nonbelievers] will influence us, but not the same way as God's Word.

SSC staff members struggle to teach their disciples to be true to their version of Christian truth and to spread these ideals, without allowing ideological differences to impede conversation or make them appear antagonistic. Bridging the gap between SSC students' espoused values and their actions is another enormous challenge for staff members as they help students remain true to Jesus. Don offered numerous examples of this gap:

> Students redefine things. Students can take truth and change it and believe the lie in their heart. . . . Students say there is an absolute truth—the Bible—then go against it. Sadly, their truth is different from biblical truth. Some guys are addicted to poker online, and they lose money online. Video games are addictive; they're not just playing, but playing them 10 hours a day. They are not getting their homework done. Students are dropping out. Pornography online is a problem, an epidemic. Moral issues have gotten worse.

One of Don's Bible study participants has a huge tattoo of a cross on his chest. Don reminded the student that, from a biblical standpoint, Christians are not supposed to tattoo their bodies. This discrepancy did not seem to bother the student. Two men in Don's Bible study occasionally talk about getting "plastered" after playing basketball, which conflicts with biblical teachings. Their decision troubles Don.

> Biblically, there is nothing wrong with alcohol, but these guys get into how much they drink. The biblical value is just not there. They identify openly with Christianity, but the seriousness of their walk is not there. I talk to them all the time, but they still don't get it.

Regularly, the SSC staff reminds students of the importance of sacrificing to live a Christian lifestyle—advice that only a handful of "Christians" are ready to accept. They seek to live their lives as role models for students and demonstrate how students are to trust Jesus' way. Staff members sacrifice their own time and humbly ask for others to support their ministry as they put their lives in God's hands.

SSC staff members worry about the moral decay of society and Christians' passive acceptance of it. The staff uses students' response to the 2005 Terry Schiavo case as a quintessential example of some students' passive acceptance of moral decay. Don expresses grief as he discusses the case: "The Bible does not say 'do what the government wants or what the husband wants.' We need to follow the Bible. From a biblical perspective, euthanasia is not an option." Staff members bemoan students' concern for social issues, which in their opinion eclipse moral issues. Don's comments illuminate this concern: "What about the issue of abortion? . . . They are not concerned with abortion or homosexuality [i.e., moral issues] as much as they are with feeding the poor" [i.e., a social issue]. SSC staff members' views are clear—Christians need to heed God's Word, stay true to the Bible, and act accordingly if they are to remain true to Jesus. Values clarification must lead to action, not talk.

Summary

Despite these challenges related to organizational change and leadership and mentoring students, the SSC staff members remain passionate about their work. Being a part of students' lives as they change remains gratifying. Jessica expresses a collective staff view: "I had an offer to come back here. I just started doing a Bible study as a senior and was excited about continuing to grow. These folks I started with are now seniors, so it has been fun to see them grow."

Sarah's comments reveal why she continues her evangelical journey on college campuses. "We help with the maturation process of college. These are more edified people as a result of their involvement with the SSC. This is especially true with the one-on-one stuff we do. It is a positive thing for so much more than Christianity."

Aaron clarified the inner drive that sustains collegiate missionaries' passions:

> I want to make a difference through my interactions with people. That is where God has led me—to work with college students. College students are much more willing to make changes in their life. You can see it in them, which makes working with these groups meaningful. . . . We are planting a couple of seeds in their lives, and their friends are fertilizing it and watering it, making things grow faster. Collectively, we are growing as a group—not in size, but in depth. We are going to make an impact, but we may not see it. They may not make strides in college, but when they are 25, the things we told them will come to life. We are on the right track for God. God is in control; we're just the instruments for that change. . . . Most days, even the bad ones, we realize there is nothing better we would rather be doing.

In the following chapters, we make sense of our own work as we retrospectively analyze and synthesize the main themes that have emerged during this study. Like the SSC staff, we hope that our work will have an impact, and that readers will consider the questions we pose aiming at transformation and change.

12

SSC REVELATIONS AND RECONCILIATIONS

Rituals of Understanding

SSC Students' Revelations

Eighty SSC students loiter in the back of the chapel on this Friday evening. Voices resonate throughout the room and the adjourning vestibule. With the end of the academic year 2 weeks away, students' conversations mostly focus on final examinations and summer plans. SSC staff members are busy meeting and greeting students. Salutations of welcome and gratitude dominate these exchanges. Aaron and Sarah discuss their upcoming wedding. Caleb talks about his SSC summer internship that is set to begin once the academic year concludes. Ted, the keyboard player and de facto band director, informs me (Peter) that staff reduced the usual music set list from 10 to 6 songs because it is "sharing night." Despite almost 2 years of fieldwork, this variation of the worship service is unfamiliar to me.

Dressed in a sport coat, tie, and T-shirt, Bobby is this evening's master of ceremonies. He looks like a street clown as he parades around the altar, and he appears to enjoy the attention. He begins with a warm welcome and follows with a list of announcements, a medley of songs, and an acquaintanceship "ice-breaker." As the program unfolds, familiar stimuli flood my senses. A stream of light, emanating from the back of the chapel to the screen behind the altar, pierces the darkness of the room. Guitarists strum, a drummer thumps, and backup singers sway in rhythm. Attendees reach for the sky as their resounding, and occasionally melodic, voices sing Jesus-friendly lyrics.

A student's 5-minute, born-again testimony follows. I am familiar with this ritual. After an introduction and a prayer by his mentor, the student reads the story of his revelation: a Christian from birth . . . spoon-fed faith from his parents as a child . . . a wayward adolescence . . . a serendipitous encounter with an evangelist leading to a "real" Christian awakening . . . and a new life—one that is far from perfect, but a life that involves walking with Jesus each and every day.

As the applause for the testimony subsides, the familiar Friday program takes a detour of sorts. Matthew, standing on the altar and facing his congregation, explains the rationale and the format for share night. "God has been working in your lives. God opened your eyes during this academic year. We are going to share what God has been doing in your life. We want to hear from you, so our eyes and ears are open." The students' collective resistance to speaking first creates a vacuum of silence. Eventually, a brave soul speaks, and others follow:

> Going to New Orleans during spring break was cool, depressing, and definitely an experience. My biggest lesson I learned is that God has blessed us. We take so much for granted. We have electricity, but they do not. Since I have been back, I have been thinking how much God has blessed me and us.

> _____

> I'm a history major, and people ask me what I am going to do with my life. God's calling me to do something. Recently, things came together. God talked to me; I am going into the seminary. I talked it over with my girlfriend; she is cool with it.

> _____

> I went to Germany with my friend. We went there standby, which is the worst way to travel. I prayed we would get back. God answered my prayers. We got on the flight, and we got business class and they waited on us hand and foot. What I learned in Germany happened when I was by myself for two days. I was okay being alone. I wandered around. I went to a concentration camp alone, which was depressing. I went to a chapel to pray and stuff. It was awesome what God taught me alone. It was God and me in Europe, and He taught me. The end!

> _____

> I have been here 3 years, and people still do not know me. I do my own things on weekends. I did not get to know people on a deep level. I went to New Orleans and I was grateful, and I learned what I missed out on the past 2 years. The people you surround yourself with can teach you much. I am glad I got to know you all better. I missed out, but not any more.

> _____

God has been working on my patience. . . . I am not the best driver. I was at an intersection downtown. My brakes locked, and I rear-ended a car. It was a good accident; I did not hurt anyone. The big car stood its ground and laughed at my car. . . . I took my car to the body shop, and they found a used hood; I saved two-thirds of the price. Cool, God bailed me out. It is kind of cool and [I'm] learning to be patient. I am waiting to hear about admission to a Ph.D. program. God has His plans and He knows what Purdue is going to say, and I have to put my faith in His hands.

I do Navy ROTC. It allows me to be here, and I do service for them. Thursday, I was working out and I . . . tore my ACL in my knee. I'm having surgery next month. I am going to be out 5 to 6 months. I had stuff planned for the summer—a cruise and sub [i.e., submarine]. Now, I have to sit at home. The Navy will stop paying me because I am hurt. I don't have money. It is kind of funny that we think we have our life figured out, but then we don't. It has been hard for me to figure out what God has planned for me. Pray for me. Put me on your prayer list.

I am new. I look forward to meeting all of you. My oboe professor is honest, and the feedback was horrible. I practiced and tried to improve. I turned into a workaholic. All I focused on was working to improve my oboe skills. Being with God helped me relax, and my lesson plans were better.

I also went to New Orleans. . . . It was hard to see people who lost everything. So many of our possessions we don't need. All we need is God. Materials should not be our focus. God should be our focus. . . . Way back when I was deciding what to do during spring break, two options were going on: a sorority trip or going home. Aaron encouraged me to go to New Orleans. I thank Aaron and God for that.

Researchers' Revelations

The final SSC Friday worship service of the 2006 academic year showcased an eclectic array of sacred and secular lessons learned as a result of students' participation in the SSC organization. Like SSC students, we too amassed numerous insights during our research. Following the students' lead, in this chapter we share our most powerful and potent learning by introducing numerous revelations resulting from our fieldwork. In Chapter 13, we augment these insights by introducing recommendations and considerations.

Regrettably, neither the SSC students nor we as researchers are able to reveal everything learned throughout the year. We ask readers for absolution for our "sins of omission."

Sommerville (2006) noted that "we judge other religions on the basis of our own religion. Indeed, we discover what our actual religion is by the judgments we render. This does not mean, however, the prophetic (alien) voices might not sometimes break through and challenge us. Those can be exciting, uncomfortable times" (p. 70). In this chapter, we examine and comment upon intriguing and perplexing central tenets and "commandments" of the SSC, evangelism, and American higher education, with the recognition that our life experiences influence these judgments. However, we do not intend these insights to be our version of the Sermon on the Mount. Instead, we hope that our alien, subjective, and sometimes uncomfortable interpretations will aid readers in gaining greater clarity about our views and about their own convictions concerning religion and higher education.

It's All about Jesus: Faith as an Oppositional Subculture

At first glance, the SSC looks like hundreds of other collegiate student organizations. It has a recognizable niche, recruits members, schedules meetings, sponsors programs for members and constituents, offers leadership opportunities, and focuses on learning outside the classroom. SSC-sponsored programs—weekly worship service, Bible study, evangelical training, and one-on-one discipleship meetings—also resemble other Christian student organizations' offerings. But closer examination of these rituals revealed unusual and important distinctions. For the SSC, it's all about Jesus; thus, faith is the foundation of this oppositional collegiate subculture.

The SSC's unique *cocurriculum* allows members to select a level of organizational involvement that uniquely fits their faith needs. Involvement levels range from members attending the once-a-week, 90-minute Friday night worship program to a Servant Leadership Team member devoting an average of 15 to 20 hours per week to SSC-sponsored events. Regardless of a member's level of organizational involvement, the focus is unique and unswerving—it's all about Jesus.

SSC elders infuse Jesus into almost every programmatic offering, and they model how the Bible should guide members' daily actions. Leaders infuse evangelical ideals into even hard-core secular topics such as post-college financial planning and organizing spring break trips, with the hope that members will grow the Kingdom one person at a time.

SSC's persistent expression of its faith in Jesus contributes to its status as an oppositional collegiate subculture. University policies that restrict or slow SSC's outreach to non-Christians in the residence halls, as well as the student culture's sometimes hedonistic cocurricular offerings, exemplify dynamics contributing to the organization's outsider status. Despite member characteristics such as being polite, wholesome, not so image-conscious, unpretentious, deferential, dutiful, conflict-avoidant, and action-oriented, there persists the perception of an oppositional subculture worthy of closer examination.

The Origins and Nature of SSC's Oppositional Subculture

Students Serving Christ's distinctive characteristics reveal an obvious, yet often overlooked realization about higher education—namely, that numerous diverse, distinct, and competing collegiate subcultures such as the SSC and its non-Christian organizational counterparts reside and coexist on every college campus. Examining and understanding collegians at the subculture level is particularly important, given the macro-examination of students that currently dominates the higher education scholarly landscape.

One popular framework scholars use to organize and analyze college students is generational theory. Most SSC students are part of the current generation of college students known as the *millennial generation* (Howe and Strauss, 2000). Using a generational framework for categorizing students and highlighting dominant trends is an important contribution to the scholarly literature, but it comes with liabilities. Generational theory can lead to radical homogenization and essentialism, which denies or flattens differences (Omi and Winant, 1994). These views of college students have the potential to inadvertently reduce otherness, uniqueness, and singularity; reinforce stereotypes; and divert attention away from those on the margins. Likewise, research about Christian collegians is often broad, homogenized, stereotypical, and essentialized (Weingarten, 2005). Subculture theory, among other advantages, augments and challenges contemporary macro-generational discourses and illuminates the inner workings of a particular Christian student organization. We intend this subculture analysis to challenge the essentialized notions of both college students and Christian evangelical students.

We theoretically analyze the unique SSC student subculture to better understand its style, including the SSC's origins, sustainability strategies, and resistance strategies. To examine the origins and nature of the SSC subculture, we explore two questions: "Why did the SSC subculture form?" and "What function does it serve?" To better understand the notion of subculture resistance (i.e., defending one's views against a more powerful force), we examine two additional questions: "What provokes the SSC subculture resistance?" and "What are the various forms of SSC resistance?" We also use the SSC case study to paint a detailed portrait of the SSC's style (Hebdige, 1979), which challenges conventional wisdom and monolithic/one-dimensional portrayals about what is considered *normal* within the SSC and what is normal among other collegiate subcultures. The reexamination of subculture style and notions of normalcy that dictate participants' everyday lives helps answer the question, "What counts as *normal* within the SSC subculture?"

A salient feature of higher education is the proliferation of subcultures. Subcultures exist, grow, and regularly form and support new subcultures. However, we tend to take subcultures for granted. Most of us are confident in our ability to recognize subcultures, so the phenomenon seldom arouses much attention. As a result, we have no clear understanding of the nature of subcultures, why they form, and what functions they serve. In higher education, the need exists to scrutinize the importance and nature of subcultures and the reasons for their rapid spread. We need also to develop an enhanced understanding of subcultures that can benefit higher education as well as faith-based organizations affiliated with colleges and universities.

The formation of subcultures or *communities of interest* (Magolda, 2000) is often linked to the quest for community and a reaction to a sense of marginalization. Carlson (1994) noted that the dominant conceptualization of community in the United States is that of a *normalizing* community. Normalizing communities emerge when those in power define a cultural center and "natural order" that render dominant group behaviors and values acceptable, while marginalizing others. Normalizing communities confer privileged status on certain individuals, activities, roles, and relationships and portray them as *normal*. Stuart Hall (cited in Hebdige, 1979) notes that dominant cultures exert "'total social control' over subordinate groups, not by coercion or by the direct imposition of ruling ideas, 'but by winning and shaping consent so that the power of the dominant classes appears both legitimate and natural'" (pp.15–16).

Subcultures form in reaction to the hegemony of dominant groups (Hebdige, 1979). Similarly, Carlson (1994) argues that *communities of interest* (i.e., subcultures) emerge when the idea of a single "unified in thought and action" community eludes the larger social entity (e.g., college campus). In order to resist normalizing expectations, marginalized groups often form communities of support. Members form these new groups, which they base on common interests, to give themselves and their fellow members voice and identity. In the world of most SSC members, their quest for Christian community was a priority long before they stepped foot on campus as first-year students. Locating a Christian community becomes an even greater priority on campus, as new students learn about the overarching values that guide their secular university and "what counts as normal" in this context. Organizations such as the SSC act as a Christian "safe haven" to satisfy students' need for community.

Resistance to mainstream ideas and marginalization are two commonalities the SSC enclave shares with other student subcultures such as women's associations and gay, lesbian, bisexual, and transgender student organizations— groups that are traditionally at odds, ideologically, with SSC's political agenda. Each of these student organizations situates itself as a less-powerful outsider that is resisting dominant campus norms. The SSC gains strength from this marginalized status, which fuels its resistance.

Ortner (1996) problematizes resistance and advocates the need to understand complexities surrounding resistance within subcultures: "Once upon a time, resistance was a relatively unambiguous category, half of the seemingly simple dualism domination/resistance. Domination was a relatively fixed and institutionalized form of power, and resistance was essentially organized resistance to such institutionalized power. This opposition began to be refined (but not abolished) through questioning of both terms" (p. 282).

Ortner argues that groups such as SSC are fraught with internal complexities. She states that resistors (i.e., subcultures such as SSC) "have their *own* politics—not just 'chiefs and commoners' . . . categories pulled out because they parallel the macro-resistance structure that the study is focused on—but all the local categories of friction and tension: men and women, parents and children, seniors and juniors. . . . and on and on" (1996, p. 285). In other words, rarely is the study of a subculture a simple case of a unified subculture resisting a dominant force. Ortner encourages readers to explore all the intricacies of a subculture as a means to avoid romanticized conceptions.

We acknowledge that there are numerous factions within the college student culture at large, but we focus on what we perceive to be their dominant and shared understandings, apart from their internal resistance complexities.

The SSC subculture as a whole resists at least three dominant forces on its campus. First, it politely yet firmly opposes public higher education values that steer clear of religious teachings. SSC also resists the dominant student culture at this public university that shuns following religious teachings in everyday life, as well as larger, more powerful campus Christian organizations.

The Origins and Nature of SSC's Subculture Style

SSC, in an effort to create a distinct and cohesive community of interest, co-opts and redefines the dominant culture's existing symbols and values. SSC members act as bricoleurs who collect mundane objects, ideas, and symbols from the dominant societal, campus, and Christian cultures and arrange them in a fashion that is unique in meaning to their particular subculture (Clarke, 1993). Cohen (1997) elaborates: "The new meanings emerge because the 'bits' which had been borrowed or revived were brought together into a new and distinctive stylistic ensemble: but also because the symbolic objects—dress, appearance, language, ritual occasions, styles of interaction, music—were made to form a unity with the group's relations, situation, experiences" (p. 110).

SSC bricoleurs take their redefined collection of artifacts, language, and behavioral characteristics and create a distinct *style* that is pregnant with complex meaning and structures that challenge dominant groups (Hebdige, 1979). Clarke (1993) asserts, "One of the main functions of a distinctive subcultural *style* is to define the boundaries of group membership as against other groups" (p. 180). Cohen (1997) adds, "[Subcultures] jointly establish new norms, new criteria of status which define as meritorious the characteristics they *do* possess, the kinds of conduct of which they are capable" (p. 51).

SSC has a distinctive style. Students reach out to Christians and non-Christians by spreading the Word to "one individual at a time" in personal and nonconfrontational ways. An SLT team member's assertion that "we learn to share the Lord's Word in dorms, and we meet new people and build relationships with them" exemplifies SSC's style, which avoids righteous or holier-than-thou interactions.

The SSC purposely schedules its weekly worship meetings on Friday nights to offer Christian students a sacred alternative to the dominant culture's profane Friday night activities. These meetings redefine what *Friday night* means to college students. SSC members communally celebrate their faith and love for Jesus rather than expend their energies on "drugs, sex, and rock and roll" and, most interestingly, individual academic achievement. Staff members remind attendees of this subculture's need to relate to God before homework or play and to conduct their ministry work concurrently with schoolwork.

The students' down-to-earth, casual, and conservative dress of jeans, T-shirts, cross pendants, and rubber bracelets with Christian symbols, as well as their lack of concern for primping in preparation for attending public events, convey the impression that members are not defined by their attire or appearance. Instead, they define themselves by their genuine relationship with Christ and their desire to live a moral life. This style is antithetical to the values of the dominant secular college student culture, such as affluence and materialism.

As bricoleurs, SSC members (as in other evangelical subcultures) retrieve words and phrases from the dominant secular culture and give them new meaning. Language is a powerful way of providing and sustaining group identity, and it marks in-group and out-group members. "Most organizations' languages, however, have unique words, phrases, and acronyms that are unrecognizable even to others who have backgrounds in the same technology" (Ott, 1989, pp. 26–27). For example, SSC members use the word "disciple" as a verb: "I am discipling someone right now." *Illustrations* are extended metaphors that aid SSC members in describing Christian principles to non-Christians during one-on-one meetings. SSC staff and students often use the phrase *to have a heart for* in talking about ways in which they believe God directs them to passionately minister to particular people. This unique language uses the dominant culture's lexicon, yet it marks SSC group membership identity as different from the dominant culture.

Summer and spring breaks usually are times of relaxation or paid work for students in the dominant culture. These spaces in the academic schedule take on a distinct meaning for SSC members, who use these occasions to get to know God better through mission trips and retreats. SSC members spoke often about personal time or quiet time. Common examples of personal time for students in the dominant culture include watching TV or exercising; SSC students recast these terms to mean weekly blocks of time devoted to silent reflection and prayer. E-mail tag lines for the dominant student culture often include quotes of the day or quotes from popular music lyrics; e-mail tag lines for SSC members are opportunities to share scripture verses with recipients.

This unique subculture style not only distinguishes this community of interest from its secular peers, but it also distinguishes the group from other Christian organizations. SSC favors more human-scale and substantive, or in-depth interaction. The not-so-polished Friday night worship meeting contrasts starkly with other, more stylized Christian worship services that we described in Chapter 1. SSC's homemade nametags and stream-of-consciousness, student-led activities reflect the organization's preference for sincere substance, rather than excess and extravagance. SSC programs are serious in tone, but simple in construction. Similar to the way in which appearance is less important to members than their relationship with God, the ambiance and the delivery of these programs are less important than the content. Earnest SSC members defer to SSC staff and often take notes during meetings and services. They seldom worry about being "hip" as defined by the dominant student subculture. Nevertheless, in an odd way their collective "unhip" persona makes them "in vogue" within the SSC. The staff and worship facilitators are rarely charismatic orators. In a low-key and sincere manner, they embrace the Bible's charismatic message and convey high expectations for students to adhere to the Bible's teachings.

SSC leaders strongly encourage members to attend formal and informal SSC offerings daily. These activities loosely resemble secular students' and other Christian students' daily priorities, which center on spending time with friends, significant others, and family. However, these "real Christian" contexts represent the organization's resistance to its secular university and Christian organizational counterparts.

SSC prides itself in substantively getting to know all new members and comprehensively attending to members' long-term spiritual needs. Students wishing to become members of the SLT teams engage with SSC staff in a process of soul-searching and discernment about their readiness before they receive training to evangelize and disciple others. However, students not wishing to become deeply involved in the organization are reminded that they will still be "embraced and loved." Whereas larger Christian groups do not have the luxury of substantively knowing each other, SSC's approach to mentoring members while spreading the Word favors intimate relationships that encourage in-depth faith development.

Whereas the larger Christian organizations structure their Bible studies as informal conversations, SSC Bible study leaders—who must be members of the leadership team—encourage participants to complete weekly written homework assignments and memorize scriptures. SSC Bible studies showcase a purposeful, unpretentious, patient, determined approach to encouraging Christians to embrace Jesus. Quality, not quantity, matters. The SSC leaders seldom overtly criticize other Christian organizations' "obsession" with reaching out to as many people as quickly as possible. Instead, they describe larger and more dominant Christian student organizations as "different," not wrong.

SSC staff and members, as bricoleurs, create a unique, cohesive style that stands in contrast to the dominant student cultures their organization opposes. These collected ideas and objects have an internal structure and sense of coherence, or *homology* (Hebdige, 1979). Through bricolage, then, subculture members interconnect symbols in order to create a distinctive style. SSC members have created a homology that focuses on the simple, faithful life—personal relationships with Christ and deep faith development.

At the foundation of this unique SSC style is a focus on student involvement and learning, which were key aspects of the organization's success that also intrigued us throughout the study as effective practices for higher education.

Researchers' Reconciliations

As we debriefed our fieldwork and fleshed out our field notes, we frequently returned to two questions scribbled in the margins of our notebooks: "How?" and "Huh?" The "how" notation was shorthand for the question, "How did they do that?" The "Huh?" notion was shorthand for the question, "They do what!?" These notations called attention to distinctive events or dynamics that were, in our opinion, atypical, counterintuitive, and potentially problematic. For example, Bible study participants would spend more than 2 hours deconstructing biblical passages and offering their diverse and thoughtful interpretations. They would masterfully scaffold their interpretations and often reach a consensus on meaning. In the margin of my field notes, I (Peter) would initially write "How?" because these exchanges appeared like ideal examples of learning in a collegiate context. Then, as the session concluded, the facilitator would share "*the* biblical interpretation" and thus occasionally undermine the students' interpretations. The facilitator's decision to allow students to explore and co-construct interpretations for 2 hours, only to proclaim the "right answer" at the conclusion, elicited a "Huh?" response in the margin of my field notes. Exploring interpretations of absolute truths seems counterintuitive. We spent most of our post-field-work time together trying to understand and appreciate these "How?" and "Huh?" encounters.

Promising Practices

From our explorations, two unique and positive "how?" aspects of the SSC subculture emerged, focusing on the organization's ability to [1] maintain high-quality and sustained student involvement and [2] maintain an unyielding commitment to student learning. Three unique, counterintuitive, and perplexing "huh?" issues also emerged. These centered on the organization's struggles to [1] position itself as the marginalized majority, [2] remain both insular and accessible, and [3] remain true to both traditional and progressive Christian agendas. These five subculture issues and the SSC's strategies for managing them are the centerpiece of the discussions that follow.

How Did They Do That?: High Quality and Sustained Student Involvement Colleges and universities recognize the importance of providing purposeful, meaningful, out-of-class experiences for all students. In the out-of-class arena, most collegiate organizations struggle to provide high-quality and diverse offerings that address students' needs and sustain their involvement. Student organizations often attract members who, over time, become bored and disinterested in the organization's offerings, which results in organizational attrition or membership stagnation. Anecdotal data from students and staff of other organizations yielded a consensus that it is difficult to keep students interested in organizations across their time in college. For example, the largest Christian group on campus, which we highlighted in Chapter 1, does not have enough upper-class students to serve as Bible study leaders. Consequently, first-year students are tapped to serve in this leadership role.

The SSC organization struggled with this challenge too. The organization perceives itself as "a place Christians need to be," not "the place to be" for Christians. It did not simply recruit members, but instead recruited members who were serious about Jesus. At the same time, SSC was conscious of the need to have sufficient members to maintain their existence and, more importantly, to grow God's Kingdom. This ideology slowed the flow of members into the organization and potentially could accelerate their exit from it. Nevertheless, the SSC has been successful in recruiting members and offering them a meaningful, out-of-class curriculum that contributes to their prolonged involvement in the organization.

In particular, the organization's *recruitment strategies and the diversity and sequencing of its program offerings* are two distinctive elements of the SSC's style that, according to SSC members, contribute to meaningful and sustained student involvement and optimize the organization's mobilization efforts to spread God's Word.

A Purposeful and Active Recruitment Plan of Action   Most SSC members expected to join a Christian organization after arriving on campus as first-year students. Interviews revealed that many SSC students visited Christian organizations' Web sites and shopped around for the ideal organization during their first days on campus. SSC students recognize that Christian organizations are not alike; as a result, they seek peers and student organizations that subscribe to their brand of Christianity.

Although SSC reaps the benefits of new students who are predisposed to joining a Christian organization, SSC members employ a strategic and comprehensive grassroots recruitment strategy, rather than wait for Christians to find them. This process begins long before students arrive on campus and is highly active during the first few weeks of the academic year. Most SSC members whom we interviewed found the SSC, or the SSC found them, during their first weeks on campus. The SSC recruitment efforts showcased the organization's "three Fs"—faith, fellowship, and fun. Prospective students appreciated the fact that SSC recruiters did not try to be *all things to all people*. SSC recruiters unambiguously clarify the purpose of the organization to prospective members and seek recruits who subscribe to those values. After students join SSC, their involvement yields a rich harvest of learning that contributes to their satisfaction with their college experience.

SSC's *roll-up-your-sleeves-and-get-to-work* recruitment strategy shuns high-pressure tactics. It sustains and satisfies student involvement with genuine human interactions. Purposeful, active, and targeted recruitment yields peers who share similar interests, which contributes to students' persistence in SSC and college, as well as to other positive outcomes. The professional literature documenting the importance of student involvement/engagement and learning is bountiful. Cross Brazzell and Reisser (1999) posited that "the greater the opportunity for students to participate in a range of activities, the more likely they are to feel a part of their community and to become productive contributors" (p. 173). Six years earlier, Davis and Murrell (1993) drew similar conclusions: "Research during the past two decades has demonstrated that the more energy that students direct into their academic lives, including becoming engaged with their studies and campus programs, the greater the likelihood of their having a positive college experience" (p. 93). Likewise, SSC students credit their involvement in the organization with enhancing their satisfaction with their collegiate experience.

Whenever they interact with prospective members, SSC members extol the organization's modest size. Many students join because of the SSC's human scale. For SSC students, prerequisites to meaningful engagement and sustained involvement outside the classroom include a recruitment process that helps prospective members discern whether the organization is compatible with their values. Is SSC an organization that allows members to develop personal relationships and learn from one another? Does it provide opportunities that encourage members to continually grow and learn through diverse offerings—thereby avoiding what one student called, "4 years of the same old, same old"?

A well-documented result of student involvement is the formation of support networks that assist students with difficulties they encounter. The SSC curriculum attempts to cultivate a *values-based* support network for students, which has been shown to have positive effects on students' level of engagement in their collegiate experience. According to Dalton (1999), a supportive community can help college students define their ethics and values. "Students' experience with a supportive sense of community in an educational setting can contribute substantially to the development of their values. A community support system makes it easier for students to experiment and take risks" (p. 54).

Ultimately, the SSC enclave is a supportive environment that additionally provides students with abundant opportunities to reflect on and solidify their values and Christian beliefs, which encourages them to stay with the organization for their entire collegiate career. Purposeful and active recruitment also contributes to students' persistence in SSC and college by yielding a group of peers with similar interests.

A Diverse and Purposefully Sequenced Curriculum   The SSC's diverse program offerings and their sequencing involve four qualitatively different levels of involvement. This curriculum allows members to select an appropriate level of involvement compatible with their personal and evangelical needs/desires, which results in high student satisfaction and sustained involvement. Each discrete SSC program serves a particular segment of the membership, and SSC's goals center on members' sustained involvement with Christian ideals. Curricular offerings focus on learning and encourage students to remain in the organization.

The Friday night worship program is the most inclusive and the most basic SSC offering; it requires a modest degree of involvement on the part of attendees. Matthew invites these members to spend 90 minutes a week with like-minded students who enjoy singing, listening to spiritual awakening stories and sermons, and participating in prayer and spiritually healthy social activities.

During these entry-level worship programs, students learn about additional opportunities, such as Bible study, that require a greater commitment on their part. During Bible study gatherings, which represent the organization's second level of involvement, students' roles are more substantive than during the Friday worship service. Attendees lead prayer, offer and listen to multiple interpretations of the passages, cull lessons learned from the passages, and brainstorm ways to enact the Bible's lessons.

At SSC's third and fourth levels, participants build upon their self-improvement agenda, which serves as the cornerstone of the first two levels. They add an outreach/outward emphasis and include others in their improvement mission. The agenda shifts from improving oneself to improving oneself *and* others. At SSC's third level, the Servant Leadership Team (SLT) members invite Bible study attendees to participate in a 4-week, 8-hour Bridge evangelical training program. The centerpiece of this level is for SSC participants to learn the six principles for sharing the Word of God with others and a tightly scripted 10-minute biblical illustration. The aim of the illustration is to introduce Christianity in a nonthreatening manner to Christians and non-Christians. This third level provides members the tools to learn more about the Bible, themselves, and—most important—effective mobilization strategies for spreading the Word of God.

Matthew invites all members to apply to become a member of the SLT, which is the fourth level of SSC involvement (although we suspect that SSC members who completed the illustration training—the third level of involvement—would be given preference in the SLT selection process). The SLT involves two subgroups: the Evangelism Team (E-Team) for sophomores and the Discipleship Team (D-Team) for juniors. Individuals who apply and accept Matthew's invitation to join the SLT pledge a serious time commitment to the SSC organization.

For most SLT members, the SSC becomes the epicenter of their collegiate existence. Typically, these students devote between 15 and 20 hours per week to Jesus. For example, Timothy, a senior, spends 14 hours per week attending classes and about an equal amount of time studying. Beyond his academic commitments, he devotes most of his waking hours to SSC activities. Each day, Timothy prays and reads his Bible. Weekly he [1] attends the Friday worship program, including the social event that follows; [2] prepares and facilitates one Bible study group per week, as well as attending another; [3] attends a prayer meeting with peers each week, which concludes with a community dinner; [4] attends the SLT gathering; [5] disciples two students; [6] seeks discipleship counsel from Aaron; and [7] visits the residence halls to support younger SSC members as they evangelize and follow up on surveys. Every month he attends on-campus and regional training sessions or off-campus retreats. During spring breaks, he participates in week-long SSC-sponsored missionary outings, and he devotes his summers to Bible study and SSC internships. During his sophomore year, Timothy began dating a Christian woman, which allowed him to intertwine his personal and SSC responsibilities. For the 30 or so students such as Timothy who are most deeply involved in the SSC, Jesus is the top priority.

SSC rejects a one-size-fits-all formula for its members. Instead, it offers an organizational structure and series of evangelical programs that encourage varying levels of involvement. This mutually beneficial model contributes to student learning and progressively builds students' investment and involvement in SSC. Within each level of involvement, students have numerous opportunities for development of their personal beliefs, morals, interpersonal skills, and leadership. SSC creates opportunities for student learning that match each individual's level of interest and investment.

These curricular options undoubtedly benefit SSC, in that it identifies members who are deeply aligned with and committed to its political agenda. Those members serve as leaders for SSC and are a huge asset when recruiting and mobilizing members to spread SSC's ideas. Nevertheless, Matthew pledges that SSC will support members who select lower levels of involvement. This affirmation contributes to students' perceptions that the organization is welcoming, which also sustains their participation.

For SSC students, prerequisites to meaningful engagement and sustained involvement outside the classroom include a recruitment process that helps members discern whether the organization is compatible with their values; an organization that allows members to develop personal relationships and learn from one another; and opportunities to continually grow and learn through diverse offerings. For Matthew and his SLT, prerequisites for a "meaningful" organization include identifying those students who are seriously interested in following Christ; providing opportunities for Christians to learn about God, themselves, and others; and providing opportunities for members to advance God's agenda.

How Did They Do That?: An Unyielding Commitment to Learning
American higher education has traditionally subscribed to a "divide and conquer" approach to serving students. Colleges and universities artificially designate classroom experiences as the context for learning that cultivates the mind. Faculty members assume responsibility for facilitating student learning in the classroom or laboratory. Typically, student affairs professionals assume primary responsibility for experiences outside the classroom that tend to students' noncognitive needs.

Over the past few decades, American higher education has embraced a more holistic and permeable conceptualization of learning, recognizing that learning occurs both inside and outside the classroom/laboratory. Thus, the goal of educating students must involve both academic and student affairs personnel. Merging these domains of learning is in the best interest of students, given that the separation between cognitive and noncognitive domains is artificial and false in many ways.

Despite "progress" associated with this blurring of students' in-class and out-of-class learning experiences, serious and sustained learning is seldom the highest priority for most student organizations. Student organizations struggle to seamlessly meld learning with other organizational priorities, and they fear that too much emphasis on formal learning, especially outside the classroom, might unintentionally "turn off" students and result in the organization's attrition. Consequently, cocurricular activities often fall short of student affairs educators' goals to engage students meaningfully, promote their learning and development, and sustain their involvement throughout their college years.

Describing student affairs divisions that effectively infuse learning into the cocurriculum, Blimling and Whitt (1999) argue:

> Student-learning-oriented student affairs divisions can be created through good student affairs practice: engaging students in active learning, helping students develop coherent values and ethical standards, setting and communicating high expectations for learning, using systematic inquiry to improve student and institutional performance, using resources effectively to achieve institutional missions and goals. (p. 180)

SSC subscribes to many of these ideals. The organization's learning-centered curriculum and pedagogy values student engagement, emphasizes values and ethics, has high expectations for members to deepen their faith and spread the Word of God, values ongoing intellectual inquiry, and devotes organizational resources to fulfilling its mission. In this regard, the SSC is unique. It neither accepts the in-class and out-of-class learning dichotomy nor subscribes to the fear that making (Christian) learning a priority would result in an organizational exodus.

SSC's emphasis on student learning is uncommon and pervasive. Recruitment strategies not only focus on generating enthusiasm for the organization, but existing members also gently teach prospective members about the mission of the SSC, which demonstrates the value they place on teaching and learning. During "fun" Friday worship services, components such as sporadic testimonies, sermons, and songs subtly educate students about Christian ways of life in college. Bible study, evangelical training, E-team/D-team gatherings, and the LLC senior workshop exemplify the more formal and intense learning opportunities for members. The SSC's staff expectations that members evangelize and disciple peers are additional evidence of the organization's commitment to teaching and learning.

The SSC staff members cultivate a passion for lifelong Christian learning, which fuels members' passions to ultimately teach. Members begin their affiliation with SSC as learners. During Friday programs, students listen to testimonials and sermons. Bible study meetings provide attendees with opportunities to explore the roles of both student and teacher. After successfully completing the evangelical training and joining the Servant Leadership Team, members assume new roles as mentors, leaders, and coaches who lead Bible studies and disciple other students. The organization cultivates a passion for learning, which results in a passion for teaching (i.e., spreading the Word by evangelizing); this is another important component of the SSC educational curriculum.

The SSC's emphasis on human-scale activity further fosters a sustained collaborative learning environment, which Kuh et al. (2005) assert is the key to maximizing student learning. For example, peer-led SSC Bible study sessions focus on inviting students to collectively explore how biblical lessons can be applied to their lives. Likewise, the social activity that follows the Friday night worship program allows attendees to discuss the ideas advanced during the program, pose questions, and exchange perspectives. For students, assuming the dual role of teacher and learner motivates them to stay involved and advance the organization's political agenda.

The SSC's layered curriculum identifies, energizes, and organizes members to prepare for action and benefits what SSC leaders perceive to be the greater good—that is, to spread the Word of God—by strategically mobilizing members to recruit and cultivate relationships with students interested in learning more about Christ and serving Him. SSC offers meaningful opportunities to educate members to fulfill this quest. Effective mobilization does not result from simply bringing like-minded individuals together. A key component of effective mobilization is providing meaningful and sustained educational opportunities for members. An incremental educational agenda that centers on learning is essential to the SSC's success.

SSC's cocurriculum also intentionally interconnects student learning with the organization's core values: faith, fellowship, and fun. Nearly every SSC activity emphasizes the organization's unambiguous faith agenda. SSC staff sermons encourage students to abandon their self-centeredness and strengthen their relationship with and faith in Jesus. Furthermore, they offer biblical rationales for pursuing a college degree. In each sermon topic, the staff encourages attendees to learn about their faith and themselves.

The informal meet-and-greet exchanges prior to SSC Friday worship services symbolically celebrate the organization's commitment to fellowship and the need for attendees to think biblically about what counts as a community. The SSC community helps students define their ethics, values, and faith, as well as learn how to support others in their quest to learn about God. Thus, the SSC's Christian social network goes hand-in-hand with learning more about—and spreading—the Word of God. Social activities showcase SSC's third core value: fun activities aligned with Christian values. These fun activities help students learn how to balance working hard for Jesus with enjoying "clean" Christian fun.

Learning is fundamental in each activity, and the SSC encourages students to live out their faith, fellowship, and fun core values. At first glance, the program offerings seem eclectic, connected only by a shared focus on student learning. However, organization leaders have devised a plan to integrate these activities into a seamless learning experience, which is the centerpiece of the cocurriculum. As a result of SSC's purposeful, diverse, integrated, and spiritually sequenced cocurriculum, a deeply committed cadre of members emerges. These students are devoted to the core values of the SSC and to enacting the organization's espoused agenda to spread the Word of God via evangelism and discipleship activities. Students serve the greater good by modeling a Christian lifestyle and teaching others to "live with Christ."

Although at times we have taken exception to the SSC's learning content and pedagogy, the organization's relentless quest to continually provide deep learning opportunities for students outside the classroom as well as create a progressive (i.e., one that innovatively and incrementally builds toward a goal) and deep learning paradigm is unusual and noteworthy. They practice what they preach and teach.

To answer the question "How did they do that?" regarding an unyielding commitment to student learning, the SSC:

1. *Aligns the organization's learning activities with its core values,* which helps SSC students identify an organizational mission and what they hope to learn as members. As a result, they can focus their time and effort on the activities that *really matter.*
2. *Creates diverse, integrated, sequenced program offerings.* Each role or activity builds upon the previous year, so students can anticipate something new and

exciting, as well as more challenging opportunities for personal growth. In the SSC, students progressively gain leadership skills, so they are well prepared to move into peer mentor and teacher roles as upper-class students.

3. *Finds ways for students to apply the skills and self-knowledge they gain in the organization to serve the organization's conception of the greater good.* SSC students experienced deeper learning when they were given the opportunity to put their education into practice as they reached out to others. Organization advisors and leaders can assist students in finding real-world applications for the skills they learn.

4. *Encourages peer teaching and learning that center on students' experiences.* Organizational advisors can encourage students to take leadership roles, use their own experiences as a knowledge base for decision-making, and serve as teachers as well as learners, which will maximize peer and individual learning.

The four insights about the organization's successes in the learning arena echo current research such as the work of Kuh et al. (2005), which states that—in terms of student learning—the content matters less than the degree to which students are *engaged* in the learning process. SSC organizational leaders designed a progressive educational agenda focusing on teaching and learning to supplement each of the organization's levels of involvement. Thus, although SSC is a religious organization, its successes can be translated to other secular student organization contexts.

Perplexing Paradoxes

A sense of internal coherence exists within the SSC subculture, or what Hebdige (1979) refers to as homology, as evidenced by the involvement and learning discussions in the previous section. Still, as in most subcultures, paradoxes or contradictions also define and confound SSC members. In this section we analyze three "Huh?" experiences that we encountered during our fieldwork and that we perceived to have an adverse effect on the organization's effectiveness. SSC's young evangelicals hardly resemble the caricature or stereotype of righteous, nonreflective, and imposing ideologues. The SSC subculture is ideological, but there is moderation at the root of that ideology. Simply stated, SSC members blend their unyielding faith and truths with practical considerations as they live their lives and attempt to walk with Jesus, mentor peers, and evangelize. This moderation philosophy contributes to their seemingly contradictory or straddled descriptions as the "Marginalized Majority," "Insular Evangelicals," and "Progressive Fundamentalists." These oxymoronic "huh?" features represent the root of unresolved tensions in the SSC and are thus worthy of analysis.

Huh?: The Marginalized Majority Evangelical Christians wield enormous power nationwide. On this particular campus, Christianity is the most popular religious preference for students. Within the student organization context, the university catalogues 27 of the 250 student organizations (10.8%) as "religious," and 21 (77.7%) of them profess an explicit Christian emphasis. Christianity dominates the religious student organization landscape, and options for student involvement in diverse Christian organizations are plentiful and popular. Also, according to the results of UCLA's Cooperative Institutional Research Program survey (UCLA Higher Education Research Institute, 2005) of new students, 41.5% (40.3% men and 42.4% women) of students on this campus listed a Christian-related category as their religious preference. Moreover, 86 percent of survey respondents indicated that they *attended a religious service during the past year.* In essence, attending religious services is widely accepted.

Racially, the SSC organization is almost entirely (with the exception of a handful of members) White, which adds to members' status as belonging to yet another dominant campus group. Despite these demographics, the SSC—an evangelical subculture of Christians—positions itself as a not-so-powerful, outsider student organization.

Since 1975, SSC has maintained a close affiliation with its parent evangelical organization. This international organization provides name recognition, human resources support, membership training, spiritual encouragement, and most important, legitimacy to the SSC and its members. During SSC sermons, training programs, leadership meetings, and testimonials, program organizers remind attendees that if they follow the Bible and act as Christians, they are on God's side. SSC leaders frequently espouse binary categories (e.g., Christian/non-Christian) and biblical mandates that Christians choose the right and righteous side. These assertions hardly sound like the discourse of powerless outsiders.

Seifert (2007) argues that Christian privilege is deeply woven into the fabric of American higher education. University calendars (e.g., organizing semesters/quarters around Christmas), physical facilities (e.g., the presence of on-campus chapels), and high-profile public rituals (e.g., nondenominational prayers during commencement or graduation) privilege Christian collegians. SSC members acknowledge that Christians are the largest religious denomination on campus and they recognize some privilege, but they argue that whereas the university is seldom overtly hostile to Christians, their campus influence is minimal. SSC further argues that although there are thousands of self-declared Christians on campus, far fewer of them actually lead a Christian life. One finding from a 2004 national survey that the Higher Education Research Institute conducted supports SSC students' common argument: "Most college freshmen believe in God, but fewer than half follow religious teaching in their daily lives" (Bartlett 2005, A-1, A-40). SSC's feelings of marginalization mask the reality of its privilege; the organization quietly and politely laments its muted voice and influence on campus.

SSC occupies a paradoxical, conflicted position as an organization both privileged and harmed. Members' marginalization discourses, while at times incomplete and contradictory, effectively focus and mobilize the membership and create a sense of solidarity that advances the organization's agenda to evangelize. The SSC subculture vacillates on the majority–minority power continuum, and members usually situate themselves in the middle as moderates—neither powerless, nor the powerful cultural epicenter of campus life.

SSC is far less known when compared to the largest Christian organization, but is better known than the many smaller Christian organizations. The SSC talks about growing the Kingdom, yet at the same time remains hypersensitive to its desire to be a human-scale organization. This desire to remain small complicates efforts to grow the Kingdom and to create a critical mass of "real Christians" on campus. The SSC wants to alter the secular ethos of its public university, but it restrains its efforts to grow into a powerful entity on campus that can induce change. As Matthew suggests, "We work very hard to grow, while upholding our values and calling. We call attention to our smaller size in recruiting because it helps us, but we would like to at least double our current size. We believe that we could do this without sacrificing the 'high touch' quality of the ministry."

This moderate stance attracts Christian students who are neither radical progressives nor fundamentalists. The absence of radical members contributes to a sense of solidarity. At the same time, however, the organization's moderate identity creates some angst and subculture identity crises that make

it more difficult to enact its evangelical aspirations—that is, for *real* followers of Jesus to be a majority group on campus. In the end, the SSC remains
mired and comfortable as the marginalized majority.

Huh?: Insular Evangelicals   Subcultures such as the SSC originate in
opposition to the dominant culture and fill voids the dominant culture
ignores or attempts to repress (Hebdige, 1979). Thus, participation in a
subculture naturally separates members from the dominant culture, as well as
from other subcultures. This isolation provides members strength and
solidarity. Tensions arise as the subculture's members strive to remain both
distinctive and insular as well as accessible and influential to outside entities.

The SSC organization appeared to be in a perpetual state of restlessness
as it positioned itself on this expansive insularity-to-outreach continuum.
SSC narratives documented numerous instances of the SSC's preference for
an insular life. In the institutional context, the sacred SSC positioned itself
in opposition to the secular university. A variation of the classic separation of
church and state battle emerged, which resulted in the SSC affirming its
insular posture as the two distinct entities peacefully coexisted and infre-
quently engaged in superficial interactions.

In the student context, SSC students positioned themselves in opposition to the un-Godly ways of many collegians. Despite organizational
goals to reach out to non-Christians, members privileged their internal
SSC organizational activities rather than interacting with other organizations. When given the option to pursue either their more insular discipleship duties (i.e., a process involving more experienced SSC members
mentoring younger members) or their evangelizing activities (i.e., a
process necessitating SSC members to move outside their organizational
cocoon and interact with "the other"), students overwhelmingly opted for
the former.

In the Christian student organization context, SSC students positioned
themselves as the Christian *David* in opposition to the larger and higher-
profile *Goliath*—the campus-based Christian organization that boasted more
than 1,000 members and 30 staff. In the SSC versions of this myth, David's
Christian depth, developed through discipleship, triumphs over Goliath's
Christian breadth, developed through evangelism. With the SSC's prefer-
ences for discipleship and depth, its members often opted for the more insular activities. The SSC seldom formally collaborated with its Christian

neighbor; a friendly and cordial "live and let live" mentality prevailed as both groups set about doing "God's work."

As SSC members gravitated toward the insular end of the continuum, they gained a sense of solidarity and security, even though favoring the insular life undermined their missionary outreach and mobilization goals. Those goals included altering negative aspects of the student and institutional culture, ministering to non-Christians, and strengthening the campus Christian community. Because of their homogeneity—racial, ethnic, socio-economic, and religious—SSC students felt most comfortable recruiting and spending time with students in the SSC who were *just like them*. That augmented the SSC's ranks with new Christian recruits, but likely stunted the organization's evangelical efforts to attract diverse others, some of whom are resistant to the SSC's evangelizing. Bryant's (2007a) recent profile of collegiate evangelicals sheds light on this gravitational pull toward, ironically, an isolated existence.

> One of the basic tenets of evangelical Christianity is that followers should do what the name implies: evangelize. . . . I observed a handful of individuals who were, for the most part, comfortable with evangelism, but another substantial proportion of the students I interviewed expressed a great deal of ambivalence for a variety of reasons, one of which had to do with their desire to avoid classic stereotypes about Christians. Among those expressing more discomfort with respect to evangelizing strangers or evangelizing at all, the vast majority were first-year students. (Bryant 2007a, para. 21)

Most SSC students fit Bryant's profile. Much of their uneasiness with outreach stems from their peers' pervasive negative perceptions of evangelicals. SSC staff and students want to influence their peers during college, but the desire to avoid hostile or judgmental peers contributes to their reluctance to engage in outreach. Cooperman's (2007) research affirms Bryant's findings centering on outsider's perceptions of evangelicals.

> Tobin asked professors at all kinds of colleges—public and private, secular and religious, two-year and four-year, to rate their feelings toward various religious groups, from very warm or favorable to very cool or unfavorable. He said he designed the question primarily to gauge anti-Semitism but found that professors expressed positive feelings toward Jews, Buddhists,

Roman Catholics and most other religious groups. The only groups that elicited highly negative responses were evangelical Christians and Mormons. (p. A3)

Ironically, SSC evangelical students, who value interacting with "the other" in the hope of conversion, resist in-depth engagement and evangelize reluctantly. When they do evangelize, they try to counter negative evangelical stereotypes and appear to be too timid to achieve their salvation agenda. The SSC assumes a moderate position on the collegiate outreach continuum. Based on our analysis of interviews, SSC students remain more comfortable interacting with like-minded peers than converting nonbelievers.

The informal survey conducted during the initial Bridge training session illuminated this tension involving members making the SSC organization the core of their collegiate universe and reaching out to others. Bridge attendees participated in the ongoing seminar to learn the art of evangelizing, but they confessed to being uncomfortable with the ultimate expectation of conversing with and converting non-Christians. Still, they pursue this daunting task because it is God's will. According to Perry and Armstrong (2007), "confronting the stereotypes of peers and professors who don't understand them is part of life on a secular campus. They [Christians] rely heavily on the support and understanding of a like-minded community centered in and around evangelical organizations on campus" (para. 9, para. 10). In practice, students' outreach goals look dramatically different from the organization's stated evangelical goals.

Being insular is "in." SSC's weekly prayer meetings, Bible studies, socials, and training sessions allow members substantive and sustained contact with Christian peers. SSC staff members mentor SLT members, and more veteran SSC members mentor younger members. These insular activities are frequent and substantive; SSC students regularly spend weekends, spring breaks, and summers together. As a result of these interactions, students gain personal and faith-based fulfillment.

When we asked upper-class students to tell us stories that would sensitize us to what it is like to be a member of the SSC, they regularly told stories about the strong relationships members formed with one another. At times, these strong peer friendships gradually morphed into more intimate relationships. Although SSC students seldom talked about dating relationships informally or during interviews (unless asked), they regularly dated—and not surprisingly, they dated other Christians. As a subculture, SSC leaders tacitly endorse heterosexual dating as a "normal" part of the SSC experience. Dating guidelines—dos and don'ts based on biblical teachings—accompany these endorsements. The large number of SSC couples has much to do with the insular nature of the organization and the considerable amount of time members spend with one another each day. For example, all three staff couples "found" their spouses within the SSC organization. SSC members do not appear to be obsessed with finding mates, but if dating appears on a member's "radar screen," there is a very high likelihood that he or she will look inside the SSC organization and connect with another Christian. Sidanius, Van Laar, Levin, and Sinclair (2004) studied ethnic student groups and concluded that those insular organizations enhanced students' social identities, rather than their desire to engage in broader university life and to interact substantively with other organizations. Our SSC fieldwork experience mirrors these findings.

Collectively, the organization's grassroots evangelizing style makes sense in light of their stance as insular evangelicals. Whereas the larger campus Christian organization uses what Matthew frequently termed "guerrilla" tactics to gain large numbers of converts, SSC students convert peers one at a time. "Timid" is an ideal descriptor of the SSC's grassroots evangelizing persona. Unlike the stereotype of a pushy, aggressive, berating evangelical standing on the street corner warning pedestrians of their evil lifestyle and destiny in Hell, SSC students are quite hesitant and, at times, unassertive in their one-on-one evangelical efforts. Sometimes, after a brief, exploratory encounter with an SSC member, the "evangelized" non-Christians did not even recognize or characterize the encounter as evangelical in nature. SSC members as evangelists favor being too cautious and polite. Bryant (2007a) found similar struggles among other collegiate evangelical Christians:

> Do they befriend and reach out? Do they retreat? It is difficult to account for the range of responses that transpired when I talked with students about what it was like to be Christian on a public university campus . . . the experience for the majority, I would venture, can be best summarized in one word: Unease—a sentiment that is understandable given the negative stereotypes evangelical students absorb about Christians from those around them. (para. 23)

Sharlet's (2007) recounting of a radical evangelical crusader's verbal diatribe—"and we gotta be ready to fight and not be these passive little lukewarm, namby-pamby, kum-ba-yah, thumb-sucking babies that call themselves Christians. Jesus? He got mad!" (p. 50)—describes the evangelical stereotypes SSC students want to avoid. SSC's moderate stance challenges these negative stereotypes of the hard-core collegiate evangelical.

> In desiring to avoid conflictual interactions with their peers, students are tempted to retreat to the safety of a like-minded peer group. Evangelical students report a sense of 'instant intimacy' with their Christian peers, and find safe haven within the boundaries of their campus organizations. Nonetheless, students enjoy substantial rewards when they take risks, step beyond ideological borders they have established, and approach others in a spirit of openness. (Bryant, 2007a, para. 25)

SSC encourages students to be risk-takers in their evangelism, as Bryant suggested. Programs such as the senior seminar target students' hesitancy to evangelize and offer practical suggestions to overcome these apprehensions. Matthew and staff intended this seminar to help students find a new, supportive, noncollegiate Christian enclave and devise new and different evangelical strategies that will allow SSC alumni to reach out to non-Christians. SSC student interviewees agreed with the premise of reaching out to diverse others, but in the end they found it difficult to actually follow through with their stated mission.

Although the SSC espouses a balance between its inside and outside worlds, it favors being insular. As insular evangelicals, SSC students develop strong in-group relationships and buck the stereotypes of "pushy" evangelicals. Dennis commented on the ideal SSC evangelizing strategy: "They have to genuinely care about things going on in others' lives, and be trustworthy and flexible . . . not like 'it's my way or the highway,' or 'this is the law,' but able to consider other ideas and get input and stuff. . . . A lot of it seems like common sense—how to interact with them and how to value the people they are, and stuff like that." This strategy seems to "work" for SSC students, who recognize the biblical call to evangelize and are thus willing to engage in evangelism, despite their preference to avoid it. Nevertheless, their reluctance to take risks and assertively evangelize limits their ability to meet their espoused organizational mission to spread the Word.

In addition, the organization's homogeneity and insularity contribute to members' inability to view their organization in new, innovative ways. Although Matthew and Jessica moved to another university in 2007, the organization there looks remarkably the same—same structure, same type of students and directors, same messages. We do not advocate that the SSC give up its core mission and shared values. On the contrary, we argue that the infusion of new ideas and diversity into the organization could help it strive toward continual improvement in reaching its stated evangelical goals.

Huh?: Progressive Fundamentalists   Despite SSC students' preference to remain insular, they remain deeply committed to their relationship with God and continually explore ways to strategically reach out to others, challenge "misperceptions" about evangelicals, and spread God's message. They recognize that "much of religious engagement on American campuses takes place outside the classroom" (Calhoun, 2007), but they struggle with how to present their fundamentalist, Bible-based ideas in a progressive, secular world. The SSC organization appeared to be in a perpetual state of restlessness as it positioned itself on this expansive fundamentalist–progressive evangelical continuum to engage their peers in discussions about Jesus.

The SSC narratives showcased the importance of the Bible in every facet of students' life. SSC staff and students use the Bible as *the* fundamental source of inspiration and answers. Students' strict reliance on the Bible contributes to their pull toward the fundamentalist end of the fundamentalist–progressive continuum. This continuum reflects different ideologies that in turn reflect different root paradigms and assumptions. For SSC members, the Bible is literally inerrant—containing no mistakes. It is a literal account of the world and the final authority guide that SSC Christians must strictly follow. These students believe in an absolute Truth, and Bryant (2007a) elaborates on this trend:

> The notion of truth and its absoluteness is a central feature of the evangelical mindset. In interviews, most students shared reflections similar to this one: "There is something out there, whether or not I possess it, that is the truth no matter what. It doesn't change. It's not a variable. . . . There's something there that is *it,* that is the end of everything . . . It doesn't matter what you do to it. . . . All that matters [is that] it's there, it exists, it's truth, with a capital 'T.'" (para. 28)

Dalton (1980) asserts that a negative by-product of this realist ontology can be anti-intellectualism. "Despite the efforts of campus evangelical leaders to avoid the stigma of anti-intellectualism, it has often been unavoidable because of their literalist views on the authority of the Bible. The charge of anti-intellectualism is by no means a new one to evangelicals; it runs deep in their historical legacy" (p. 26). SSC students recognize the negative baggage associated with espousing evangelical fundamentalism and persuading collegiate peers to adhere to Truth. They realize that if they are to evangelize successfully, they must counter these stereotypes and embrace a more progressive outreach strategy, without abandoning their fundamental roots. As Romanowski (Sheler, 2004) notes, "They [evangelicals] exist in a hostile world and are defending their faith, particularly in personal kinds of ways, but at the same time they want control of that culture. They want their values to be the supreme ones" (p. 14). In order to influence the larger culture, SSC students understand that they must blend their reactionary, separatist identity with their responsive, integrationist identity.

When SSC members interact with each other and with outsiders, they straddle this fundamentalist–progressive continuum. The net result is a centrist positioning of the organization, and it makes many efforts to counter evangelical stereotypes. SSC's Friday worship service is intentionally different from conventional church services. The casual dress, silly and fun acquaintanceship experiences, games, house band, inclusive ethos, and "youthful pastor" are purposeful strategies to appear more progressive to college students. At the same time, however, organizers intermix these contemporary components with serious, Bible-based sermons and born-again testimonies, which creates a centrist ideological persona for the organization. Likewise SSC's evangelical "rules of engagement" (e.g., asking permission to share the Bridge illustration at the outset) are the organization's attempt to convey a biblically based illustration using contemporary and progressive strategies that are less dogmatic—strategies that challenge the in-your-face, polarizing, street-corner proselytizing that is commonly associated with evangelicals.

Matthew's discussions with seniors about their Christian life beyond college reveals the organization's attempt to blend and package traditional and fundamental biblical ideas in new and different ways, so the SSC can be biblically grounded, responsive, and relevant. Bryant (2007) summarizes key constructs of this outreach strategy:

The evangelical movement both on campus and beyond has taken strides to communicate the Christian faith to spiritual seekers through culturally relevant, "postmodern" approaches. Some authors have coined the phrase "new paradigm" churches to reflect evangelical congregations that meet in a casual and celebratory atmosphere and use sophisticated technology to create an "engaging multimedia worship experience" (Shibley, 1998, p. 75). (para. 7)

Miller (1998) comments on the irony of theologically conservative evangelicals defying traditional worship environments at the same time that theologically liberal mainline Protestants maintain those traditions: Liberals modernized the message of Christianity, but they left relatively untouched the medium through which the message was being communicated. . . . In contrast, conservatives—and particularly the new paradigm churches—modernized (and continue to reinvent on a weekly basis) the medium, but they have refused to tinker with the supernaturalism inherent in the New Testament narratives. (p. 209)

Like Bryant's respondents, SSC students experiment with modes of packaging the message, and their approaches to outreach reflect their progressive leanings. Although this progressive mode makes the message more palatable and less contentious, it tends to muddle the message in an attempt to achieve "balance." Students attempt to be righteous and respectful interpreters of Truth and—at the same time—counterculture conservatives. SSC students adhere to biblical Truth while trying not to sound too absolute. They position their subculture as not too righteous and not too relativistic. They are opposed to, as they say, an "anything goes" brand of Christianity, yet they work hard to distance themselves from the absolutes commonly associated with radical fundamentalism. This "progressive fundamentalism" makes the evangelizer uneasy at times, and it occasionally confuses the evangelized.

This progressive–fundamentalist tension regularly emerged during our fieldwork. In regard to gender roles, Matthew is the subculture's spiritual leader, but women play a central role in SSC's evangelical training, Bible studies, and worship programs. These *progressive* (in the context of the evangelical community) gender roles appear to be more progressive than in some conservative Christian sects, which exclude women entirely from formal religious leadership positions (Bryant, 2007b). However, the views expressed by a male student during an interview reveal how gender inequity is "alive and well" within the SSC, provided the inequity is biblically defensible: "I think men are natural leaders for women . . . as in the Bible." Men expressed similar views during their Bible study discussion described in Chapter 7. They struggled with the complexities inherent in the SSC subculture's efforts to "be true to the Bible" and resist appearing sexist. According to Shibley (1998, cited in Bryant, 2007):

> Many evangelical students also approach their personal relationships with the opposite sex using a traditional framework for understanding gendered realties and roles. By and large, leadership opportunities in religious contexts and dating and marriage relationships are girded by beliefs in essential, God-ordained gender differences and guided by the complementation perspective, which maintains that men should be the initiators and primary leaders in the dual realms of church and home, while women occupy the submissive, "helping" roles in relation to male religious leaders and, in marriage, to their husbands. (p. 75)

The desire to apply ancient biblical foundations to contemporary times leads to confusion and uneasiness as members attempt to respect both biblical and modern views of women. Bryant (2007) found that evangelical Christian students experienced great tension as they attempted to blend their traditional Christian gender roles with the liberal, feminist values that surrounded them on a public university campus. This tension was likewise a constant struggle for SSC students.

In addition to sidestepping tensions related to gender roles, SSC students seldom explicitly raise hot-button issues such as abortion and homosexuality. When such issues arise, usually during Bible studies, members quietly yet firmly offer their opposition, always on biblical grounds. Shibley (1998, cited in Bryant, 2007) commented:

> On political matters, evangelical student organizations are decidedly quiet when it comes to specific stances on various issues so as to avoid fragmentation . . . One student reported that she was "moderate, because there are some issues that I feel very liberal about and others I feel very conservative about." Another expressed distaste for political labels: "I would say that I'm conservative, but I don't really like saying Republican or Democratic." Revealing their conservative side, evangelical students are predominatly in

favor of the pro-life agenda, whereas their liberal inclinations emphasize the importance of providing for the welfare of economically disadvantaged people, protecting the environment, implementing gun control, and abolishing the death penalty. (p.75)

SSC students, though often quite conservative in their views, also publicly embraced a quiet and mostly moderate viewpoint; they did not appear to harbor any obsessive distain for those whose views differed from their own. Still, a sense of pity seemed to linger after political discussions subsided. Students seem to embrace a progressive "live and let live" attitude, with the hope that someday those who oppose God's will shall "see the light."

The SSC resists trendy Christian movements, instead favoring traditional evangelical teachings based on the Bible. SSC members expressed skepticism with spirituality movements that are currently pervasive on American campuses, especially those whose spirituality does not involve the Bible. They favor a working-class approach to "just doing it (God's work)" while gently critiquing the "doing what feels right" movements. Although SSC students desire to see their peers enhance their spiritual lives and engage in spiritual activities, they struggle with the balance between being "respectful" of the other and being "right" when engaging with their peers in discussions centering on faith and spirituality.

Interestingly, the SSC appears to be more progressive than its peer evangelical groups and more closely aligned with its "spirituality colleagues" as related to the role of organized churches in the life of students. Both camps de-emphasize membership in organized churches. The SSC, like its spiritual counterparts, encourages students to explore their faith and elevates an individual's personal spirituality (among SSC students, this is their "relationship with Jesus") over formal church affiliations. Matthew and the other leaders of the SSC are not active members of any local church. They encourage students, as in the Learning to Live with Christ senior seminar, to focus on one's personal relationship with Jesus.

In the secular world of college student organizations, SSC adopts a moderate power structure that respects hierarchy and abhors bureaucracies. During weekly leadership meetings and larger gatherings, coordinators of these events devote virtually no time to the administrative structures that are common in most student organizations. The only two leadership positions are president and treasurer, which the SSC "elects" because the university requires recognized student organizations to have them. There are no other officers. During meetings and gatherings, *Jesus is the agenda;* there is no new business, old business, Robert's Rules of Order, motions, or votes. The Servant Leadership Team is as close as the organization gets to a governing body, but most of their work centers on supporting and educating members and performing outreach, not administration. The staff manages most administrative tasks.

Still, the SSC retains classic elements of traditional bureaucracies. For example, Matthew serves as the traditional, all-powerful male leader, as designated in the Bible. Even though SSC staff members encourage students to "make the SSC their own," they are also informed during Bridge training that they "must agree with all decisions made by the leaders of SSC." Matthew sets the tone for the organization, determines whether the organization accepts students into its leadership teams, and decides whether students can attend organizational events. As traditionalists, the students are engaged followers and conform to Matthew's expectations. The organization tries to mediate the progressive–fundamentalist leadership struggle by adopting a moderate stance, whereby leadership is sometimes progressive (e.g., students take charge in Bible study) and sometimes traditional (e.g., Matthew takes the lead in SLT meetings).

In addition to Matthew's role as a powerful, traditional leader, the organization's reliance on the Bible creates additional struggles as the SSC seeks to create progressive, member-generated learning opportunities. Often, conflicts arise between the group's *ontology* and its *epistemology*. Guba and Lincoln (1989) define ontology as an individual or group's view of the nature of reality. According to Guba and Lincoln, ontologies fall into two broad categories: realist, referring to a belief in one authority, or Truth; and relativist, implying that multiple, socially constructed truths exist and are valid. Epistemology is the relationship between the knower and the known (Guba and Lincoln, 1989) and relates to *how* an individual or group creates or discovers knowledge.

As Christians, most SSC members subscribe to a realist ontology because they believe in the ultimate authority of God's Word as Truth. Since ontology and epistemology are connected, it follows that SSC members also hold to a dualist objectivist epistemology, in which there is a prescribed way to find the Truth. For these Christian students, the way to Truth is through God's Word in the Bible. Thus, the overarching aim of the SSC is for students to come to a fuller grasp of God's Word, with the hope of learning God's Truth for how the world should *be*. Students believe in the authority of God's Word in the Bible, so multiple coexisting interpretations are acceptable if they can be biblically supported.

For example, it seemed that a relativist ontology and subjectivist epistemology prevailed in 90 percent of the Bible study meetings. Attendees offered multiple interpretations of what was said during discussions and debates, which resulted in the co-creation of knowledge (Guba & Lincoln, 1989). Why, we wondered, would the SSC encourage this type of relativist, progressive-oriented collaboration when the group's mentors could (and often did) simply provide students with "the Truth?" We suspect that this pedagogy may stem from a combination of the historical structure of the Christian religion, which relies on the wisdom of spiritual mentors, and the authoritative word of the sacred biblical text (i.e., a strict realist ontology). Bible study leaders intend this collaborative pedagogy to bring students closer to the Bible and its absolute teaching, not to bring multiple realities to the surface. SSC leaders intend to teach students how to study the Bible on their own by skillfully using hermeneutic principles, so that they can arrive at these conclusions on their own. Students seemed comfortable with this sometimes confusing (especially to outsiders) pedagogy and did not appear to be bothered by it.

Regardless of its roots, the way students' progressive learning pedagogy is "cut short" by the fundamentalist SSC leaders and the biblical truths they convey is worth noting. Baxter Magolda (1992) found that students at less-complex levels of development commonly defer to authority and seek one "Truth" or "right answer." It is difficult for these students to consider multiple perspectives simultaneously. In order to grow and develop cognitive complexity, they must be able to appreciate, integrate, and evaluate multiple perspectives. As researchers, we interacted with SSC students who used more complex ways of thinking and operating in the world. A nagging concern persists, however, that some students' analytical and critical thinking skills—which will be invaluable as they enter the diverse, multicultural workplace—may be "stunted" as they rely exclusively on the authority of the Bible and their spiritual mentors in their quest for the Truth. The seemingly incongruent epistemologies of Christian organizations and those of established student development theory (e.g., Learning Partnerships Model) display a difference that the SSC welcomes and accepts, despite the constant tension that results.

As a result of these simultaneous pulls toward the progressive and the fundamentalist ends of the spectrum, SSC assumes a centrist stance that is similar to other Christian organizations. On a nationwide level, evangelicals are moving similarly toward the center. A *Newsweek* article documented the rise in evangelicals supporting more centrist political views and moving more toward the left than their predecessors (Miller, 2006). Like the insular–accessible tension, however, the fundamentalist–progressive tension also creates problems for SSC students when they attempt to evangelize and gain new members into the organization. If students go too far to the fundamentalist side, potential converts will be turned off. If they go too far to the progressive side, their message and Bible-based beliefs are lost. The SSC recognizes that the middle ground on campuses is shrinking; most students classify themselves either as having a "strong religious affiliation" or "no religious affiliation" (Leland, 2004). Thus, they must precariously position themselves in the center to gain middle-ground and nonbeliever converts.

The SSC will likely never lose its fundamentalist tendencies; to do so would of course mean losing its identity as an evangelical Christian organization. But we also agree that the SSC is moving in a positive direction by adopting some more progressive means of reaching other students. The SSC should continue to search for the proper balance between mandating God's Word and encouraging (and accepting) the exploration of individual students' beliefs.

Conclusion: Understanding Jesus-centered Subcultures

The tensions and paradoxes we presented in this chapter illuminate the challenges of working with and understanding college student subcultures, as well as the challenge associated with treading the tumultuous waters of religion in higher education. Like the SSC, we suspect that all student organizations have some things they do well and other "Huh?" qualities that could use further thought. Communities of interest, such as the SSC, on college campuses offer many benefits, including providing members with voice and identity. At the same time, however, these communities have liabilities. Although communities of interest create space for marginalized groups, their existing power structures remain undisturbed. In addition, these discrete autonomous groupings seldom engage in public dialogue centering on the public interest (Magolda and Knight Abowitz, 1997). Dialogue about the public good—transcending Christians and non-Christians as well as SSC and other Christian organizations—was virtually nonexistent in the case study. We not only embrace the establishment and sustainability of subcultures, but we also advocate the formation of *communities of difference* (Tierney, 1993). These communities provide space for subcultures to form and prosper, while rupturing borders that separate camps into neat categories and initiating a public dialogue across and about difference.

In the chapter that follows, we provide considerations for a variety of readers as they embark on the work of enhancing students' learning experiences. We hope to begin *dialogues of difference* in an attempt to help diverse readers—those working in Christian organizations, students involved with secular organizations, and higher education professionals—reassess their activities and gain more "faith" in their efforts as they devote their lives to college students' learning, satisfaction, and success.

13

CAPSTONE PRINCIPLES

Exit Rituals

It's All about Jesus: The Next Generation

Jessica, the SSC staff intern and alumna, makes her way to the altar. After gingerly arranging her Bible and notes on a nearby music stand, she stares into the sea of SSC worshipers' smiling faces. Students gradually face forward and their fidgeting ceases. The din of their laughter gives way to almost complete silence as Jessica begins her sermon, discussing periods in her life when she did not fully trust God. She speaks candidly about her struggles the past few months as she transitioned from SSC member to a full-time intern, including failing to solicit sufficient donations to fund her internship, difficulty finding housing, working long hours, and grappling with health issues. She explains, "I'm not telling you this so you can feel sorry for me; I want to help you see your life just can't work without God."

A few women in front of me (Kelsey) hunch over their tiny notebooks and record Jessica's message, which she delivers in an informal, conversational tone. "Last year I depended on grades and external affirmation from my teachers. My life was displeasing to God. I was not spending enough time praying, choosing to sleep instead of having quiet time with God." She effortlessly recites multiple Scripture verses from memory while stressing a familiar theme—the need to embrace Jesus. From time to time, she emits a nervous giggle and interjects a humorous quip, which lightens the somber, yet realistic moral of her story: Make God the highest priority. She concludes with a prayer, "Lord, thank You for bringing us together tonight to praise You. Help us to remember to trust You. Umm, please hear our prayers and help us to build Your kingdom in this week ahead and to come to know You better. . . . Amen."

Jessica reminds students about the importance of setting priorities as she proffers a moral imperative to attendees—make Jesus their top priority every day during college and beyond. She acknowledges that this is no easy task, however. Like Jessica, we also recognize the importance of priorities. Accordingly, we base our secular *principles of good practice* on our priorities and focus on what we deem to be good. We, too, acknowledge at the outset that there are numerous challenges associated with enacting these principles.

SSC narratives and interpretations spark numerous moral questions—all centering on what is "good." In order to help clarify these "goodness" considerations, we present in this chapter a series of principles for readers to consider. Our moral questions and principles target three audiences: [1] higher education faculty and staff, [2] parachurch staff, and [3] college students, both believers and nonbelievers. For higher education scholars and practitioners, we ask: What is the appropriate role of religion in a public university? What is the optimal distance between higher education and religion? What role should parachurches play on college campuses? For parachurch staffs, we ask: Should these organizations expand members' understanding of diverse Christian discourses? For students, both believers and nonbelievers, we ask: What counts as meaningful and sustained involvement in the cocurriculum? How can learning take center stage in cocurricular activities? How can evangelical students remain true to their faith and be more reflective?

Kuh, Kinzie, Schuh, and Whitt (2005) noted a commonality among exemplary institutions that excel in helping students succeed in college. "Never quite satisfied with their performance, they continually revisit and rework policies and practices to get better. They are restless in a positive way" (p. 146). We offer our *principles for good practice*, an exit ritual of sorts, in the spirit of invoking a positive restlessness among readers to think differently and to rework their everyday practices.

Principles For Higher Education Scholars and Practitioners

Universities can do more than just familiarize students with the world's religions in survey-course fashion. The rise of religious fanaticism stems in part from a failure of intellectuals within various religious traditions to engage the faithful of their traditions in serious and reasoned reflection, inquiry, and dialogue. The marginalization of faith within universities contributes to this failure. (Jenkins and Burish, 2006, A-21)

Clarify the Role of Religion and Faith in the Curriculum

On many public university campuses, religion's "appropriate" place appears to be in the Religious Studies classroom or a university lecture hall. It is *normal* for universities to sanction religion professors or visiting religious scholars to discuss faith. Other higher education faculty and staff tread lightly (or not at all) when broaching religion topics. Ironically, public higher education's segregated and marginalized positioning of faith appears antithetical to reasoned reflection, inquiry, and dialogue—three cornerstones of academia.

We invite university communities to explicitly contemplate the role of faith in the formal curriculum. In particular, we invite faculty from all disciplines to explore the intersection of faith with their discipline and, when appropriate, to explicitly engage, rather than implicitly avoid the topic. The dearth of faith conversations in the classroom exacerbates the simplistic and entrenched binary views (e.g., theologians vs. scientists) of some faculty and students. These binary views sustain ignorance and breed prejudices, which disadvantages the next generation of students who are expected to think and act globally in a world where avoiding religion and faith is no longer an option.

Opportunities to discuss faith in the classroom are plentiful, and they are often squandered. For example, during our fieldwork there were several SSC students who majored in teacher education and aspired to do God's work in both Christian and public schools. Their curriculum, however, did not provide space for students to explore, for example, the merits and liabilities of teachers proselytizing in public school classrooms. Two moral questions arise from this void: [1] Should Christians who teach in public schools be evangelizing or proselytizing? [2] Should professors integrate such questions into the curriculum?

Romano's (2007) response to the first question is "no," but his response to the second one is "yes." He invites aspiring teachers to find ways to celebrate their religion without imposing it in their classroom, and he urges them to refrain from attempting to bring their students to salvation. Sommerville (2006), like Romano, advocates that faculty explicitly discuss the role of religion in the curriculum. He urges secular universities to foster a climate in which religion doesn't rule, but religion is not ruled out. We concur with Romano's and Sommerville's sage advice. This teacher education exemplar is but one of a multitude of academic disciplines that could easily explore the role of faith along with traditional academic discourses.

During their Wingspread Conference on Religion and Higher Education, the Society for Values in Higher Education (2005) encouraged the academy to "examine how it teaches about religion; how welcoming it is to students of diverse religious views and spiritual interests; and how it will factor religion into its educational programs and initiatives to strengthen deliberative democracy, all the while preserving standards of intellectual inquiry, public reason, and academic freedom" (p. 1). Similarly, Rice (2006) urges universities to address students' religious illiteracy and argues that students need exposure to religion across a wide range of academic disciplines.

Heeding this advice will allow higher education staff and faculty to help students discuss diverse religious views that will augment and enrich students' disciplinary studies and, more importantly, model ways to negotiate, rather than avoid difference. We invite faculties to create an ethos in the classroom that encourages students to cross borders and speak, write, and listen to the "other." This border pedagogy provides opportunities for professors and students to deepen their understandings of the discourses of various "others" and to recognize and appreciate their own politics, values, and pedagogy (Giroux, 1992).

Nevertheless, skeptics persist. "Some faculty members worry that students who arrive at college holding fast to religious beliefs are conditioned to resist the "liberal learning" curriculum and may graduate without seriously reexamining their beliefs and values" (Kuh and Gonyea, 2006, p. 40). Extending discussions about religion beyond religious studies seminars and the occasional guest lectures can actually facilitate liberal learning and encourage religious reflection and understanding on the part of all students. Infusing religion into the curriculum will certainly not guarantee that all students will sufficiently reflect on their own views, but the possibility that it may enhance students' understanding of themselves and the diverse world around them warrants its introduction. Simply stated, a public university should refrain from favoring or supporting one religion over another. It should, however, encourage discussions (voluntary not compulsory) about religion—recognizing such dialogue as essential to students' identity development and essential to living out American higher education's ideals.

Infuse Issues of Faith and Religion into the Cocurriculum

"College is a critical time when students search for meaning in life and examine their spiritual/religious beliefs and values" (Bryant, Choi, and Yasuno, 2003, p. 726). Despite the importance of religion and faith in the lives of collegians, public universities' infusion of faith and religion into the cocurriculum is the exception rather than the rule. Universities keep their distance from faith-based initiatives by relegating primary responsibility for religious and faith matters to individual students, religious denominations, or parachurches (Miller and Ryan, 2001). Even public universities with formal campus ministry offices acknowledge that they have insufficient staff to substantively respond to students' diverse faith needs. Collegians at public universities have looked to off-campus agencies such as Hillel, Newman Centers, and parachurches to fill this faith void.

Although college students have many off-campus options for religious counsel, parachurches have gained significant ground on conventional off-campus denominational churches during the past two decades. As Brinton (2007) notes, "independent congregations [e.g., parachurches] are slowly chipping away at the 'trusted brands' as the Christian faith becomes more like Wikipedia and less like Encyclopedia Britannica" (p. 15A). In our case study context, approximately 30 full-time parachurch staff members, none of them university personnel, interact year-round with more than 1,000 evangelical students in the largest Christian organization on campus. Of these students, few involve themselves in local churches. Perry and Armstrong (2007) reveal what students gain from their affiliation with parachurches:

> Students find participation in parachurch organizations appealing because they provide social activities, meaningful friendships, adult mentorship, guidance building romantic relationships, safe and low-stakes opportunities to meet possible romantic partners, and non-adversarial ways to relate to the opposite gender. (para. 5)

Perry and Anderson's finding affirms Dalton's (1980) and Kim's (2006) earlier research on this topic, which concluded that collegians gravitate toward evangelical groups to worship, continue their spiritual journey, acquire new like-minded friends, gain approval from peers and parents, reflect upon identity development issues, and relieve pressures they encounter in the class-room. Evangelicals affiliated with parachurches such as the SSC, report:

> "It's a daily battle, you know, we feel pressure from all areas. We are sur-rounded by a lot of people in classes who choose to go out and get drunk and sleep with whoever they please." Their community provides an alter-native to the sex and alcohol-infused party life on campus. And this alter-native is a total package: different people, different social activities, different rhetoric, different relationship norms, and a different set of valued behavior. (Perry and Armstrong, 2007, para. 11)

Like parachurches, college cocurricula aspire to provide safe space for stu-dents to focus on issues such as developing their identity, honing interpersonal and intellectual competencies, managing emotions, developing integrity, avoid-ing high-risk behaviors, and finding purpose in one's life. Regularly, public uni-versities' cocurricula seek to accomplish these aims by making certain that faith issues do not creep up—an unnatural separation for collegians who seek to develop their faith. We recommend that universities clarify what role religion and faith should play in the cocurriculum, with the hope that they will be pur-posefully and thoughtfully woven into the fabric of the cocurriculum and will become a part of the rich tapestry of life outside the classroom.

Forge Alliances with Parachurches Based on Difference

Religious organizations, grounded in morality and theology, profoundly shape students' sense of self (Hoekema, 1994). Still, public higher education remains uneasy about forging alliances with off-campus, faith-based organi-zations. Instead, it embraces a variation of the United States government's "separation of church and state" doctrine, which intentionally de-couples these two entities. This informal doctrine and the litigious nature of our soci-ety contribute to universities' reluctance to substantively collaborate with faith-based student organizations (Miller and Ryan, 2001). In the SSC con-text, university staff members neither encourage nor discourage students' involvement in parachurches; they simply acknowledge that these two colle-giate worlds co-exist.

In our study, one senior student affairs member joked that a doctrine of "don't ask and don't tell" best describes the relationship between the university and nearby parachurches. Leaders from both institutions recognize that they subscribe to different ideologies and favor different constituents. As a result, they seldom exchange unsolicited information. University and parachurch leaders know enough about the inner workings of each other's organization to not get too close, thus avoiding ideological conflicts that might warrant a resolution. What happens in parachurches stays in parachurches.

Although there are obvious reasons for this estrangement, there are even more compelling reasons for universities and parachurches to forge strategic alliances. The kind of alliance we recommend is built on difference and requires that staff people from universities and parachurches move beyond their borders, or venture outside their comfort zones. Collaborators must recognize the other group's potentially differing ideologies and competing goals, as well as recognize the value in exploring these differences and developing border literacy. Forging such alliances will position differences front and center and will lead to what Tierney (1993) calls "tolerable discomfort" with one another as the organizations confront their differences. Dialogue and subsequent action based on celebrating difference is generally agreed to be a worthwhile venture for all engaged in public higher education.

Engaging in critical dialogue will allow higher education professionals and parachurches to better understand the views and problems that deeply concern students. For example, several SSC students commented on the great discomfort they feel as Christians on this particular college campus. An understanding of Christian students' views (and those of other diverse student subcultures) will help higher education administrators as they develop policies and practices to better educate and engage students. A by-product of this proposed alliance is the cultivation of a spirit of critique and respect for human dignity, whereby participants in the alliance learn from each other and reflect and reevaluate their own beliefs and practices.

A Principle for Parachurches: Expand Members' Understanding of Christian Discourses

> The evangelical subculture, which prizes conformity above all else, doesn't suffer rebels gladly, and it is especially intolerant of anyone with the temerity to challenge the shibboleths of the religious right. . . . Despite their putative claims to the faith, the leaders of the religious right are vicious toward anyone who refuses to kowtow to their version of orthodoxy, and

their machinery of vilification strikes with ruthless, dispassionate efficiency. (Balmer, 2006, para. 3)

The SSC brand of evangelism is dramatically different from that of the evangelicals Balmer describes. Although the SSC subculture similarly values conformity and social conservatism and adheres to a particular evangelical orthodoxy, their typical response when encountering evangelical hostilities is to retreat, not antagonize or vilify. SSC members quietly enacted their espoused conservative values in their everyday collegiate life, and their brand of evangelical outreach, which targets Christians, is more moderate, flexible, and accepting (especially when compared to the groups to which Balmer refers).

If a nonbeliever or a nonpracticing Christian appeared receptive or at least ambivalent about participating in the Bridge illustration, for example, the evangelizer would purposefully and cautiously establish a personal relationship with the individual—a prerequisite to that individual's establishing a personal relationship with Jesus. During these Jesus-courting processes, human relationships took center stage. SSC evangelicals spent considerable time getting acquainted, which more regularly brought nonpracticing Christians and occasionally nonbelievers into the fold. Over time, the evangelizer and the evangelized learned each other's life stories, but when discussing Christianity, the emergence of a less-balanced dialogue was more common. SSC students devoted more time to introducing nonpracticing Christians or nonbelievers to the SSC's evangelical Christian world than learning about their peers' (both Christian and non-Christian) religious beliefs and practices.

The SSC curriculum and cocurriculum seldom included opportunities for members to learn about other Christian traditions. Instead, the SSC's brand of evangelical Christianity was the epicenter of this learning-centered curriculum. These teaching and learning opportunities centered on a particular Christian tradition that uses the Bible as a guide for leading an evangelical life. The United States is the most religiously diverse nation in the world, however, with numerous kinds of Christian traditions as well as numerous strands of evangelical Christianity. Practically speaking, if evangelizing and reaching out to nonpracticing Christians and "getting to know these students" are core SSC values, it seems sensible for aspiring evangelicals to not only know about their own brand of Christianity, but also to substantively learn about other strands of Christianity as well.

As Robert Coles (1989) chronicled his medical school residency in the psychiatric unit of a hospital, he conveyed the importance of listening to others' stories. During a meeting about a phobic patient, one of his supervisors, Dr. Binger, urged Coles to read more extensively in the psychiatric literature so as to understand better the nature of the patient's phobias. Binger wanted Coles to diagnose and treat the patient correctly. Dr. Ludwig, another supervisor, offered contrasting advice. During supervisory meetings, Ludwig listened carefully to Coles' stories and seldom talked. Ludwig encouraged Coles to do the same with his patients. Ludwig urged Coles to view patients as human storytellers, not as subjects that he had to "get a fix on." Ludwig argued that patients' stories contained reservoirs of wisdom that were essential to the physician's understanding and subsequent provision of care. In Ludwig's model, patients actively participated in the diagnosis and prognosis phases of recovery. Coles eventually modeled his practice after Ludwig's model.

In most evangelical encounters we observed, SSC evangelicals resembled Dr. Binger. When interacting with nonpracticing Christians and the occasional nonbeliever, SSC members transmitted information about the Bible and Jesus as though they intended to diagnose and treat (i.e., save) the sinner. The Bridge illustration illuminates this philosophy in practice. We invite parachurches to consider Ludwig's model that values teaching and listening, which would allow evangelists to better understand and appreciate *all* Christian experiences, and ultimately to provide better care.

Undoubtedly, the SSC is all about Jesus. We encourage the SSC to systematically learn more about how other Christian denominations and traditions deal with biblical exegesis and how these other traditions attract adherents. Engaging in dialogue with other Christian traditions (i.e., evangelical Black churches, Latino evangelical traditions, Korean Baptists, Catholics, and Lutherans) would reveal diverse theological underpinnings, faith traditions, and interpretations of the Bible. Such dialogues would explicitly demonstrate the roots of these diverse Christian traditions' biblical authority. These Christian subcultures are all under the Jesus umbrella, yet they also advance alternative Christian approaches and worldviews. An understanding of these diverse views could enrich SSC members intellectually and spiritually—and vice-versa. The SSC embraces a hermetic view of what it means to be a Christian. In short, there's no engagement with the outside, except for the rather tentative Bridge presentation that is likely to draw in only like-minded Christians.

We suspect that a root of the perceived emphasis on diagnosing rather than listening is that SSC evangelicals, like many parachurches, view religion through an exclusivist lens (Eck, 2002). That is, they regard their brand of religion as completely true. We posit another root: the fear of encountering new and perhaps appealing ideas by listening to others, and thus being tempted to question what one has always viewed as Truth.

SSC-like parachurches acknowledge that some other Christian traditions have some things right, but in the end, members conclude that those other belief systems are fundamentally flawed. This exclusivist lens differs from a pluralist lens (Eck, 2002), which views all religions as legitimate, valid, and "true" (i.e., when viewed from within) and honors all faiths equally. Eck argues that viewing religion through a pluralist lens leads to engagement and substantive interfaith dialogues (in this instance, with other Christian subcultures). We contend that even exclusivists should heed Ludwig's advice and recognize the value of others' stories, not simply their own.

We recognize that parachurches share systems of language, dress, music, rituals, and other cultural identifiers that provide a valuable, safe space for members. Still, we encourage parachurches to encourage members not only to share their evangelical beliefs, but also to listen and learn more about those of others. Expanding members' intellectual curiosity about other Christian traditions will benefit all parties. These dialogues will likely debunk stereotypes, challenge monolithic views of "other" Christians, and increase respect and appreciation of the other. More importantly, these potentially messy dialogues will enhance one's understanding of one's own Christian beliefs and will allow participants to be distinctively themselves—even in relationships with others. We urge parachurches to critically examine their own traditions, and then to understand and appreciate (not necessarily agree with) the Christian traditions of others.

> Cultural discernment, that is, teaching students the best of what secular culture has to offer and providing them with the tools for examining it themselves, requires constant vigilance and a lot of forethought from religious college leaders, but the rewards for success are tremendous. Striking the right balance means producing graduates who are unafraid of the world, can participate in some aspects of it, change other parts of it, and all the while maintain their religious grounding. (Riley, 2005, p. 189)

Riley's (2005) insights about Christians interacting in a secular world apply to exchanges between groups and individuals who value the sacred (e.g., Christianity) but who conceptualize the sacred differently. Maintaining one's beliefs while learning about those of the other are not mutually exclusive efforts, and such activities would likely enhance both students' learning and the organization's overall effectiveness on this public campus.

Principles for Students: Believers and Nonbelievers

The importance of the cocurriculum in the lives of college students, especially as it relates to providing students with powerful learning opportunities, cannot be overstated. Higher education scholars and practitioners are keenly aware of the struggles that student leaders face, for example, as they attempt to infuse learning into the cocurriculum—often as their peers resist. Many student organizational leaders struggle to sustain members' long-term involvement in the organization. As students progress through college, they tend to "outgrow" some organizations and disaffiliate. Enhancing student learning and sustaining student involvement are perennial challenges for student organizational leaders and advisors.

Nonbelievers: Look to Evangelicals for Ways to Enhance Student Learning and Sustain Student Involvement

Prior to this SSC study, had student leaders and advisors asked us to consult about student learning and involvement, we would not have recommended parachurches as a source of inspiration and guidance. Now that we have completed this ethnographic study, we think differently.

As noted in Chapter 12, SSC's recruitment strategies, human scale, and the diversity and sequencing of its program offerings encourage learning and sustained student involvement. Purposeful and active recruitment brings in peers who share similar interests, which contributes to students' persistence in the organization. SSC program offerings also attend to human scale and allow for intimate and active engagement and meaningful discussions, which in turn foster active and collaborative learning with peers. The SSC offers an organizational structure and programs that encourage varying levels of involvement, which contributes to student learning and sustains students' investment and involvement in SSC. Whereas other student organizations experience difficulty sustaining members' interest, SSC creates opportunities for student learning that match each individual's level of interest.

The SSC faith-based case study has implications for secular organizations. This particular parachurch reminds all organizations to understand the organization's mission, develop a purposeful and comprehensive recruitment strategy for new members, recognize the power of a human-scale organization, offer students numerous involvement options, and develop a progressive curriculum and cocurriculum that focus on teaching and learning. Although the SSC offers valuable lessons for both secular and sacred student organizations, it certainly does not hold all the keys to student organization success. The SSC case study reminds student leaders to look for suggestions for improvement in unlikely places. It is probable that other organizations on campus, both recognized and "hidden," have additional lessons that would help student leaders improve their organizations.

Evangelicals: Look to the Secular World for Ways to Become More Reflective

If there is a primary reason that we decided to change our plans and study an evangelical student organization midway through our original study of the political actions of college students, it would undoubtedly be that we got to know the SSC students. These collegians, admittedly unlike students with whom we had interacted as undergraduates, intrigued and educated us. Their genuineness, coupled with evangelical passion, acted as a magnet and drew us toward them. We learned as much about them as we did about ourselves. We hope that our narratives and analysis reveal the many positive aspects of these students. As we look at principles aimed at encouraging different thinking in the future, we would be remiss if we did not mention one aspect of this student culture that we do not fully understand—one that gnawed at us during and after our fieldwork. It is our hope that evangelical collegians will respectfully ponder this principle.

Often, when an important decision was on the horizon for SSC students, they prayed before acting. There was hardly an instance when SSC students recounted how they made important decisions that did not involve praying and seeking the counsel of God, and when they retrospectively made sense of life events, they often attributed the outcomes to "God's will." If a student applied for a summer internship and did not get the job, he or she would maturely accept the decision. Often, they attributed the decision exclusively to God's will, or to God calling them to do something else. The good news is that such disappointments seldom deterred these students from pursuing other opportunities. The troubling news is that their analysis often attributed all of their life outcomes to God's will, while ignoring their own influence (i.e., human agency) on the decisions. This lack of retrospective processing seemed to inhibit potent learning opportunities that would help students gain knowledge about themselves and the world around them and re-examine their actions. One SSC student offered this commentary when asked directly about the apparent lack of human agency as students publicly make sense of events in their lives:

> There are people who use God to skirt responsibility. There are younger believers who are not following Jesus as much as He would desire. These students are not dedicated to God. When they apply for a job . . . and they are not spiritually mature enough, they say it is God's will and God put it in other people's mind to reject them. If the person was spiritually mature enough in the first place, they would have likely gotten in. They could be using it as a crutch. . . . Part of this is that God is all powerful and in control.

Can a student both think critically and be committed to a particular faith perspective? We argue that the answer is yes. We encourage SSC students to continue to embrace their faith while not obstructing their capacity to think critically and accept some responsibility for their actions.

Endings

The Wingspread Declaration on Religion and Public Life: Engaging Higher Education (Society for Values in Education, 2005)—a manifesto of sorts concerning the role of religion on college campuses—advocates for religious literacy. We concur that infusing the topic of religion into the curriculum is sage advice. But we extend their recommendation by advocating religious literacy in the cocurriculum as well, because collegians' out-of-the-classroom learning is equally potent. As the findings in this book suggest, initiating discussions that respect secular viewpoints and the viewpoints of all religions is challenging for all individuals, from the religiously devoted student to the atheist.

College students are deeply concerned about finding purpose and meaning in life, and many collegians, like SSC members, use a faith-based lens to interpret their life experiences. For universities and colleges interested in both students' personal development and their cultural competence in a global world, providing students with a seamless environment in the curriculum and cocurriculum in which to explore their own and others' religion and sense of purpose is a worthy pursuit. Madeleine Albright (2007), former U.S. secretary of state, argues that religious literacy is a must for diplomats. Such knowledge is essential when seeking to understand world conflicts. Students, then, need opportunities to engage in difficult religious discussions that challenge their personal value systems and provide them with the skills they need to take leadership roles in our society and be effective democratic citizens.

We hope that this modest study enriches readers' religious literacy. It is also our hope that higher education institutions, parachurches, college students, and educational researchers—regardless of their own beliefs—will contemplate our findings and heed Albright's advice to develop their religious literacy and act on this new learning, with the goal of enhancing all students' educational experiences. Citing Desmond Tutu, Madeleine Albright (cited in Maher, 2006) noted, "Religion is like a knife; you can either use it to cut bread, or stick it in someone's back" (para. 6). Let us . . . not necessarily pray together, but instead cut bread and share with one another as we work collectively to better understand more of the diverse viewpoints and individual experiences on our campuses.

14

IT'S ALL ABOUT JESUS

The Last Word

The Last (SSC) Supper

As I (Kelsey) round the stairs leading to the third floor of the student center, I pause to glance at my reflection in the stairwell window and give myself a tentative nod of approval. After changing my outfit a few times, I settled on a printed skirt and dressy top. The e-mails from Matthew about tonight's SSC End-of-Year Banquet called for "semiformal" attire, and I am hypersensitive about wearing something too dressy or casual for the occasion or not appropriate for this Christian crowd, even though my wardrobe is relatively conservative. Most of my encounters with SSC students have been at informal gatherings where they wear T-shirts, jeans, or sweatpants. I am anxious to see how the SSC students look "in their Sunday best." More importantly, I wonder how the SSC uses this ritual to mark the end of the school year.

Noticing that it is already 6:00 p.m., I hurry toward a large set of wooden double doors that open into one of the university's banquet rooms. The polished wood floors, ornate light fixtures, and beautiful place settings with shiny glassware and folded cloth napkins surprise me. I am overcome with a sense of formality and grandeur that rarely accompanies the small-scale, homegrown SSC events.

"Welcome!" Aaron, seated near the door to collect attendees' dinner fees, finishes his conversation with a male student and turns his attention toward me. I greet him and hand him a check to cover the cost of my dinner. He thanks me as I enter the lively crowd of about 80 SSC students who are already inside the banquet room. The clean-cut, smartly dressed students impress me; several are barely recognizable. All the men are wearing ties and button-up shirts. The women's attire ranges from summer print skirts to more formal attire.

I talk with Kiley about her summer plans and with Leslie about her job search for teaching positions. The room is buzzing with activity as students flit back and forth between clusters of friends; they snap photos, giggle, and tell stories. There is almost a flirtatious feel to the air as students size one another up and delight in the near-completion of their academic coursework for the year. By 6:15, I realize that organizers have designated the first half-hour as social time. Matthew, Jessica, Don, and Nancy "work the crowd" as they shake hands, hug students, and pose for photo opportunities.

Students begin to hover around the tables. Each place setting features a different flavor of cheesecake, so students spend a few minutes in diplomatic debate and discussion about their favorite desserts. Bethany approaches me and asks if I have selected a seat. I answer "No," so she offers to sit with me. I notice that the rest of her sophomore friends are already seated around a table with one seat remaining, so I decline her gracious offer so that she can sit with her peers. Most students I know are seated at full tables, so I elect to sit at a table of first-year students with whom I am less familiar. I introduce myself as a graduate student, and one woman with long brown hair replies with a giggle, "Thank you for adding age diversity to our table." Her comment amuses me.

Don makes his way to the podium at the front of the room. It bears the logo of the university—an unusual juxtaposition of a stalwart Christian against a secular backdrop. As Don bows his head, students quickly wrap up their conversations. "Lord, we thank You for each other, the seniors, and the food we will have to strengthen our ministry . . ." Following the prayer, attendees immediately return to their conversations. Two chatty women at my table exhibit the usual SSC bubbly conversation style. They talk about all the fun times they have had in the SSC and the academic courses they have enjoyed. All of them are "regulars" at Bible study, and one plans to attend an SSC summer training program.

Rebecca tells me excitedly about a game called Star Wars that she and other SSC students play in a campus building. It's basically a mix of Capture the Flag and Hide and Seek that they play in the dark building after midnight, when few students are around. She tells me, with a look of childish mischief in her eyes, "We're pretty sure it's *legal*." Silently, I laugh. Is this their form of "rebellious college behavior?" In the larger scheme of aberrant college behavior, it's a rather dorky activity. It reminds me of myself in college; the things I thought were "wild and crazy" really weren't—like the time my friend and I stole free ice cream cone coupons out of the campus recycling bin after careless students emptied their mailboxes.

Students throughout the room behave as formal dinner guests, with the exception of the usual suspects. Amateur photographers circulate from table to table and interrupt conversations for the sake of that "Kodak moment." Each time a photographer arrives at a table, diners scoot together at one side and lean in very close to one another. I feel a bit awkward participating in these photos.

Just as the last crumbs of cheesecake disappear, Matthew walks to the podium and starts the formal program. He thanks Henry for preparing a slideshow with photos from the year, and then flicks off the light switch. The show is set to Christian music—both rock songs and slower ballads. Surprisingly, the students around me immediately start singing along to the music. They appear extremely entertained by the photos—all of which feature SSC students with beaming faces hugging one another or hamming it up for the camera with silly expressions and poses. Amid the singing and laughter, collective "awww" sounds arise from the crowd when photos of hugging students appear. There are many pictures from the New Orleans spring break trip, including the van ride, a trip to a Creole restaurant, and students cleaning up the community.

After the slide show, Matthew announces that he will be recognizing some individuals. In his usual measured tone, he thanks Aaron for being an intern and Don and Nancy for "taking time out of their schedules to be with us to disciple people and lead studies." Then he asks students in the evangelism, discipleship, and senior teams to stand and be recognized for their faithfulness and strength. Matthew briefly mentions the first-year students. He thanks them for their participation, but identifies them only collectively in relation to the upper-class students. "The freshmen are here as a result of upper-classmen's labor and the answer to their prayers that there would be a strong freshman class this year." Symbolically, Matthew communicates the importance that SSC places on "growing the Kingdom" and getting more deeply involved in the organization.

After this brief recognition of the student congregation at large, Jessica joins Matthew at the podium as they prepare to recognize tonight's featured guests of honor, the seniors. Matthew speaks fondly about the strength of the seniors' faith, and even though his personality seems to inhibit him from becoming too emotional in public settings, I can tell he's attached to this group. They were freshmen during his first year as SSC director. Like a proud parent he proclaims, "This group was a small, faithful group of freshmen that had a vision for the future, and through their faithfulness, the ministry grew." Matthew announces the men, Jessica names the women, and they hand each student a gift wrapped in shimmery paper. Both keep their remarks short and provide one scripted, yet genuine compliment about each person: "This woman has such a loving heart." "This guy is really good at relating to other guys." They also share brief anecdotes about when and where they first met each student. In a few cases, they mention that the student was not originally a part of SSC but joined as an upper-class student, when "God really took hold of his heart and his life." By honoring the seniors, who are the most highly involved students in the organization, Matthew clearly communicates to first- and second-year students the importance of making their college journey a progressive walk with Jesus.

Subsequently, I am completely taken by surprise when Matthew pauses and says, "There is one more person here who is graduating, and she knows more about us than we know about ourselves and the SSC." The students I have come to know very well all turn their glances toward me and smile, while the students with whom I have spent little time this year appear befuddled. They search the room and try to guess the identity of the recipient of Matthew's praise. "Kelsey has been with us for the past 2 years studying us for her graduate degree, and she will finish next week. We've enjoyed having her around and getting to know her and wish her luck." I can feel myself blushing and squirming a bit in my seat; I am surprised and overwhelmed with gratitude for their thoughtfulness, yet I also struggle with how to respond now that I am the center of attention, something I have successfully avoided for 2 years. I walk to the podium and accept my gift and a warm handshake from Matthew and Jessica.

As I return to my seat, Matthew launches into a final, powerful mini-sermon to conclude the year. "The seniors had a vision 4 years ago," Matthew begins, and he follows by citing several examples from the Bible about various peoples' visions and how "Jesus helped people to see." He speaks passionately and asks everyone to think about the vision they have for themselves and for the future of the ministry. "Although they [the seniors] have grown a lot in the past 4 years, this is just a beginning, and there is much more work to be done. . . . There is a whole campus full of people drowning out there, waiting for you." His vivid language of students "drowning" in a campus sea of secularism, hedonism, and materialism serves as a moving call to action.

Matthew weaves together the SSC's core values, which include strengthening one's own personal faith while using evangelism and discipleship as ways to help peers know Jesus. He also challenges students to set goals and create a vision of the kind of person they would like to be by the end of their college career—yet another indication that the SSC values student learning. He makes it clear that students accomplished much during the past year, but God calls each of them to do more in the years to come—whether that is with the SSC, at home over summer vacation, or in the seniors' new postgraduate pursuits. I suspect his message moves the young evangelists sitting around me; they lean forward in their chairs and hang on his every word.

"Let's pray." Matthew concludes his sermon with a prayer and then invites everyone to take a summer address list on their way out so that "we can support each other through the summer." Students begin jumping up to continue their photo frenzy. "Sophomore guys' Bible study over here!" shouts Warren. "Senior women over here!" yells Leslie, as she lines up her peers with the taller women in the back, the shorter ones in front. Students hug and scurry about, seeking out friends. First- and second-year students make particular efforts to connect with the seniors; sadly they hug, promise to stay in touch, and wish them luck. I work my way through the crowd to Jessica, Kiley, and Leslie, thanking them and wishing them the best. Jessica says that she looks forward to her upcoming 6-week trip to Thailand with Matthew this summer.

The students remain engrossed in taking photos, and I feel decidedly awkward posing in more photos, so I prepare to leave. Before pushing the double wooden doors open, I pause and look back at the students within the banquet room. I feel a sense of appreciation for my experiences with this group and am saddened to exit the field. Even though I did not always agree with SSC students' views, I have a strong respect for them and truly enjoyed and gained much from the experience.

En route to my car, I open my gift, which is a book entitled *The Search for Significance,* by Robert McGee. Curious about what is in the accompanying envelope, I tear it open and remove the card. On the front is a photo of a country road; on the inside, I read: *Kelsey, Congratulations on your upcoming graduation! We've enjoyed having you around the past couple years and getting to know you some. Your smile and gentle demeanor will be missed. We pray that your time around us has challenged and encouraged you in your own journey with God. Please enjoy this book; it is a classic as it looks at how to tap into a life of fulfillment and significance. We will remember you in our prayers. By His grace, Matthew and Jessica for SSC.*

Matthew's and Jessica's note signals that they have a strong interest in others' (both Christians' and non-Christians') growth and personal learning. I hope that they have the same interest in learning about themselves and their organization as a result of reading our book.

The Last Word

We conclude the book with this brief story of the SSC's last supper for numerous reasons. First, the story reveals how the organization brings closure to its academic year and recognizes its accomplishments and star performers. Second, the story provides glimpses into the student–student friendships and student–staff relationships that are the cornerstone of the organization's existence. Third, the story reveals Matthew's never-ending quest to perpetually teach whenever possible and the students' desire to learn, even during a celebratory social event. Finally, the story reveals the evolution of the relationship between one researcher and the research participants, which grew and strengthened over time based on mutual respect for similarities and differences.

Although many points of agreement exist between the SSC and us, most differences resulted from our use of secular interpretations within sacred fieldwork contexts. Imbedded in the preceding chapters are *our* interpretations, which reflect how we negotiated these differences. We conclude the book with SSC members' interpretations of our interpretation. Specifically, we invited select SSC members to read a draft of the book and offer their reactions, including their points of disagreement. The intent of this unusual chapter is to continue the conversation and to fully capture all participants' enriched understanding of this complex research phenomenon. Our intent is not to engage in a point-counterpoint debate to determine the "right" interpretation. Too often researchers and authors—by virtue of the power of the pen (or computer)—get the last word. Instead, in this chapter we invite SSC students and staff to have the last word.

The SSC's End-of-Year Banquet inspired students and staff to go forth and continue their spiritual journey. The banquet also inspired us researchers to "*spread our words*" to a wider audience. It is our hope that the lessons learned from this SSC study (both our interpretation and SSC members' interpretations)—in the spirit of Matthew's and Jessica's wish for continued self-improvement—may improve the lives of college students and administrators, as well as Christian organization leaders and participants. This chapter showcases the SSC's reactions to our tales and interpretations, and the sections are in the individuals' own words. We encourage readers of this book to continue the conversation by offering and sharing their interpretations with others. May the journey continue.

Sarah: In Her Own Words

As I read this book, it is very interesting to hear a different interpretation of something that has been such a huge part of my life for the last 5½ years. Although some of the "rituals" we practiced regularly were not specifically things I had done before college (e.g., Bible study, Servant Leadership Teams, Friday night worship times), they were never weird to me. I knew that I wanted to get to know other Christians on campus who could encourage me and challenge me in my faith, and this seemed like a good way to achieve that goal. The different side that I see now is that the ultimate goal of the SSC is *not* to encourage me and challenge me in my faith during college; the goal ultimately is to expand God's Kingdom. As a freshman, I had no idea what that meant, probably much like Peter and Kelsey. The difference between us was that I had heard this phrase before and knew I wanted to be a part of anything God wanted me to do.

The researchers focused on what the SSC is doing to add to or take away from the collegiate experience. Although this is a byproduct of the ultimate goal, it is way too narrow of a view. It reminds me of the comparison in Isaiah 49:6, which says, "He [God] says: 'It is *too small* a thing for you to be my servant to restore the tribes of Jacob and bring back those of Israel I have kept. I will also make you a light for the Gentiles, that you may bring my salvation to the ends of the earth'" (emphasis added). It is too small a thing for the SSC to be a social gathering and teaching center for Christians on a campus. God brought about the SSC to bring salvation to the ends of the earth, wherever that is.

The SSC helped me become a "lifelong laborer." I have gladly taken the challenges, lessons, and encouragements that I got from the SSC and plan to use them for the remainder of my life. Unlike the other organizations the researchers studied, the SSC has a much greater goal. Whereas other organizations (e.g., sororities, fraternities) desire to improve society, practice leadership, and build friendships, we believe that the goal of the SSC is eternal. As Christians, we experience the love that God has for us in such a way that we can't help but want others to experience that same love. This is a major issue absent in this manuscript. The reason behind everything that goes on is not for our gain, our reputation, our friendships, our career ideas, or our futures. The reason behind it all is that God loves us.

2 Corinthians 5:14 says, "For Christ's love compels us, because we are convinced that one died for all, and therefore all died." To unpack this verse, we can first see that Christ's love is the force behind all of the SSC "rituals." If Christ didn't love us, there would be no reason to study Him and His Word. If Christ didn't love us, there would be no reason to want to bring other people closer to Him. If Christ didn't love us, there would be no reason to worship Him on a Friday night, or any other day for that matter. And, if Christ didn't love us, there would be no reason to spend time with Him in a personal relationship.

The second part of the verse explains how we *know* beyond a shadow of a doubt that Christ loves us. "One died for all, and therefore all died." The One who died was Christ. He gave His life because He loves us and wants us to spend all of eternity with God. The "all who died" is us. Galatians 2:20 explains this: "I have been crucified with Christ and I no longer live, but Christ lives in me. The life I live in the body I live by faith in the Son of God who *loved* me and gave Himself for me" (emphasis added). I fully believe that my life is not mine, but that because I have accepted Jesus as my *Lord* and *Savior,* He is exactly that to me. A lord . . . one who rules, governs, provides for, and owns me. And a savior . . . one who rescues, protects, gives, and keeps me from evil, Hell, and eternity away from God. 2 Corinthians 5 continues and encourages me in this belief, "And He died for all, that those who live should no longer live for themselves, but for Him who died for them and was raised again"(verse 15) . . . then in verse 20, "We are therefore Christ's ambassadors, as though God were making His appeal through us. We implore you on Christ's behalf: Be reconciled to God."

What may look from the outside as forceful, intrusive, or close-minded is simply sharing with others something that has become so dear to us because of love. If when Thomas Edison invented the light bulb, he only shared it with his family, we might still be living in the dark. In the same way, if I have found the way to eternal life full of love, grace, forgiveness, compassion, justice, and mercy . . . a much more important find . . . why would I not want to share it? One of my favorite passages, 1 John 4:7–21, says it this way: "This is how God showed His love among us: He sent His one and only Son into the world that we might live through Him. This is love: not that we loved God, but that He loved us and sent His Son as an atoning sacrifice for our sins . . . if we love one another, God lives in us and His love is made complete in us" (verses 9, 10, and 12). Sharing the love of God with someone is inviting them to meet God, know Him, experience His love and forgiveness, and spend all of eternity with Him.

Aaron: In His Own Words

I have two initial reactions to *It's All about Jesus*. The first is the researchers' keen observational skills and insightful interpretations. Admittedly, I have limited experience with books, articles, or other documents of this genre; nonetheless, I commend Peter and Kelsey for their disciplined work, understandable writing, and clear focus. Being a part of this organization for a long time, I truly feel they give the reader a good vicarious experience of what our group looks like and offer some startlingly accurate conclusions—especially as aptly self-proclaimed outsiders. The "slippery slope" they encountered and reflected on throughout the book was the challenge of making secular conclusions about sacred practices, leading to my second initial reaction: that we (the SSC) and the researchers view our ministry through very different lenses.

The authors' choice for the book's title, *It's All about Jesus: Faith as an Oppositional Subculture,* unveils deeper truths about the nearly 2,000-year struggle that followers of Christ have encountered. Jesus himself was oppositional to the culture and conventional wisdom of the day. Let me offer only the example of his death. The ruling Roman Empire of Jesus' day was strong and vibrant, not yet experiencing any indications of its eventual fall. To maintain stability and peace within its borders, they used force. The invention and use of the cross was a warning for those who opposed the Empire. By shedding the blood of the rebellious, the Romans made peace. Jesus also used the cross to make peace for His Kingdom by voluntarily going to the cross; He flipped the cultural norm by shedding his own blood. Jesus declared that He was not a part of the world and that those who follow Him were equally going to be strangers and aliens in their culture. Any good student of the Bible would tell you he or she accepts, but also expects, to be an "oppositional subculture."

Many question this oppositional subculture status by pointing out that Christianity has been the dominant religion of the western culture since Constantine made it the official religion in the 4th century. Yet, those claiming to be Christians often do not follow in the path of Jesus. Do the tactics of the Crusades really remind you of the man Jesus Christ? Would He have applauded when early reformer John Hus was burned at the stake in 1415 for speaking against the moral corruption of the Catholic Church and the belief that all followers of Christ should have the right to preach the Good News to friends and neighbors? Mankind is notorious for using religion to seek power and control, and alleged Christians are perhaps the guiltiest. But even when "Christians" have the power, followers of Jesus and his teachings almost always oppose the dominant culture.

This truth about the Christian subculture is most recognized today through our thinking. In a pluralistic and relativistic society, many consider Christians' belief in one absolute truth close-minded and sometimes offensive. Again, if we look at the man Jesus, most humans considered His whole way of thinking as close-minded and offensive, so much so that in John, chapter 6, many of His followers deserted Him. His teachings and opposition to the way of thought in His day eventually cost Him His life.

The characterization of the SSC as progressive fundamentalists is strikingly accurate, and I applaud the authors' presumed appreciation for our struggle of finding that delicate (and ever-changing) balance. We truly believe we have a message in Jesus that offers the means to a fulfilled life, for now and for eternity. From my studies and research, I believe Jesus *is the only way* to that life because His death and resurrection—according to the Bible—is the only sufficient way of dealing with our sins against a perfect God (described in more detail in Chapter 8). Our (SSC's) dilemma is: How can a counter-cultural and initially offensive message (just as in Jesus' day), become relevant and understandable in our present culture? We're fundamentalists because we believe Scripture is inerrant and we should proclaim the message. But we're also progressive in our belief that we can learn from the methods used to proclaim the message in scriptures millennia ago, but we should not necessarily follow them literally. Let me illustrate this, knowing that with these complexities I will certainly make generalizations, and definite holes in my argument will become apparent.

Let's say that you are walking with a peer on a tall bridge, and he trips and begins to fall over the edge. He grabs on with one hand, with his feet dangling over the edge. Most people would argue that they would reach out and try to save him from inevitable doom. If we see this as the evangelical's plight in a pluralistic culture, there are two general responses, with neither being sufficient. The progressive way would be to do nothing, allowing the fallen friend to determine the best way to save himself so as to be sure to not offend him. The fundamentalist might even consider tactics to push his friend closer to the edge to show him how much he needs to be "saved," and then save him. To me, Christ's way would be to offer a hand of help with the understanding that upon grabbing it, they'll need to learn a new way to "walk" in their life. The dangler has the option of grabbing the hand or trying to manage on his own. Do we want to be relevant and effective in our culture? "Yes." Will we undoubtedly offend and step on others' toes? "Yes." That is where we are; to do nothing would be to not follow Christ.

Finally, I want to comment on the book as a whole. What I perceived as the authors' purpose for writing this book was to increase the discourse, learning, and understanding among campus evangelicals, parachurches, non-Christians, and higher education institutions. With this honorable intent, the authors based their observations, interpretations, and conclusions on how mankind can benefit from better understanding and interaction. Although the SSC also sees the numerous benefits of more dialogue, our first and utmost purpose in all we do in our ministry is for God. As followers of Christ, we are completely indebted to the gift of eternal salvation, and our response is to serve Him, not because we want to pay Him back, but because of our loving gratitude. We believe that what best serves Him is for the people He has created and loves with infinite depth to love Him and follow his son Jesus in return. We want our impact not just to benefit humans here and now, but to impact eternity. This human-centered vs. God-centered perspective between researchers and subjects is worth noting, as that is the lens from which the entire book is written.

In the end it is for us, the SSC, "All about Jesus." To us, following Him is different than identifying your religious preference as Christian. It means trying our best to live like the man Jesus was and impacting people the way He impacted them.

Matthew: In His Own Words

"Why?" It's an important question that SSC students knew would be coming out of my mouth whenever we discussed beliefs, observations, or methodology. Of course, the question is always coupled with an observation or perceived fact, like, "Why do you like basketball?" or "Why do you believe there is no truth?" or "Why does it snow?" When used properly, the "why" question is an important tool that helps us process the empirical data we've collected.

Reading this book frustrated me. Personally, I like Dr. Magolda and Ms. Gross, and I know how much work they invested in this project, but after reading the manuscript, I thought the book lacked an accurate understanding of many underlying objectives in our ministry. The text shows the authors directed the majority of their "why" questions to themselves as opposed to individuals and leaders within the cultural community they wanted to understand (i.e., the SSC). This author-centrism led to several core assumptions and misunderstandings about SSC. As a result, the researchers based *many* of their critiques upon false interpretations or entirely different perceptions of reality. These practices subvert one of their main stated goals: "A goal of this study is to help SSC members and readers understand what we think are the contradictions inherent in the SSC ideology; in essence, we share what we think is 'really going on'" [Chapter 1]. The first and most crucial step toward accomplishing this goal is to *accurately* understand SSC ideology and the convictions that drive that ideology. Once the authors attain an accurate understanding, they are in a position to help SSC make changes that align with SSC goals, ideology, and ontology. Unfortunately, the authors repeatedly offer critiques that center on *their* ideology and ontology.

As the director of SSC, I had great freedom to set the goals and priorities of the ministry. Although I'd graduated as a member of SSC from the same campus, I recognized there were several aspects of the ministry that needed to change. One of my first actions as director was to survey the students about their SSC experience. The survey results revealed students lacked a sense of community and clear vision for their lives. I spent a lot of time praying and seeking wisdom regarding where to lead the ministry. I then devised and implemented growth and learning opportunities that would develop these young men and women into Christian laborers equipped with heart, vision, and skill. Did our ministry succeed? I won't know for another 20 years. The SSC staff and I had to make choices based on what we thought would best prepare students to follow Jesus for a lifetime, not just for a few years in college. I repeatedly reminded SSC students the ministry defined success by looking at their lives 25 years from now. This is our primary goal. Why? Because Christ has instructed us to "Go and make disciples of all nations," teaching them to obey everything Jesus taught His disciples (Mt. 28:19–20). If we bear the name "Christian," then our lives and priorities must reflect His.

Our ministry developed and grew in each of my 5 years (and continues to grow after my departure in 2007). One verse that outlines an important value and philosophy for SSC is Luke 16:10: "Whoever can be trusted with very little can also be trusted with much, and whoever is dishonest with very little will also be dishonest with much." The SSC staff built the ministry upon levels of opportunity. As students increase their voluntary involvement in SSC opportunities, so too does the required level of commitment or sacrifice [increase]. Students freely choose their level of involvement. However, if they have not been faithful with the opportunities they accepted, then SSC staff does not offer them the opportunity to access greater levels of opportunity. Each level of opportunity offers students more in-depth and personal attention and training. Each level also demands that students surrender more of their rights and make a higher level of commitment to living their faith.

There are four levels of opportunity in our ministry, but these levels differ from those the authors describe. The first level includes opportunities [that are] open to all yet require no additional commitment. The only cost to students is the time they devote to attending the event. Our Friday large group meeting, prayer meetings, and social events exemplify this level of opportunity. The second level includes opportunities that are open to everyone but require additional commitment, often in the form of preparation. Bible studies and Bridge Building training sessions fall into this category. If students desire to be involved at the second level, [the] staff expect[s] them to complete the preparation associated with that level. If they choose not to complete the preparation, they can continue on this level but will not be permitted to partake in third-level opportunities. The third level of opportunity is the Servant Leadership Team. This umbrella group includes the Evangelism

Team (E-Team), the Discipleship Team (D-Team) and the Senior Team (S-team). These teams are sequentially organized; faithful completion of one team is necessary to move to the next. Students at this level commit to a weekly 75-minute meeting and a short assignment, as well as continuing and faithful participation in the first two levels of opportunity. The fourth and final level is to be discipled/mentored by an SSC staff member. Staff extends this level of opportunity to the few who are making the most of the other three levels of opportunity. For reasons I don't understand, in the book the authors insist that the Bridge Building training sessions be classified as a separate level and largely ignore the staff discipling level.

The SSC involvement structure works for both SSC staff and students because it provides each with its needs. Students want to be trained and developed. For SSC staff, these opportunities reveal the students who are most likely to be the best investment of our time and energy to accomplish our stated meta-goal. It also upholds the biblical principle that those who lead must be willing to sacrifice rights (e.g., the right to watch TV/play video games/hang out with friends *whenever I feel like it*) in exchange for influence/leadership. This trade-off is always made by leaders—Christian or non-Christian; influence with individuals costs a leader personal freedom, and his influence is limited by his own willingness to sacrifice that freedom.

As the authors clearly assert, SSC students view the Bible as *the* authority on life and how to live. This belief reflects a worldview that embraces Truth as a constant force, not a malleable, subjective idea. A clear understanding of our meta-goal, structure, and ontology is vital as I discuss the critiques offered by the authors in the "three huhs" section of Chapter 12 and throughout the book.

"Huh" #1—The Marginalized Majority As I read this section, the authors' assertion that SSC really was part of a majority on the campus amazed me. Although I cannot refute the demographic statistics they cite supporting this assertion, I also cannot refute their many statements that clearly *depict SSC students as distinct and unlike the majority* of students on campus. Americans claim Christianity in much the same way that Thai people claim Buddhism . . . "I know I'm not Hindu or Jewish or Muslim, so I must be Christian." Noted Christian researcher George Barna (barna.org) has found that while 83 percent of Americans identify themselves as Christians, 54 percent believe that a place in Heaven can be earned through

good works.[1] Salvation by grace (rather than good works) is a hallmark of the Christian faith and is a hallmark difference between Christianity and other world religions. Clearly, there is a wide range of meaning when people identify themselves as Christian. Positioning SSC students as a part of the majority would lead us to believe that the Christian label yields similar lifestyles and behaviors; however, this is not the case.

It would be easy for me to proclaim the many ways that the lifestyle of an SSC student is far removed from that of the dominant campus culture, but the authors' words will do better to refute their own claim that SSC students are a part of the privileged mainstream on campus. Throughout the text the authors, too, position SSC students as distinct, different, and out of the dominant mainstream campus culture. I have added italics for emphasis.

- "we explore how the SSC, as a subculture, opposes the dominant campus groups that determine legitimacy and "weirdness" on this campus." [Chapter 5]
- "Praying, singing, listening to a sermon, and playing chess—these are unlikely images one would conjure up when brainstorming college students' activities on a Friday night. As unusual as these components of the SSC's Friday worship service may seem to outsiders, SSC members purposely and voluntarily participate in these activities to distinguish themselves from their collegiate peers." [Chapter 6]
- "The SSC opposes and resists the *natural order* of its public, secular university that typically steers clear of religious teachings." [Chapter 6]
- "The SSC's university is known for enrolling a disproportionate number of image-conscious, affluent, competitive, high-achieving, highly involved, and academically successful students. Frequently, SSC's Christ-centered values clash with materialism, hedonism, and individualism—dominant values of the larger student culture." [Chapter 6]
- "Although many SSC students describe themselves as high achievers and mirror the mostly Caucasian, traditional-age demographics of the campus, they otherwise do not fit the dominant profile. Instead, they have created their own subculture and have their own SSC "dominant profile." [Chapter 6]
- "This is perhaps the most salient point of divergence between the SSC and the dominant secular student culture; many students on this campus shun religious teaching in their everyday lives. This attitude differs sharply from SSC members' Christ-based lifestyle." [Chapter 6]

- "This style is antithetical to the dominant secular college culture, which endorses materialism and affluence." [Chapter 6]

Obviously, the authors acknowledge that SSC students are in fact *not part of the dominant campus culture*. From their values to their dress, from the way they interact with their faith on a daily level to how they define success and achievement, SSC students live a life that is in the minority on the campus and in the culture at large.

In this "huh" section the authors draw a binary much like the ones they deem harmful in our organization. By saying, "SSC occupies a paradoxical conflicted position as both privileged and harmed," the authors imply that a person or group must be either privileged or harmed by a society or culture. I believe that many Black men or White women or White gay men, among other social strata, could easily point out ways they have been both advantaged by an aspect of themselves that positions them in the majority of our culture yet at the same time are harmed by another aspect that positions them on the outside looking in. In fact, I would argue that all of us could find at least one way we have been both part of the privileged majority and part of the harmed minority by our culture. SSC is no different. The organization does enjoy some benefits from operating on a campus within a predominantly Christian culture, yet at the same time, it's easy to see that overall the SSC student does not fit well within the cultural mainstream.

"Huh" #2—Insular Evangelicals   I agree with the authors that there is a very real tension in SSC between reaching out to others and spending too much time within our own community. However, a couple "why" questions regarding the frequency that we met together or a clearer understanding of our meta-goal, among others, would have helped the authors to bring clarity to this "huh" issue.

SSC staff has been well aware of this tension for years. As director, I kept a close eye on this problem and took efforts to ensure it remained as minimal as possible. Since I agree with the authors on the tension/problem, this section provides fertile ground to explore my contention that the authors did not take the time to ask the staff "why" questions, which resulted in a shallow and misguided interpretation of the goals of SSC.

In this section, the authors don't understand why SSC members prefer to stay within the group rather than to go out and "evangelize," which is the preference of other Christian groups on campus. Despite the seemingly obvious fact that humans prefer to spend time with people more similar to themselves rather than less, there are other factors that contribute to this tension in SSC, which were not on the authors' radar. One factor is our overarching goal of preparing and equipping students to minister for the rest of their lives. To accomplish our overarching goal, we believe that we must frequently meet together. As a result, the more time students spend in training sessions, the less time they have to be with non-Christians.

Another factor is our theology of evangelism. In the book, the authors position the SSC against an evangelical Christian group that views evangelism as an event and teaches students how to proclaim the Gospel and then bang the drum of "get out there and share." There is no doubt that if SSC staff adhered to this evangelistic philosophy, students would spend much less time meeting or socializing together and more time proclaiming the Gospel message to anyone who would listen. Instead, SSC students learn how to live the Gospel among non-Christians so that people actually ask them to share about God.

As the authors make these comparisons between the SSC and other Christian groups, they reveal that they understand little of our evangelistic theology or the "why" behind methods that we employ. This is clearly seen, as the authors state: "Sometimes, after a brief, exploratory encounter with an SSC member, the "evangelized" non-Christians did not even recognize or characterize the encounter as evangelical in nature" [Chapter 12]. Traditional evangelistic methodology posits that it's the job of Christians to verbally proclaim the Gospel to everyone who will listen. Some of the underlying convictions of this methodology include: the belief in conversion as primarily an event, the belief that ignorance is what's preventing non-Christians from becoming Christians, and that the goal of evangelism is to bring a message. When Christians act on these beliefs, there is little doubt whether an individual has been "evangelized." SSC, on the other hand, believes that conversion is an event, but one that's preceded by a process. We believe that some non-Christians will become Christians with the right information, but many others already have that information and still do not believe. Thus, only a part of our evangelism responsibilities is to bring a message. To my knowledge, there were no questions about why we evangelize the way that we do.

SSC accepts the fact that America is the most Gospel-saturated culture in the history of the world. Individuals are hard pressed to avoid hearing the

Gospel as they live in our culture. The Gospel is on the radio, on television, in music, and is accessible for millions of Christians who reside in the United States. Our nation does not suffer from a Gospel information problem; we suffer from a Gospel application problem. SSC views faith in Christ as a journey. Some have it and are already growing in their faith that Jesus is their Lord and Savior, while others are far away and become angry or withdrawn when individuals introduce the subject of religion. Within SSC evangelistic theology, the job of a Christian is to help each person take *the next step* toward faith in Christ. It's only toward the end of this evangelistic process that a proclamation of the Gospel and call to faith are prudent.

Unfortunately, the authors don't seem to understand or are even aware of these viewpoints. Instead, their assumptions lead them to make statements about our evangelistic methods such as, "Nevertheless, their reluctance to take risks and assertively evangelize limits their ability to meet their espoused organizational mission to spread the Word" and "[On the contrary,] we argue that the infusion of new ideas and diversity into the organization could help it strive toward continual improvement in reaching its stated evangelical goals" [Chapter 12]. The authors' summary statements show that they never really understood our stated evangelical goal of helping each person we encounter take *the next step* toward faith in Christ.

While the authors view this tension as one mainly created by the students, in my view it is more a result of our meta-goal and SSC evangelistic theology. I believe that all organizations have problems. While we work hard to minimize this particular problem, it exists largely because of conscious choices and convictions.

A Problem with Ontology/World View　　My focus in this section is not to refute the claim of the third "huh," but rather to extricate examples of author-centric critique. There are several points throughout the book where the authors seem to have difficulty accepting the SSC worldview, one that adheres to the existence of Truth. This difficulty manifests itself in critiques of methods and commentary about how we view non-Christians and ourselves.

Christians are often slammed for thinking that everyone who doesn't accept Jesus as Lord and Savior will spend eternity in Hell. In a time when mainstream America promotes a relativistic view of truth, offense is often taken when others deem truth to be a constant that can be known. The ironic nature of these criticisms has been widely noted and can be summed up by the question, "If you really believe truth is relative, then why can't I believe truth is fixed and knowable?" The contradictory nature of the relativist worldview is uncovered in the criticisms of those who hold that Truth is constant.

The authors communicate the same inconsistency by saying, "Rather than viewing non-evangelical Christian students with 'pity' because they are not 'on the path to salvation,' SSC participants could engage in dialogues with other organizations aimed at developing a deeper understanding and appreciation of their differences" [Chapter 9]. While I would not contend that we couldn't benefit from dialogues that lead to deeper understanding, the implication is that after these dialogues we will no longer "pity" people, and instead, we will appreciate their opposing views on truth.

Our "pity" of non-Christians is a theme that seems to bother the authors. They mention it several times throughout the book, most notably—"SSC students continue to pray for and be friendly toward students unwilling to adopt their Christ-centered lifestyle, but they harbor pity and disapproval of their sinful ways" [Chapter 6]. Those who believe that Jesus is the Son of God also agree with Him that He is the only way to God and eternal life (John 14:6, 17:3). The authors do not consider that given our worldview, if you believe someone is going to spend eternity in Hell, then we can either feel compassion, apathy, or hate toward them. Feeling hate or apathy toward individuals in that situation would be on par with the mindset of Hitler or Stalin. In fact, compassion (or "pity," as the authors state) and love are by far the most noble responses a Christian can have toward those who do not follow Jesus.

The authors' relativist leanings are on full display as they examine our methods in Bible study and training. While SSC aims to help students properly understand the Bible in its context, the authors advocate allowing the students to find meaning for themselves. Again, this does not take into account our worldview or the fact that the Bible is the most widely read and deeply studied book in all of history. When the authors claim that we should allow students to "construct their own beliefs, values, and identities internally rather than encourage students to adhere to existing beliefs" [Chapter 7], they are advocating for us to allow students to believe the Bible is saying whatever the individual student believes it is saying. While this fits the authors' ontology well, it completely violates and ignores ours.

When knowable Truth exists, there are those who know it and those who don't. In fact, our entire educational system is founded upon the presumption that some people know XYZ and others don't know. As a result, there are many instances where it is neither practical nor desirable to have a system in which meaning is mutually constructed by teachers and learners. I would argue that such study of the Bible would lead to frequent misunderstanding of God and biblical situations. SSC works hard to teach students hermeneutical principles to help them engage with the Bible. As students follow these principles, there is plenty of room for interpretive disagreement. Theologians have been debating many issues for centuries using these principles and supporting their arguments biblically.

Although we use different teaching methods from those of the authors, their stated goal of having "learners eventually come to construct their own perspectives from this process" [Chapter 7] seem[s] to be fulfilled through our approach. As Stacey said, "They wanted to help us learn things for ourselves, instead of telling us. That really represents the way that SSC is based on a smaller group setting and you developing your own faith rather than someone telling you." And as Leslie said, reflecting on what she had learned through Bible study, "Just being able to open to a chapter and learning. Just feeling confident and being able to read the Word and get something out of it instead of waiting for someone to tell me, or waiting for the preacher to tell me something on Sunday to get me through the whole week."

The authors seem to believe that exclusivists cannot recognize value in the experiences of others; yet, it is unclear what they mean by value. They say:

> We suspect that a root of the perceived emphasis on diagnosing rather than listening is that SSC evangelicals, like many parachurches, view religion through an exclusivist lens (Eck, 2002). That is, they regard their brand of religion as completely true. We posit another root: the fear of encountering new and perhaps appealing ideas by listening to others and thus being tempted to question what one has always viewed as Truth.
>
> SSC-like parachurches acknowledge that some other Christian traditions have some things right, but in the end, members conclude that those other belief systems are fundamentally flawed. This exclusivist lens differs from a

pluralist lens (Eck, 2002), which views all religions as legitimate, valid, and "true" (i.e., when viewed from within) and honors all faiths equally. Eck argues that viewing religion through a pluralist lens leads to engagement and substantive interfaith dialogues (in this instance, with other Christian subcultures). We contend that even exclusivists should heed Ludwig's advice and recognize the value of others' stories, not simply their own. [Chapter 13]

This seems to imply that SSC *should* adopt a worldview that surrenders Truth in exchange for relativism. Obviously, this critique is one that cannot be adopted without an ontological shift.

On balance, this book falls short of the stated goal I'm in a position to evaluate: helping SSC and other parachurch organizations understand ideological contradictions and make improvements. As I reflect on our ministry, there are plenty of areas that need improving, [and] at least one was accurately identified in this text. I agree with the authors that insularity is a main weakness of our ministry, and it may threaten the core of what SSC is trying to accomplish if we do not monitor and address it regularly. Yet the authors' other ideas for improvement seemed to be consistently centered on their worldview, rather than the SSC/Christian worldview.

I appreciate that the authors did not blatantly misrepresent or belittle us for our differences. In person they treated us with a high level of professionalism and respect, and they did the same in the text. When Dr. Magolda first approached me about studying our organization, neither of us expected that a book would result. Over the course of the years Peter and Kelsey spent around us, we were able to develop a relationship that was characterized by mutual respect and warm interactions. The students decided to participate in this study because we viewed it as an opportunity to impact two individuals who we wouldn't otherwise get to influence. As I read this book, it was evident that the authors were forced to consider the foundations of their life and faith. Despite my qualms with the book, I'm proud that the descriptions of SSC will also impact others as they consider their own educational methods, life values, and faith journey.

It's been a year now since I passed on the reins of SSC on this campus, and I remember my time as director of the ministry very fondly. I'm now working among Buddhist students at another university for SSC. Reading this book has brought back many great memories, and I'm proud of the work that SSC continues to do on that campus.

Leslie: In Her Own Words

I can summarize my SSC experience in one sentence: SSC equipped me to engage in relational ministry, where my goal is to reproduce my love of God in others by trying to get everyone I meet (Christian or not) closer to Christ. Plus, we had fun. In a nutshell—that's what I learned and how I live my life.

Here I sit, almost 2 years out of college, reflecting. What difference did this all make? A ton, it turns out. I am noticeably different in my life and faith, especially when interacting with people I meet at work, church, and social settings. SSC trained me to push past my reluctance and shyness to love people with my heart. I go out of my way to do my best and show individuals that I care in meaningful ways. Christ's strength has motivated me to survive the tumultuous waters of my career so far.

Several weeks ago I had coffee with a friend from SSC who graduated the same year as me. We talked about how much our SSC experience makes us stand out at work. Only 2 months into her new job, my friend's coworkers have noticed that she treats people differently—she treats them exceedingly well. She is not simply friendly, and it's clear to them that she's not there just to do her job. Her love for Christ motivates her to do small things for coworkers and clients. She is already making an impact on her workplace.

Kelsey and Peter asserted, "Matthew's dualistic and divisive rhetoric . . . is troubling," but I've seen it to be a reality in my life. It was and is comforting to know that I'm not supposed to feel like I fit in; I'm supposed to feel different. As I realize who I am in relation to Christ and in relation to others, I can engage those dichotomies to find out more about others and me. By talking to people who don't know Christ, I get to know Him better and learn more about the most effective ways to love and serve everyone I meet. A dichotomy is disturbing when two groups scowl staunchly at each other from either side of a barbed wire fence, but dichotomies that cause people to engage with each other in openness and honesty are healthy and beneficial.

Did the seminar for seniors prepare us for the real world? Hardly. Nothing can. Graduation was the rockiest transition of my life, and I'm still trying to steady my boat after the storm. However, I don't think Matthew's intent was a comprehensive preparation workshop. He could have spent weeks and months telling me everything I would need to know, but I wouldn't have listened because I couldn't fully understand the reality until I experienced it. For example, my older sister told me again and again how difficult and lonely it was in the post-college world. And I truly did believe her and Matthew, but it wasn't until several months after college that I realized the magnitude of what they'd told me. Their purpose and goal was to give me a snapshot of what life would be like so that I could begin preparing. They aimed to give me the knowledge and tools that I needed, so when life sent my little boat rocking on the waves, I could stay focused and get things under control.

SSC as a marginalized majority: this is a seeming contradiction. Most students on our campus would say they're Christians, but many of those same students were living blatantly non-Christian lifestyles. There was and is a difference between wearing the label of Christianity and living the life of Christianity. The life of Christianity involves more than attending church or being nice to others. A passionate and devoted love for Christ fuels our all-encompassing, ever-striving sacrificial life. So while most students wore a Christian label, we chose to live a different Christian life.

The authors introduce the term "progressive fundamentalists." Thank you. I've been in search of a term to describe the balancing act that is my spiritual life—and my social life, too, for that matter. I've often thought, "Am I conservative?" "Am I liberal?" and felt confused when I felt I could answer "yes" to both, at least sometimes. As confusing as "progressive fundamentalists" is, I think it fits perfectly.

Kelsey and Peter criticized the effectiveness of our evangelism. In my time with SSC, that was the biggest area of growth I saw in the organization as a whole. During my freshman year, SSC was a tight-knit group that didn't branch out. As the years went by, especially as a result of Matthew's leadership, we became more and more effective at reaching out to other people. Are we model evangelists yet? Absolutely not. So in that way, you are right to wonder about our effectiveness. Many of us are, in fact, still "too cautious and polite." But I also believe that we were (and continue to be) a group capable of "inducing change" on our campus. Our goal is to help individuals make huge changes in their lives, and we do that. Although this may not have an earthquake effect on campus, as our waves of change grow, they ripple out to touch life after life. Our primary aim is not to be a big bang of attention with little lasting change. Our impact is slower and deeper. All the same, people must be willing to be bold and take risks to fuel this change, and that is an area where many current and past SSC students need to continue to grow. Thanks for reminding me of a challenge for my life.

Sexism and gender roles are another area where I saw SSC grow in my time there. It seems to me your portrayal focuses more heavily on the male perspective. Several times you wonder what the women were thinking, so in the next two paragraphs, I offer my take.

Biblically, Jesus loved and lifted up women in ways that were highly uncommon for his time. I know by the way I'm treated in SSC that I'm not viewed as lesser than men, no matter what lifestyle choices I make as a woman. SSC equips women with the same skills and knowledge as men. Each individual enacts his or her role differently, regardless of gender. Choosing submission (which applies truly to marriage) does not relegate a woman to simply childbearing and cooking. If a husband loves a wife like Christ loved the church (that He died for) and knows God intimately, there is no reason that a wife should feel doomed to silence and following. Just like God listens to people and does what is best for them, a husband listens to his wife and does what's best for her. This makes it all the more important that I seek after God to find a man to marry. I want a man who is led by God so I can be confident that God is leading our marriage.

Early on in my time in SSC, students butted heads over how to relate to the opposite sex, or simply slipped into avoidance of the topic and interaction. Leaders and upper-class students struggled to teach practical ways to honor and respect the opposite sex. As a stubborn woman, I was reluctant to accept anything that seemed like someone was looking down on me. I didn't know how to encourage men, and they didn't know how to encourage me. Our good intentions spurred frustration; yet over time, we learned to boldly communicate. Women talked to women about how we want men to treat us. Men talked to other men. I talked to my guy friends and to Matthew to help them understand how they could best show us they care, and they shared with me the genuine intentions behind their actions. We all admitted we didn't know how to best show our support and admiration for each other. So we learned. Just like any other aspect of becoming Christlike, it takes time, practice, and work. We learn to love and show honor and respect for each other; it's a process and a struggle. Over my 4 years in SSC, I learned the joy of serving, but I also learned the joy of being served, by both genders. It's this mutual serving that I hope to have in marriage someday.

Thanks for your time and your observations. They've helped me to reflect on who I am.

Don: In His Own Words

Since much of the study shows the value we place on the Word of God, let me start with the verses from Proverbs 24:30–34: "I passed by the field of a sluggard, by the vineyard of a man without sense; and lo, it was all overgrown with thorns; the ground was covered with nettles, and its stone wall was broken down. Then I saw and considered it; I looked and received instruction. A little sleep, a little slumber, a little folding of the hands to rest, and poverty will come upon you like a robber, and want like an armed man."

It isn't often that an organization like SSC has the privilege to receive some unbiased critique after 2 years of direct observation. But if the writer of Proverbs could learn from an inanimate, broken-down stone wall, how much more should I be able to learn from two highly motivated researchers who have intimate access to almost everything that happened in our organization over 2 years and tried to make deductions based on these observations, with nothing to gain by being biased?

Sometimes it grieves me to admit I'm part of the parachurches that the researchers talk about in here. As part of SSC, I see some of the results; they are alarming, disturbing, aggravating, even maddening, and need attending to, yet I also see many results as reason to rejoice that we are doing a good job at what God has been leading us to do. We can always get better.

We are involved with students to help them get to know the person of Jesus Christ, and then they in turn help others do the same. One of our past leaders said evangelism is "taking a look at Jesus and telling others what you see." This isn't a pursuit to build SSC or to make us feel good about what we are doing, but it is in direct obedience to what God seems to be doing here on this earth to build laborers for a lifetime and build His kingdom. We usually have only a small part in the students' lives (3–4 years, max), but hopefully we (with God's help) will have an impact that will last a lifetime.

Two things stick out to me about the observations. First, the observers do not seem to comprehend the power that the believer has within them through the indwelling Holy Spirit (Ephesians 1:13), and second, they don't quite understand the fact that the Bible isn't just a good guidebook, but is in fact (from God's perspective), the living Word of God (Hebrews 4:12).

I've heard that to train someone to find counterfeit money, they study real money, not the different counterfeits. Thus, we try to saturate those involved with us with the Word of God and a desire to know Him personally, not focus on different religions or groups. When studying the Bible for discussion group, I may have a little more insight because of more preparation and maturity, but when I spend a couple of hours with the students after they have studied, I learn as much from them as they may from me. They look to me not because I have some preconceived idea, but because I've walked with the Writer of the Book longer. Sometimes, there are definite interpretations of the scriptures that they can't figure out, but it isn't because I'm the "leader" that I can give a definitive answer. Sometimes I have walked away and said to them, "I don't know, but I'll try to find the answer."

It is very obvious that a leader of SSC and any other organization of this type could use his or her position for good or bad, depending on their motives and desired outcomes for their work. There is no perfect organization. We need to hold carefully the authority and influence given to build what God may be doing, not what we may selfishly want to see happen. Sometimes our desires and God's desires may not be the same, but hopefully they are.

Looking at the researchers' conclusions is very insightful. I see how SSC as an organization can grow and change to better meet its God-given goals, which can vary and add value to the university and its subcultures, as well as individual SSC students' overall life learning.

I would love to have the researchers spend time with other SSC branches on other campuses, as each ministry is a reflection of its leader's bents, student needs, and campus culture. They might come to some other conclusions in other places. However, from reading this book, I will enjoy trying to implement some of the recommendations for SSC here, and I'm sure other SSC staff could gain valuable insight from such observations. Hopefully, they can read this book and gain something from this valuable research. I'm looking forward to sitting down and dialoguing more with the researchers in the near future.

It's my desire that God will use this book to advance His Kingdom and help bridge the gap between secular and sacred in our universities.

Jessica: In Her Own Words

"Everyone, this is Kelsey, and she'll be observing us tonight and maybe for a while." Every time I said this to a group or Bible study I was leading, I felt a familiar knot of apprehension. Not only was I a little concerned how the students would react to me inviting a stranger to observe their deepest thoughts and issues, but I was also wary of the final result. How would we as an organization, in the big picture, and a Bible study, on a small scale, measure up? Would an observer really be able to understand our goals and our heart behind those goals? I think many Christians and Christian groups feel a similar tension about letting people study them at their most intimate and vulnerable moments. Most of us could share numerous stories of criticism and ridicule, and we often feel very misunderstood, even within our local communities. This is absolutely not unique to Christians, but the experience has taught us to be cautious of inviting outside critique.

After reading a draft of the manuscript, I regret to say that some of my fears were substantiated. Although the factual statements about what occurred during our meetings were usually correct, more often than not the authors misinterpreted the spirit and heart behind what we were trying to accomplish. For example, Chapter 8 focuses on what the authors call our "Outreach Ritual" and what I call a helpful tool to share our faith with our friends and other interested individuals. The first point the researchers missed in their discussion of the Bridge Building workshop was the purpose of teaching the illustration. The primary reason we sponsored this class was to help interested students learn a clear and concise way to share their faith. The authors repeatedly used the word "mechanical" to describe both the teaching and the students' practice sessions. I'm not sure what they expected, since the goal of the 4-week workshop was for students to be able to share the illustration. It's difficult to learn something like the Bridge illustration without practice and repetition. We repeated numerous times that we didn't expect the students to repeat verbatim what we showcased. We encouraged them to eventually adapt it to their personality, but in order to learn it, they needed to initially follow our lead. A problem I have with describing the class and students as "mechanical" is that it implies that we discourage critical thinking or discussion, which couldn't be farther from the truth. In addition, the description does not capture the students' heart; they did want to learn the lessons the SSC staff taught.

The authors also assume that during my role-play as a non-Christian, I didn't ask more questions about the cross because "the idea of salvation through the cross, a cornerstone of the Christian faith, is likely so ingrained at this point that they may not realize what types of questions non-Christians may raise about this tenet of faith." What they did not realize was that when I've shared the Bridge illustration with students who indicate they're interested in learning more about the Bible, their responses are very similar to what I modeled during the workshop approximately 95 percent of the time. Far from assuming that everyone accepts salvation through the cross, I was merely demonstrating a realistic situation students might encounter. SSC's goal is not just to share the Bridge illustration once, dispense our wisdom to the student, and leave; we're trying to build relationships. Even if students don't ask many questions during initial meetings but seem interested, I will ask if they would like to get together again to discuss their questions or issues with Christianity.

I take exception with the authors' misunderstanding of gender roles in the SSC. Throughout the manuscript, they interject comments about how gender plays out in the SSC. Again referring to Chapter 8, when we were initially sharing the Bridge and asked the participant to describe "man," Peter commented that he silently wondered about "woman." To me this suggests oversensitivity on his part, rather than a misstep on our part. It's fairly clear presenters meant *mankind,* and they weren't trying to exclude women from the discussion. As a woman, I keep my eyes open for unfair treatment of women within Christian circles. No doubt, some Christian groups are certainly guilty of marginalizing and even outright discriminating against women. However, it doesn't have to be that way for Christians, and I firmly believe it isn't that way in the SSC.

We believe what the Bible says about gender roles. Without going into too much detail, the Bible teaches that men and women are equal in their worth and identity; they just have different jobs or roles. This is not meant to demean women or to give men all the power. Both are taught to respect one another. The SSC men respect the women, and although they may not demonstrate it perfectly, they do their best. Almost every Valentine's Day the men bring roses or make treats for the women. They try to be gentlemen by carrying heavy bags—do whatever they can do to help. It is quite admirable for men in this generation to show such consideration and care for women. Instead of criticizing us for inadvertent remarks, I had hoped the authors would have noticed the care and respect we express to one another and more fully incorporate this positive quality into the manuscript.

In the end, I am glad we agreed to be a part of this research project. We all learned valuable lessons about the way others perceive us and ourselves. I'm proud of the way SSC students opened up their hearts and minds to Kelsey and Peter. I hope that in the future, both Christians and non-Christians respond to one another with more understanding and empathy.

Kiley: In Her Own Words

I am surprised to say that I learned a lot while reading this book. I learned more about people's perspectives when listening to things that I have to say, and I even gained insight on my own beliefs. It was a little strange to read how Kelsey and Peter perceived some of what I said. Sometimes they interpreted what I had to say differently than I intended, and this reminded me that everyone hears things differently.

While reading this book, one thought crossed my mind: I never got to know the people interviewing me. Granted, we would sit down for hours at a time occasionally and talk, but I never got to know their opinions. There was never much discussion about what Peter and Kelsey thought about what I had to say. Looking back, I wish there would have been. I would have gained a better understanding of what was going through their heads as we were talking to one another. After reading the personal testimonies of Kelsey and Peter, their reactions to some of what I had to say make more sense to me.

There are a lot of stereotypes about Christians, and I find this very upsetting. I felt this way before reading this book, but reading parts of it confirmed my feelings. While reading about what the researchers thought SSC was going to be like, I realized that because of these stereotypes, Christianity probably turns off a lot of people who have not come to know Christ. I want to shout to the world that these stereotypes do not apply to everyone, and that Christianity is really about a personal relationship with God. In my opinion, it is the worst thing in the world when a person is turned off from knowing our Savior because of certain actions of others. From time to time, we all question our faith and what we believe. This is evident in hard times and with things that we just don't understand. This does not mean, however, that we lose our faith.

Reading about one's own life can provide an interesting perspective. It has been a few years since some of these interviews took place. I am a senior now, and some of these interviews occurred during my sophomore year. When I was reading everything I had to say in response to questions Kelsey and Peter posed, my confidence shocked me. I always considered myself to be a shy, quiet person. Being a part of SSC really opened me up to my own faith. I had to grow as a result of wanting to be a good example for girls in my Bible study, and also just wanting to make Christ's name known.

Shortly after I finished reading this book, I sat at my kitchen table, just thinking. These last 2 years have been hard for me spiritually, and I have lost something and want it back. The immediate feeling I got from the character "Kiley" was true joy. Somewhere along the way, I feel like I have lost some of that joy. As time goes on, people get busier and busier. School has begun to steer me away from my dedication, and this made me realize after reading about myself that I need to once again change my life priorities. Life is too short and you need to live for the moment. Never have regrets. Everything you do reflects your character and helps you grow as a person. Many times, people get so caught up in living their own lives that they forget their real purpose for being on this earth. This book, in certain ways, gave me a better understanding of myself, and for this I am very thankful.

NOTES

Chapter 1

1. We changed the name of all evangelical groups and their members to address anonymity concerns.

Chapter 2

1. A version of this narrative originally appeared in Magolda, P., and Ebben, K. (2007, June). Students serving Christ: Understanding the role of student subcultures on a college campus. *Anthropology and Education Quarterly,* 38(2), 138–158.

2. Throughout the book, we use the term "nonbelievers" to signify our status as subculture outsiders.

Chapter 3

1. A version of this narrative originally appeared in Magolda, P., and Ebben, K. (2007, June). Students serving Christ: Understanding the role of student subcultures on a college campus. *Anthropology and Education Quarterly,* 38(2), 138–158.

2. Van Maanen (1988) defined a confessional tale as an attempt to "explicitly demystify fieldwork or participant-observation by showing how the technique is practiced in the field. Stories of infiltration, fables of fieldwork rapport, minimelo-dramas of hardships endured (and overcome), and accounts of what fieldwork did to the fieldworker are prominent features of confessions" (p. 73).

Chapter 5

1. A complete description and explanation of this biblical illustration appears in Chapter 8.

Chapter 6

1. A version of this narrative originally appeared in Ebben, K., and Magolda, P. M. (2007, July–August). Thank God it's Friday: Evangelical Christians preach a new cocurriculum. *About Campus, 12*(3), 8–15.

Chapter 7

1. A version of this narrative originally appeared in Magolda, P. M., and Ebben, K. (2006, May–June). College student involvement and mobilization: An ethnographic study of a Christian student organization. *The Journal of College Student Development, 47*(3), 281–298.

Chapter 8

1. A version of this narrative originally appeared in Magolda, P., and Ebben, K. (2007, June). Students serving Christ: Understanding the role of student subcultures on a college campus. *Anthropology and Education Quarterly, 38*(2), 138–158.

Chapter 9

1. A version of this narrative originally appeared in Magolda, P. M., and Ebben, K. (2006, May–June). College student involvement and mobilization: An ethnographic study of a Christian student organization. *The Journal of College Student Development, 47*(3), 281–298.

Chapter 11

1. A version of this narrative originally appeared in Magolda, P. M., and Ebben, K. (2006, May–June). College student involvement and mobilization: An ethnographic study of a Christian student organization. *The Journal of College Student Development, 47*(3), 281–298.

Chapter 14

1. (www.barna.org/FlexPage.aspx?Page=Topic&TopicID=2) "Atheists and agnostics comprise 10% of adults nationwide (2007)." "7% of the U.S. population identify with a faith other than Christianity (2007)."

REFERENCES

Adler, J. (2005, September 5). In search of the spiritual. *Newsweek, 46*–64.

Albright, M. (2007). *The mighty and the almighty.* New York: Harper-Collins.

Angrosino, M. V. (2005). Recontextualizing observation: Ethnography, pedagogy, and the prospects for a progressive political agenda. In N. K. Denzin and Y. S. Lincoln (Eds.), *The Sage handbook of qualitative research* (3rd ed., pp. 729–745). Thousand Oaks, CA: Sage.

Astin, A. W. (1993). What matters in college? [Electronic version]. *Liberal Education, 79* (4).

Dadei, M., and Duxlei, M. (2003). An interview with Steve Earle. *Tikkun, 18*(2), 59–62.

Balmer, R. (2006, June 23). Jesus is not a Republican. *Chronicle of Higher Education,* p. B-6.

Barley, N. (1983). *The innocent anthropologist: Notes from a mud hut.* London: British Museum Publications.

Barna, G. (1996). *Index of leading spiritual indicators.* Dallas: Word Publications.

Bartlett, T. (2005, April 22). Most freshmen say religion guides them. *Chronicle of Higher Education,* pp. A-1, A-40.

Baxter Magolda, M. B. (1992). *Knowing and reasoning in college: Gender-related patterns in students' intellectual development.* San Francisco: Jossey-Bass.

Baxter Magolda, M. B. (2004a). Preface. In M. B. Baxter Magolda and P. M. King (Eds.), *Learning Partnerships: Theory and models of practice to educate for self-authorship* (pp. xvii–xxvi). Sterling, VA: Stylus.

Baxter Magolda, M. B. (2004b). Learning partnerships model. In M. B. Baxter Magolda and P. M. King (Eds.), *Learning partnerships: Theory and models of practice to educate for self-authorship* (pp. 37–62). Sterling, VA: Stylus.

Berkowitz, M. W., and Fekula, M. J. (1999, November–December). Educating for character. *About Campus, 4,* 17–22.

Blimling, G. S., and Whitt, E. J. (1999). Identifying the principles that guide student affairs practice. In G. S. Blimling and E. J. Whitt (Eds.), *Good practice in student affairs: Principles to foster student learning* (pp. 1–20). San Francisco, CA: Jossey-Bass.

Boyer, E. L. (1987). The college as community. Paper presented at the meeting of the Freshman Year Experience—West, University of California, Irvine.

Bramadat, P. (2000). *The church on the world's turf: An evangelical Christian group at a secular university.* Oxford: Oxford University Press.

Braskamp, L. A. (2006). The religious and spiritual journeys of college students (p. 16). Loyola University.

Braskamp, L. A., Trautvetter, L. C., and Ward, K. (2006). *Putting students first: How colleges develop students purposefully.* Bolton, MA: Anker Publishing.

Brinton, H. (2007, October 29). Do-it-yourself Christianity. *USA Today,* p. 15A.

Bryant, A. N. (2005). Evangelicals on campus: An exploration of culture, faith, and college life. *Religion and Education, 32*(2), 1–30.

Bryant, A. N. (2006). Assessing the gender climate of an evangelical student subculture in the United States. *Gender and Education, 18*(6), 613–634.

Bryant, A. N. (2007a). A portrait of evangelical Christian students in college. *Essay forum on the religious engagement of American undergraduates.* Retrieved July 22, 2007, from http://religion.ssrc.org/reforum/.

Bryant, A. N. (2007b). *Negotiating complementarianism in evangelical student organizations: A longitudinal exploration of college student gender ideologies.* Paper presented at the Association for the Study of Higher Education Conference, Louisville, KY.

Bryant, A. N., Choi, J. Y., and Yasuno, M. (2003). Understanding the religious and spiritual dimensions of students' lives in the first year of college. *Journal of College Student Development, 44*(6), 723–745.

Burnett, J. H. (1976). Ceremony, rites, and economy in the student system of an American high school. In J. L. Roberts and S. K. Akinsaya (Eds.), *Educational patterns and cultural configurations: The anthropology of education* (pp. 313–323). New York: McKay.

Butler, J. (1989). An overview of religion on campus. In J. Butler (Ed.), *Religion on campus* (pp. 3–16). San Francisco, CA: Jossey-Bass.

Calhoun, C. (2007). Preface. *Rise of religion on campus: Online guide.* Retrieved November 20, 2007, from http://religion.ssrc.org/reguide.

Carlson, D. (1994). Gayness, multicultural education, and community. *Educational Foundations, 8*(4), 5–25.

Cherry, C., DeBerg, B. A., and Porterfield, A. (2001). *Religion on campus.* Chapel Hill: University of North Carolina Press.

Clarke, J. (1993). Style. In S. Hall and T. Jefferson (Eds.), *Resistance through rituals: Youth subcultures in post-war Britain* (pp. 175–191). London: Routledge.

Cohen, A. K. (1997). A general theory of subculture. In K. Gelder and S. Thornton (Eds.), *The subculture reader* (pp. 44–54). London: Routledge.

Coles, R. (1989). *The call of stories: Teaching and the moral imagination.* Boston: Houghton Mifflin Company.

Coomes, M. D. (2004). Understanding the historical and cultural influences that shape generations. In M. D. Coomes and R. DeBard (Eds.), *Serving the millennial generation* (pp. 17–31). San Francisco: Jossey-Bass.

Cooperman, A. (2007, May 5). Is there disdain for evangelicals in the classroom? *Washington Post,* p. A-3.

Creswell, J. W., and Miller, D. L. (2000). Determining validity in qualitative inquiry. *Theory into Practice, 39*(3), 124–130.

Cross Brazzell, J., and Reisser, L. (1999). Creating inclusive communities. In G. S. Blimling and E. J. Whitt (Eds.), *Good practice in student affairs: Principles to foster student learning* (pp. 157–177). San Francisco, CA: Jossey-Bass.

Dalton, J. C. (1980). Student evangelicals: Campus activism from the right. *NASPA Journal, 17*(1), 22–27.

Dalton, J. C. (1999). Helping students develop coherent values and ethical standards. In G. S. Blimling and E. J. Whitt (Eds.), *Good practice in student affairs: Principles to foster student learning* (pp. 45–66). San Francisco: Jossey-Bass.

Dalton, J. C. (2001). Career and calling: Finding a place for the spirit in work and community. In M. A. Jablonski (Ed.), *The implications of student spirituality for student affairs practice* (pp. 17–25). San Francisco: Jossey-Bass.

Davis, T., and Murrell, P. (1993). *Turning teaching into learning: The role of student responsibility in the collegiate experience.* Washington, D.C.: George Washington University School of Education and Human Development.

Denzin, N. K. (1989). *Interpretive interactionism* (Vol. 16). Newbury Park, CA: Sage.

DeWalt, K. M., and DeWalt, B. R. (2002). *Participant observation: A guide for fieldworkers.* Walnut Creek, CA: AltaMira Press.

Ebben, K., and Magolda, P. M. (2007, July–August). Thank God it's Friday: Evangelical Christians preach a new co-curriculum. *About Campus: Enriching the Student Learning Experience, 12*(3), 8–15.

Eck, D. (2002). *A new religious America: How a "Christian Country" has become the world's most religiously diverse nation.* San Francisco, CA: Harper Collins.

Eims, L. (1978). *The lost art of disciple making.* Grand Rapids, MI: Zondervan Corp.

Eisner, E. W. (1998). *The enlightened eye: Qualitative inquiry and the enhancement of educational practice* (2nd ed.). New York: Macmillan Publishing Company.

Ely, M., Anzul, M., Friedman, T., Garner, D., and Steinmetz, A. M. (1991). *Doing qualitative research: Circles within circles.* London: The Falmer Press.

Fetterman, D. M. (1998). *Ethnography: Step by step* (2nd ed.). Thousand Oaks, CA: Sage.

Finder, A. (2007, May 2). Matters of faith find a new prominence on campus [Electronic version]. *New York Times.* Retrieved November 20, 2008, from http://www.nytimes.com/2007/05/02/education/02spirituality.html.

Foley, D. (2002). Critical ethnography: The reflexive turn. *Qualitative Studies in Education, 15*(3), 469–490.

Fontana, A., and Frey, J. H. (2005). The interview: From neutral stance to political involvement. In N. K. Denzin and Y. S. Lincoln (Eds.), *The Sage handbook of qualitative research* (3rd ed., pp. 695–727.). Thousand Oaks, CA: Sage.

Geertz, C. (1973). *The interpretation of cultures.* New York: Basic Books.

Giddens, A. (1997). *Sociology.* London: Polity Press.

Giroux, H. (1992). *Border crossings: Cultural workers and the politics of education.* New York: Routledge.

Glaser, B. G. (1965). The constant comparative method of qualitative analysis. *Social Problems, 12,* 436–445.

Glesne, C., and Peshkin, A. (1992). *Becoming qualitative researchers: An introduction.* White Plains, NY: Longman.

Grahmann, R. G. (2001). *Understanding the way Christian students at secular universities perceive and practice Bible study.* Unpublished dissertation, Trinity International University, Deerfield, IL.

Guba, E. G., and Lincoln, Y. S. (1989). *Fourth generation evaluation.* Newbury Park, CA: Sage.

Guba, E. G., and Lincoln, Y. S. (2005). Paradigmatic controversies, contradictions, and emerging confluences. In N. K. Denzin and Y. S. Lincoln (Eds.), *The Sage handbook of qualitative research* (3rd ed., pp. 191–215). Thousand Oaks, CA: Sage.

Hansen, C. (2005, September). The holy and the ivy. *Christianity Today, 49,* 64–69.

Harding, S. G. (1991). *Whose science? Whose knowledge?: Thinking from women's lives.* Ithaca, NY: Cornell University Press.

Harrison, M. D. (2002). *Narrative based evaluation: Wording toward the light.* New York: Peter Lang.

Hebdige, D. (1979). *Subculture: The meaning of style.* London: Routledge.

Henderson, J., & Casper, M. (2007). *Jim and Casper go to church: Frank conversation about faith, churches, and well-meaning Christians.* Carol Stream, Ill.: Barna Books.

Hodder, I. (2000). The interpretation of documents and material culture. In N. K. Denzin and Y. S. Lincoln (Eds.), *The handbook of qualitative research* (2nd ed., pp. 703–715). Thousand Oaks, CA: Sage.

Hokema, D. A. (1994). *Campus rules and moral community: In place of in loco parentis.* Lanham, MD: Rowan and Littlefield.

Howe, N., and Strauss, W. (2000). *Millennials rising: The next great generation.* New York: Vintage Books.

Hunt, M. J. (1993). *College Catholics: A new counter-culture.* New York: Paulist Press.

Jablonski, M. A. (Ed.). (2001). *The implications of student spirituality for student affairs practice.* San Francisco: Jossey-Bass.

Jenkins, J. I., and Burish, T. (2006, October 23). Reason and faith at Harvard. *Washington Post,* p. A21.

Jones, G. (2005). The soulless university. *Christian Century, 122*(1), 35.

Jorgensen, D. L. (1989). *Participant observation: A methodology for human studies* (Vol. 15). Newbury Park, CA: Sage.

Kim, R. Y. (2006). *God's new whiz kids?: Korean American evangelicals on campus.* New York: New York University Press.

Kuh, G. D., and Gonyea, R. M. (2006). Spirituality, liberal learning, and college student engagement. *Liberal Education, 92*(1), 40–47.

Kuh, G. D., Kinzie, J., Schuh, J., and Whitt, E. (2005). *Student success in college: Creating conditions that matter* (1st ed.). San Francisco: Jossey-Bass.

Kuh, G. D., and Umbach, P. (2004). College and character: Insights from the National Survey of Student Engagement. In J. C. Dalton and T. Russell (Eds.), *New directions in institutional research: Assessing character outcomes in college* (p. 197). San Francisco, CA: Jossey-Bass.

Kuh, G. D., and Whitt, E. J. (1988). *The invisible tapestry: Culture in American colleges and universities.* Washington, D.C.: Association for the Study of Higher Education.

Lather, P. (1986a). Research as praxis. *Harvard Educational Review, 56*(3), 257–277.

Lather, P. (1986b). Issues of validity in openly ideological research: Between a rock and a soft place. *Interchange, 17*(4), 63–84.

Laurence, P. (1999, November–December). Can religion and spirituality find a place in higher education? *About Campus, 4*(5), 11–16.

LeCompte, M. D., and Preissle, J. (1993). *Ethnography and qualitative design in educational research* (2nd ed.). San Diego, CA: Academic Press.

Lee, J. J. (2002). Religion and college attendance: Change among students. *Review of Higher Education, 25*(5), 369–384.

Leland, J. (2004, May 16). Christian cool and the new generation gap. *New York Times,* p. 1.

Lewis, C. S. (1945). *Mere Christianity* (Rev. and enl. ed.). New York: Macmillan.

Lincoln, Y. S., and Guba, E. G. (1985). *Naturalistic inquiry.* Newbury Park, CA: Sage.

Lincoln, Y. S., and Guba, E. G. (1989). Ethics: The failure of positivist science. *The Review of Higher Education, 12,* 221–240.

Lowery, J. W. (2000). *Walking the halls of ivy with Christ: The classroom and residential experiences of undergraduate evangelical students.* Unpublished dissertation, Bowling Green State University, Bowling Green, OH.

Lowery, J. W., and Coomes, M. D. (2003). The residence hall experiences of undergraduate evangelical students: Not always the best place to be a Christian. *Journal of College and University Student Housing, 32*(1), 31–38.

Magolda, P. M. (2000). The campus tour ritual: Exploring community discourses in higher education. *Anthropology and Education Quarterly, 31*(1), 24–36.

Magolda, P. M. (2003). Saying good-bye: An anthropological examination of a commencement ritual. *Journal of College Student Development, 44*(6), 779–796.

Magolda, P., and Abowitz, K. K. (1997). Communities and tribes in residential living. *Teachers College Record 99*(2), 266–310.

Magolda, P. M., and Ebben, K. (2006). College student involvement and mobilization: An ethnographic study of a Christian student organization. *Journal of College Student Development, 47*(3), 281–298.

Magolda, P. M., and Ebben, K. (2007). Students Serving Christ: Understanding the role of student subcultures on a college campus. *Anthropology and Education Quarterly, 38*(2), 138–158.

Maher, H. (2006). U.S.: Albright speaks out on religion, politics, and Bush. Retrieved November 25, 2007, from http://www.rferl.org/featuresarticle/2006/10/49e3ba46–8c1b-4203-aaee-d38a7f26a889.html.

Main, B. (2003). *If Jesus were a senior: Last-minute preparations for postcollege life* (1st ed.). Louisville, Ky.: Westminster John Knox Press.

Malley, B. (2004). *How the Bible works: An anthropological study of evangelical biblicism.* Walnut Creek, CA: AltaMira Press.

Marsden, G. M. (1992). The soul of the American University. In G. M. Marsden and B. J. Longfield (Eds.), *The secularization of the academy* (pp. 9–45). New York: Oxford University Press.

Marsden, G. M. (1997). *The outrageous idea of Christian scholarship.* New York: Oxford University Press.

Martin, J. (1992). *Cultures in organizations.* New York, NY: Oxford University

McLaren, P. L. (1985). The ritual dimensions of resistance: Clowning and symbolic inversion. *Journal of Education, 167*(2), 84–97.

McLaren, P. L. (1986). Making Catholics: The ritual production of conformity in a Catholic junior high school. *Journal of Education, 168*(2), 55–77.

McMurtrie, B. (1999, December 3). Pluralism and prayer under one roof. *Chronicle of Higher Education,* p. A-48.

McMurtrie, B. (2001, May 18). Crusading for Christ, amid keg parties and secularism. *Chronicle of Higher Education,* p. A-42.

Miller, D. (2003). *Blue like jazz: Nonreligious thoughts on Christian spirituality.* Nashville: T. Nelson Publishers."

Miller, L. (2006, November 13). An evangelical identity crisis. *Newsweek,* 30–37.

Miller, M. A. (2006, March/April). Religion on campus. *Change,* 6–7.

Miller, T. E., Bender, B. E., and Schuh, J. H. (2005). *Promoting reasonable expectations: Aligning student and institutional views of the college experience* (1st ed.). San Francisco, CA: Jossey-Bass.

Miller, V. W., and Ryan, M. M. (2001). *Transforming campus life: Reflections on spirituality and religious pluralism.* New York: P. Lang.

Moran, C. D. (2007). The public identity work of evangelical Christian students. *Journal of College Student Development, 48*(4), 418–434.

Nasir, N., & Al-Amin, J. (2006, March/April). Creating identity-safe spaces on college campuses for Muslim Students. *Change,* 38, 22-27.

Omi, M., and Winant, H. (1994). *Racial formation in the United States.* New York: Routledge.

Ortner, S. B. (1996). Resistance and the problem of ethnographic refusal. In T. McDonald (Ed.), *The historic turn in the human sciences* (pp. 281–305). Ann Arbor, MI: University of Michigan Press.

Ott, J. S. (1989). *The organizational culture perspective.* Chicago: Dorsey Press.

Patton, M. Q. (1990). *Qualitative evaluation and research methods.* Newbury Park, CA: Sage.

Patton, M. Q. (2002). *Qualitative research and evaluation methods* (3rd ed.). Thousand Oaks, CA: Sage Publications.

Peacock, J. (1986). *The anthropological lens: Harsh light, soft focus.* Cambridge, UK: Cambridge University Press.

Perry, E. M., and Armstrong, E. A. (2007). Evangelicals on campus. *Essay forum on the religious engagement of American undergraduates.* Retrieved July 22, 2007, from http://religion.ssrc.org/reforum/.

Peshkin, A. (1986). *God's choice: The total world of a fundamentalist Christian school.* Chicago: The University of Chicago Press.

Peshkin, A. (2000). The nature of interpretation in qualitative research. *Educational Researcher, 29*(9), 5–9.

Quantz, R. A. (1992). On critical ethnography (with some postmodern considerations). In M. D. LeCompte, W. L. Millroy and J. Preissle (Eds.), *The handbook of qualitative research in education* (pp. 447–505). San Diego: Academic Press.

Quantz, R. A. (1999). School ritual as performance: A reconstruction of Durkheim's and Turner's use of ritual. *Educational Theory, 49*(4), 493–513.

Quantz, R. A., and Magolda, P. M. (1997). Nonrational classroom performance: Ritual as an aspect of action. *Urban Review, 29*(4), 221–238.

Quebedeaux, R. (1974). *The young evangelicals: Revolution in orthodoxy.* New York: Harper and Row.

Redman, M. (2005). Blessed be your name. On *Blessed be your name: The songs of Matt Redman* [Album]. Brentwood, TN: EMi CMG.

Reinharz, S. (1997). Who am I? The need for a variety of selves in the field. In R. Hertz (Ed.), *Reflexivity and voice* (pp. 3–20). Thousand Oaks, CA: Sage.

Rhoads, R. (1994). *Coming out in college: The struggle for a queer identity.* Westport, CT: Bergin and Garvey.

Rice, E. (2006). Faculty priorities: Where does faith fit? Unpublished contribution to a symposium. Faculty Work and the New Academy: Emerging Challenges and Evolving Roles Conference, Association of American Colleges and Universities, Chicago, IL.

Richardson, L. (2000). Writing as a method of inquiry. In N. K. Denzin and Y. S. Lincoln (Eds.), *Handbook of qualitative research* (2nd ed., pp. 923–948). Thousand Oaks, CA: Sage.

Riley, N. S. (2005). *God on the quad: How religious colleges and the missionary generation are changing America* (1st ed.). New York: St. Martin's Press.

Romano, T. (2007, February 3). Keeping faith with public education. *Cincinnati Enquirer,* p. B-6.

Rorty, R. (1999). Religion as conversation-stopper. In R. Rorty (Ed.), *Philosophy and social hope* (pp. 168–174). New York: Penguin.

Rudolph, F. (1962). *The American college and university: A history.* Athens, GA: The University of Georgia Press.

Schwandt, T. A. (1990). Paths to inquiry in the social disciplines: Scientific, constructivist, and critical theory methodologies. In E. Guba (Ed.), *The paradigm dialogue* (pp. 258–276). Newbury Park, CA: Sage.

Schwandt, T. A. (2001). *Dictionary of qualitative inquiry* (2nd ed.). Thousand Oaks, CA: Sage.

Schwehn, M. (2005). A dying light or a newborn enlightenment: Religion and higher education in the twenty-first century. *History of Education Quarterly, 45*(3), 454–460.

Seifert, T. (2007, May–June). Understanding Christian privilege. *About Campus, 12*(2), 10–17.

Senge, P. M. (1990). *The fifth discipline: The art and practice of the learning organization* (1st ed.). New York: Doubleday/Currency.

Shaffir, W. B., and Stebbins, R. A. (1991). Getting in. In W. B. Shaffir and R. A. Stebbins (Eds.), *Experiencing fieldwork: An inside view of qualitative research* (pp. 25–30). Newbury Park, CA: Sage.

Sharlet, J. (2007, April 19). Teenage Holy War. *Rolling Stone,* 50–67.

Sheler, J. (Writer). (2004). An interview with William Rominowski [Television series], *Religion and ethics news weekly:* United States: PBS.

Sidanius, J., Larr, C. V., Levin, S., and Sinclair, S. (2004). Ethnic enclaves and the dynamics of social identity on the college campus: The good, the bad, and the ugly. *Journal of Personality and Social Psychology, 87*(1), 96–110.

Society for Values in Education. (2005). *Report: Wingspread declaration of religion in public life.* Racine, WI.

Sommerville, C. J. (2006). *The decline of the secular university.* Oxford: Oxford University Press.

Spaid, E. L. (1996, September 6). More colleges opt for religion 101. *Christian Science Monitor, 88,* 1.

Spradley, J. P. (1970). *You owe yourself a drunk: Ethnography of urban nomads.* Boston: Little, Brown and Company.

Spradley, J. (1979). *The ethnographic interview.* Fort Worth: Holt, Rinehart, and Winston.

Spradley, J. (1980). *Participant observation.* New York: Holt, Rinehart and Winston.

Strange, C. C., and Banning, J. H. (2001). *Educating by design: Creating campus learning environments that work* (1st ed.). San Francisco: Jossey-Bass.

Swidey, N. (2003). God on the quad: New England's liberal college campuses have become fertile ground for the evangelical movement [Electronic version]. *Boston Globe.* Retrieved June 23, 2007, from http://www.boston.com/news/globe/magazine/articles/2003/11/30/god_on_the quad/.

Tierney, W. G. (1993). *Building communities of difference: Higher education in the twenty-first century.* Westport, CT: Bergin and Garvey.

UCLA Higher Education Research Institute. (2003). *The spiritual life of college students: A national study of college students' search for meaning and purpose (preliminary report).* Los Angeles: UCLA Higher Education Research Institute.

UCLA Higher Education Research Institute. (2005). *The spiritual life of college students: A national study of college students' search for meaning and purpose.* Los Angeles: UCLA Higher Education Research Institute.

van Gennep, A. (1960). *The rites of passage* (M. B. V. G. L. Caffee, Trans.). Chicago: The University of Chicago Press.

Van Maanen, J. (1988). *Tales of the field: On writing ethnography.* Chicago: The University of Chicago Press.

Warren, R. (2002). *The purpose-driven life.* Grand Rapids: Zondervan.

Weingarten, T. (2005). Campus Christians: Not always at ease. *Christian Science Monitor, 97*(42), 12.

Whyte, W. F. (1997). *Creative problem solving in the field: Reflections on a career.* Walnut Creek: AltaMira Press.

Witherell, C., and Noddings, N. (Eds.). (1991). *Stories lives tell: Narrative and dialogue in education.* New York: Teachers College Press.

Wolfe, A. (1997, September 19). A welcome revival of religion in the academy. *Chronicle of Higher Education,* p. B4–5.

Wolly, B. (Writer). (2006). College students look beyond institutionalized religion [Television], *PBS: Generation Next.* United States: PBS.

Young, R. B. (1999, September–October). Reexamining our rituals. *About Campus,* 4(4), 10–16.